THE FABER POCKET GUIDE TO
Greek and Roman Drama

John Burgess

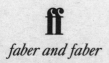

faber and faber

First published in 2005
by Faber and Faber Limited
3 Queen Square London WC1N 3AU
Published in the United States by Faber and Faber Inc.
an affiliate of Farrar, Straus and Giroux LLC, New York

Typeset by Faber and Faber Limited
Printed in England by Mackays of Chatham, plc

A CIP record for this book
is available from the British Library

ISBN 0–571–21906–3

10 9 8 7 6 5 4 3 2 1

The Faber Pocket Guide to Greek and Roman Drama

John Burgess is a freelance director and lives in London. He worked for fourteen years at the National Theatre where he directed works from the classical, romantic and modern repertoires as well as many new plays. He helped found the NT Studio in 1984 and was the National Theatre's Head of New Writing 1989–94. He has directed abroad in Switzerland, Scandinavia and North America.

For Hilda and Freda

Contents

Introduction

Tragedy

> In tragedy, the received mythical way of thinking engaged with the new rationality, folk culture engaged with high culture.
>
> Christian Meier, *The Political Art of Greek Tragedy*

What is the origin of tragedy? There are two answers – a short one and a long one. The short answer is that we don't know. One historian put it trenchantly when he wrote, 'I shall not concern myself the shadowy first decades about which there is hardly any information and consequently endless speculation, both ancient and modern, none of which I find either persuasive or illuminating' (M. I. Finley, *The Idea of a Theatre: the Greek Experience*). Any theory involving such things as scapegoats, rituals, initiation, fertility rites, satyrs or ecstatic religion should be treated with scepticism: *there is no evidence.*

The longer answer is (of course) more complicated. It's perhaps worth looking first at the reasons why the information has gone missing. There is nothing particularly mysterious about it. Ordinary fallibility plays a part. We know very little about the life of William Shakespeare, for example, yet he died only four hundred years ago, in an age when literacy was widespread and printing had been in existence for over a century.

The second reason is that there was, at the time, no real way of recording such an event as the 'birth of tragedy'. When the first tragedies were being composed classical Greece was still an oral culture. Laws and treaties might be carved in stone, as a way of remembering what had been agreed, but the main business of government was carried out by word of mouth. Literature was not written to be read, it was composed for performance, whether spoken or sung.

The Homeric epics were meant for listeners, not readers. All literary forms were in verse of one kind or another, because verse is memorable and can be readily grasped at first hearing. Prose had yet to be invented – or rather the first glimmerings of prose were a strange radical avant-garde affair to do with scientific enquiry in the east Greek cities on the coast of Asia Minor. Herodotus' prose *History*, itself an extremely innovative departure, lay nearly a hundred years in the future. This meant that, supposing someone had understood the significance of tragedy at the moment when it first appeared, there was no easy way of recording the fact for posterity. Neither epic nor lyric, nor choral song, nor the poetry of political advocacy provided a viable template.

A third reason why the event received no particular notice is that the early Greeks had not yet developed a concept of progress, as we understand it. Progress is such a central notion for the modern world that it is difficult to 'unthink' it. The Greeks in the sixth century, however, imagined themselves, not as surpassing what had gone before, but as trying to live up to the great achievements of the past. Innovation was not considered automatically interesting.

The idea of progress was itself an innovation, thrown up as a result of the rapid developments taking place during the fifth century, and we can see dramatists such as Aeschylus and Sophocles struggling to understand its implications. A hundred years later still, Aristotle became the first thinker to put growth and change at the centre of his thought. Plato regarded form as an unchanging archetype; for Aristotle it was a guiding principle of development. Aristotle focused his thought on the process of unfolding: why does an acorn become an oak tree and not a sycamore? He was also interested in how cultural forms developed. He wrote several books on constitutional history, for example, and in his celebrated and problematic work *Poetics* he offers a description of what tragedy is and how it evolved. The *Poetics*, though, was written two centuries after the first tragic performances and much had been lost or forgotten in the meantime.

What we think of as the 'birth of tragedy' may have passed unnoticed by the Greeks for another reason too: because they were already familiar with the tragic view of life through the great Homeric epics, *The Iliad* and *The Odyssey*.

Aristotle described Homer as 'the most tragic of poets'. In the *Iliad* Book 24, the Greek hero Achilles mourns his friend Patroclus. The death had been unnecessary, brought about by Achilles' pride and stubbornness. Now the funeral games are over and the other warriors return to their everyday lives.

And the games broke up, and the people scattered to go
    away, each man
to his fast-running ship, and the rest of them took
    thought of their dinner
and of sweet sleep and its enjoyment; only Achilleus
wept as he still remembered his beloved companion, nor
    did sleep
who subdues all come over him, but he tossed from one
    side to the other
in longing for Patroklos, for his manhood and great
    strength
and all the actions he had seen to the end with him, and
    the hardships
he had suffered; the wars of men; the hard crossing of the
    big waters.
Remembering all these things he let fall the swelling
    tears, lying
sometimes on his side, sometimes on his back and now again
prone on his face . . .
    tr. Richmond Lattimore

Later, Achilles and the Trojan King Priam sit in Achilles' tent. Priam has come to ransom the body of his son Hector whom Achilles, in his rage, has killed in revenge for Patroclus. He has underlined his triumph by dragging the dead body behind his chariot round the city walls. Achilles is the greatest warrior in the Greek army, a young man whose whole life has been war. He is soon to die in battle. Priam is old and has lived long enough to see all his fifty sons die before him. The proper relationship between youth and age is reversed as the old man humbles himself before the younger.

> But now Priam spoke to him in the words of a suppliant:
> 'Achilleus like the gods, remember your father, one who
> is of years with mine and on the door-sill of sorrowful old
>   age.
> And they who dwell nearby encompass him and afflict him,
> nor is there anyone to defend him against the wrath, the
>   destruction.
> Yet surely he, when he hears of you and that you are still
>   living,
> is gladdened within his heart and all day he is hopeful
> that he will see his beloved son come home from the
>   Troad.
> But for me my destiny was evil. I have had the noblest
> of sons in Troy, but say not one of them is left to me.
> Fifty were my sons, when the sons of the Achaians came
>   here.
> Nineteen were born to me from the womb of a single
>   mother
> and other women bore the rest in my palace; and of these
> violent Ares broke the strength in the knees of most of
>   them,
> but one was left me who guarded my city and people, that
>   one
> you killed a few days since as he fought in defence of his
>   country,
> Hektor; for whose sake I come now to the ships of the
>   Achaians
> to win him back from you, and I bring gifts beyond number.
> Honour then the gods, Achilleus, and take pity upon me
> remembering your father, yet I am still more pitiful;
> I have gone through what no other mortal on earth has
>   gone through;

I put my lips to the hands of the man who has killed my
    children.'
So he spoke and stirred in the other a passion of grieving
for his own father. He took the old man's hand and
    pushed him
gently away, and the two remembered, as Priam sat hud-
    dled
at the feet of Achilleus and wept close for manslaughter-
    ing Hektor
and Achilleus wept now for his own father, now again
for Patroclus. The sound of their mourning moved in the
    house.

Achilles then tries to console the old man.

There is not
any advantage to be won from grim lamentation.
Such is the way the gods spun life for unfortunate mortals,
that we live in unhappiness, but the gods themselves have
    no sorrows.
    tr. Richmond Lattimore

All the ingredients of tragedy are present here, except
drama. Tragedy, we can say, is something which looks at the
relationship:

- between man and his own death and other men
- between man and the immortal gods and things that do
  not change
- between man and the passions that live inside him.

Aeschylus, Sophocles, Euripides – each of the three great
dramatists was to handle this set of concerns in their own way,
giving it a deeply personal inflection.

If we know nothing about the moment when tragedy
began, we know a good deal about the force field which produced it. Tragedy in the form we know it might never have
arisen if it were not for the establishment of two great civic
festivals at Athens towards the end of the sixth century BC.
There had been since ancient times a yearly celebration

called the Panathenaia in honour of the city's patron goddess Athena. In 566 BC the tyrant Peisistratus grafted an essentially secular addition on to the already existing cult, founding a great cultural and athletic festival. The thing that singled out this particular festival from others which took place elsewhere in the Greek world was that it featured a competition for performers who recited the works of Homer. This ran in parallel with a competition for musicians, and for other performers who sang to the accompaniment of the lyre or the oboe. The establishment of the Panathenaia was followed just over thirty years later in 535 BC by that of the Great Dionysia, where once again a civic celebration was grafted on to an already existing religious cult, this time in honour of Dionysus. The competition featured performances of tragedy and dithyramb (a choral poem honouring the god).

The effect of these two great festivals was to bring together in Athens every year (the Dionysia) or every four years (the Panathenaia) leading performers and practitioners of the literary arts from all over the Greek world. Lyric poetry, sung to the accompaniment of the lyre, had been invented in Lesbos and Sparta; singing to the accompaniment of the oboe in Phrygia and Argos; public recitals of the Homeric poems had developed in East Greece; and choral lyrics originated in the Peloponnese.

The singular nature of tragedy as we know it is that it represents a fusion of all these different genres into a new whole. It brings together diverse art forms from all over Greece to make something new and specifically Athenian. The dialogue and the speeches of the central characters are in a kind of iambic verse associated with the politician Solon – a civic poetry designed as a vehicle for ideas and persuasion, whose function was to admonish and convince. The choral lyrics, which came from the Peloponnese, are written in a different, softer dialect. (To use a crude analogy – if the spoken parts of tragedy are in 'Received Pronunciation', then the lyric sections might sound as if they were set in the west of Ireland.) The lyric outbursts which the leading actors sing come from a different tradition again and have their origin in the poetry of Sappho and Alcaeus from the islands in the Ionian Sea. The subject matter and the way of dividing up a narrative into striking scenes, focused on an encounter between two characters, comes from the Homeric epic. A dramatized version of the scene between Priam and Achilles quoted above formed the centrepiece of a lost play by Aeschylus called *The Ransoming of Hector*.

It is unlikely that tragedy emerged fully fledged in all its Aeschylean splendour. Aristotle, describing early examples of the genre, speaks of 'little plots and laughable diction': but once the form had taken hold, development was rapid. *The Persians*, the first surviving tragedy, dates from 472 BC, over sixty years after the first performances were instituted, and there is nothing primitive about it.

We are so used to thinking of tragedy in terms of Aeschylus, Sophocles and Euripides that it is worth remembering that there were other playwrights writing too. Here are some – but by no means all – of their names: Phrynichus, Pratinas, Aristarchus, Euphorion, Hippias, Ion, Iophon, Callistratus, Philocles, Datis, Melanthius, Neophron, Menecrates, Theognis, Polyphrasmon, Xenocles, Agathon, Critias, Meletus, Aristias, Achaeus, Acestor and two more Euripides.

Democracy

> We may also imagine a state that has so brought up its citizens that their works, by their existence alone, will demonstrate the eminence of that state and so declare its praise.
>
> George Seferis, *On the Greek Style*

Tragedy in its origins and first development is Athenian. It is not Spartan, Theban, Argive or Corinthian – although poets who wrote tragedies came to Athens from all over the Greek world. There is no Persian, Egyptian, Hittite or Phoenician tragedy. Drama by its very nature presents a series of competing voices. It is different from the solitary outpouring of the lyric poet or from a single performer reciting a Homeric epic in front of an aristocratic audience. As Hegel saw, the distinguishing characteristic of the dramatic form is that it is unmediated: 'It presents an action completed in the past as actually happening before us, as emanating from the inner life of self-directed characters' (*The Philosophy of Fine Art*, tr. F. B. P. Osmaston). There is no single voice directing our reactions: the reader/spectator is left to make up their own mind. Democracy is built into the very fabric of the work.

Athenian democracy was not a representative democracy in the modern mould; it was a participatory democracy. This meant that ordinary citizens were involved in running the state and administering the law to a quite extraordinary degree. Power at Athens was vested in the people, that is to say all male citizens over the age of twenty. The full assembly met ten times a year. In the great war against Sparta it met more often: forty times a year on average, almost once a week. No quorum was required for ordinary business. The record of one vote that has come down to us shows 3,461 in favour with 155 against – a total attendance of 3,616. Unfortunately we have no way of knowing whether this was typical or not.

Obviously some delegation was necessary; thousands of people cannot run a state; but to ensure maximum involvement the system was arranged as follows. The population was divided into ten tribes and each tribe was carefully spread across the whole of Athenian territory – the coast, the city and the rural hinterland. Each tribe then voted for a number of representatives to govern the city on their behalf. Any male over the age of thirty was allowed to stand. The number for each tribe was then reduced to fifty by the process of drawing lots. Fifty men from each of the ten tribes made up the Council of 500 or the *Boule* and this was the government for a year, charged with the supervision of everyday business. The council prepared motions to be put before the Assembly and dealt with day-to-day affairs. Selection by lot was an important part of civic ideology. It said that beyond a certain level everyone was equally capable of holding office. A talent for military leadership, then as now, was not widespread. The ten generals were chosen by election only: lottery played no part.

All five hundred members of the council did not convene every day. A steering committee of fifty people was on duty each month. Seventeen of them came in each day, so they did one day on and two days off. Every day the chairman of the council was chosen by lot; the President for the day was the result of a lottery. Any important business that arose was dealt with by fifty-nine people – the fifty on duty plus one representative from each of the other tribes. In case of emergency the full five hundred could be convened at any time.

The legal system worked in a similar way. There were no lawyers, no judges, no body of precedent or case law. Each of the local parishes in Attica nominated men to serve as jurors, and once again the final choice was made by lot – six thousand men in all, six hundred from each tribe. Cases were tried before a jury of two hundred and one men: this provided safety in numbers and made bribery or intimidation impossible. Each case lasted a day and was decided by a majority vote.

It has been calculated that in any given year one sixth of the adult male population was active on state business. This meant that the diffusion of expertise through the citizen body was both thorough and cumulative. The system demonstrated enormous confidence in the ability of the ordinary person to decide things in a responsible way. It would after all be these same citizens who would have to bear the consequences of their decisions. Athens' enemies were quick to spot this growing self-assurance and sense of adventure.

An Athenian is always an innovator, quick to form a decision and quick to carry it out . . . Athenian daring will outrun its own resources; they will take risks against their better judgement and still in the midst of danger remain confident . . . If they win a victory they follow it up at once, and if they suffer a defeat they scarcely fall back at all. As for their bodies they regard them as expendable for their city's sake, as if they were not their own; but each man cultivates his intelligence with the view to doing something notable for his city. If they aim at something and do not get it, they think they have been deprived of what belonged to them already; whereas if their enterprise is successful, they regard their success as nothing compared with what they will do next. Of them alone it may be said that they possess a thing almost as soon as they have begun to desire it, so quickly with them does action follow on decision. Their view of a holiday is to do what needs doing: they prefer hardship and activity to peace and quiet. In a word, they are by nature incapable of living a quiet life themselves or allowing anyone else to do so.

Thucydides, *History of the Peloponnesian War, Book I,*
tr. Rex Warner

Democracy did not spring up fully formed overnight. The transfer of power from an aristocratic oligarchy to the sovereign people took place over a century and a half. The first step was taken in 594 BC with the reforms of Solon, which opened state office to a wider range of citizens. The seizure of power by the tyrant Peisistratus was a further blow to aristocratic power but the decisive, radical shift came with the reforms of Cleisthenes in 507 BC, twenty-eight years after the first tragic performance took place at Athens. One historian sums up Cleisthenes' achievement like this:

Earlier statesmen in Athens and elsewhere in Greece had tinkered with this or that feature of the traditional political structures. Cleisthenes on the other hand, in effect coolly dismantled the entire fabric and assembled a new one, partly from the old components and partly from his own devising. Latent in this achievement was a philosophical and religious as well as a political revolution; if man's intellect could thus restructure his social environment at will, what could it not restructure in the long run?

John Herington, *Aeschylus*

From the time of Pericles, anyone engaged on state business was paid a *per diem*. This was less than the daily wage for a skilled craftsman but it meant that the poorest citizens were not excluded from the political process on the grounds of income.

The democratic culture of argument – making arguments, listening to them, evaluating them, weighing up the intentions of the speaker – is an important shaping factor in how tragedy was written and received. The arguments between Antigone and Creon, between Medea and Jason, between the two sons of Oedipus in *The Phoenician Women*, between Athena and the Furies in *The Eumenides*, and the pleasure the audience took in listening to these scenes – all this has its origin in the everyday life of the law courts and the Assembly. It has been argued that tragedy was something the Athenians *needed*: from it 'democracy gained the sort of support which early monarchies derived from their world-views and early aristocracies from tradition'.

Religion

There is little sign in Greece of the metaphysical ascetic tradition we find in the cults of Christianity, Islam, Shiva and Buddha. The Greeks never went so far as to renounce the world by opening monasteries, espousing virginity, practising yoga or fasting for long periods of time in an attempt to gain psychic power

James N. Davidson, *Courtesans and Fishcakes*

For the time of life is short and once a mortal is hidden beneath the earth he lies there for all time.

Sophocles, *Tantalus*, tr. Hugh Lloyd-Jones

Greek religion, like Greek democracy, was an affair of many voices. There was not one god, there were many gods. Each had their own territory and privileges, and they were often in dispute. Hippolytus worships Artemis but that doesn't prevent him being destroyed by Aphrodite for disrespecting her powers. Orestes obeys Apollo's command to kill his mother but is persecuted for it by the Furies. Oedipus' life is shattered in its prime but touched with redemption at the very end. Greek religion is good at awe, but bad at despair. Whatever is going on, there is always a second opinion.

It's difficult for spectator/reader in the modern West to enter into the religious world view of the Greeks. The Greeks for example, had no scriptures: there was no 'word of God'. There was no established church, either Anglican or Catholic, no Pope, no papal bulls, no prophets, no saints, no martyrs, no original sin and no redemption.

This goes deeper than the simple fact that this was a world without Sundays. For one thing the sense of time is different. The Judaeo-Christian tradition orders the world around three moments when God makes himself manifest in time – firstly when he creates the world, secondly when he sends his son to redeem the world and thirdly when he appears at the end of time to judge the world. This sense of life structured according to a single divine purpose, which is revealed to mankind in a holy book, runs deep and is difficult to set aside. Even in a secular culture the feeling that life is there as something subject to judgement is very strong.

Perhaps the most important difference between Greek religion and the Christian/Muslim tradition is that the Greeks had no concept of the afterlife. There was an underworld but it was imagined as a sort of damp cave in which the souls of the dead fluttered about like bats. The clearest expression of what it meant to be dead comes in Book XI of *The Odyssey*. Odysseus goes to consult the ghost of the prophet Teiresias about his return home. His men dig a trench which they fill with the blood of two slaughtered sheep.

> The dark blood flowed, and the souls of the dead came flocking upwards from Erebus – brides and unmarried youths, old men who had suffered much, tender girls with the heart's distress still keen, troops of warriors wounded

with brazen-pointed spears, men slain in battle with blood-stained armour still upon them. With unearthly cries, from every quarter, they came crowding about the trench until pale terror began to master me . . . I drew the keen sword from beside my thigh, seated myself and held back the strengthless presences of the dead from drawing nearer to the blood before I had questioned Teiresias.

tr. Walter Shewring

The dead are nerveless, almost transparent: it is only when they have drunk the blood that they have the strength to speak.

Amongst the crowd is the ghost of Achilles, once the greatest warrior in the Greek army.

The soul of fleet-foot Achilles knew me, and in mournful tones he uttered these words in rapid flight: 'Son of Laertes, subtle and overbold Odysseus, what venture will ever tempt your mind more reckless than this? What daring has led you down to the house of Hades, the dwelling place of the dead who have no understanding, of the wraiths of mortals who have perished?'

So he spake and I answered him: '. . . But you, Achilles – no man has been more blest than you in days past, or will be in days to come; for before you died we Achaeans honoured you like a god, and now in this place you lord it among the dead. No, do not repine in death, Achilles.'

So I spoke, but at once he answered: 'Odysseus, do not gloss over death to me. I would rather be above ground still and labouring for some poor portionless man, than be lord of all the lifeless dead.'

tr. Walter Shewring

Life is the thing. Even if it means being desperately poor and powerless it is infinitely preferable to fame and heroic status among the dead. There is only one life and it is here and now. When Iphigeneia begs her father 'Do not send me into death before my time. It is sweet to see the light. Do not make me look at what is under the earth', the death she is confronting is something final and conclusive. All we know of existence is here, and in this world. Iphigeneia is not like Joan of Arc: there is no reward waiting for her in heaven. There is, in fact, no other heaven than here on earth. The third Homeric Hymn contains the description of a religious festival on the island of Delos where the predominant note is one of delight and celebration of human beauty, strength, dignity and material possessions.

> But it is in Delos, Apollo, that your heart most delights, that is the place where the Ionians assemble for your glory, wearing their long robes, together with their children and their honoured wives. Having you in mind, they delight you with boxing and dancing and song, each time they set up their gathering. A man who came upon the Ionians at that time, when they were all together, would say to himself that they were immortal and forever ageless; for he would see then the charm of them all, and his spirit would delight as he looked at the men, and at the beautifully girt women, and at the swift ships, and at the many possessions of them all.
>
> tr. John Herington

This is a religion remarkably free of zealotry and paranoia. There is an intriguing passage in Polybius, a Greek historian writing in the second century BC in which he remarks on the superstitiousness of the Romans and on its usefulness in preserving the status quo.

> What in other nations is looked upon as a reproach, I mean the scrupulous fear of the gods, is the very thing which keeps the Roman commonwealth together. To such an extraordinary height is this carried among them both in private and in public business, that nothing could exceed it . . . In my opinion their object is to use it as a check upon the common people.
>
> Polybius, *History VI. 6ff*, tr. E. S. Shuckburgh

This Roman attitude obviously struck him as unusual enough to be worth commenting on.

Perhaps most important for our understanding of tragedy is that there is in Greek religion no sense of the individual soul being subject to judgement and differential treatment after death. The desire to interpret characters in terms of the expiation of some 'fatal flaw' has led to many misreadings of what is going on in Greek drama. The Greeks were more interested in characters' behaviour – the kind of choices they made, their reasons for making them and how they dealt with the consequences of what they had chosen – than in the state of their souls. As one critic put it:

> The question raised by wrongdoing was not so much 'How can this *person* be dealt with fairly?' as 'What reaction to this *situation* will safeguard the interests of the community?'
>
> K. J. Dover, *The Greeks and their Inheritance*

Theatre

> An amazing aural and visual experience . . .
> Plutarch, *On the Glory of Athens*

Aristotle tells us that tragedy originally had one actor. Aeschylus added a second and Sophocles a third. The chorus was made up of twelve members, which Sophocles increased to fifteen.

Music was an important part of the tragic performance. The chorus chanted and sang elaborate songs with oboe accompaniment. The principal actors sang as well, often in shared laments with the chorus. Sometimes events were presented twice – emotionally as song and then rationally as dialogue. Euripides was specially fond of this device. In our contemporary speech-based theatre the choruses often seem an embarrassment – something to be got through before the action can begin again – but in the original productions they formed one of the high points of the action. A Greek friend remarked to me that when she saw performances of the plays (in modern Greek translation) she always looked forward to the choruses because they were the most beautiful and exciting bit of the evening.

The tragedies presented each year at the festival of the Great Dionysia were part of a competition. Three dramatists would be entered, each submitting three tragedies and one satyr play. (A satyr play is a tragedy as written by Sancho Panza. It deals with the same mythological subjects as tragedy but the treatment is earthy, materialistic, funny – a worm's eye view.) Aeschylus liked to link his four plays together to tell an unfolding story with a comic afterpiece. Sophocles and Euripides seem to have preferred to stage three separate tragedies, though sometimes they were linked thematically, as with Euripides' Trojan War trilogy. The judges were chosen by the usual Athenian process of selection for public office. A panel of people was nominated (to ensure expertise) and the final choice was made by lot (to ensure fairness).

Performances took place over five successive days in late March. Each of the three contenders had a day to present his three plays and the satyr play. There were also competitions between ten men's choruses performing odes in honour of Dionysus, as well as ten boys' choruses, and a competition between five comic playwrights, each of whom presented one play. Some time the previous year the poets who wished to compete presented their ideas (or perhaps a completed play) to the city magistrates, who chose three to go forward to the competition and nominated a sponsor to bear the costs of the performance. The sponsor was a well-known wealthy citizen who was singled out for this special windfall tax. The duty of sponsoring a set of productions was seen as a great honour, particularly if they won first prize. One reason the plays each year were first performances was because only something new and never-seen-before was considered likely to please the god.

The dramatists not only composed the play but directed and choreographed it into the bargain, and most probably wrote the music too. How the plays were composed we don't know. It is interesting that when the central character in Aristophanes' play *Clouds* goes to call on Euripides, who is busy working on his next play there is no mention of any writing materials.

The theatre itself was on the southeast slope of the Acropolis in central Athens. The audience, about 15,000 in number (almost certainly, but not definitely, all men) sat divided into their ten tribes looking down at the circular dancing floor – the *orchestra*. At the back of the *orchestra* was a low raised stage, quite narrow, that ran across the width of the playing area. This was backed by a rectangular building known as the *skene*. (The Greek word means 'tent' or shack' and suggests something impermanent). The *skene* most often represented a palace but it could equally well be a tent, a cave, or a temple. In *Prometheus Bound* it represented a crag at the end of the world. It had a set of double doors in the centre which opened inward. Interior scenes could be presented by means of the *ekkyklema*, a wooden trolley which could be rolled out to display a tableau, such as Ajax surrounded by the carcases of the animals he had killed, or Heracles in Euripides' play, sitting among the bodies of his slaughtered family. Actors could appear on the roof (as in Aeschylus' *Agamemnon* or Euripides' *Orestes*) or make aerial entrances, swung in by a crane concealed behind the palace walls (like the two goddesses who frame the action of *Hippolytus*). Apart from through the central doors, entrances were made by means of two walkways at either side of the dancing floor.

Performances were in broad daylight, in the open air, under the 'clear impartial light of the sun'. The numbers involved were not small. One historian has done the sums:

Each tribe presented a dithyrambic chorus of fifty men and one of fifty boys (10 x 2 x 50 = 1,000). Each comedy had 24 chorusmen (5 x 24 = 120). Sophoclean and Euripidean tragedies had15 chorusmen, but the total numbers are less certain: perhaps three sets x 15 = 45, but it may be that each tragedy and satyr play had different chorusmen, i.e. 3 x 4 x 15 = 180. Add to these the various trainers and organisers, costumers and musicians (not to mention the actors and mask-makers involved in formal drama), and a noticeable proportion of the free male population would have been involved.

J.R. Green, *Theatre in Ancient Greek Society*

With performances occurring regularly every year, the spread of expertise and first-hand experience through the citizen body must have been thorough and wide-ranging. This had obvious implications for the way the audience watched the plays.

The actors were all men. They wore masks to make their faces legible in the large open space. The masks covered the whole head and were quite naturalistic. Costume for the principal actors was a colourful long-sleeved tunic reaching to the ground and decorated with strange patterns of whorls, zigzags, even animal figures. These were clothes that belonged to the heroic world and were quite separate from everyday dress.

The festival of the Great Dionysia took place annually at the end of March, that time of year when the spring sowing has been completed and the seas are open for travel again after the winter storms. This was the moment when Athens showed off her power to the world. The five days of performances were preceded by two days of processions. The first day was a re-enactment of the arrival of the god Dionysus in the city. His statue was carried out to a shrine on the road outside Athens. Sacrifices were offered and the statue was escorted back to his temple inside the city walls. On the second day, there was a great procession leading up to a sacrifice in the temple precinct. Allied to these ceremonies was the *proagon* (the 'preview'), where each poet appeared in public surrounded by his actors and chorus to announce the subject of the plays he was about to present.

On the opening day of the festival, a libation to Dionysus was offered by the ten generals – the city's most powerful military and political leaders. They very rarely appeared in public all together and when they did the occasion was very special. This was followed by a display of tribute from the Athenian allies and then the children of those who had died in battle were brought onstage. These orphans had been raised at state expense. The fourth-century orator Aeschines describes what happened next.

> Once on this day, when tragedies were about to be performed, in a time when the city had better customs and followed better leaders, the herald would come forward and place before you the orphans whose fathers had died in battle, young men clad in the panoply of war; and he would utter that proclamation so honourable and such an incentive to valour: 'These young men, whose fathers showed themselves brave men and died in war, have been supported by the state until they have come of age; and now clad thus in full armour by their fellow citizens, they are sent out with the prayers of the city, to go each his way; and they are invited to seats of honour in the theatre.
>
> *Against Ktesiphon*, tr. C. D. Adams

Because the seas were open, the audience at the Great Dionysia included representatives who had travelled to Athens from other Greek cities. Athenian democracy was putting on this display not just for its own citizens but also for the rest of the Greek world.

There was another dramatic festival, also in honour of Dionysus, called the Lenaia. This took place in December and focused mainly on comedy. Five comic poets competed, each with one play, and there were two tragic poets, each with two plays. Travel by ship was impossible in the winter and this festival was a more purely Athenian affair.

Comedy

Greek comedy, unlike Greek tragedy, was in its early form intensely topical. It drew its subject matter from contemporary life, not from the heroic past. Its principal characters were not legendary figures such as Agamemnon, Ajax or Medea but ordinary citizens – often defiantly ordinary in their liking for a quiet life and their determined pursuit of pleasure. This closeness to the everyday meant that comedy changed and developed as Athens itself changed and developed through the fifth century and beyond. Three separate periods can be distinguished – Old Comedy (486–c.404 BC), Middle Comedy (c.404 –c.321 BC) and New Comedy (c.321 BC onwards). These are dealt with more fully below: see pages 247 and 287.

Translations

First, a note of caution. Beware of anything that can be downloaded for free off the web. There is generally a good reason why it's free. These are mostly nineteenth-century versions now safely out of copyright. The original plays are so submerged in a glue of sub-Shakespearean verbiage that their outlines are barely discernible. Much the same is true of the relatively cheap Dover Press editions.

It's a pity that Penguin, a prestigious imprint and widely distributed, has such a poor track record in this area. The old Philip Vellacott and E. F. Watling translations were never very good and are now long past their sell-by date. There are some new prose versions published more recently which might do as literal translations but cannot be read with any pleasure: the experience is a little like eating sand. (The same is true of the recent prose versions of Greek plays published in the Oxford World Classics series.) The exceptions to these strictures are Robert Fagles' translations of the *Oresteia* and Sophocles' *Theban Plays*, the Menander of Norma Miller, the Aristophanes of Alan Sommerstein, and the Plautus and Seneca of E. F. Watling

The versions published by the University of Chicago Press are still doing useful service after nearly half a century, though some of the diction is now beginning to show its age.

The Oxford series Greek Tragedy in New Translations, designed as a replacement, varies between the excellent (*Ajax, The Persians, The Women of Trachis*) and the frankly pedestrian (*Antigone, Hippolytus*). The most accessible translations are those by Kenneth McLeish (sometimes in collaboration with Frederic Raphael): they are also eminently actable. Their faults are a certain rhythmic monotony, a tendency to make all the playwrights sound the same, and a preference for translating what the dramatist means instead of what he says.

The Everyman paperbacks edited by Michael Ewans provide a reliable guide to Aeschylus and Sophocles. There is no Euripides as yet. The developing series Cambridge Translations from Greek Drama looks very promising and includes an excellent *Philoctetes*. There are a number of fine translations that have been made for particular modern productions and these are noted below under the entries for the individual plays.

Readers looking for a literal translation can consult either the Loeb Classics Edition (Harvard University Press) or the Aris and Philips editions of individual plays. Both have the original language on one page and English on the other.

Aeschylus (Aischylos), 526/5–456/5 BC

Life

When Aeschylus was sixteen, the tyranny that had governed Athens (often progressively) for half a century was overthrown and the democratic constitution restored and expanded. When he was seventeen, the Spartans invaded, overthrew the new democracy and installed an oligarchy in its place. A counter-coup threw the Spartans out. The next threat was more menacing. Darius, ruler of the mighty Persian Empire, decided to add Greece to his possessions. Aeschylus, aged thirty-five, was one of the Athenian infantry that defeated the Persian army at the battle of Marathon. His brother Kynegeiros was killed in the fighting.

Ten years after their defeat at Marathon, the Persians came again, more determined, and in greater numbers. The Athenians abandoned their city, which they had no hope of defending, and withdrew to the island of Aegina, taking with them their families and everything they could carry. In the autumn of 480 BC the Athenians and their allies won a conclusive victory over the Persian navy at the battle of Salamis. The Persians withdrew, but not before they had reduced Athens to a heap of rubble. The Athenians returned home and set about rebuilding their city from the ground up.

It's clear from this brief account that Aeschylus' life was unusually eventful – and not just outwardly. The reforms of Cleisthenes, which re-founded democracy in Athens after the tyranny, were an intellectual happening as much as a political one. One historian described their effect as 'a philosophical and religious as well as a political revolution; if man's intellect could thus restructure his social environment at will, what could it not restructure in the long run?'

Aeschylus' particular quality as an artist is that he looks both ways. He was part of the new fifth-century world, full of possibility, excitement and intellectual adventure, but his childhood and early life had been part of the old sixth-century Athens, before the Persians came, with its ancient temples and its more traditional way of life – an Athens which was just one Greek city among many and not, as it later became, the centre of a powerful empire.

Seven of his plays have come down to us – *Persians*, *Seven Against Thebes*, *Suppliants*, *Agamemnon*, *The Libation Bearers*, *The Eumenides* – these three form the trilogy called the *Oresteia* – and *Prometheus Bound*. He began writing for the theatre about 499/6 BC and won his first victory in 484. *The Persians* (his first play to have survived) was composed when Aeschylus was already in his fifties.

Aeschylus wrote over ninety plays in all – both tragedies and satyr plays – an enormous body of work, several times the length of the *Iliad* and the *Odyssey* combined. The fragments of these all-but-vanished works form an enticing shadow world surrounding the plays which have survived. What would Aeschylus' *Oedipus* have been like? Or his *Pentheus*? Or his *Iphigeneia*? An ancient critic writing about his *Philoctetes* said that it showed 'the grandeur of Aeschylus' spirit and his antique dignity; the sternness of its ideas and diction seemed to me appropriate to tragedy as well as to the character of the hero, for there was nothing contrived, no idle talk for talk's sake, nothing base' (tr. John Herington).

There was a trilogy about Ajax, another about Odysseus. *The Archer Maidens* is about Actaeon, hunted to death by Artemis; *Athamas* is about the Thracian king who was driven mad by Hera and killed his own son; *Phorkides* is about the killing of the Medusa and features the Graeae, three ancient hags with one eye and one tooth between them (Aristotle classed it as one of the 'spectacular' tragedies). *The Lemnian Women* and *Hypsipyle* dramatize the cruel legend in which the women of Lemnos rose up and massacred their menfolk – all except Hypsipyle who spared her father's life. What is perhaps surprising is that the fragments show that Aeschylus had a powerful gift for comedy and the grotesque: it's a pity that none of his satyr plays has come down to us intact.

If tragedy explores the relationship
- between man and his own death and other men
- between man and the immortal gods and things that do not change
- between man and the passions that live inside him,

then each of the three great dramatists approached these problems in his own particular way. Aeschylus is concerned to show how everything is related to everything else. He experiences the universe as a living breathing whole, whose balance, if disturbed, will ultimately reassert itself. This is one of the reasons he had a liking for trilogies: he needed space to show how actions ramify. In his play *The Daughters of the Sun* he wrote:

> Zeus is air, Zeus is earth, Zeus is heaven,
> Yes, Zeus is all things and whatever is beyond them.

In *The Persians* the sin of seeking to dominate the sea as well as the land is punished by a terrible defeat and the cosmic equilibrium is restored. In the *Oresteia* the blood feud in the house of Atreus is resolved because the king of the gods himself institutes a new form of justice.

At some point between 472 and 468 Aeschylus visited the wealthy West Greek settlements in Sicily and wrote a play, *The Women of Aetna*, celebrating the newly founded city of that name. He returned to Sicily, this time to Gela, in 458 or later, and died there in 456/5. His epitaph makes no mention of his work in the theatre, recording simply that he fought at Marathon.

The Persians (*Persai*)

∾ The legend

The Persians is based not on myth or legend but on historical events.

In the fifty years from 550 to 500 BC the Persians conquered most of what is now the Middle East – Iran, Iraq, Turkey, Syria, Lebanon, Palestine, Egypt and Libya. They overran the Greek cities on the coast of Asia Minor and reached northwards towards Bulgaria and the Crimea.

In 492 BC the Persian king Darius sent his armies to invade Greece: Thrace and Macedonia were subdued and formed the base for future campaigns. In 490, however, the Athenians defeated a large Persian expedition at the battle of Marathon. The expansion of the Persian Empire had met its first major check. Darius died in 486 BC. Six years later, his son Xerxes set off at the head of a second and larger expedition to subdue Greece. This was to be a two-pronged attack by land and sea.

After their victory at Marathon the Athenians knew that the Persians would try again. They knew too that they could not hope to match the power of their enemy on land. When silver mines were discovered outside the city it was voted that the revenue should be used to build a fleet. As the Persian army drew near, the Athenians abandoned their city to the enemy and evacuated the whole population to the nearby island of Aegina.

The Persians destroyed the city of Athens but could not touch the Athenians themselves, who were protected by the wooden walls of their new fleet. At the battle of Salamis in the autumn of 480 BC the Athenians and their allies destroyed the Persian navy, which greatly outnumbered theirs, by means of superior tactics and fighting skills.

Xerxes abandoned his expedition and fled back to his capital. The remains of his ground forces were defeated in the summer of the following year by the Spartans and their allies at the battle of Plataea. These two victories removed the Persian threat and marked the beginning of the great flowering of fifth-century Greek civilization.

∾ The story

The action of the play takes place in Susa, the capital of the Persian Empire.

It is months since Xerxes and his great expedition left for Greece. The Persian elders are apprehensive. No news has reached them and they fear that disaster has occurred.

Xerxes' mother Atossa has a dream. Xerxes is trying to yoke two women, one Greek and one Persian, to his chariot. The Persian woman submits gladly but the Greek woman throws off the yoke and destroys the chariot. The elders advise Atossa to pray to the gods for deliverance.

A messenger arrives from Greece bringing news of the Persian defeat at Salamis. In the longest messenger scene in Greek tragedy he gives a circumstantial account of the battle, the destruction of the Persian fleet, and the losses suffered by the army as it makes its way homewards through the wintry landscape of northern Greece.

Atossa offers libations on the grave of her dead husband Darius. She and the elders summon his ghost for comfort and advice. Darius appears from the underworld. He understands that the Persian defeat is god's judgement on overweening pride. He recalls a prophecy to the effect that the Persian power would be humbled but he had not expected it to be fulfilled for many years.

Darius returns to the world of the dead. Atossa leaves for the palace. Xerxes enters alone and unaccompanied. No trace now of the mighty army he led forth to war. He and the elders join in a tremendous lament for the fallen warriors and their own shattered hopes.

∾ About the play

The Persians is the earliest surviving tragedy, but there is nothing primitive about it. At the time of its first performance, tragedies had been composed at Athens for over fifty years. A similar span of time in Renaissance England encompasses Elizabethan drama from *Gorboduc* (1562) to *The Tempest* (1612) or, in the more modern period, the development of film from Edison's first kinetoscope (1893) to *Citizen Kane* (1941). When he wrote *The Persians*, Aeschylus was already in his fifties and had been composing for the stage for roughly twenty-five years: two thirds of his dramatic output lay behind him.

The play is unusual in that it is based on events in the comparatively recent past: the battle of Salamis had taken place only eight years before. Most tragedies draw their subjects from a body of inherited myth but it was as if the struggle between the Greek cities and the mighty Persian Empire had been so colossal, so outside any previous experience, and its outcome so magnificent and beyond all hope, that it had become a kind of legend, like the war at Troy that forms the subject of *The Iliad*.

Aeschylus is reputed to have said 'his tragedies were slices from the mighty feasts of Homer'. He was unusual among the tragedians in attempting to grapple directly with the Homeric legacy. He wrote a trilogy about Achilles, another about Odysseus, another still about Ajax, as well as single plays about Palamedes and Philoctetes. But it wasn't simply the subject matter. Aeschylus was quick to understand the dramatic possibilities of the Homeric scene, and to learn from the poet how to select episodes from a wider narrative and present them with maximum expressive power. *The Persians* is full of echoes of *The Iliad*. There are the same lists of champions, the same evocation of armies in their splendour, the same unsparing description of death in combat and the same feeling for the defeated enemy. Above all, Homer's legacy declares itself in the management of suspense and the establishing of the action within the wider framework of divine justice.

There are two other plays that we know of that took as their subject episodes from the Persian Wars. The first, *The Sack of Miletus*, dealt with the capture and destruction of the city by the Persian army. When it was first performed Herodotus tells us 'the audience in the theatre burst into tears. The author was fined a thousand drachmas for reminding them of a disaster which touched them so nearly and they forbade anyone to put the play on again.' The same author, Phrynichus, also wrote a play called *The Phoenician Women* which, like *The Persians*, dealt with the victory at Salamis looked at from the point of view of the losing side. The Phoenician women of the title were the widows of sailors killed in the battle and the play began with a eunuch setting out cushions for a meeting of Xerxes' counsellors and announcing news of the defeat.

Aeschylus proceeds quite differently. Instead of giving everything away immediately, he builds an atmosphere of doubt and suspense.

CHORUS: King royal army blazoned in gold
WILL THEY COME HOME?
                                My heart's ragged beat
prophesies doom:
        all Asia's strong sons
are gone gone
                        and now rumours bruit
the young king's name
but not one runner and not on rider
        brings word to Persia's capital.
    tr. Janet Lembke and C. J. Herington

The Persian elders try to overcome their fears by recalling the power and the splendour of the expedition when it left home.

Men sprang forth like Amistres and Artaphrenes
Megabates and Ataspes
commanders of the Persians,
kings subject to the great King,

guardians of the enormous army,
invincible archers and horsemen,
terrifying to look at and formidable in battle,
in the steadfast resolve of their spirit.
[. . .]
From all Asia there follow tribes
wielding the sabre
at the dread summons of the King.
Such is the flower of manhood, such the flower of the
Persian land which has gone.
    tr. Edith Hall

Aeschylus was to take up this atmosphere of dread and unease
with old men waiting for the uncertain outcome of a foreign
expedition and rework it with memorable effect at the opening of *Agamemnon* fourteen years later – only this time the
army, the Greek force sent to conquer Troy, was travelling in
the opposite direction.

The general foreboding is increased still further with the
entry of the Empress Mother. Her speech takes up and develops these twin themes of confidence and unease.

Nothing
       guards my inmost self
              against the fear
that vast Wealth,
       kicking up dust
              as it pelts headlong
may overturn
       continued joy
              in the prosperity
Darius
       by some god's grace
              lifted high.
    tr. Janet Lembke and C. J. Herington

The Queen expresses here a thought that the ghost of Darius
will make explicit later in the play, namely that good fortune is

given to men by god alone: the habit of prosperity can engender a recklessness and over-confidence which can prove fatal.

The remainder of the play's first half is taken up with the messenger's report on the defeat at Salamis. Aeschylus himself fought in the battle and his eyewitness account is of an unforgettable vividness.

> The sea was swamped with wreckage, corpses,
> The beaches, dunes, all piggy-backed with dead.
> Our ships broke ranks, tried one by one
> To slip the line. The Greeks, like fishermen
> With a haul of tunny netted and trapped,
> Stabbed, gaffed with snapped-off oars
> And broken spars, smashed, smashed, till all the sea
> Was one vast salty soup of shrieks and cries.
> At last black night came down and hid the scene.
>   tr. Frederic Raphael and Kenneth McLeish

The play is now half over, but before the story is complete two further developments are needed. Firstly there needs to be an explanation: why did the catastrophe occur? And secondly we need to see the consequences of the disaster with our own eyes. It is the ghost of Darius, summoned from the dead in an eerie ritual, which puts events into perspective. A wise and powerful ruler in his life, now in death he has become a kind of god, looking before and after.

> Alas! How swiftly oracles have been accomplished. Zeus
> has hurled down on my son consummation of prophecies.
> I trusted, I suppose, that the gods would bring them to
> fulfilment in some far distant time. But when someone is
> hasty, god lends assistance too. Now it seems that the
> fountain-spring of misery has been discovered for all those
> dear to me. And this was achieved by my son, uncompre-
> hending in his youthful audacity, the man who thought he
> could constrain with fetters, like a slave, the sacred flowing
> Hellespont, the divine stream of the Bosporos. He altered
> the very nature of the strait, and by casting around it

hammered shackles furnished a great road for his great
army; although only a mortal, he foolishly thought he
could overcome all the gods, including Poseidon. Surely
this must have been some disease affecting my son's mind.

tr. Edith Hall

When Darius speaks of the bridge across the Hellespont he
touches on one of the central images of the play – that of the
yoke. It is the chariot yoke that Atossa dreamed about, which
the Greek woman threw off: 'and she /shatters the yoke mid-
span /and he falls, /my son falls . . .' It represents an unholy
desire to tame and master nature (including human beings)
that is bound to come to grief. Aeschylus gives us two striking
images to drive this home. Atossa first enters dressed in ceremonial robes, mounted on a chariot and accompanied by
attendants. At her second appearance, after the news of the
disaster, she enters on foot, dressed in black. Instead of the
artificial symbols of her royal power she now carries humble
natural offerings of milk and wine and water for Darius' grave.

The disaster has been prophesied but it is human agency
that brings it about.

So great the piles of bones
even to the third generation they shall be
seen by human eyes as speechless warnings
that those who must die
                              not overreach themselves;
when stubborn pride has flowered, it
ripens to self-deception
and the only harvest is a glut of tears.

tr. Janet Lembke and C. J. Herington

This restates a theme that the Empress Mother had broached
earlier. Material wealth is a sign of divine favour but the
impious and greedy exploitation of good fortune brings swift
retribution.

Aristotle says, 'Aeschylus brought the number of actors
from one to two.' Looking at *The Persians* we can see why.

The extra actor allows the playwright to expand his action both in space (the messenger) and time (the ghost of Darius), so that its meaning can be explained. We can see here already a recognizable Aeschylean pattern that was to repeat itself most memorably in the *Oresteia* – the movement from the past into the present; from narrative and interpretation into contemporary action.

The whole of *The Persians* works as a preparation for Xerxes' final entry. By the time he appears we understand what he has done and what it was that led him to do it; but it still remains for us to see the man, to look at the human aspect of calamity. It is in this final scene that the images which run through the play achieve their resolution. Over and over the chorus lists the mighty generals that went with Xerxes to the war and evokes the numberless hosts that followed them. Now in place of this vast assembly we see a single man. The chorus have often referred to the land being emptied of its people; now we can see what that looks like. The desolation is underlined when Xerxes displays his quiver empty of arrows, all its forces spent. Clothes too are important in the play. The rending of garments is another leading image and reference is constantly made to the finery of the Persian court. Xerxes' appearance draws these two images together into a single point as he comes onstage with his royal garments torn and shredded.

It only remains for this desolation to be generalized and this is what happens in the great final lament when the chorus rend their own clothes and claw their cheeks and tear their beards. Darius' blessing is for them cruelly negated.

Though evil surrounds you
give joy to your souls
all the days that you live
for wealth is
useless to
      the dead.
   tr. Janet Lembke and C. J. Herington

∾ Translations

The Persians is one of Aeschylus' thorniest works from the point of view of language, so there's something to be said for approaching it by means of a scrupulous literal such as that provided by Edith Hall in her edition of the play (Aris and Philips). The best literary translation is by Janet Lembke and C. J. Herington (Oxford). Michael Ewans (Everyman) and Frederic Raphael and Kenneth McLeish (Methuen) both provide good straightforward versions, though the latter fails to match the lyric intensity of the final scene.

∾ In performance

The Persians was first performed in 472 BC as part of a trilogy with *Phineus* and *Glaucus at Potniae*: the satyr play was *Prometheus*. The producer was Pericles and Aeschylus won first prize. A production by Karolos Koun was seen at the World Theatre season in 1965. More recently the play was staged by the Berliner Ensemble in 1983, and at the Mark Taper Forum in 1993, directed by Peter Sellars.

Seven Against Thebes (Hepta epi Thebas)

∾ The legend

Three times Apollo warned Laius, king of Thebes, not to have children. The safety of the city depended on it. But Laius, 'led by his own unwisdom', disregarded the warning of the god.

When his child Oedipus was born, Laius abandoned the boy on a mountain outside the city. Oedipus was rescued by a shepherd and many years later returned to Thebes. On the journey he encountered Laius at a junction where three roads met. The two men quarrelled and Oedipus killed his father, not knowing who he was.

Oedipus delivered Thebes from the Sphinx, a monster that was terrorizing the city, and as a reward was made king and married to Queen Jocasta, Laius' widow and his own mother. The incestuous marriage produced two sons, Eteocles and Polyneices. When Oedipus discovered what he had done he put out his eyes. Jocasta killed herself. Oedipus laid a curse on his two sons who were also his brothers.

Eteocles and Polyneices fell out over their inheritance and Eteocles forced Polyneices into exile. Polyneices married the daughter of the king of Argos and returned at the head of a mighty army to conquer Thebes. The invaders were defeated and the two brothers killed each other in the battle, thus bringing to an end the family curse.

∽ The story

The Argive army is besieging Thebes. Inside the city Eteocles, the commander, rallies the citizens to defend the walls and despatches a scout to bring him news of the enemy's dispositions. He prays that the city may be spared from the effects of his father's curse and the avenging Fury that is fated to destroy his family.

The female population of Thebes is struck with panic. They fear disaster will overwhelm the city and desperately implore the gods to rescue them.

The scout returns and describes Argive preparations for the forthcoming battle.

Seven champions are to attack the city's seven gates. The enemy fighters are Tydeus, Capaneus, Eteoclus, Hippomedon, Parthenopaeus and the prophet Amphiaraus. Eteocles responds by matching each enemy with a defender of his own.

Polyneices has chosen to attack the seventh gate; Eteocles decides to fight his brother. The chorus plead with Eteocles not to go but he sees that the fatal encounter cannot be avoided. Eteocles and Polyneices kill each other but the Argives are defeated and the city saved. The chorus lament over the bodies of the two young men. They are to be buried together in the Theban earth. Their father's curse has been fulfilled. Now they have equal shares in the city's wealth and territory.

∾ About the play

The air is full of the noise of battle. We hear the scream of the chariots' ungreased axles, the thunder of stones battering at the walls, the neighing of horses, the stamping of hooves, the clanging of shields, the sound of trumpets, the weird amplified snorting made by Eteoclus' chariot teams, the wailing of women, the rattle of spears. *Seven Against Thebes* is one of the greatest war poems ever written – a grim, armour-plated play which matches the sardonic, practical tones of Eteocles against the frenzied wailing of the female chorus. In Aristophanes' play *Frogs*, where Aeschylus is a character, he is made to boast that his writing here is 'full of the War-God'.

Thebes is likened to a ship in a storm; the city's walls become the planking of the hull, pounded by massive waves and liable to give way at any moment. The whistle of weapons and the screams of the horses are like the raging of the wind and the attacking armies like the monstrous sea that threatens to overwhelm the vessel. This is the portrait of a community *in extremis*, placed there by the folly of the ruling house. At the helm stands Eteocles. In front of him are ranged the male citizens of fighting age. Behind him or beside him stand the images of the gods – Zeus, Athene, Poseidon, Ares, Aphrodite, Hera, Apollo, Artemis. These voiceless reminders of divine authority are present throughout the play, a sign of powers and purposes that are other than human.

Eteocles sends the men out to fight. When he is left alone he prays for the city's deliverance with the uneasy knowledge that it is his father's curse that has brought about this deadly war.

Zeus, Earth, Olympian gods, this city's defenders,
my father's Curse, and you who will bring it to pass,
Fury, whose power is great,
let not this war capsize us
or overturn our city to ravaged desolation –
our city where the mother tongue of Hellas
rings in the sanctuary of our homes.
    tr. Anthony Hecht and Helen H. Bacon

Seven Against Thebes is the last part of a trilogy. It represents the conclusion of an action – the working out of a family curse that goes back three generations. The two plays that precede it are *Laius* and *Oedipus*. Of these only the merest fragments survive. It is uncertain, for example, whether the first play dealt with the curse on Laius and his determination to have children in defiance of divine prohibition or with the murder of Laius and the fatal encounter at the crossroads. *Oedipus* must have covered much the same territory as Sophocles' play but with the addition that Oedipus cursed his offspring, so that the action was not complete in itself but spilled forward into the future.

As Eteocles leaves the chorus enters, and the stage is flooded with female emotion. The rhythm of the Greek at this point is of an extreme jaggedness and agitation. The verse is not divided into the stanzas that are the usual pattern for the chorus's first entry; the opening thirty lines are in a metre usually reserved for extremes of violent feeling. There must have been a wild frenzy to the dancing here that matched the frenzy of the storm at sea or the chaos of the battlefield that had been described earlier. The total destruction of a city and a community was not simply a theory to the play's first audience. Some twenty years earlier, Athens had been in just such peril before the battle of Marathon. And thirteen years previously, just before the victory at Salamis, the whole population had been forced to evacuate the city and sail across the sea to a foreign refuge while the enemy destroyed the place they had left from the ground up.

The women surge round the statues of the gods, imploring them for mercy.

> Yoh! Yoh!
> Gods, goddesses, it rears,
> Evil, turn it aside.
> O-ah!
> It hurls on the walls.
> Surging shields, dazzling,
> White shields pound Thebes.
> Which god? Which goddess?
> Who our champion?
> Whose altars? Where kneel?
>   tr. Frederic Raphael and Kenneth McLeish

It takes an unusually firm intervention from Eteocles to calm this frenzy. His male rationality is set in opposition to the female emotion of the chorus – a polarity which will be reversed with powerful effect later in the play. The content of Eteocles' remarks recalls the calmness and good sense of Oedipus in Sophocles' play when he confronts the plague that threatens his city. Perhaps there is a sense here that Eteocles is behaving in the statesmanlike manner of his father, calming the plague-stricken citizens in the earlier part of the trilogy. But there is intemperateness to his tone which is unsettling.

> Good times or bad
> Who'd live with women?
> On top they're unendurable; done down,
> They pull the town around their ears.
> Our soldiers, look! Scream panic in every street,
> You rip the heart out of them.
>   tr. Frederic Raphael and Kenneth McLeish

This fierceness and settled contempt make it impossible for Eteocles to listen to the women's advice when he needs it later.

The central section of *Seven Against Thebes* is an extraordinary *tour de force*. Present on stage are Eteocles, the Scout and the chorus. These simple means are used to conjure effects of enormous complexity and power. The scene has a structure that is repeated seven times. The Scout describes each of the Argive champions that threaten Thebes; Eteocles meets his description with a calm response; the chorus sing and dance their fears.

We have already encountered the furious determination of the Argives to destroy the city.

> This night there were seven men, violent, terrible, captains,
> they slit the throat of a bull, catching the blood
> in an inverted shed bound with black iron.
> They splashed their hands in bull blood, they swore
> by the trinity of battle, Ares, god of strife,
> Enyo, goddess of frenzy and Phobos, god of fear,
> either to sack and gut this city
> or by dying smear and defile
> this life-giving land with their blood.
>
> tr. Anthony Hecht and Helen H. Bacon

Now the images of threat and violence are intensified as we come face to face with the individual commanders. The sense of being at the mercy of a raging and implacable enemy is very powerful.

> But Tydeus, raving and gluttonous for battle
> bellows like a chimera in noonday clangor.
> He abuses and berates Apollo's priest Amphiaraos,
> alleging that he licks the hand of fate and avoids battle
> out of cowardice. Shouting such things as this,
> he shakes the three crests of his helmet,
> and, behind the rim of his shield,
> brass-forged bells clash fear.
>
> tr. Anthony Hecht and Helen H. Bacon

The seven Argives are a portrait gallery from hell. One is monstrous, another blasphemous, a third consumed with restlessness, a fourth beautiful and corrupt, a fifth hellish and the sixth, Apollo's prophet, a good man helpless in evil company.

The colourfulness of these warriors is part of their savagery. Each champion has a blazon on his shield.

> Upon the shield he bears this arrogant device
> engraved; the sky at night blazing with stars,
> and in the middle, standing out a full clear moon,
> eye of the night – greatest and most eminent of stars.

Eteocles, however, refuses to be impressed.

> As for that night you say is blazoned on his shield,
> sparkling with all the stars of heaven,
> stupidity so great might have prophetic power.
> If he dies night descends upon his eyes;
> then rightfully and properly this overboastful sign
> would live up to the omen of its name.
>
> tr. Michael Ewans

His tone is consistently sober. He has no lyrics: all his utterances are spoken.

The Argive champion for the seventh gate is Polyneices: Eteocles decides to face his brother. Now his role and that of the chorus are reversed. He is the one who is behaving unreasonably and it is the chorus who are urging restraint. To mark the transition they neither sing nor chant: their pleas are spoken in ordinary speech. They beg Eteocles not to fight but to send someone else in his place. But Eteocles is unmoved. His free will and the family curse coincide.

> Oh maddened, greatly hated by the gods,
> Oh utterly lamented race of Oidipous!
> Oh me, for now my father's curses are fulfilled.
> Still I must not cry out aloud or weep;
> that might give birth to even greater suffering.
>
> tr. Michael Ewans

Yet there is also an unnerving hunger for death which drives him on, despite what the chorus say.

CHORUS: Do not let blind desire for combat fill your soul

and carry you
away; banish this dreadful love before it starts.
ETEOCLES: The god urges this on – so let us go,
  swept by the wind, bound for the river Kokytos;
  Apollo hates the whole of Laios' race.
    tr. Michael Ewans

The hurricane that threatened the city now comes to sweep away the son of Oedipus.

The brothers die; Thebes is saved. The end of the play is a long lament for the destruction of the cursed family. The funeral dirge the women sing is more restrained than that of the Persian elders in *The Persians*, but they are not personally at stake. The danger for them is past; they have survived the cataclysm. The community in peril has become the community restored by the gods. It is easy to forget the statues of the eight Olympians who have been watching over the action but they are as present at the end of the play as they were at the beginning.

The chorus's lament now goes back over the whole history of the house of Laius from the beginning. Aeschylus' poetic mastery is at its most evident as he takes up for the last time all the play's leading images, giving them a deathly cast. In the opening speech Eteocles spoke of the city as a ship; now the souls of the two brothers are being ferried to the underworld on a very different kind of boat.

CHORUS: Dear friends, now row down the wind of sighs
  striking around your heads the splash of oars to speed
  them on their way, music that always crosses Acheron
  sending the black-sailed sacred ship to land
  upon the shore the god of Healing never sees,
  the dark place where we all must go.
    tr. Michael Ewans

He spoke too of the earth as a bounteous mother.

For when you were infants on all fours
dandled upon her nourishing hills and valleys,

she welcomed the familiar burdens of child-rearing,
tended you, brought you up so that
you would be filial keepers of her house.

> tr. Anthony Hecht and Helen H. Bacon

But the riches of the earth lie squandered, fruitless.

Under their bodies will lie
the bottomless wealth of the earth.

> tr. Michael Ewans

The earth also features in one of the play's most unforget-table images, which could perhaps stand as a summing-up of the whole trilogy: '*The soil of delusion brings forth the harvest of death.*'

Sometime after the playwright's death, an extra eighty or so lines were added to the end of the play by some unknown writer who knew the continuation of the story in Sophocles' *Antigone* and Euripides' *Phoenician Women* and sought to bring Aeschylus' work into line with what his successors had done. The added passage introduces Oedipus' daughters Antigone and Ismene and the decree forbidding the burial of Polyneices, which prolongs the conflict into the next generation. This works contrary to Aeschylus' intentions. For him the family curse was closed by the death of the two brothers. The pattern of *Seven Against Thebes* is complete at this point. The antiphonal grieving of the chorus as they carry the two dead young men away to bury them marks the true end of the play.

ᵔ Translations

Given the linguistic complexity of the original there is a good deal to be said for a clear and faithful version such as that by Michael Ewans (Everyman). Anthony Hecht and Helen H. Bacon's translation (Oxford) is more literary and highly-worked and is good at the 'war music' of the play: it comes complete with some tendentious stage directions and includes the spurious ending. The version by Frederic Raphael and

Kenneth McLeish (Methuen) is lively and speakable but sometimes rather lightweight for such an ironclad play.

∽ In performance

Seven Against Thebes was first performed in 467 BC as part of a trilogy with *Laius* and *Oedipus*: the satyr play was *The Sphinx*. Aeschylus won first prize. The play was staged at the Berliner Ensemble in 1968 as a protest against the Soviet invasion of Czechoslovakia. Einar Schleef's production in Frankfurt in 1986 twinned the work with Euripides' *Suppliants* which deals with what happened to the survivors of the invading army. The play was also seen at the Wiener Festwochen in 1987 in an adaptation by Heiner Mueller.

The Suppliants (*Hiketides*)

∽ The legend

Io was priestess in the temple of Hera at Argos. Hera's husband Zeus, king of the gods, fell in love with her and took her virginity. When Hera discovered this she set out to take revenge.

First she changed Io into a cow. Zeus promptly transformed himself into a bull so that their lovemaking could continue. Hera then set Argus, a creature with a thousand eyes, to keep watch over the girl-cow. Zeus responded by getting Hermes to kill Argus. Hera sent a horsefly to sting and torment Io, who was driven to wander restlessly through the world until finally she came to Egypt. There Zeus soothed her pain and by a gentle stroking made her conceive. Her child Epaphos (the name means 'Touch' or 'Caress') was born.

Epaphos founded a dynasty. He had a daughter called Libya and she had a son called Belos or Baal. Baal had two children Danaus and Aegyptus. Danaus had fifty daughters;

Aegyptus had fifty sons. The sons of Aegyptus wanted to marry the daughters of Danaus against their will but the women fled across the sea to seek sanctuary in Argos, the homeland of their ancestor Io.

The sons of Aegyptus pursued the daughters of Danaus to Greece, defeated the Argives in battle and killed their king. The daughters of Danaus were forced to marry their cousins after all, but on the wedding night they concealed daggers in their hair and stabbed their new husbands to death. Only one girl out of the fifty took pity on her bridegroom and spared his life. Her name was Hypermnestra: his name was Lynceus. They went on to have children together who became the new royal family of Argos.

∾ The story

The action takes place in the territory of Argos, at a shrine somewhere between the city and the sea. The daughters of Danaus (the Danaids) arrive seeking sanctuary. They beg Pelasgus, king of Argos, to protect them and take them in. This presents the king with a dilemma. Either he will need to fight a war on the refugees' behalf or his city will be punished by the gods for violating the laws of hospitality.

Pelasgus decides to let the young women stay but he needs to seek approval for his decision from the full assembly of the citizens. While Pelasgus is absent, the Egyptian fleet arrives. A herald enters accompanied by soldiers and tries to snatch the Danaids away by force. Pelasgus returns with his own army and drives off the intruders.

The girls are accepted into Argos as resident aliens, entitled to the full protection of the community. Danaus counsels his daughters to behave well and modestly in their new home. As the Danaids set out for the city there is a debate about marriage which pits the reluctance of the young women to be forced against their will against an acknowledgement of the sexual nature of all living things and the need for the world to be peopled.

ᕦ About the play

The Suppliants is one of the strangest and most strangely beautiful of all Greek tragedies, rich and suggestive out of all proportion to its length. Its singular feature is that it has a leading part for fifty people – or at least fifty people as represented by the twelve members of the chorus. The preponderance of choral lyrics meant that for many years *The Suppliants* was considered to be an early, rather primitive piece. The chance discovery of a papyrus fragment in 1952 led to a sharp revision of this theory. It turns out that *The Suppliants* is a work written comparatively late in Aeschylus' career, just before the *Oresteia*.

In one sense the play is quite straightforward. It is about helplessness and need and what it means to stand up for those who are defenceless. This is a responsibility not to be entered into lightly as Pelasgus understands.

> If I help you, I pay the price;
> If I refuse, I pay the price.
> What should I do? Intervene?
> Leave it to fate? Either way, I am afraid.
>   tr. Frederic Raphael and Kenneth McLeish

The Danaids present the king with a difficult problem. The refugees are women and foreigners; they arrive unannounced, unaccompanied and unsponsored; but at the same time, and contrary to appearances, it turns out that they are Greek by descent. They have some claim on the city through their ancestor Io: to defend them will mean committing Argos to a war. Yet they cannot simply be turned away, because they also trace their descent from Zeus, king of the gods. Refusing them, Pelasgus and his people risk more than the usual punishment reserved for those who trespass against the laws of hospitality.

Coming from a different, absolutist culture the women insist that the decision is for Pelasgus alone to take.

You   the people!   You   the government!
A pharaoh chosen, unimpeachable you
sustain the fire blazing on the country's altarhearth
         with single-voiced decrees, your own,
and single-handed from the sovereign bench   you
bring all debts to final reckoning.

  tr. Janet Lembke

But this is Greece and the king is quite rightly not prepared
to take a decision without consulting the citizens.

I've told you once before I would not act in this
without the people even though I rule; may they never say,
if some disaster falls on us, 'Paying respect
to strangers you destroyed your native land'.

  tr. Michael Ewans

The women's fear and desperation make them difficult to
deal with. At the beginning of the play their father Danaus
counsels them how to behave.

                You must talk as suppliants should;
show reverence and need, pour sorrows out
and make it plain that you are exiles but have not shed
  blood.
Your voice must have no hint of boldness,
nothing wild; your faces must look sensible
and in your eyes there must be calm.
Do not become too forward in your speech.

  tr. Michael Ewans

But when it comes to it these words count for nothing. The
women's pleas to Pelasgus become wilder and wilder, until
finally they threaten to commit suicide if he will not give
what they want, and to do it in such a way as to bring maximum pollution on the city – by hanging themselves from
the statues of the gods at the altars where they have taken
sanctuary. The king's beleaguered reason is brought face to
face with a seething mass of female emotion.

I need deep thought to save myself,
plunge like a diver down into the depths,
sharp-sighted, sober, so that this affair
brings no destruction on my city.
    tr. Michael Ewans

The girls are no respecters of persons. They have previously issued the same threat to Zeus himself – that if the supreme god will not give in to their wishes they will go to the underworld and seek satisfaction there.

The Suppliants is the first surviving example of the 'asylum play'. Euripides took up the form again in the *Children of Heracles* and *The Suppliant Maidens*, both of which glorified Athens as protector and champion of the weak. These works share a common outline. A group of refugees arrive seeking protection; they pose a problem for the city to which they come for help; their pursuers follow them threatening violence; there are long speeches leading up to the ruler's decision to take them in; finally the city extends its protection and sees off the intruders. Each play raises the question of where justice lies. Sophocles memorably placed the theme of sanctuary at the centre of his final masterpiece *Oedipus at Colonus*. In that play Oedipus confers a blessing on the city that takes him in. In Aeschylus' play too there is the sense that the women, difficult though they are, bring something valuable to Argos. The city will benefit from domesticating all this wildness, as Athens does by incorporating the Furies at the end of the *Eumenides*.

Aeschylus is a great poet of distances. Space in his plays always has an important role. In *The Persians* there is not just the sense of the distances covered painfully in the terrible retreat from Salamis, but also of distances covered hopefully, as the mighty Persian army comes together from all the corners of the Empire. Space is compressed in *Seven Against Thebes* as the invading army crowds against the city walls and expanded in *Prometheus Bound*, where the action involves the whole known world from Egypt to the Caucasus and from the Caspian to the Atlantic.

The Suppliants begins with an account of the heroines' journey:

> This voyage of women   who set sail
> where Nile twists through saltpolished
> sand   Hallowed netherland whose sunbruised
> boundaries graze desert.
>> tr. Janet Lembke

The strange beauty of their starting-point is mirrored in the girls' appearance.

> What kind of group is this – not clothed like Greeks
> but in fine linen clothes and headbands – an exotic garb.

Yet this outlandish exterior is matched with an inner daring.

> You reached this land unharmed, without the help
> of heralds ambassadors or guides;
> how did you dare to come?
>> tr. Michael Ewans

This is contrasted with Pelasgus' rooted kingdom, which he defines by its limits, closed in by mountains, forests and the sea.

The story of Io and her wanderings is one of the central images of the play. Her settled life in Argos was disrupted by the intervention of two powerful gods, yet her sufferings ended in the birth of a child and the founding of a new kingdom across the sea. The journey of the Danaids retraces Io's steps and their irruption into the life of Argos will result in the birth of a new ruling family. Just as Zeus brought Io's troubles to an end at last with his healing touch, he will see her descendants safely established in their new home.

The Suppliants marks a new development in Aeschylus' work. In *The Persians* and *Seven Against Thebes* the scheme of values was comparatively straightforward. Pride and arrogant disregard of the gods led in both cases to disaster. *The Suppliants* stands closer to the *Oresteia* in the complexity of its characterization and ideas. The suppliants themselves are not simple victims, to be pitied. They are shown to be by turns

stubborn, fearful, bold, pious, threatening, violent, blasphemous, terrified and utterly single-minded. Pelasgus and his
people are blameless, yet they become embroiled in a war
which is none of their seeking. It's a sign of this new feeling
for the two-sidedness of things that *The Suppliants* has more,
and more elaborately developed, dialogue scenes than any of
Aeschylus' previous plays.

Zeus himself is not exempt from the general climate of
ambiguity. The Danaids repeatedly appeal to him as supremely
wise and just.

> Force is not in his armory,
> For all that a God does
> Is freed from labor. Sitting in his place
> He executes his will
> From there, from the pure throne.
>   tr. John Herington

Yet this is also the god who overpowered the temple-maiden
Io as the pursuing sons of Aegyptus plan to overpower the
Danaids when they catch them.

It is here that the play reaches out beyond the simple
drama of escape and rescue to engage with the wider matter
of the relationship between men and women, and specifically
with male violence and the female response to it. The sons of
Aegyptus are portrayed from the outset as predatory and
without pity.

>   But the night-thick
> manswarm   self-vaunting, spawned out of Egypt
>   let them die
> before they can man themselves   decency forbid!
> in cousin-beds, in bodies seized and
>   brutally entered.
>   tr. Janet Lembke

When the herald and his soldiers appear this impression is
confirmed.

Go, go down to our ship
as quick as you can.
Well then!
Tearing, tearing, branding;
pools of blood,
severed heads.
Go, go you bitches, down to our ship.
 tr. Michael Ewans

The enemy soldiers are seen as reptiles or insects.

He leads me seaward
Like a spider, step by step.
A dream!
A black dream!
 tr. John Herington

Thirty years or so before Euripides' *Medea*, Aeschylus starts in this play to make the relationship between the sexes one of the central preoccupations of his work. This is something he was to take up and develop in his next trilogy, the *Oresteia*, where violence between men and women is a central part of the story: a father kills his daughter, a wife kills her husband, a son kills his mother. His lost play *Hypsipyle* told the story of the women of Lemnos who, angry because their husbands had taken Thracian concubines, killed every man on the island.

The antagonism between the sons of Aegyptus and the daughters of Danaus cannot be resolved quickly or easily. *The Suppliants* is the first part of a trilogy. We know next to nothing about the other two parts, though a surviving description of *Amymone*, the accompanying satyr play, seems to reveal a common theme of sexual union carried out by a powerful male on the body of an unwilling or resisting female. The second play, *The Sons of Aegyptus*, most probably dealt with the arrival of the invading army, their victory over the Argives and the death of Pelasgus. The final play, *The Daughters of Danaus*, seems to have picked up the story after the murder of the bridegrooms and led somehow to a reaffirmation of the power of sexual love. We have a fragment of a speech of the goddess Aphrodite.

> Now the pure Heaven yearns to pierce the Earth;
> Now Earth is taken with longing for her marriage.
> The rains showering from the mating Sky
> Fill her with life, and she gives birth, for man,
> To flocks of sheep and to the lifegiving wheat.
> And from that liquid exultation springs,
> Perfect, the time of trees. In this I share.
>   tr. John Herington

∾ Translations

The clearest and most straightforward introduction to the play is Michael Ewans's translation (Everyman). Janet Lembke (Oxford) is denser and more literary. There is a rapid speakable version from Frederic Raphael and Kenneth McLeish (Methuen) and a fluent modern adaptation from James Kerr (Oberon Books) which cuts the entire end of the play. The Chicago translation (S. G. Bernadete) can no longer be recommended.

∾ In performance

If the scholars' reading of the papyrus is correct *The Suppliants* was first performed in 463 BC as part of a trilogy with *The Sons of Aegyptus* and *The Daughters of Danaus:* the satyr play was *Amymone*. Aeschylus won first prize and Sophocles came second. An adaptation of the story called *The Danaids*, incorporating other parts of the legend, was performed by the National Theatre of Craiova in 1996 directed by Silviu Pucarete. The play was last seen in London at the Gate Theatre in 1998. An adaptation by Charles Mee entitled *Big Love* was staged at the Actors' Theater Louisville in 2000.

Agamemnon (*Agamemnon*)

✤ The legend

The king of Argos had two sons, Atreus and Thyestes. Thyestes seduced his brother's wife. Atreus punished him by killing Thyestes' children and giving the butchered remains to their father to eat. When Thyestes discovered the trick that had been played on him, he cursed his brother and his brother's family.

Atreus had two sons, Agamemnon and Menelaus. They married two sisters Clytemnestra and Helen. When the Trojan prince Paris seduced Helen and took her away with him to Troy, Agamemnon and Menelaus raised a mighty expedition to fetch her home. On the journey out the Greek fleet was held up by gales. Agamemnon sacrificed his daughter Iphigeneia to the goddess Artemis to secure a fair wind.

After a ten years' siege the Greeks captured Troy and razed it to the ground. Agamemnon returned in triumph home to Argos where he was murdered by Clytemnestra and her lover Aegisthus, the youngest of Thyestes' children and the only one to have survived the murder of his siblings.

✤ The story

The action takes place in Argos, outside the royal palace. It is ten years since the Greek army set sail and those who stayed behind are waiting anxiously for news. Clytemnestra has stationed a watchman on the palace roof to look out for the blazing beacon which will signify the fall of Troy.

The fire-signal brings news of the Greek success and the citizens assemble in front of the palace. The chorus, old men past the age for military service, are apprehensive. They fear the outcome of an expedition that has claimed so many lives, including that of the innocent Iphigeneia. They are also uneasy because they know of Clytemnestra's adultery and fear what will happen when Agamemnon returns home.

A herald brings news of the sack of Troy and the disasters which overtook the Greek fleet on the way home. Clytemnestra prepares a welcome for her husband.

Agamemnon arrives in his chariot accompanied by his concubine Cassandra. Cassandra is a prophetess. The god Apollo gave her gift of foretelling the future in exchange for her virginity. When she reneged on the bargain, it was too late to withdraw the gift but Apollo rendered it useless by arranging that no one would believe her.

Clytemnestra tempts Agamemnon to walk into the palace on a carpet of rich purple hangings, delicate fabrics suitable only for the gods. He lets himself be persuaded and goes into the palace to his death. Cassandra is granted a vision of the horrors of the house of Atreus, the slaughtered children and the feuding brothers. She sees that Clytemnestra will murder Agamemnon and that she too will be struck down in her turn.

Clytemnestra appears standing over the slaughtered bodies of Agamemnon and Cassandra and proudly justifies what she has done. She is joined by Aegisthus her lover and fellow conspirator. The murderous couple are now the new rulers of the kingdom.

∽ About the play

Aeschylus is the great creator of the drama of fear.
  Thomas G. Rosenmeyer

Why, why at the doors
Of my fore-seeing heart
Does this terror keep beating its wings?
  tr. Louis MacNeice

If Aeschylus is the dramatist of fear, then *Agamemnon* is undoubtedly his masterpiece. The foreboding of the chorus in *The Persians* and the outbreaks of naked terror in *Seven*

Against Thebes and *The Suppliants* are pale in comparison with the sustained atmosphere of dread and apprehension in *Agamemnon*.

The play begins in the final hours before dawn. The watchman is waiting for the light of the signal fire to pierce the darkness. He thinks back over the year of nights he has spent watching on the palace roof too terrified to sleep:

> Yet when I take my restless rest in the soaking dew,
> My night not visited with dreams –
> For fear stands by me in place of sleep
> That I cannot close my eyes in sleep –
> Whenever I think to sing or hum to myself
> As an antidote to sleep, then every time I groan
> And fall to weeping for the fortunes of this house.
>   tr. Louis MacNeice

The fear is a twofold. Anxiety about what is happening at Troy is coupled with knowledge of what has gone wrong at home. This double tension drives the play. The beacon blazing out brings news of success but sets in train a chain of events at least as deadly as anything that has gone before. The relief of the victory-fire is short-lived. As the chorus enter their narrative takes us back in time to the very beginning of the conflict. We know the war is ended but the old men make us feel that it is to do all over again, and that victory is still a distant prospect. They take the story back to before the war, when the great Greek expedition was assembling.

> An omen figures forth the fall of Troy.
> Kings of the birds to our kings came,
> One with a white rump, the other black,
> Appearing near the palace on the spear-arm side
> Where all could see them,
> Tearing a pregnant hare with the unborn young
> Foiled of their courses.
>   tr. Louis MacNeice

The power and majesty of the great eagles is set against the softness of the hare and the vulnerability of the foetuses torn from her womb.

This feeling for the suffering of the innocent is intensified by the horrible killing of Iphigeneia.

> Then dropping on the ground her saffron dress,
> Glancing at each of her appointed
> Sacrificers a shaft of pity,
> Plain as in a picture she wished
> To speak to them by name, for often
> At her father's table where men feasted
> She had sung in celebration for her father
> With pure voice, affectionately, virginally,
> The hymn of happiness at the third libation.
> The sequel to this I saw not and tell not.
>   tr. Louis MacNeice

Artemis is protector of all defenceless things. When she demands the death of Agamemnon's daughter it is as if it is down payment for all the innocent lives that will be lost in the coming war.

The action we see takes place in Argos but in order to put it in its context Aeschylus embarks on great sweeps through time and space. The war and its grisly prelude are condensed into a series of unforgettable film-like images. The picture of Iphigeneia begging for her life, her pale defenceless body standing out in relief against the armour of the surrounding soldiers, is matched by the portrait of Menelaus wandering restless through his empty palace.

> Through desire for her who is overseas, a ghost
> Will seem to rule the household.
>   And now her husband hates
>   The grace of shapely statues;
>   In the emptiness of their eyes
>   All their appeal is departed.
>   tr. Louis MacNeice

But pain is not the special property of the ruling house.

Once the war gets under way, it brings grief to every home.

> But the money-changer War, changer of bodies
> Holding his balance in the battle
> Home from Troy refined by fire
> Sends back to friends the dust
> That is heavy with tears, stowing
> A man's worth of ashes
> In an easily handled jar.
>> tr. Louis MacNeice

Clytemnestra gives a picture of Troy in the aftermath of its capture.

> The Trojans all tearful, their arms round their fallen
> embracing cold corpses, the widows, the orphans,
> knowing their own lives mean only bond-chains
> keen for their bloodkin, their nearest their dearest;
> the Greeks, their whole night spend in harsh skirmish,
> famished for breakfast swoop down onto Troy,
> no billets allotted, all discipline broken,
> each man for himself, the luck of the straw lot,
> they bed themselves down in the houses they've captured,
> free of the nightfrost the beds in the open,
> sleep, for once without sentries, and wake up refreshed.
>> tr. Tony Harrison

The herald fills in the detail of the ten-year campaign with realism that even Homer never rivalled.

> If I were to tell of our labours, our hard lodging,
> The sleeping on crowded decks, the scanty blankets,
> Tossing and groaning, rations that never reached us –
> And the land too gave matter for more disgust,
> For our beds lay under the enemy's walls.
> Continuous drizzle from the sky, dews from the marshes,
> Rotting our clothes, filling our hair with lice.
> And if one were to tell of bird-destroying winter
> Intolerable from the snows of Ida

Or of the heat when the sea slackens at noon
Waveless and dozing in a depressed calm –
But why make these complaints? The weariness is over . . .
tr. Louis MacNeice

When Agamemnon finally enters in his war chariot halfway through the play he brings this history with him. Too many people have died trying to mend a single broken marriage and he bears much of the responsibility. The chorus fear that there is a price to be paid for all the destruction: 'the gods are not unwatchful of those who cause much bloodshed'.

Part of the play's uncanny atmosphere comes from the feeling that time has somehow been compacted or has collapsed upon itself like matter in a neutron star. The story of the *Oresteia* covers three generations but the years seem pressed together so that Agamemnon, who sacrifices his daughter, merges with Atreus, the child-killer; Aegisthus, repeating the adultery of his father, blends with Thyestes; Clytemnestra is Helen's destructive sister. And the pattern persists into the next generation: Electra, vengeful and haunted by the past, becomes a version of Clytemnestra; Orestes takes on the spirit of his dead father. It's as if the characters are not surrounded by air but by some thicker, more resistant medium, which they have to wade through. Agamemnon himself seems to be wading in blood as he walks into the palace along the delicate, expensive purple hangings his wife's maids have laid out for him – his own blood, the blood of his daughter and of all the men whose deaths he oversaw. The stream flows into the palace and mingles with the blood that has been spilled within the house.

If the other characters feel to be sleepwalking, Clytemnestra is full of terrible energy – a woman with the mind of a man. Cassandra calls her a two-footed lioness, and it is her will that drives the action forward, exerting an inexorable grip over the play's second half. The returning warrior steps straight into a new form of contest – the struggle between male and female. At first he refuses to walk on the purple fabric.

It is the gods who should be honoured in this way.
But being mortal to tread embroidered beauty
For me is no way without fear.

But Clytemnestra is implacable.

CLYTEMNESTRA: And how would Priam have acted in your place?
AGAMEMNON: He would have trod the cloths, I think, for certain.
CLYTEMNESTRA: Then do not flinch before the blame of men.
AGAMEMNON: The voice of the multitude is very strong.
CLYTEMNESTRA: But the man none envy is not enviable.
AGAMEMNON: It is not a woman's part to love disputing.
CLYTEMNESTRA: But it is a conqueror's part to yield upon occasion.
AGAMEMNON: You think such victory worth fighting for?
CLYTEMNESTRA: Give way. Consent to let me have the mastery.
AGAMEMNON: Well, if such is your wish, let someone quickly loose
My vassal sandals . . .

    tr. Louis MacNeice

Agamemnon enters the palace and the chorus break out in a paroxysm of anxiety. But Aeschylus doesn't let the murder happen yet. Clytemnestra reappears to order Cassandra, her husband's concubine, into the house. Transferring the focus here to Cassandra is a dramatic masterstroke. She has been sitting silent in Agamemnon's chariot throughout the previous scene. It is only when Clytemnestra has withdrawn that she begins to speak. Her tormented ravings introduce a new tone into the play. This is the voice of naked vulnerability. Because her vision goes backwards and forwards in time, she is able to grasp in one intuitive flash the full horror of the trap which she has entered. Her lament releases all the emotion that has been kept suppressed so far. She grieves for herself but also for those who have died before. For the first time in

the play the story reaches back to include the slaughtered
children of Thyestes.

> Clues! I have clues! Look! They are these.
> These wailing, these children, butchery of children;
> Roasted flesh, a father sitting to dinner.

She sees Agamemnon's death before it happens.

> Quick! Be on your guard! The bull –
> Keep him clear of the cow.
> Caught with a trick, the black horn's point,
> She strikes. He falls; lies in the water.
> Murder a trick in the bath. I tell what I see.

She sees the destruction of her native city.

> Oh trouble on trouble of a city lost, lost utterly!
> My father's sacrifices before the towers,
> Much killing of cattle and sheep,
> No cure – availed not at all
> To prevent the coming of what came to Troy
> And I, my brain on fire, shall soon enter the trap.
>> tr. Louis MacNeice

The whole narrative of the play is recapped in these flashes
of fear, in poetry of great lyric intensity. Eventually the terror
blows itself out and Cassandra prepares herself calmly to face
her death. She strips off her prophetess's clothing and goes
towards the palace. She can see clearly now the ghosts of the
slaughtered children gathered at the threshold.

> Do you see these who sit before the house,
> Children, like the shape of dreams?
> Children who seem to have been killed by their kinsfolk,
> Filling their hands with meat, flesh of themselves,
> Guts and entrails, handfuls of lament.
>> tr. Louis MacNeice

She goes to her death with great dignity, clear eyed.

CASSANDRA: No escape, my friends,
  not now
CHORUS: But the last hour should be savoured.
CASSANDRA: My hour has come. Little to gain from flight.
CHORUS: You're brave, believe me, full of gallant heart.
CASSANDRA: Only the wretched go with praise like that. ·
    tr. Robert Fagles

Agamemnon is killed and the chorus's brief attempt at revolt
is quickly snuffed out. Clytemnestra and Aegisthus are triumphant. But this new settlement is only provisional.
Cassandra has told us this will not be the end of the story.

But witness you my words after my death
When a woman dies in return for me a woman
And a man falls for a man with a wicked wife.
    tr. Louis MacNeice

Agamemnon begins in darkness and is a play shot through
with ambiguity. Clytemnestra is a murderer but she is avenging
the murder of her daughter. Aegisthus is an adulterer but he's
avenging the death of his siblings. Helen destroys a city and
many lives yet is only being true to her own immoral beauty,
like the lion cub which grows from family pet to natural killer.
Agamemnon himself is a child-murderer and impresario of
slaughter, yet the Trojan War and the Greek victory in it are
willed by the gods: when it comes to the sacrifice of Iphigeneia
he is said to have 'put on the halter of Necessity'. There is no
easy way out from these complications and it will take the two
remaining plays of the trilogy to resolve them.

∿ Translations

The reader is spoiled for choice. There are two very fine and
very different translations from two poet-scholars, Louis
MacNeice (1936) and Tony Harrison (1981) – both published
by Faber. Faber also publish freer translations by Ted Hughes
and Robert Lowell, (the latter abbreviated and very free

indeed). There are reliable versions from Michael Ewans (Everyman), Peter Meineck (Hackett Publishing), Robert Fagles (Penguin), Alan Shapiro and Peter Burian (Oxford) and Frederic Raphael and Kenneth McLeish (Cambridge), and an academically respectable translation from Hugh Lloyd-Jones (Duckworth). Eduard Fraenkel's great edition comes complete with a literal, and the generally useful Cambridge Translations from Greek Drama series has a new version in the pipeline. Richmond Lattimore (Chicago) is no longer the automatic first choice.

∾ In performance

The *Oresteia* trilogy – *Agamemnon*, *The Libation Bearers* and *Eumenides* – together with the satyr play *Proteus* was first performed in 458 BC. It won first prize. For subsequent stage history see below under *The Eumenides*.

The Libation Bearers (*Choephoroi*)

∾ The legend

Agamemnon, King of Argos, was the leader of the great Greek expedition against Troy. In order to secure a wind for the fleet to sail, he sacrificed his daughter Iphigeneia.

The war lasted ten years. When Agamemnon returned home, his wife Clytemnestra killed him with the help of her lover Aegisthus and took over the kingdom.

Agamemnon and Clytemnestra had two children, a daughter, Electra, and a son, Orestes. Electra became a powerless spectator of the new regime. Orestes was living in exile at the time of his father's murder. The god Apollo sent him to revenge his father's death, which he did by killing his mother.

This sin against the most basic of all human bonds summoned terrible snake-haired creatures from under the earth to punish the man who committed it. These creatures were called the Furies (perhaps 'Ragers' would be a better translation). Orestes was forced to throw himself on the mercy of Apollo, god of Light, to escape the anger of these terrifying monsters of the dark.

∿ The story

Orestes returns to Argos to kill his mother, following the instructions of the god Apollo. He and his friend Pylades visit Agamemnon's grave to ask the dead man's spirit for help.

Clytemnestra has a dream about a deadly snake that came to drink her blood. She sends her daughter Electra and a group of slave women – the Libation Bearers of the title – with offerings to the dead king's tomb. Electra discovers a lock of hair that Orestes has placed on the grave.

Brother and sister are reunited. Electra, Orestes and the chorus invoke the shade of Agamemnon and the powers above and below the earth to sanction the death of Clytemnestra and her lover Aegisthus.

Orestes and Pylades pose as strangers and seek hospitality in the palace. Orestes tells Clytemnestra that her son has died in exile. Clytemnestra despatches Orestes' old nurse to fetch Aegisthus and his soldiers to hear the news. The chorus persuade the nurse to leave out the part of the message relating to the soldiers so that Aegisthus arrives unaccompanied. He is killed inside the palace.

Clytemnestra begs her son not to kill his mother. Orestes hesitates but Pylades reminds him of his duty, saying that it is 'better to offend the whole human race than the gods'. In a deliberate echo of *Agamemnon*, Orestes appears standing over the slaughtered bodies of Aegisthus and his mother. But his triumph is short-lived. He sees the deadly Furies, with their eyes dripping blood and their hair of snakes, closing in on him. Clutching a suppliant's olive branch he runs out to seek sanctuary at Apollo's temple in Delphi.

∾ About the play

Nothing will wash away this blood.
So much blood has fallen on our earth,
it is caked and hard and nothing drains off.
  tr. Robert Lowell

        Blood of the murdered
Cries from the earth for blood.
The gods have fixed that law.
The Furies, screaming for blood,
Rise like a miasma
From the fallen blood.
  tr. Ted Hughes

In *The Libation Bearers*, blood – spilled blood, caked blood, blood soaked into the earth, clotted blood – is omnipresent. Blood is mentioned so often you can almost taste it. The only way of scrubbing out the old stains is to use fresh blood to do it. The Furies that pursue Orestes have eyes that drip more blood.

From the opening the play is directed towards a single end: the murder of Clytemnestra. The first half represents a slow gathering of powers. The gods above, the gods below and the human agents all rally to the task. The second half has a swifter and more headlong rhythm, as the gathered powers are unleashed.

The opening of the play focuses on revenge for Agamemnon's murder. Electra, sent to her father's grave with offerings, hesitates to pray for her mother's safety.

When I pour these burial offerings, what should I say?
What would be right? How can I pray to my father?
Should I say I bring dedications from a loving wife
to her beloved husband when they come from my
    mother?
Or should I recite the customary saying:
'Repay those who send these honors'

for they deserve a gift that matches their evil.
> tr. Peter Meineck

But where Electra hesitates the chorus is quite clear:

CHORUS: Pour the wine and pray for those you can trust.
ELECTRA: Those I can trust. Who can I trust?
CHORUS: Yourself. And all who hate Aegisthus.
ELECTRA: For myself. And for you? Shall I make this prayer
    for you?
CHORUS: You know the truth of my words. You decide.
ELECTRA: What other can there be – that I can trust?
CHORUS: Pray for Orestes. Pray for far-off Orestes.
ELECTRA: Orestes! Yes! For Orestes!
CHORUS: And for the murderers pray –
ELECTRA: Yes, pray what?
    What shall I pray for the killers? What?
CHORUS: Pray
    That a god or a man
    May come, bringing justice.
ELECTRA: To judge, to convict, to condemn.
CHORUS: To kill! Blood for blood. Pray for that.
ELECTRA: Can God hear a prayer for assassination?
CHORUS: Evil for evil is justice
    And justice is holy.
> tr. Ted Hughes

The need for vengeance is clearly stated. Savagery seems to have the blessing of the gods. Electra calls for the killers to be punished.

> Bring the avenger into the light,
> let Justice kill the killers.
> In the midst of my prayers for good
> I say for them a prayer for evil.
> > tr. Peter Meineck

It is at this point that she discovers the lock of hair that Orestes has placed on the grave. In Sophocles' *Electra* the recognition scene between Electra and the brother that she thought had died forms the climax of the play. Orestes' appearance is like a miracle, as unexpected as if Agamemnon himself had come back to life. After the emotional intensity of this encounter the murder of Clytemnestra is almost incidental. Aeschylus by contrast has brother and sister reunited early in the action. The scene is affecting but it is a prelude not a climax. It is only the first step on a journey.

Orestes arrives knowing what needs to be done. Apollo's oracle has ordered Clytemnestra's death and the Furies will punish any backsliding.

> He told me what their unappeased anger
> Spills into men's homes.
> The ulcers that gnaw the human shape
> To an oozing stump.
> The white fungus that flowers on the ulcers.
> Then he told me
> What the unavenged blood of a murdered father
> Presents to the eyes of a negligent son.
> The Furies, forcing their way out of thick darkness,
> Drunk with the fumes of that blood,
> Their arrows flying in the darkness,
> Insanity flung like a net,
> Their night horrors dragging the sleeper awake,
> Hunting him from collapse to deeper collapse,
> Lashing him from city to city
> With whips of bronze wire.
>
>   tr. Ted Hughes

But it is important that Orestes is not seen simply as a puppet. He pauses to consider whether he is right to trust in oracles and concludes that with or without the oracles the deed must still be done. He has desires of his own.

> I have many motives of my own that drive me;
> The god's command, the great sorrow I feel for my father,
> and the burden of the stolen birthright.

And what of my people, the finest of men,
who conquered Troy with their sterling spirit?
They should not be ruled by a pair of women!
>   tr. Peter Meineck

The will of the gods and the free choice of a human being
come together here.

There follows an extraordinary scene – a mixture of
singing, chanting, dance and the spoken word. It is part
lament, part invocation, part threat and part an affirmation of
solidarity. It is in passages like this that the huge range of formal resources open to the Greek tragedians permits a very
deep kind of realism. Orestes and Electra have already
reached a decision. What follows is a revisiting of all the
emotions that went into its making. Different facets are taken
up and considered but lyrically, not reasonably. The different
emotions succeed one another; they are not ranged in a hier-
archy. The scene has another purpose too. Brother and sister
stand together but there is another family member – the
shade of Agamemnon – whose help they need.

ORESTES: O Earth, send up my father to survey the battle!
ELECTRA: O Persephassa, grant him beauteous victory!
ORESTES: Remember the bath in which you were murdered
     father!
ELECTRA: Remember the new sort of covering they
     devised!
ORESTES: Do these shameful words not rouse you father?
ELECTRA: Do you not raise erect your beloved head?
>   tr. Hugh Lloyd-Jones

Electra and the chorus were sent with offerings to the dead
king's grave because Clytemnestra had had a dream. Aeschylus
waits till now to tell us what it was.

CHORUS: She dreamed she gave birth to a snake, she said it
     herself!
ORESTES: A snake? What else?
CHORUS: She laid it down and wrapped it like a baby.

ORESTES: What? Did she see this creature feeding?
CHORUS: She dreamed that she suckled it herself.
ORESTES: But, a snake? It must have slashed her breast?
CHORUS: It sucked her milk clotted with blood.

Orestes sees instantly what the dream means.

> The snake came from the same place as I.
> She wrapped it in the same cloths that I wore.
> It suckled at the breast that nurtured me . . .
> As she has raised this gruesome omen,
> so she must die. I am the snake,
> I will be the one to kill her and fulfil this dream.
> tr. Peter Meineck

Everything has now converged: Apollo's oracle, the urging of the Furies, Agamemnon's spirit from beyond the grave, Orestes' own wishes and finally this portent from the mind of Clytemnestra herself. From this point on the action uncoils like a spring. The second half of the play moves in quite a different way to the first. There is a rapid succession of short scenes: exits and entrances follow one another in accelerating rhythm. Orestes' first encounter with his mother is shot through with eerie tension. Will she recognize her son? Will he flinch from carrying out his plan? In *Agamemnon* it is Clytemnestra who tricked her husband into entering the palace, luring him inside to his death. This time the roles are reversed: the deceiver becomes the deceived.

At this point Aeschylus suddenly alters the focus. The entry of the Nurse, like that of the Herald in *Agamemnon*, brings a refreshing glimpse of life as it is lived outside the deadly circle of the ruling family. The Herald has survived the ten years' war at Troy and is unaffectedly glad to be back home. His simple pleasure at having escaped alive and come back safe is something King Agamemnon can never know. The Nurse's grief at the news of Orestes' pretended death puts Clytemnestra's show of mourning into perspective. In the moments before the matricide, we have a reminder of

Orestes' humanity and of the simple universal facts of child-care.

> A baby's like a little animal, it can't think for itself,
> it needs to be nursed. You have to know its mind.
> I mean, when he was that small he couldn't talk,
> so he could tell me if he was hungry or thirsty,
> or when he wanted to pee, and a baby's insides are a law
> unto themselves, let me tell you! I had to foresee
> his every need, and a lot of the time I was wrong,
> then I would have to wash out his little baby clothes.
> Washerwoman and childminder all rolled into one,
> I was an expert at both . . .
>   tr. Peter Meineck

This innocent and helpless child is now required to kill the woman who gave him birth.

Through the first half of the play the emphasis is on the need for vengeance: the fact that vengeance means the murder of a mother by her son is deliberately left vague. It is not until Clytemnestra and Orestes are face to face that the full horror of the deed strikes home. Faced with the unescapable reality, Orestes hesitates. Aeschylus does something totally unexpected here. Orestes has been accompanied throughout the play by a silent companion, Pylades. This other young man, a friend from the time of exile, has shadowed his every move yet never said a word. At this crucial moment this silent figure acquires a voice.

ORESTES: Pylades, what should I do? How can I kill my own mother?
PYLADES: And what then becomes of the oracles of Apollo declared at Delphi, or the unbreakable oath we took?
Better to be hated by every man on earth than hated by the gods.

When Orestes turns to his friend he uses the word 'mother' for the first and only time in the play. Pylades never speaks again, but his intervention has been enough.

CLYTEMNESTRA: My son, I think you mean to kill your
    mother.
ORESTES: You are the killer, not I. You kill yourself.
CLYTEMNESTRA: Then beware the vengeful hellhounds of a
    mother's curse.
ORESTES: And how would I escape my father's if I failed?
[. . .]
CLYTEMNESTRA: Ah! I suckled this serpent, I gave it life!
ORESTES: Yes, the terror you saw in your dream was true.
    You should not have killed, now suffer what you should
    not.
    tr. Peter Meineck

Clytemnestra is spoken of by the chorus as the serpent that
struck down the eagle Agamemnon. Now Orestes has taken
on his mother's snake-like nature and entered into his inheritance. The young man who entered with such hope has now
become another link in the chain of murder. The chorus refer
to Orestes as bringing light into the darkness but it isn't long
before the light is extinguished. Through most of the play
Aeschylus has been careful not to refer to events that preceded
Agamemnon's death: the killing of Thyestes' children and the
sacrifice of Iphigeneia are passed over in silence. Only after
the murder of Clytemnestra does the chorus draw attention to
the deadly, continuing and seemingly unstoppable pattern and
poses the question: where will it end? There are no humans
left to carry on the feud but there is still no relief. The perse-
cuting and deadly snakes now belong to the Furies who are
hunting Orestes to avenge the spilled blood of his mother.

∿ Translations

Ted Hughes' version (Faber), though often quite free, catches
a good deal of the original's barbaric power. The most reliable reading texts are Peter Meineck (Hackett Publishing),
Michael Ewans (Everyman) and Alan Shapiro and Peter
Burian (Oxford). There is an academically sound translation

from Hugh Lloyd-Jones (Duckworth) and useful modern versions from Robert Fagles (Penguin) and Frederic Raphael and Kenneth McLeish (Cambridge). The poet-scholar Tony Harrison's translation formed the basis of Peter Hall's National Theatre production of 1981. Robert Lowell (Faber) is fiery but abbreviated. Richmond Lattimore (Chicago) is now at the back of the queue.

∿ In performance

See above, under *Agamemnon*, and below, under *The Eumenides*.

The Eumenides (*Eumenides*)

∿ The legend

Orestes was ordered by the god Apollo to kill his mother Clytemnestra. After the murder he was pursued by the Furies and sought the protection of Apollo's shrine at Delphi. Following Apollo's advice Orestes went to Athens where he was put on trial for murder and acquitted.

The plot of *The Eumenides* is made up of two different legends put together and is largely Aeschylus' own invention. Early versions of Orestes' story came to an end with the death of Clytemnestra (see above under *The Libation Bearers*). Sometime in the sixth century the narrative was expanded to include Orestes' madness and recovery or (in an alternative version) his pursuit and persecution by the Furies. According to one account he travelled to Athens where he was put on trial before a jury of the gods.

Aeschylus took this story and combined it with an account of the founding of the Areopagus, which was the Athenian court for trying murder cases. Perhaps the most important change he made to the legend is that in his play the jury are made up of human beings not of gods.

∾ The story

After the murder of his mother Orestes fled for sanctuary to Apollo's shrine at Delphi. The Furies have followed him there and surrounded the altar where he has taken refuge. Apollo tells Orestes that he must go to Athens and throw himself on the mercy of Athene.

Orestes makes his escape while the Furies are sleeping. The ghost of Clytemnestra appears and appeals to the dark goddesses for help. Apollo drives the Furies from his temple and they set out once more to hunt their prey.

Orestes arrives in Athens followed closely by his pursuers. He begs Athene to help him. She summons a jury of Athenian citizens to hear his case. At the trial the Furies act as counsel for the prosecution; Apollo acts as counsel for the defence. The jury is equally divided and Athene decides the matter by casting her vote for Orestes to be acquitted.

The Furies consider they have been cheated and threaten the city of Athens with terrible consequences. Athene wins them over with promises of honourable treatment and they finally consent to stay in Athens and give the city their blessing and protection.

The title *Eumenides* means 'the kindly ones' and is a euphemistic way of referring to the Furies.

∾ About the play

The doer must suffer his deed.
  Agamemnon, tr. Anne Lebeck

Through suffering, learning.
  Agamemnon, tr. John Herington

The vampires bless the city
  poster for a German production, 1975

The Eumenides is a play about change and transformation. In *Agamemnon* and *The Libation Bearers* events had the quality of nightmare; they were menacing and inexorable; there seemed to be no way out. In *The Eumenides* all this alters. What appeared to be absolute becomes subject to compromise; what was fixed is seen as alterable.

When the play opens any kind of harmony seems remote. Light and Dark, Male and Female, Heaven and Earth, New and Old confront each other in stark opposition. The Furies, daughters of Night, are hunting Orestes; Apollo, god of Light, is protecting him. Orestes avenged his father by killing his mother. It was the male god Apollo who ordered him to commit the murder. The Furies, female goddesses, are seeking vengeance for the murdered woman. They come from under the earth. Apollo is one of the new gods whose home is in the sky. The feud within the house of Atreus has gradually come to polarize the universe.

The action falls into four separate parts. Firstly there is the confrontation at Delphi. Secondly there are the preparations for the trial at Athens, which establishes a framework within which the conflict can be resolved. The third part is the trial itself. The final movement, taking up a quarter of the play's length, is devoted to reconciliation. In it Athene persuades the Furies to abandon their deadly anger and to bless the city. What is dramatized in *The Eumenides* is the difficult, gripping and grown-up process of hammering out a compromise to which all parties can agree.

At the start of the play Orestes turns to Apollo for help. The god promises his protection.

> No, I will never fail you, through to the end,
> Your guardian standing by your side or worlds away!
> I will show no mercy to your enemies!

He looks down on Orestes' pursuers as primitive and barbaric.

> They disgust me.

These grey ancient children never touched
by god, man or beast – the eternal virgins.
Born for destruction only, the dark pit,
they range the bowels of the Earth, the world of death,
loathed by men and the gods who hold Olympus.

    tr. Robert Fagles

As Orestes makes his escape the ghost of Clytemnestra
calls on the sleeping Furies to follow him.

You sleep? What use are you asleep?
It is because of you that I am dishonoured by the dead.
They charge me with the killings, accuse me –
I who suffered the cruellest pain from my closest kin.
There is no angry god to avenge me,
slaughtered by those mother-killing hands.
See my wounds – let them tear your hearts.

    tr. Peter Meineck

The battle lines are drawn: each side in turn has invoked their
supernatural sponsor. Apollo concludes the sequence by
chasing the Furies from his temple.

Out, I tell you, out of these halls – fast! –
set the Prophet's chamber free!

                          Or take
the flash and stab of this, this flying viper
whipped from the golden chord that strings my bow!
Go where heads are severed, eyes gouged out,
where justice and bloody slaughter are the same.
castrations, wasted seed, young men's glories butchered,
extremities maimed, and huge stones on the chest
and the victims wail for pity.

    tr. Robert Fagles

This encounter marks the end of the play's first movement
and is the first sign of an emerging compromise. Although
the language is violent and the confrontation full of threats,
no actual violence is committed – and this is something new.

The dispute is referred to a third party for settlement; it will be brought before the court of the Areopagus at Athens.

The action moves to Athens and the balance of forces shifts again. Apollo is replaced as Zeus' representative by Athene, who adopts a more conciliatory tone. The Furies too show that they have another side to them. So far they have been seen as merely savage and repellent. Now they claim to be a necessary part of civilization. The terror they engender is creative; without them there can be no such thing as justice.

> How can the man
> or city that has no fear
> to nourish the heart
> ever have respect for justice?
>   tr. Frederic Raphael and Kenneth McLeish

A community without fear is a community where there are no sanctions. The result can only be anarchy or repression, with no place for a civilized middle way. There is more at stake in the trial of Orestes than the fate of a single individual. The whole rule of law is being called into question. What is being decided is nothing more or less than the fate of human society itself.

Justice – *Dike* in Greek – is one of the keywords of the trilogy. At first it means little more than payback. Agamemnon and Menelaus get payback from Troy for the abduction of Helen; Clytemnestra gets payback from Agamemnon for the murder of her daughter; Orestes gets payback from his mother for the murder of his father. When it comes to the murder of Clytemnestra, Apollo breaks the cycle. He promises that Orestes will escape the consequences of the killing: 'The oracle told me: do it and go unpunished'. Zeus, through the agency of his son, has set aside his law that 'the doer must suffer his deed'. But the Furies, who enforce the code, have not been consulted and do not agree to the change. They are conservatives, upholding the old order that Zeus himself has left behind. The old law and the new law now come into conflict – and it is not immediately clear what the new law is, except that Zeus has intervened to protect the young man who carried out his orders. *The Eumenides* sees Athene establish a new definition of justice: guilt or acquittal depend on the verdict of a court of human beings who have carefully weighed the evidence. *Dike* now acquires other more civilized meanings – 'trial' and 'justice'.

'Through suffering, learning.' Zeus revised the old law when he saw that it did not take sufficient account of complexities; something more supple and more adequate was needed. Here is another of the play's transformations. The gods have come to understand that they have obligations that go beyond the mere exercise of their power. Apollo says,

> I will defend my suppliant and save him.
> A terror to gods and men, the outcast's anger,
> once I fail him all of my own free will.
>   tr. Robert Fagles

Athene sees that whichever way the verdict goes, she will be held responsible. She will incur the anger of Zeus and of Apollo if she condemns Orestes. If she acquits him the Athenians will blame her for the disasters visited on them by the angry Furies. One of the *Oresteia*'s most perceptive critics has written that the trilogy dramatizes 'the necessity of disastrous choice'. Athene wisely decides to share the burden: the citizens of Athens will be affected by the outcome so it is only right that they should help decide.

> Because this case has become my responsibility
> I will appoint the exemplary men of my city
> as magistrates over murder, bound by a solemn oath,
> for now and ever to serve this sacred court.
>   tr. Peter Meineck

This widening of the decision-making powers, so that the responsibility belongs not to an individual but to a group, is an important step towards the final settlement. It is important too that justice is something that gods and human beings make together.

The Eumenides moves beyond the old simplicities to embrace a new sense of complexity, so it is fitting that the trial of Orestes is full of imperfections. Both the counsel for the prosecution (the Furies) and the counsel for the defence (Apollo) exaggerate their arguments and attempt to threaten or to bribe the jurors. The Furies quickly get Orestes to admit his crime.

CHORUS: Will you tell us how you killed her?
ORESTES: I held my sword at her neck and slit her throat.
CHORUS: Who persuaded you to do this, who advised it?
ORESTES: It was the god's word, he will testify to that.
CHORUS: The prophet guided you to kill your own mother?
ORESTES: Yes, and as yet I have no regrets.
CHORUS: You will when the verdict places you in our grasp.
> tr. Peter Meineck

Apollo defends Orestes by a piece of extremely specious reasoning.

The son is said to belong to the mother –
But she isn't the real parent.
She is the nurse.
She is like the soil in the pot
Where the seed germinates, and the plant springs,
The seed planted there by the father.
If the child lives, the mother
Continues to tend it, and nurse it –
As the plant is kept in the pot till it flowers.
The mother is incidental.
She may be entirely unnecessary . . .
> tr. Ted Hughes

But despite its imperfections, the process works. The jury, split down the middle, recognizes that there is truth on both sides. The verdict is a collaborative effort between gods and humans. When the decision is tied Athene casts her vote in favour of acquittal, and Zeus' purpose is fulfilled. But the manner of its fulfilment has been important and this leads into the final section of the play.

Just as the new Olympian gods have changed, the Furies cannot be allowed to continue in their old ways either. There can be no exceptions to the rule 'Through suffering, learning'. However it is not enough for Zeus simply to batter them into submission by force. Since there can be no justice without their contribution, their consent is vital. The task is too important to be left to Apollo to deal with. His feelings of revulsion are only too apparent: 'You repulsive hags! The gods detest you.' It is Athene who has to do the job.

> You were not defeated, the votes were even,
> it was an honest verdict, there is no disgrace. . . .
> I swear by Justice that you will receive your due respect.
> I will give you a shrine of the earth in this righteous land
> and seat you on gleaming thrones beside an altar,
> where my citizens will worship you with honor.
> tr. Peter Meineck

The verdict has left the Furies unreconciled, and subduing them is not an easy task. What follows is a scene like that between Eteocles and the terrified women in *Seven Against Thebes*: one side is full of vivid emotion, a turmoil that is sung and danced with jagged vehemence; the other side is spoken, calm, conciliatory – and this is the side that in the end wins out.

The Eumenides is a deeply political play in more ways than one. Not only does it offer an account of the struggle between what might be called liberal and conservative forces, it is also tied more closely than most Greek tragedies to a particular political context. For many years the Areopagus had functioned as a form of Athenian senate. Membership was made up of the former archons – that is the two men who every year served as the senior representatives of the state. The Areopagus chose the new archons and supervised the appointment of the other magistrates. It is not surprising that it exercised a strong conservative influence. Four years before the *Oresteia* was written, the Areopagus was stripped of these supervisory powers and returned to its original more limited function as a court of law dealing with cases of homicide.

Sovereign power was now vested in the full assembly of the citizens: Athens had become a full democracy at last.

But the man who had carried through the reforms was murdered shortly after in circumstances that were never cleared up. The honour paid to the vanquished conservative forces expresses a strong contemporary need and Aeschylus pays tribute to the importance of the Areopagus by making it the focus of the action. The Furies' blessing on the city contains a pointed warning.

> May faction, sedition,
> for ever flesh-hungry,
> civil disturbance,
> cycles of slaying,
> never bray in this city,
> its dust never gulp
> the blood of its people,
> the state get ripped open
> by rages of bloodgrudge,
> a chainlink of murder.
> Let the linking be love-bonds,
> common likes, common hatreds,
> a group bond against
> the troubles men suffer.
>   tr. Tony Harrison

The play is a celebration of the creative powers of the universe. It shows gods and men united in their concern for justice. And it says that a city cannot prosper unless it can manage to harness the forces of the irrational.

> Go to your home, children of Night,
> Honoured with music and torchlight.

> *Silence while the Kind ones pass*

> Grave powers, gracious and kindly,
> Attended by torches follow us home.
>   tr. Tony Harrison

∾ Translations

See above, under *Agamemnon* and *The Libation Bearers*.

∾ In performance

In the nineteenth century, the *Oresteia* trilogy stands behind Herman Melville's *Moby Dick* and Richard Wagner's *Ring of the Nibelungen*. Eugene O'Neill wrote *Mourning Becomes Electra* in 1931 and Jean-Paul Sartre *The Flies* in 1943. Modern productions of the *Oresteia* have been directed by – among others – Jean-Louis Barrault (Paris 1955), Vittorio Gassman (Syracuse 1960), Tyrone Guthrie (Minneapolis 1966), Luca Ronconi (Venice 1972), Karolos Koun (Epidaurus 1980), Peter Stein (Berlin 1980), Peter Hall (London 1981), Ariane Mnouchkine (Paris 1990–92), Silviu Pucarete (Craiova 1998) and Katie Mitchell (London 1999).

Prometheus Bound (*Prometheus Desmotes*)

∾ The legend

In the beginning, Ouranos (Heaven) married Gaia (Earth). They gave birth to a race of primordial giants called Titans, among whom were Okeanos (Ocean) and Kronos. Kronos castrated his father and took his place as king of the gods. Kronos in his turn had many children and was eventually deposed by his son Zeus.

A colossal war broke out between Zeus and the Titans, which Zeus won. Prometheus (the name means Foresight) was a Titan, son of Earth. He understood that intelligence not violence, would become the ruling power in the universe and chose to side with Zeus, helping him to secure victory. Kronos and the other defeated Titans were imprisoned under the earth.

Full of suspicion, Zeus planned to destroy the human race and begin again with a new creation that he himself had made. Prometheus rescued mankind from destruction and gave human beings two gifts – the gift of fire and the gift of hope – which together made civilization possible. Zeus punished Prometheus for these transgressions by chaining him to a desolate rock for thirty thousand years.

Prometheus, who could see into the future, knew that one day Zeus would need him again and come to seek his help. There was a sea nymph called Thetis, of whom it was foretold that any son she had would be greater than his father. If Zeus had a child by her he would be overthrown and his reign as king of the gods brought to an end. Secure in the possession of this knowledge, Prometheus endured all the torments that Zeus could inflict on him until eventually the passage of time brought about a reconciliation.

∾ The story

The play is set in Scythia, at the outer limits of the known world. Violence and Power, Zeus' henchmen, bring their prisoner Prometheus to a lonely crag where Hephaistos, the god of ironwork, shackles him to the rock.

Prometheus, being immortal, cannot die. He determines to wait out Zeus' anger, knowing that one day his rival will come begging for his help. When his tormentors have left Prometheus is visited by a group of sympathizers – the daughters of Okeanos. They have heard the sound of hammering in the cavern where they live under the sea and have come to see what the matter is. They ask Prometheus what he has done to deserve such a terrible punishment.

Their father Okeanos appears and says that he will to intercede with Zeus on Prometheus' behalf. Prometheus is furiously angry with Zeus for his unjust treatment and refuses point blank to beg for his freedom. Prometheus is so contemptuous of any compromise that Okeanos is forced to withdraw.

The next visitor to arrive is Io, another of Zeus' victims. She was the beautiful daughter of the king of Argos. Zeus fell in love with her. When she would not yield to his advances, Zeus punished her by changing her into a cow, and his wife Hera, jealous of the girl, sent a stinging fly to torment her and set her wandering through the world.

Prometheus foretells what will happen to Io on her journeying – how after many difficulties she and Zeus will be reconciled. She will bear the god a son and found a dynasty which in the thirteenth generation will produce the demi-god Heracles. Heracles will return to the lonely mountain where Prometheus is chained and kill the eagle that Zeus has sent to feed on Prometheus' liver. (The liver grows again and is eaten again, so the pain is constant and unending.)

Prometheus boasts of the knowledge that he has which is vital to Zeus' safety. Zeus overhears him and sends his messenger Hermes to threaten Prometheus into giving up the secret. Prometheus refuses to collaborate. Zeus sends his thunderbolt to shatter the mountain and send the defiant Titan plunging into the abyss.

∾ About the play

THE YOUNG SOLDIER: It's no use your talking. I won't stand for injustice!

MOTHER COURAGE: You're quite right. But how long? How long won't you stand for injustice? One hour? Or two? You haven't asked yourself that have you?

Bertolt Brecht, *Mother Courage*, tr. Eric Bentley

To defy Power, which seems omnipotent;
To love and bear; to hope till Hope creates
From his own wreck the thing it contemplates:
Neither to change, nor falter, nor repent.

Percy Bysshe Shelley, *Prometheus Unbound*

The action of *Prometheus Bound* takes place near the dawn of time and at the outer limits of the known world. The actors are superhuman: everyone in the play, except for Io, is immortal. Prometheus in particular has vast reserves of physical strength, endurance and mental toughness. The play is about resistance to authority – a resistance so determined, heroic and long lasting that it ends by bringing about a change in the nature of God himself.

Zeus, the new ruler of the universe, never appears but we learn something of his nature from the quality of his servants, Power and Violence – just as we learn something about Prometheus from the pity that Hephaistos feels for him.

POWER: Now the unfeeling tooth of a spike of adamant!
 Use all your strength and drive it right through his breast!
HEPHAISTOS: Ah Prometheus! I am sorry for your pain.
POWER: Will you shrink back and be sorry for Zeus's
   enemies?
 Take care. You may have to moan for yourself one day.
HEPHAISTOS: You see a sight most hard for eyes to look
   upon.
   tr. Rex Warner

In the great war that precedes the play Prometheus changed his allegiance and sided with Zeus because his brother Titans refused to listen to reason. But Zeus has taken on the defects of his vanquished enemies; he has come to believe that violence is the answer to everything. Prometheus knows that it solves nothing. It is the tension between this belief and this knowledge that drives the play. Ouranos mistreated his offspring and was castrated and imprisoned under the earth. His successor Kronos was similarly cruel and his children rose up to overthrow him. Unless Prometheus comes to the rescue, Zeus will beget a child more powerful than himself, who will treat him just as he treated his own father. The cycle of violence cannot be broken unless Zeus himself relents. Prometheus, secure in his knowledge of the future, is resolved to wait for his opponent to see sense.

He's savage, I know. He keeps
justice in His fist.
But with this hammer blow
he'll soften. He'll calm down
His blind stubborn rage.
He'll come to me, as a friend,
I'll love my friend again.
   tr. James Scully and C. J. Herington

In *The Eumenides* Aeschylus had dramatized the conflict
between liberal and conservative forces in the universe.
Enlightenment won the day and supporters of the old order
were coaxed into surrender. In *Prometheus Bound* the struggle
between the two sides is bleaker and more bitter: this time the
forces of progressive intelligence are on the losing side.
Prometheus sees what will happen, what must happen, but is
for the time being powerless to bring it about.

Prometheus is nailed to a rock: he can neither move about
nor leave the stage. Since he cannot go to the action, the
action has to come to him. The first to arrive are the daughters of Okeanos. They are young women innocent of the
ways of the world, like the chorus in Sophocles' *Women of
Trachis*. They accept the status quo: Zeus' power fills their
whole field of vision. They cannot see beyond it or understand that it might be vulnerable and subject to decline. Their
father Okeanos too has made his peace with the new dispensation. He offers to plead Prometheus' case but is finally
more interested in his own safety than in standing up for a
friend.

OCEAN: Your advice is clear: 'Go home'.
PROMETHEUS: Or you'll earn hatred too.
OCEAN: From his new high lordship?
PROMETHEUS: Watch out for him. Do nothing to rouse his
   rage.
OCEAN: Your suffering, Prometheus, teaches me that.
PROMETHEUS: Go then. Before you change your mind.
   tr. Frederic Raphael and Kenneth McLeish

There are strong echoes in the play of Sophocles' suffering heroes. Prometheus has the lonely intransigence of Ajax, Oedipus and Philoctetes. He suffers physical agonies like the poisoned Heracles. Okeanos' position resembles the more accommodating stance of Ismene and Chrysothemis (the timid conventional sisters of Antigone and Electra).

Prometheus, now powerless to help himself, was in former times the great helper of mankind.

> They had eyes but saw nothing, ears
> But could not hear. Like dream-people
> They blundered from birth to death.
> They built no houses, from brick or wood:
> Termites they scrabbled underground
> In runs and hollows, sunless.
> They knew no seasons – winter, flowery spring,
> Abundant summer passed them by.
>
> Life without reason. Then I helped them.
> I showed them the stars' elusive movements,
> Rising and setting. I taught them numbers,
> Skill of skills, and writing,
> All-memory, mother of arts.
> I tamed wild animals, yoked them
> To drudge for mortals . . .
> I gave them ships, sail-carts
> With wings to ride the sea.
> These were my gifts to mortals –
> Who can find no cleverness to help myself.
>   tr. Frederic Raphael and Kenneth McLeish

It is at the play's midpoint that Io, Prometheus' fellow-sufferer, appears. His punishment is to be nailed down; hers is to be fretted with continual motion. Her wild dancing is in the strongest possible contrast to Prometheus' immobility.

> E! E!
> Gadfly, sting, afraid,
> Worn witless, why?

Cinder me, smother me,
Bait me for sharks,
I pray, I pray,
O hear me, lord.
Wandering, wandering,
Learning, but still no way
To end this pain.
  tr. Frederic Raphael and Kenneth McLeish

The scene with Io represents an enormous expansion of the play's imaginative boundaries. It covers huge distances in time and space. There is a powerful sense of the inter-connectedness of things, the strange unpredictability of life. A young girl's beauty can result in a journey that takes her for hundreds of miles through Southern Russia, the Caucasus, Turkey, Syria and Egypt. The actions of a powerful Titan, blessed with a knowledge of time to come, can lead to him spending thousands of years penned in one place, with only his mind free to roam. The chorus in *Prometheus Bound* have comparatively little to do. Their function of looking before and after, setting the present action in context, evoking origins and consequences, has in this play been allocated to the principal actor.

Io's travels are not simply a matter of miles covered: they're a way of making the audience 'see' time. Her journey takes her from the Peloponnese to Egypt, clockwise round the world, on foot. Imagining the days, the months, the years involved, helps to create the length of Prometheus' captivity. The dynasty, which in the thirteenth generation will produce his helper Heracles, cannot begin until Io reaches the banks of the Nile. In *Agamemnon* Aeschylus uses distance to compress time; a chain of beacons brings the news of victory from Troy to Argos within a single night. The litany of place names as the fire flashes across the intervening space gives a sense of almost supernatural speed. Here the effect works the other way: time is being stretched out through distance.

When Io leaves, the chorus close the scene with a song about the powerlessness of human beings compared with the power

of the gods. They pray that they may be spared her fate.
Prometheus is roused to reveal that Zeus' power is not unlim-
ited. He boasts that he alone possesses the key to its survival.

> I tell you this; for all the boldness of his mind,
> Zeus will be humbled. Such is that act of sex which he
> now seeks to consummate, which will soon cast him
> from tyrant throne to his extinction; then the curse
> of father Kronos will be utterly fulfilled.
> Zeus's troubles are so great, no other god
> could show him clearly his escape except for me;
> I know both when and how.
>   tr. Michael Ewans

This leads to another confrontation with the powers of
Olympus as Zeus sends down Hermes to threaten Prometheus
with further violence unless he gives up his secret. Prometheus
refuses and is swallowed up in an earthquake.

> Wind leaps on wind,
> Howling, tearing,
> Sky drinks sea.
> Zeus did this. His storm.
> Themis, mother!
> Sky-wheel that turns the stars!
> See how unjust my suffering.
>   tr. Frederic Raphael and Kenneth McLeish

Surviving fragments of the successor play *Prometheus
Unbound* give us a glimpse of the future. Thousands of years
have gone by. Zeus has released the Titans from their captivity under the earth. The giants come to visit Prometheus on
his crag. They are the chorus of the new play. But
Prometheus' sufferings are unending. Zeus has devised a new
torment for him.

> And always on the third day, for me, the light of day
> is black,
> when Zeus's horrible pet glides in at me –

the EAGLE
that digs in with crookt claws
gouging out
             her feast, until her crop's
bloated rich with liver.
                          Then
screaming
             wheeling skyward . . . her tail feathers
drag through blood,
my blood.

   tr. James Scully and C. J. Herington

The fragments of *Prometheus Unbound* reveal many parallels with the present work. Instead of Okeanos, Prometheus' mother Gaia appears and tries to persuade her son make peace with his tormentor. Instead of Io, there is Heracles, whose journeyings round the world from East to West Prometheus foretells, as he foretold Io's travels from West to East. Heracles killed the eagle that was eating Prometheus' liver but how the play ended we do not know.

The names of three Prometheus plays have come down to us – *Prometheus Bound*, *Prometheus Unbound* and *Prometheus the Fire Bearer/ Fire Carrier*. If they form a trilogy it is not certain which order they are in. Was *Prometheus the Fire Bearer* first, dealing with the theft of fire and Zeus' battle with the Titans? Or did it come last and deal with Prometheus' readmittance to the society of the gods and the foundation of a festival at Athens in his honour? There is a feeling in *Prometheus Bound* that Zeus is resentful of human progress and sees it as a threat to his power: it would be fascinating to know how this resentment was resolved.

The play is a case study in the difficulties and uncertainties that surround Greek tragedy. It is by no means certain that it is by Aeschylus at all. Scholars are divided on the subject and the most recent Oxford edition attributes the play to 'author unknown'. The discovery of a papyrus fragment in the sands of Egypt could resolve the controversy overnight.

∾ Translations

The sharpest and most gripping version is by Frederic Raphael and Kenneth McLeish (Methuen). There are also useful translations by Michael Ewans (Everyman) and by James Scully and C. J. Herington (Oxford): the latter has the benefit of a brilliant introduction and an appendix containing the fragments of *Prometheus Unbound*. The Rex Warner (The Bodley Head) and the David Grene (Chicago) are now over fifty years old but still in their different ways give good accounts of the play.

∾ In performance

If the play is by Aeschylus, then it most probably dates from the end of his career, sometime between 460 and 456 BC. If the play is not by him, then a date around 440 is more likely. *Prometheus Bound* exercised a strong fascination for the writers of the Romantic Movement. It influenced Shelley's *Prometheus Unbound*, Byron's *Manfred* and Goethe's *Faust* and caught the imagination of Karl Marx and Victor Hugo. One writer called Prometheus 'the patron saint of the proletariat'. *Prometheus Bound* was staged at Delphi in 1927 directed by Eva Palmer-Sikelianos and at Syracuse in 2002 directed by Luca Ronconi. Other modern productions include Yale Repertory Theater (1967), translated by Robert Lowell, and the Salzburg Festival (1974), translated by Peter Handke. There are operas by Carl Orff (1968) and Luigi Nono (1984) and a film by Tony Harrison (1998).

Sophocles (Sophokles) 497/6–406/5 BC

> Blessed Sophocles, who lived a long life, a happy man and
> a clever one. He composed many fine tragedies and died
> well, without enduring any misfortune.
>
> Phrynichus, tr. Bernard Knox

Life

Sophocles had his first performance and his first victory in
468 BC, when he was twenty-nine. Aeschylus was fifty-seven;
Euripides just seventeen; it was nearly seventy years since
tragedy had first begun. Sophocles was too young to have
fought in the Persian Wars; as a youth he was part of a choir
which celebrated the Greek victory at Salamis. His life
coincides almost exactly with the great Athenian century and
he died just before the city suffered its final humiliating
defeat at the hands of Sparta in 404 BC.

When Sophocles was in his twenties Athens consolidated
its naval power by building the Long Walls, which link the
city to its harbour in the Piraeus. When he was in his early
thirties Ephialtes carried out his reforms which brought
about full participatory democracy, with all the offices of state
open to each citizen. The playwright's fifties coincided with
the ascendancy of the great statesman Pericles that marks the
high point of Athenian power and confidence. The bitter war
between Athens and Sparta which polarized the whole Greek
world broke out when Sophocles was in his mid-sixties and
continued till his death twenty-five years later.

Unlike Euripides, and what we know of Aeschylus,
Sophocles took a full part in public life. In 443/2 he was treas-
urer of the Delian league, the defensive alliance of Aegean
states formed to counter the threat of Persian invasion. In
441/39 he served with Pericles as a general in the war against
Samos: it is said the Athenians gave him the job because they

liked his play *Antigone* so much. Later in life Sophocles was a commissioner in the interim government set in up 413 in the aftermath of the disastrous failure of the Athenian expedition against Sicily. He also took part in the religious life of the city. He was a priest of Halon, a minor deity who looked after the sick, and in 420, when the cult of Aesculapius was installed at Athens, Sophocles sheltered the god in his own home until a proper sanctuary could be built. In recognition of this service Sophocles was known after his death as a 'bringer of blessings' and was given the name of Dexion, the Receiver.

According to the sources Sophocles wrote one hundred and twenty-three plays: the real total may be smaller as some works are known by more than one title. The seven plays that survive are *Ajax*, *The Women of Trachis*, *Antigone*, *Oedipus Tyrannus*, *Electra*, *Philoctetes* and *Oedipus at Colonus*. Plutarch writing in the first century AD records Sophocles' reflections on his career: 'Sophocles used to say that after practising to the limit the pomp of Aeschylus and then the harsh artificiality of his own manner of elaboration, he turned finally to the kind of style which was best and most expressive of character.'

As with the two other major dramatists, the works that have survived are surrounded by a halo of tantalizing fragments. What would Sophocles' *Phaedra* have been like? Or his *Iphigeneia*? Or his *Ion*? There was a sequel to *Philoctetes*, called *Philoctetes at Troy*, and a trilogy about the Argonauts – *The Women of Colchis*, *The Root-Cutters*, and *The Scythians*. There were plays too about the house of Atreus – *Tantalus*, *Thyestes*, *Atreus*, *Niobe* – and it would be fascinating to have the complete text of Sophocles' Trojan plays – *Priam*, *Troilus* and *Polyxena*.

Like Shakespeare, and like Molière, Sophocles was an actor. He had a particular success in the title role of his own play *Nausikaa* as the young princess playing ball with her companions, and was remembered for his lyre-playing in *Thamyris*, about a Thracian bard who set himself up against the Muses and was punished with blindness.

If tragedy explores the relationship:

- between man and his own death and other men

- between man and the immortal gods and things that do not change
- between man and the passions that live inside him,

then each of the three great dramatists approached these problems in his own particular way. Sophocles is interested in how a person faces death (Ajax, Deianeira, Heracles, Antigone, Oedipus) and in the relations between gods and men. One of his major themes is time – how the time of the immortals is different from the time of men and what happens when the two come into contact. The two different kinds of time proceed separately side by side, each moving to a different rhythm and each with their own particular logic. It is when the two times coincide that something happens – either terrible (*The Women of Trachis, Oedipus Tyrannus*) or wonderful (*Philoctetes, Oedipus at Colonus*) or a mixture of the two (*Electra*).

Aristotle in his *Poetics* says that Sophocles increased the number of actors from two to three and the number of the chorus from twelve to fifteen. The presence of the third actor is vital to the shaping Sophocles' work; it enabled him to give his narratives tremendous speed and energy as they drive towards their close. This brings a whole new rhythm to dramatic storytelling. Sophocles, apart from the odd exception, seems to have turned away from the Aeschylean preference for developing a narrative over three linked plays, preferring to concentrate the action within the span of a single work.

Ajax (Aias)

∾ The legend

Ajax was the son of Telamon, king of Salamis, one of the heroes of the first Trojan War. Ajax followed in his father's footsteps and became a commander in the second Greek expedition against Troy. He was known as 'the bulwark of the army' because of his physical strength and his tenacity in defence. He stood a head taller than the other warriors and was noted for his prowess in battle. When the Greeks needed a champion to fight Hector in single combat it was Ajax that they chose. As a fighter he was second only in the Greek army to Achilles, who according to some accounts was his cousin. Ajax commanded the left wing of the Greek army and Achilles the right.

When Achilles was killed, there was a question over what to do with his magnificent armour, which had been specially made for him by the gods. Who should inherit it? The two contenders for the honour were Ajax and Odysseus. When the decision was made in favour of Odysseus, Ajax was enraged and plotted to kill Agamemnon and Menelaus, whom he felt had treated him unfairly.

Athene, Odysseus' patron goddess, intervened to protect her favourite and the other generals. She scrambled Ajax's senses so that instead of murdering the Greek commanders he turned instead against the sheep and cattle in the camp and massacred both the animals and the herdsmen who were guarding them. When Ajax came to his senses and saw what he had done he killed himself.

After his death Ajax became one of the tutelary heroes of the Athenian people. When the Greek fleet defeated the Persians in 480 BC at the battle of Salamis it was felt that Ajax had an important part in the victory.

ᴄ᷾ The story

The play begins on the morning after Ajax's assassination attempt on the Greek high command. Odysseus, puzzling over who can have killed the army's sheep and cattle and murdered the men who were guarding them, has followed the tracks back to Ajax's tent. There he is met by Athene who explains how she has deliberately made Ajax blind in order to humiliate him and protect the Greek generals from his attacks.

Ajax emerges from his tent covered in blood, gloating over his supposed success. He boasts how he intends to torture his surviving prisoners before killing them.

Odysseus is appalled by the transformation of his former colleague from noble warrior to this blood-smeared assassin. Athene points out that this is the fate that lies in wait for all mortals who get above themselves.

Ajax comes to his senses surrounded by the dismembered bodies of the animals he has slaughtered. Not only has he failed in his revenge but he has failed in a particularly humiliating manner. His disgrace is so great that there is no way out except to kill himself. Tecmessa, the Trojan slave who shares his bed begs him to go on living in order to protect her and their small child Eurysaces ('Broad Shield'). Ajax says goodbye to the boy, gives his last instructions and goes into his tent. He re-emerges apparently transformed and announces that he is going down to the shore to wash himself and to bury the sword that has been the agent of so much destruction.

Teucer, Ajax's half-brother, returns from a military expedition just too late to stop him leaving. It has been prophesied that Athena's anger will last only for one day, so that if Ajax remains in his tent he will be safe. Teucer, Tecmessa and the chorus scatter to look for him.

The scene changes to the seashore. Ajax commits suicide by falling on his sword. Tecmessa finds the body and covers it. Teucer who has assumed the care of his brother's family sends her to fetch the child Eurysaces. He embraces his brother's body and grieves for his death.

Menelaus tells Teucer that Ajax is a criminal and a murderer and his body must remain unburied. Teucer defies him and Menelaus leaves. Tecmessa, Eurysaces and Teucer place offerings on Ajax's dead body and Teucer goes off to choose a place for his brother to be buried.

Agamemnon tries to assert his authority by trying to deny Ajax burial. Teucer stubbornly defends his brother and recalls Ajax's many heroic deeds and how he saved the Greek ships from being set on fire by the Trojans. In the end Odysseus intervenes. Ajax was his enemy but nothing, even hatred, lasts for ever. The time has come for reconciliation. It would be an act of injustice to pursue the dead man further. Agamemnon leaves and Odysseus expresses a desire to help with the funeral. Teucer denies him this as being displeasing to the dead but invites him to be present as a spectator. Little Eurysaces rests his hand on his father's body as Teucer and the chorus carry the hero out to bury him.

∾ About the play

When one does away with oneself one does the most estimable thing possible: one thereby almost deserves to live.
  F. Nietzsche

To stop breathing is bad.
So the gods judge
For they do not stop breathing.
  Sappho

Ajax begins with a catastrophe. The playwright brings us immediately face to face with the physicality of death and slaughter. First there is the sheer effort of killing. Athena speaks of Ajax 'his head and sword-slaying hands still dripping sweat'. Then there is its grisly aftermath. Odysseus tells of a witness who saw the hero 'leaping across the field alone, swinging a wet sword'.

Sophocles has a special feeling for the suffering of the body, whether human or animal.

The beasts were tied up, he dragged them inside,
  threw them to the ground and cut their throats
        or tore them apart barehanded.
Then he seized on two quick-footed rams,
slashed out the tongue of one, cuts its head off
and threw the carcass aside; the other
he bound to a stake and lashed
with a heavy leather harness,
a hissing two-thonged whip . . .
  tr. Herbert Golder and Richard Pevear

This is recognizably the poet who portrayed the physical agonies of Philoctetes and the poisoned Heracles.

The opening of *Ajax* is packed with images of death and torture. The pain is inflicted on harmless animals but what is evoked is the damage of combat, the savagery of the hero and the terrible frailty of mortal flesh. Ajax often speaks about the sharpness of his sword: when he is about to impale himself these references to metal slicing into softness come back to haunt him.

> The killer, the sacrificial knife,
> is set now to be most cutting.
>   tr. Herbert Golder and Richard Pevear

The animal nature of the human body is underlined again at the end of the play. As Teucer and the child Eurysaces lift Ajax's body up to bury it the dark blood is still pouring out.

> Help me lift your father – gently.
> The black life force is still flowing
> out of his warm veins.
>   tr. Herbert Golder and Richard Pevear

Earlier Ajax had asked for the boy to be lifted up to him in the shambles that was now his home. Surrounded by dismembered carcasses, he introduces the child to raw flesh and blood, the realities of his human inheritance.

> Lift him up, lift him to me. He won't be frightened,
> Even by seeing this fresh-butchered gore,
> Not if he really is my son. Break in
> The colt straight off to his father's rugged ways;
> Train him to have a nature like his sire.
>   tr. John Moore

Athene, who is immortal and untouchable, remains detached from all the pain and mess. She has struck down Ajax to avenge her honour and to protect her favourite, Odysseus. The spectacle of Ajax's suffering is something that she can use to point a moral.

> Know that the gods
> Love men of steady sense and hate the proud.
> > tr. John Moore

It is left to Odysseus to feel compassion – that distinctly human emotion – for his humiliated opponent.

> Yet I pity
> His wretchedness, though he is my enemy,
> For the terrible yoke of blindness that is on him.
> I think of him, yet also of myself.
> > tr. John Moore

Athene is simply pleased with the evidence of what she has achieved and expects Odysseus to share her pleasure. Odysseus is neither immortal nor invulnerable. He pities the victim of divine power: he can imagine being on the receiving end.

Once the catastrophe has happened there is no going back. It is not just that Ajax has been slighted by the award of Achilles' armour to his rival Odysseus; his attempted revenge on his enemies has resulted in utter humiliation. This is a man who prided himself on his self-sufficiency.

> His father had advised him to pray
> for victory with the Gods' blessing
> but he boasted that anyone could conquer
> > like that
> he intended to make his own glory
> > by himself.
> Athene came once   standing by him
> > in the battle
> > told him what to do   again
> he replied in words
> > no mortal tongue should speak
> and told the Goddess to protect those who needed her   he
>   could
> hold the line alone.
> > tr. Robert Cannon

He has lived his life full of godlike confidence, with a frank relish for his uncommon powers; how can he now begin to remake himself into the man he once was?

> It's contemptible to want to live for ever
> When a man's life gives him no relief from pain.
>> tr. John Moore

Sophocles makes suicide a special theme. In his seven surviving plays there are six suicides – Ajax, Deianeira, Antigone, Haemon, Eurydice, and Jocasta. It's interesting that all these deaths come in the first half of Sophocles' output: the second half focuses on endurance.

> Strangely the long and countless drift of time
> Brings all things first from darkness into light
> Then covers them once more. Nothing so marvellous
> That man can say it surely will not be –
> Strong oaths and iron intent come crashing down.
>> tr. John Moore

Ajax recognizes the changeableness of things only to reject it. He knows he has sustained a defeat but he does not intend to survive the passing of his old, inflexible, powerful self.

His death has an effect on other people. By choosing suicide he abandons those who depend on him – his young son Eurysaces and his war-wife Tecmessa.

> If you die and abandon me
> know I'll be taken the same day
> and dragged off with your son
> to eat slave's food. And the Greeks
> my masters will throw bitter words
> in my face: 'Do you see that woman.
> Once she was concubine to Aias,
> the strongest man in the army . . .
>> tr. Herbert Golder and Richard Pevear

Tecmessa isn't the only one to be affected. Ajax's death will also harm his brother Teucer.

What will Telamon our father say?
What will he look when I return? A man
who never smiled in happy hours!
Call me a war-slave's bastard
coward in your time of need
a traitor to our family
or worse

tr. Robert Cannon

Sophocles is clear about the harmful consequences of Ajax's action but he also makes us see that to go on living would be intolerable. That is one of the reasons the play is structured as it is. The petty, gloating swagger of Menelaus and the harsh unyielding stance of Agamemnon make it plain how unbearable Ajax's life would have been if he had survived. And Ajax is still visibly present in the scene. His dead body dominates the closing stages of the play just as his living presence has dominated the rest of it.

Agamemnon and Menelaus have not shared Ajax's shattering experience – indeed they are proud to have avoided it – but this means that they don't share his understanding either. Sophocles creates an effect here that he was to use again in *Oedipus at Colonus*. As the hero moves into death his opponents seem to shrink, as if seen through the wrong end of a telescope. They bustle about their business with self-regarding energy – an energy that looks increasingly trivial, hectic, misapplied. Unlike the hero, news about their own mortality doesn't seem to have reached them yet. Even Teucer's defiance, admirable though it is, seems to have a certain tinny ring to it.

Aeschylus wrote a trilogy on the Ajax story. The first play *The Award of Arms* showed Ajax and Odysseus arguing their respective claims before the tribunal. The second play *The Thracian Women* dealt with Ajax's suicide. The death wasn't presented directly as in Sophocles but related in a messenger speech. The last play *The Women of Salamis* traced the action home to Salamis, where Teucer had to face the anger of King

Telamon. It ended with him going into exile to found a new city of Salamis elsewhere.

Aeschylus typically works out the implications of the struggle for Achilles' armour over time. He follows the effects of the action as they ripple out from a central point and shows how a dispute between soldiers at Troy leads to the founding of a city in Cyprus. Sophocles works to a different pattern. The action and its consequences have to be resolved within the confines of a single play. The content of *Oedipus Tyrannus* and *Oedipus at Colonus* – the dismantling of a hero followed by his recuperation – is in *Ajax* fitted into a single span. Sophocles achieves this by relating everything to an overall pattern of change which governs the universe. Ajax recognizes this law but refuses to bow to it. Odysseus, observer of his great opponent's fate, has the intelligence to draw the lesson and apply it fruitfully to his own life; the two experiences taken together make a complete whole.

> I know now to hate an enemy
> just so far, for another time
> we may befriend him. And the friend
> I help I will not help too greatly,
> knowing that one day may find him
> my enemy.
>   tr. Herbert Golder and Richard Pevear

These are Ajax's words but he is unable to make anything of them. He dies cursing those who have done him wrong and calling on the Furies to destroy the whole Greek army. Odysseus is the one to put them to some use. The pity that had been provoked in him by the sight of Ajax's madness finds a meaningful outlet when he gets Agamemnon to renounce his claim to vengeance. Ajax's body is to be buried by the ever practical Teucer but the spectators at the graveside will be those who stand to learn most from witnessing his end – Odysseus and little Eurysaces.

∾ Translations

The translation by Herbert Golder and Richard Pevear (Oxford) is outstanding. Also useful are Robert Cannon (Methuen), John Moore (Chicago) and Michael Ewans (Everyman). There is a version by Robert Auletta made specially for Peter Sellars' 1986 production.

∾ In performance

The year of the first performance is unknown. A range of dates between 468 and 435 BC is possible. Some time between 458 and 448 is most plausible. A Latin version *Ajax Flagellifer* was rehearsed in 1564 to be presented before Queen Elizabeth I but she proved too tired in the end to view the actual performance. The play was staged at the National Center for the Performing Arts Washington in 1986 directed by Peter Sellars and at the Théâtre de Gennevilliers in 1991.

The Women of Trachis (*Trachiniai*)

∾ The legend

There was a beautiful princess called Deianeira. Two suitors fought for her hand – Achelous, the most powerful river god in Greece, and Heracles, son of Zeus by a mortal woman. Heracles won and obtained Deianeira for his wife.

As Deianeira and Heracles were on their way to their new home they came to a river. The ferryman was a centaur called Nessus. He was enormously strong and simply carried travellers across the torrent in his arms. He got halfway across with Deianeira and was so overcome with her beauty that he tried to rape her. Heracles shot him dead with an arrow that had been dipped in deadly poison from the snake-headed Hydra.

The marriage of Deianeira and Heracles was not a happy one. Heracles was always absent while Deianeira stayed at home worrying about his safety.

On his travels Heracles encountered Iole, daughter of Eurytus, king of Oechalia, and fell passionately in love with her. He challenged her father to an archery contest with Iole as the prize. When Heracles won, Eurytus reneged on his bargain, claiming that Heracles' bow had supernatural power so that it was not a fair contest. Heracles, enraged, assembled an army, killed Eurytus and his sons, destroyed his city and captured Iole for himself.

Deianeira, fearing that she was about to be replaced by a younger woman, tried to win back her husband with a love charm. She sent him a garment smeared with the blood of the dead centaur Nessus. He had told her that if she did this her husband would never look at any other woman. The words of the dying centaur were a trick, meaning that Heracles would die. The blood was contaminated by the Hydra's venom.

The garment ate into Heracles' flesh and he was consumed with agony. Deianeira was horrified when she discovered what she had done, and killed herself. Heracles, tormented by the poisoned robe, entrusted his son Hyllus with the task of building a pyre of oak wood, sacred to his father Zeus, and burning him alive.

∿ The story

Deianeira is living in exile in Trachis. Heracles in his feud with Eurytus had killed one of his sons by treachery and so the family had to leave their home to avoid defilement.

Heracles has been away for fifteen months. Deianeira is waiting anxiously for his return. She is buoyed up by an ancient prophecy, which says that if Heracles survives these fifteen months then his troubles will all be at an end.

A herald, Lichas, arrives with a group of captured slave girls, among them Iole. He announces that Heracles has won a mighty victory over King Eurytus and destroyed his city. In deference to his master's wife, Lichas does not mention the true cause of the quarrel, saying simply that Heracles was avenging a slight to his honour.

A second messenger contradicts this story and gives the true reason behind the war, namely Heracles' all-consuming passion for the beautiful Iole. It is now clear what the role of the new slave girl is to be.

At first Deianeira reacts philosophically. Her husband has a large sexual appetite and there have been mistresses before; besides she feels genuinely sorry for the girl. But she fears to lose her husband's affection altogether. With some misgivings she sends him a present of new robes, smeared with a charm made from the blood of the dead centaur Nessus which she thinks will win her husband's feelings back.

Deianeira's misgivings are justified. A piece of wool that she had used to apply the ointment catches the sunlight and bursts into flame. Deianeira realises what she has done and kills herself.

The meaning of the prophecy is now clear. Heracles' troubles are at an end in the sense that he is going to die. Heracles remembers another prophecy, namely that he couldn't be killed by anything that lives and breathes. When he is told that the deadly ointment came from the dead centaur Nessus he finally understands what has happened to him. He orders his son Hyllus to marry Iole and found a dynasty and to prepare a pyre for him on a high mountain on which he is to be burnt alive.

∾ About the play

Anyone who tries to see two days ahead
or more, is mad.
There's no tomorrow at all
until the day we're in is suffered through.
    The Women of Trachis, tr. C. K. Williams and Gregory W.
    Dickerson

A reversal is a change from one state of affairs to its
opposite.

Aristotle, *Poetics*, tr. T. S. Dorsch

The Women of Trachis is the first of Sophocles' surviving plays to
express his particular feeling for the vulnerability and uncertainty of human life – the sense that whatever your life is when
you get up in the morning, by nightfall everything about it
could have changed utterly. In this sense it looks forward to his
two great masterpieces *Oedipus Tyrannus* and *Electra*.

Events in the play seem sudden and unforeseen, yet turn
out to have been predicted long ago. The drama presents us
with a slow process of understanding. The characters learn by
experience what they already have a way of knowing but
haven't fully grasped.

Knowledge is made real by suffering. The action is
watched by a chorus of young unmarried girls, who by definition have yet to enter on the world of grown-up experience.

All sweet things growing in their good places,
the sun's burning never touching them, or the rain or wind;
living their happy little joyfulness, until the virgin's name
is wife and then she knows anxiety and the night . . .

tr. C. K. Williams and Gregory W. Dickerson

In the very first lines of the play Deianeira seems to be
preparing herself to face disaster:

It's a long established saying among men
That no one knows his fate before he's dead.

tr. J. Michael Walton

This basic truth was in some ways a commonplace in the
Greek world where 'Call no man happy till he is dead' was a
famous saying. Rather surprisingly Deianeira seems to think
that though she is miserable, the worst is already over:

Well, I know mine. It will not take my dying
To recognize my life as ill-starred, full of grief.

tr. J. Michael Walton

The action will show how badly she is mistaken. Deianeira has a long journey to travel before the full truth of what she says here has worked itself out. She thinks her sufferings are all in the past: she has no inkling that worse is still to come.

Two prophecies underpin the play. The first is that at the end of a fifteen-month period all Heracles' trouble will be at an end. The second is that Heracles cannot be killed by anyone who lives and breathes. Both seem to promise happiness and good fortune: both turn out to mean the opposite. The twin themes of knowledge and time are in some ways the master narratives of Sophocles' art. All the characters in *The Women of Trachis* are drawn into this pattern. Deianeira discovers too late the nature of Nessus' fatal ointment; Lichas discovers the nature of the gift he carried from Deianeira to his master; Hyllus, Deianeira's son, discovers that the mother he has cursed is in fact innocent; Heracles discovers the way his life was meant to end.

The first half of the play is a psychological study. Deianeira's principal experience of her beauty is one of bewilderment and fear. It provokes in men a terrifying violence. Achelous and Heracles fight for possession of her – a fight Deianeira is too frightened to watch. Then, as she is travelling with her new husband, the centaur Nessus tries to rape her. Finally the marriage itself has been one long experience of anxiety, with her husband continually in danger and away from home.

> We had children, of course.
> He sees them the way a farmer sees his back fields
> he drops a seed and comes back once in awhile
> to check the harvest
> tr. C. K. Williams and Gregory W. Dickerson

Now the useless uneasiness that was her beauty has begun to fade; only the fear remains – the fear of losing the only man she has ever known. No wonder that she looks on the newly enslaved Iole with sympathy.

You, who are you poor woman? A virgin? A mother?
You look so innocent . . . are you a princess?
Lichas, whose daughter is this one?
Who are her mother and father? Tell me . . .
there's something about her . . . I feel sorrier
for her than for the rest. She seems to know
what's in store for her

    tr. C. K. Williams and Gregory W. Dickerson

The famous anecdote in Plato's *Republic* shows that
Sophocles knew only too well the savagery and craziness of
sexual passion.

How well I remember the aged poet Sophocles when in
answer to the question, How does love sort with age
Sophocles, are you still the man you were? Peace, he
replied, most gladly have I escaped the thing of which you
speak. I feel as if I had escaped from a mad and furious
master.

    Plato, *The Republic*, tr. A. F. Jowett

The destructive power of Eros is as great in this play as in
Euripides' *Hippolytus*. Desire drives Heracles to sack
Oechalia, wipe out a family and destroy a kingdom. Desire
brings Nessus to his death. And it is desire to avoid abandonment that leads Deianeira to kill the man she married. The
raging venom that runs through Heracles' body is a way of
making physical this notion of an all-devouring, all-destruc-
tive passion. The poison is harmless as long as it lies in the
dark, but bring it out into the light and it consumes everything it touches.

Deianeira and Heracles stand in strong contrast to one
another. The female anxiety that has characterized Deianeira
gives way to the violet irruption of Heracles' physical suffering. 'All stoicism is undramatic', said a famous nineteenth-
century critic. Heracles' agonies are anything but stoical.

Why are you touching me? Don't
touch me! You're killing me! Killing me!

You've woken up what was asleep.
It has me . . . Again. It's lungeing through.
Where are the Greeks? Ungrateful!
I wore my useless life out
clearing monsters from your woods
and seas and where are you now? Somebody
put a sword to me! Set fire to me!

tr. C. K. Williams and Gregory W. Dickerson

One of the recurring images in Euripides is an innocent young person (usually a girl) who is killed as a sacrifice or who offers him/herself to be sacrificed. Sophocles by contrast has a special feeling for grown men in physical agony. In this sense Heracles looks forward to the sightless Oedipus and to Philoctetes. The play also contains another Sophoclean motif, that of suicide. It is striking that Sophocles' surviving seven plays contain six suicides (seven if Heracles' death on the funeral pyre is counted too). Euripides, though many more of his plays have come down to us, has only four. And these suicides are all from the first half of Sophocles' career: after that he concentrates on figures like Electra and Philoctetes characterized by their powers of endurance.

Aeschylus might have approached the story in a different way, spreading his material out over a complete trilogy – devoting one play, say, to the marriage of Deanaiera, another to the sack of Oechalia and the suffering of Heracles, and a third to the hero's death and apotheosis. The justice of Zeus would have been shown working itself out over time. Sophocles has adopted a different tactic, compressing the story into the framework of a single play. This gives a different sense of how the world is ordered. For Sophocles the gods move on a quite different timescale to individual human beings and their purposes are wholly mysterious. What brings grief to mortals is their inability to see more than a small fragment of the whole. The philosopher Heraclitus expressed this in another way when he wrote, 'Men find some things unjust and other things just; but in the eyes of God all things are beautiful and good and just.'

Heracles, of course, is the son of Zeus by a mortal woman Alcmene, so he, if anyone, ought to be favoured and protected. He is given two oracles which foretell what will happen to him. But the humans in the play choose to interpret them in the most favourable sense, according to their hopes; and this is a perfectly reasonable use of the divine gift – to sustain an aspiration to a happy and settled life. Only at the end are the gods' real purposes revealed. It is by no means plain however that life for Deianeira and Heracles would have been better if both had lived their lives in dread of the catastrophe to come.

Sophocles has no quarrel with the way things are: such a quarrel would have seemed to him childish and futile. Life is magnificent and terrible in equal measure but it is the only life we have and there is no point in trying to run away from it. The basic fact to be grasped is that the universe is not organised for the convenience of human beings and there is little they can do to influence its course. All that is open to them is to try to understand and accept it. Two quotations express this uniquely Sophoclean combination of pain and radiance. There is Heracles' cry as finally everything becomes clear to him:

> What
> SPLENDOUR,
> IT ALL COHERES.
> tr. Ezra Pound

And there is Hyllus' speech that closes the play.

> You've seen dying, dreadful, and agony today
> and hideous suffering and nothing is here,
> nothing,
> none of all of it, that is not Zeus.
> tr. C. K. Williams and Gregory W. Dickerson

ᗞ Translations

The best translation is by C. K. Williams and Gregory W. Dickerson (Oxford). It deals well with the play's overall patterning and with the scene of Heracles' madness; it comes rather unstuck with the choruses. Michael Jameson (Chicago) is good over the first two thirds of the play and makes a much better fist of the choruses but comes unstuck in the scene with Heracles. Graham Ley (Everyman) is also useful and has good notes. The Methuen (J. Michael Walton) is sound but dull. There is also an eccentric and thought-provoking version by Ezra Pound (Faber). The edition by Pat Easterling (Cambridge) has an excellent introduction and notes.

ᗞ In performance

The year of the first performance is unknown. A range of dates between 457 and 430 BC is possible. Most scholars place the play in the earlier part of the period. A version of the story, *Hercules Oetaeus*, is attributed to Seneca and dates from the year AD 60 or thereabouts. There is an opera *Hercules* by Handel (1745). In modern times an adaptation *Dianeira* by Timberlake Wertenbaker was broadcast by the BBC in 1999. The play was staged at the Young Vic Theatre, London in 2004 in a version by Martin Crimp entitled *Cruel and Tender*.

Antigone (*Antigone*)

ᗞ The legend

Oedipus, King of Thebes, unknowingly killed his father Laius and married his mother Jocasta. When he discovered what he had done he put out his own eyes: Jocasta hanged herself.

Two sons, Eteocles and Polyneices, and two daughters, Antigone and Ismene, were born to this incestuous marriage. The two sons fell out over their inheritance. It was originally agreed that they should govern turn and turn about but Eteocles, the elder, refused to relinquish his rule and drove his brother into exile.

Polyneices married the daughter of the king of Argos and returned with a foreign army to take his inheritance by force. In the final encounter of the battle the two brothers killed each other. Since the direct male heirs were dead, the rule of the city fell to Creon, who was Jocasta's brother. He ordered that Eteocles be buried with full honours but pronounced that Polyneices' body should remain unburied. This meant that his soul would be denied passage to the world of the dead: it was the Greek equivalent of eternal damnation.

∾ The story

The action begins on the morning after the battle. Antigone has just heard of Creon's decree. She resolves to defy the edict and bury Polyneices herself. She tries to get her sister Ismene to help her.

Creon outlines the reason for his decision. He considers it fitting punishment for a traitor who tried to destroy his native city and tried to enslave its inhabitants. One of the soldiers stationed to guard the body announces that someone somehow has performed a rudimentary burial rite, sprinkling the corpse with dust. Creon orders him to find and arrest the culprit.

Antigone is captured trying to complete what she had started. She defends her action: Creon's determination to seek revenge beyond the grave is not only unjust but also blasphemous. He may claim to speak for the city but there are fundamental human values that he is ignoring. Creon, furious, condemns Antigone to death. She is to be walled up in a cave with just enough food for her to slowly starve to death.

Creon's son Haemon, who is betrothed to Antigone, pleads with his father to spare her life. Father and son quarrel bitterly and Haemon leaves, saying that his father will never see him again. Antigone is taken out to be buried alive.

The prophet Teiresias warns Creon that his actions are contrary to the will of the gods. The pollution spread by the unburied corpse is affecting the whole city. Creon refuses to listen and accuses the prophet of being in the pay of his enemies.

Once Teiresias has gone Creon changes his mind and hurries out to bury Polyneices' body and free Antigone. But he comes too late. Antigone has hanged herself; Haemon commits suicide over her body. When Creon's wife Eurydice hears the news she too kills herself. The play ends with Creon, a broken man, surrounded by the bodies of his wife and son.

The Greek name Creon means Ruler; Antigone means Childless; Haimon means Bloody and Eurydice means Broad Justice. An ancient commentator tells us that *Antigone* is Sophocles' 32nd play.

◡ About the play

CREON: An enemy is never a friend, even in death.
ANTIGONE: I was born to love and not to hate.
CREON: Go then to the world of the dead
  Since it is the dead you love.
    tr. C. A. Trypanis

Antigone is one of the most complex and thought-provoking of all Greek tragedies. Its swiftness and compression add enormously to its power. The themes of state and family, power and gender, the relationship of gods to human beings, are brought together within the confines of a single work.

The opposition at the outset is clear-cut. Polyneices has returned at the head of a foreign army to invade his home-land. If he had been victorious, it would have meant disaster for the city.

But his brother Polyneices
Who found his way back from exile
To burn down his father's city

And shatter the temples of the gods
And drink his brother's blood
Dragging those who survived into slavery
Must we honour him with burial?
  tr. C. A. Trypanis

A family feud has endangered a whole community and its
gods: Creon's edict seems to have justice on its side. A century
later the orator Demosthenes quoted Creon's opening speech
as an example of the way a statesman should behave. When
Creon says,

The state is like a ship in which we sail
Only if she prospers in her journey
Can the passengers make good friends . . .

he is expounding a piece of political wisdom which
Sophocles' friend Pericles was to take up again in his famous
funeral speech celebrating the glories of Athenian civilization. Creon's treatment of Polyneices is severe but not
extraordinary, given the nature of the provocation.

The Athenian statesman Themistocles, who had been the
city's saviour in the Persian War, died in exile after being
found guilty of collaborating with its enemies. His family
were refused permission to bring his body home to be buried
in Athenian territory. The reaction is likely to have been even
more severe if he had entered the country at the head of an
invading army.

Creon's calm statement of his position, however, has been
preceded by Antigone's rejection of his edict. It is her passionate response to his proclamation that opens the play. The
first thing the audience encounters is not Creon's reasoned
arguments but something more urgent and emotional.

ANTIGONE: Will you share the danger?
ISMENE: What danger? What is in your mind?
ANTIGONE: Will you help these hands to carry the dead?
ISMENE: But will you bury him? Forbidden to the whole of
  Thebes?

ANTIGONE: My brother – yes, your brother too . . .
I will not betray him.
ISMENE: You are talking wildly. Creon has ordered –
ANTIGONE: What right has Creon! I know my duty.

> tr. C. A. Trypanis

No sooner has Sophocles established this opposition between the calm elder statesman and the passionate young woman than he begins to modify and develop it. When Antigone and Creon are brought face to face, it is Creon's composure that cracks first.

CREON: Insolent when she disobeyed my orders
Now she adds a second insult by her boasting
Being proud of what she did.
If she will go unpunished, she is the man,
Not I. But child or no child of my sister
The closest of those who worship Zeus
In my home, she and her sister shall die a painful death.

> tr. C. A. Trypanis

What begins to be evident here is Creon's outrage at having his power challenged by a woman and his stubborn insistence on being right no matter what. This becomes even plainer in the following scene where Creon is confronted by his son Haemon.

CREON: Must the disobedient go unpunished? be honoured?
HAEMON: Injustice commands no respect.
CREON: But she has acted unjustly.
Haemon: The whole of Thebes denies it.
CREON: Must Thebes tell the king how to rule?

> tr. C. A. Trypanis

Creon's authority, which had earlier seemed to speak for the whole city, now becomes simply naked self-assertion. There is no question of right and wrong any more, only a particular individual's wish to impose himself at any price. Creon has replaced the consensus of the citizens with his own personal fiat.

Antigone's position also emerges as more complicated than it first appeared.

> Had I lost a husband
> I could have married again,
> I could have had other children
> From some other man
> But now, with my mother and father
> Hidden in Hades, no brother
> Could ever blossom for me again.
> By such a law I honoured you first.
>> tr. C. A. Trypanis

Sophocles shows that Antigone's principled stand has a very particular motivation, just as he had shown her unusually headstrong and unconventional character in the scenes with her sister Ismene. And he does not shirk her terror at the thought of her approaching death.

It is finally the voice of the gods which reveals that Creon is in the wrong, although these same gods leave Antigone quite uncomforted at the last. When the condemnation comes it is unequivocal.

TEIRESIAS: Your judgement has made the city ill.
> Our altars, our hearths, are clogged with the foodscraps of birds and dog-meat, scraps from the dead son of Oedipus. The gods can no longer receive our prayers or fire from the burning of meats.
>> tr. Timberlake Wertenbaker

But Creon is now entrenched in his own stubbornness. He insists that the advice Teiresias is giving him is not disinterested but the result of bribery and he rejects the prophet in the most wounding terms. His earlier remark that 'the king must listen to the best advice' has been long forgotten.

Greek civilization, which accorded such a central place to human reason, was at the same time fascinated by those limits beyond which reason failed to hold. One of the main preoccupations linking all three tragedians is with those moments when reasoning stops and emotion takes over. Euripides in his *Medea, Hippolytus, Hecuba* and *The Bacchae* paints an unforgettable picture of sudden irruptions of violence which break through the surface of everyday life. In *Antigone* Sophocles shows how an impulse grounded in personal feeling can result in a principled action that is pleasing to the gods, while a position which started out as reasoned and reasonable can by degrees become dangerous and destructive when it is persisted with in defiance of all opposition. Some twenty years or more before Euripides wrote his great studies of the politics of unreason, *Orestes, The Phoenician Women* and *Iphigeneia in Aulis*, Sophocles had posed one of the central questions which any political system must address – how to achieve a proper balance between reasoned policy and those darker, uncontrollable forces which lurk beneath the surface.

> The flexible tree survives
> The weight and rush of the winter stream and saves its
>   wood;
> The stiff-necked perish root and branch.
> If a sailor never slackens his sail,
> His boat capsizes and floats with an upturned keel.
>   tr. C. A. Trypanis

Antigone is in some ways a tricky play to read from our Christian or post-Christian perspective. The Greeks were not interested in how the individual soul would fare on judgement day, weighed in the scale of good and evil. They were interested in situations and the choices people made within them. In the *Oresteia*, for example, Agamemnon at Aulis is caught in a situation where he has either to sacrifice his daughter Iphigeneia or see the Greek expedition fail. His son Orestes has to choose between murdering his mother and disobeying the commands of the god Apollo. In the final play of the trilogy the goddess Athene has to choose between disobeying her father and incurring the anger of the Furies when she acquits Orestes of the matricide. These are all situations in which there is no obvious right way of choosing.

The characters have to make their decisions and then live with the consequences.

To this way of looking at things, Sophocles brought his own fascination with the incommensurability of divine and human time. All the right decisions that Oedipus makes in human terms – leaving Corinth to spare his 'mother' and his 'father', ridding Thebes of the Sphinx, hunting down the murderer of Laius – bring him inexorably closer to that terrible moment – foretold from birth – when his time would collide with the time of the gods. In the same way in *Antigone*, Creon is right in human terms, but not on the timescale of the immortals. Antigone is right on the superhuman scale of things, but comes into conflict with ordinary human justice. Creon is right to uphold the law and must suffer the consequences when he refuses to back down. Antigone is right to break the law but she also has to bear the penalty for what she's done. It is this double action – equally weighted – that makes up the meaning of the play. To make Antigone the heroine or turn Creon into a psychotic bully is to misunderstand what Sophocles is about.

It's interesting to see how the playwright has shaped inherited material to suit his purposes. As far as we can tell *Antigone* makes several departures from the story as traditionally told – not the least of which is the prominence given to Antigone herself. Earlier accounts had focused principally on the issue of the Argive dead. The issue was a political one between cities, and the Thebans were eventually made to hand over the bodies by the intervention of an Athenian army. Sophocles' first innovation is to centre the story round the burial of an individual, Polyneices, and to make the action something internal to Thebes. Setting the struggle within a single city not only intensifies the conflict but also leads to the development of the character of Antigone to be Creon's opponent and so to the contrast between her and her more conventionally minded sister Ismene. Haemon's role is to form a bridge straddling the two camps and the character of Creon's wife Eurydice is supplied to be the autocrat's final victim. It is quite possible that, Creon apart, all the other characters are given their definitive form for the first time in this play. Euripides' version written many years later seems to have been closer to the world of New Comedy, in that it featured a pair of young lovers defying parental authority. Antigone and Haemon performed the burial together and were arrested together. The play had a happy ending, engineered by the god Dionysus, and featured a debate on marriage and the behaviour fitting for a wife – Antigone's daring obviously made her exceptional.

The chorus is made up of Theban elders who have been summoned by Creon to witness the new dispensation. Their entrance song is a hymn of deliverance, giving thanks for the victory over the foreign invaders. They behave circumspectly throughout but, however mild their demeanour when confronted with established power, their responses are generally accurate and to the point. They are quick to grasp that Polyneices' burial may have something to do with the will of the gods. They side with the mature man Creon against the youth Haemon, but are able to see, as Creon cannot, that Haemon has valid points to make. Their intervention saves Ismene from being executed along with her sister. They sympathize with Antigone in her last moments and remind Creon that Teiresias has a proven record of truth telling. Their words here guide the king towards revoking his decisions.

CHORUS: Son of Menoeceus, you must be brave
　　And wise.
CREON: What must I do . . . tell me . . . I will follow your
　　advice . . .
CHORUS: You must go yourself and free Antigone
　　From her hollow prison, and you must make a tomb
　　For the unburied man.
CREON: Must I do that . . .
CHORUS: Yes, King Creon, for the punishment of the gods
　　Pounces on men's folly . . . .
　　　　tr. C. A. Trypanis

∾ Translations

There are two excellent translations by C. A. Trypanis (Aris and Philips) and by Seamus Heaney (Faber). Timberlake Wertenbaker (Faber), Kenneth McLeish (Cambridge), Michael Ewans (Everyman) and Brendan Kennelly (Bloodaxe) are all useful. Don Taylor (Methuen), Elizabeth Wyckoff (Chicago) and Richard Emil Braun (Oxford) are less good. Tom Paulin's version *The Riot Act* sentimentalizes the play by turning Creon into a villain.

∾ In performance

Antigone was first performed around 445/42 BC. A Latin translation was performed at Cambridge *c.*1583. There is a play by Jean Anouilh (1944), an adaptation by Bertholt Brecht (1948) and an opera by Carl Orff (1949). Recent productions have included the Living Theatre (1967), the Freehold (1971), the National Theatre London (1983/4), Krakow (1984), the Royal Shakespeare Company (1991), the Old Vic (1999), Northern Broadsides (2003) and the Abbey Theatre (2004). Nelson Mandela played the part of Creon in production on Robben Island and Athol Fugard's play *The Island* uses *Antigone* as its central image.

Oedipus Tyrannus (*Oidipous Tyrannos*)

∾ The legend

Laius, king of Thebes, was warned that if he had a son, that son would grow up to kill his father.

When Oedipus was born Laius pierced the child's ankles, bound them together and gave him to a servant to abandon on the mountain outside the city. The servant spared the baby's life and gave him to a passing shepherd to look after.

The shepherd took the boy to Corinth where he was adopted by the king and queen, Polybus and Merope, who had no children of their own. They brought him up to be their heir. When Oedipus grew to manhood he was taunted by a drunk with not being the true son of his parents. He went to Delphi to consult the oracle and learned that his fate was to kill his father and sleep with his mother.

Oedipus was horrified and resolved never to return to Corinth. Making his way north, he encountered an older man in a chariot who tried to push him off the road. There was a fight and Oedipus killed the man and his attendants. Without knowing it he had just struck his father Laius dead.

Later in his wanderings he came to Thebes which was being attacked by a strange monster, part woman and part animal, called the Sphinx. Oedipus overcame the monster by answering the riddle it posed: 'What goes on four feet in the morning, two feet at noon and three feet in the evening?' The answer is man.

The grateful Thebans made Oedipus king of their city. He married Laius' widow Queen Jocasta – and so the second part of the prophecy was fulfilled. They had four children together – two boys, Eteocles and Polyneices, and two daughters, Antigone and Ismene. When after many years Oedipus came to discover what he had done, he put out his eyes. Queen Jocasta hanged herself.

The name Oidipous in Greek means Swell-Foot but it also incorporates the Greek word *oida* which means 'I know'.

∽ The story

The action takes place on the last day of Oedipus' rule at Thebes.

The city has been visited by a terrible plague. Oedipus has sent to ask Apollo's oracle about the cause of the infection. The answer comes back that Thebes is being polluted by the presence of King Laius' murderer. Oedipus determines to find the criminal and punish him.

At first his thoughts turn to conspiracy. Why was the killing never fully investigated? Perhaps there was a plot from within the city. The prophet Teiresias knows who the murderer is; why has he kept silent for so long? Teiresias tells Oedipus that the criminal he is looking for is himself but Oedipus refuses to listen. Reports had said that Laius was killed by a group of brigands, not a single man.

Oedipus accuses Creon, his wife Jocasta's brother, of being part of the conspiracy. Jocasta tries to calm the two angry men. She tells Oedipus that, contrary to what he had always believed, when King Laius was killed one of the men escorting him survived. Oedipus immediately sends a messenger to fetch this vital witness.

Jocasta prays to Apollo for deliverance from her troubles. As if in answer to her prayers a messenger arrives from Corinth, bringing news of the death of King Polybus and Oedipus' succession to the throne. Oedipus is unwilling to return home since his mother Merope is still alive. The Corinthian messenger tells him to have no fear on that score: Merope was not his real mother.

The messenger turns out to have been the man who rescued Oedipus on the mountain years ago. He tells the king the story of his rescue and how he brought him safe to Corinth. When Jocasta hears about the child with the fettered feet, she realises the truth at once and runs into the palace. Laius' surviving bodyguard supplies the last piece of the puzzle. He tells how he spared the child he had been ordered to kill and gave him to a foreigner to care for.

All the elements in the story are now accounted for. Oedipus has finally learned the truth about himself. He rushes into the palace to look for his mother, who is also his wife. He finds her hanging from a beam and with her brooches puts out his eyes. He will never look on anything from his former life again.

∾ About the play

> What a piece of work is a man. How noble in reason,
> how infinite in faculty . . . In action how like an angel, in
> apprehension how like a god. The beauty of the world,
> the paragon of animals . . . .
>
> Shakespeare, *Hamlet*, Act II, Scene 2

> This horror is mine and I alone am strong enough to
> bear it.
>
> *Oedipus Tyrannus*, tr. E. R. Dodds

Oedipus Tyrannus is the most perfect expression of Sophocles'
feeling for the uncertainty of the world – the awareness that
everything that seems settled in life can be overturned within
the space of a single day. The play explores the paradox that
human beings are at one and the same time both powerful
and helpless. The way the two poles of this opposition are
held in perfect balance gives *Oedipus Tyrannus* its special mixture of terror and exhilaration.

Pages and page have been written trying to pin down
Oedipus' 'transgression' or his 'fatal flaw' – all of them in
vain. The Greeks did not share the Christian fascination with
sin and guilt and how the individual soul would stand on
judgement day. They were interested in situations and the
choices people make within them.

The images associated with Oedipus are active: they make
him by turns hunter, helmsman, cultivator, mathematician,
scientist, doctor and lawyer. But these qualities have their
opposites. Oedipus is the hunter but also the prey, the scientist but also the experiment, the doctor but also the patient,
the lawyer but also the criminal, the man who measures and
the thing that is measured, the cultivator who sows his seed in
his own mother's womb.

Oedipus' speed, decisiveness and fearless use of intelligence were all recognized in the fifth century as belonging
specifically to the inhabitants of democratic Athens. The his-

torian Thucydides makes the Corinthians describe their northern neighbour with a mixture of awe and apprehension.

An Athenian is always an innovator, quick to form a decision and quick to carry it out . . . Athenian daring will outrun its own resources; they will take risks against their better judgement and still in the midst of danger remain confident . . . If they aim at something and do not get it, they think they have been deprived of what belonged to them already; whereas if their enterprise is successful, they regard their success as nothing compared with what they will do next. Of them alone it may be said that they possess a thing almost as soon as they have begun to desire it, so quickly with them does action follow on decision. Their view of a holiday is to do what needs doing: they prefer hardship and activity to peace and quiet. In a word, they are by nature incapable of living a quiet life themselves or allowing anyone else to do so.

tr. Rex Warner

It is uncanny how much of this description applies to Sophocles' hero. There is no firm date for the play but it was most probably written sometime between 430 and 423 BC, just after the beginning of the Peloponnesian war, when Athenian power and confidence were at their peak. The play takes a man at the height of his success and shows how swiftly and easily that success can be overturned. It is one of the work's many paradoxes that it is Oedipus, the representative of human reason, who provides the most striking confirmation of divine power.

'Not from the beginning did the gods reveal everything to mankind. But in the course of time by research men discover improvements' (Xenophanes). *Oedipus Tyrannus* was written at a period when, for the first time in history, the idea of progress began to develop. The traditional view held that the present was a sad falling off from a former Golden Age. But there was another way of looking at things – namely that civilized life was not a decline at all but an improvement. The author of a fifth century text *On Ancient Medicine* was clear, for example, about the superiority of a proper diet over raw food gathered in the wild. As for the cure of diseases: 'Many splendid discoveries have been made over the years, and the rest will be discovered if a competent man, familiar with past findings, takes them as the basis for his enquiries'. Knowledge was seen as something cumulative, capable of improving the lot of human beings far into the future.

This increasing sense of mastery over nature had unsettling implications. If man is truly the measure of all things, what place is there left for the gods? Perhaps their power is simply an illusion. This is what the chorus are afraid of.

> I will go to Delphi no longer
> To worship at the pure navel of the Earth,
> If these oracles never come true,
> If men cannot point at them clearly.
> [. . .]
> The old prophecies of Laius are failing,
> No more to be trusted;
> Apollo is no longer honoured;
> The worship of the gods is withering away.
>   tr. C. A. Trypanis

It seems at first that the chorus are right to be afraid. A messenger arrives from Corinth with news that Oedipus' supposed father Polybus has died a natural death. Oedipus is quick to see the implications.

> O god! Then why should one look
> To the hearth of the Pythian seer
> Or to the birds that scream over our heads!
> Did they not say that I would kill my father?
> But he is dead, hidden under the earth,
> And here I am, not having touched a spear!
> Unless he died of longing for me –
> Then I could be guilty . . . .
>   tr. C. A. Trypanis

Oedipus at least attempts to provide a rational explanation: perhaps he was guilty of the old man's death in so far as Polybus 'died of longing for me'. Jocasta is more radical. She sees a world that is not only unpredictable but also has no pattern to it – a world governed by blind chance.

> How can a man fear the accidents of chance? No one has access to the future. It is best not to plan too carefully but to live as well as one can . . . The one who does not take any of this too seriously bears life more lightly.
>
> tr. Timberlake Wertenbaker

But Oedipus' belief that he has escaped his fate is only a temporary lull before the final cataclysm in which, after this moment of maximum doubt, the power of the gods is seen to reassert itself.

The metaphysical dizziness evoked by these passages is a long way from the earliest form of the story, which appears in Homer's *Odyssey*. Odysseus is meeting ghosts from the underworld.

> I saw the mother of Oedipus, the fair Epicaste, who committed an enormity in ignorance, marrying her son. He married her after killing his father. But in time the gods made matters known to men. He ruled the Cadmean people in lovely Thebes in sorrow, through the dreadful will of he gods, and she went to strong-gated Hades, after stringing a high noose from the top of a room, gripped by her own misery, leaving behind for him many causes of pain, and all the things that the avenging spirit of a mother brings about.
>
> tr. R. D. Dawe

Aeschylus wrote a tetralogy on the story – *Laius*, *Oedipus*, *Seven Against Thebes* and the satyr play *The Sphinx*. His version turned on the working out of an ancestral curse over three generations. Euripides' *Oedipus*, written late in his career, seems to have been a sensational piece about political violence. The discovery of Laius' murder becomes the pretext for a coup in which Creon seizes power. Oedipus doesn't blind himself but has his eyes put out by Creon's henchmen, like Gloucester in *King Lear*. Sophocles shows us something else – how Oedipus unmakes himself, how his restless intelligence will not be satisfied until it has uncovered every secret and come face to face with truth. As a great German scholar put it:

> The daimonic, continual and unconscious reaching over out of the realm of appearance into the realm of truth is the human element which was not supplied by the legend and had not been linked with the figure of Oedipus before Sophocles.
>
> Karl Reinhardt

'In time the gods made matters known to men' says Homer. Sophocles' Oedipus by contrast is the active agent who drags things from obscurity into the light. Teiresias, who knows the truth, tries to keep his knowledge hidden. Jocasta, whose mind runs ahead of her husband's, begs him to stop.

> JOCASTA: Listen to me, I beg you. Don't go on.
> OEDIPUS: I must. I must find out the truth.
> JOCASTA: I know I am right. I warn you for your own good.
>
> tr. C. A. Trypanis

The shepherd who possesses the last piece of information knows what is coming and tries to keep silent.

> SHEPHERD: Must I answer? I am afraid to speak.
> OEDIPUS: And I am afraid to hear. But I must hear.
>
> tr. C. A. Trypanis

Oedipus is an explorer, not a victim.

At the end of the play he is reborn into knowledge, both of himself and of the world; and, being reborn, his actions are his own. His blindness is something freely chosen.

> OEDIPUS: Apollo. It was Apollo, friend, who completes these terrible things, this evil I must suffer.
> But it was my hand that struck, not his.

The gods are immortal and invulnerable –they always win. But the experience of change is uniquely human; it is something the gods can never know. How each man endures his defeat is his own business. Unlike Ajax, Deianeira, Antigone, the leading characters in Sophocles' earlier plays, Oedipus makes the decision to live on.

∾ Translations

The best translations are by C. A. Trypanis (Aris and Philips) and Timberlake Wertenbaker (Faber). The Kenneth McLeish (Nick Hern Books) is powerful but a little short-breathed. Gregory McCart (Everyman), David Grene (Chicago), and Don Taylor (Methuen) are also useful There is a version by W. B. Yeats, first performed in 1926, which was completed by the poet Richard Murphy for the Abbey Theatre production in 1973. The translation by Ranjit Bolt (into rhyming couplets) is to be avoided.

∾ In performance

We don't know the date of the first performance – sometime between 430 and 423 BC seems most likely. There are plays by Seneca (c.AD 50), Jean Corneille (1659), John Dryden and Nathaniel Lee (1667/8), a comic version *The Broken Jug* by Heinrich von Kleist (1811), and a Nigerian adaptation by Ola Rotimi *The Gods Are Not To Blame* (1968). There are operas by Stravinsky (1927), Georges Enescu (1936) and Wolfgang Rihm (1987). In 1585 the play was the opening production of Palladio's Teatro Olimpico at Vicenza. There have been notable twentieth-century productions by Max Reinhardt (1910), Michel Saint Denis, with Laurence Olivier in the title part (1945), Tyrone Guthrie (1957), and in Prague with designs by Josef Svoboda (1963). The play was staged at the RSC and by Tara Arts (both 1991), the National Theatre in 1998 and by Northern Broadsides in 2001.

Electra (*Elektra*)

∾ The legend

> The curses are at work: the buried live; blood flows for
> blood, drained from the slayers by those who died of yore.
> *Electra* tr. R. C. Jebb

The story of the house of Atreus is one of bloodshed from the
start. Tantalus, son of Zeus, was founder of the line. He killed
his son Pelops and offered him to the gods to eat. The gods
punished him by condemning him to eternal thirst, with a
glass of water just out of reach, and eternal hunger, with food
in front of him that he could not grasp.

Pelops was brought back to life. He killed his bride's father
in a chariot race and then murdered the man who helped him
do it. Pelops had two sons, Atreus and Thyestes. They fell
out over their inheritance. Thyestes stole Atreus' kingdom
and his wife; Atreus retaliated by killing Thyestes' children
and giving them to their father to eat.

In the next generation, Atreus' son Agamemnon was
forced to sacrifice his daughter Iphigeneia to secure a wind
which would enable the Greek fleet to sail to Troy. When
he returned at the war's end, he was murdered by his wife
Clytemnestra, avenging Iphigeneia, and her lover Aegisthus,
Thyestes' son, avenging his dead brothers.

Agamemnon had three surviving daughters, Electra,
Chrysothemis and Iphianassa, and a son, Orestes. Orestes,
with Electra's help, killed his mother Clytemnestra and her
lover Aegisthus.

∾ The story

The action takes place on the day when Orestes returns from
exile to kill his mother. He arrives in Argos accompanied by
his Tutor and his friend Pylades. They plan how to proceed.

The Tutor will bring news of Orestes' supposed death. The two young men will then be able to enter the palace unsuspected and take their revenge.

Electra, alone of Agamemnon's daughters, has refused to come to an accommodation with her father's murderers, the new rulers of the kingdom. She lives in the palace, ragged, lonely, childless, keeping alive her father's memory, existing only for the day when her brother will return from exile. Aegisthus is so weary of her complaints that he threatens to have her confined in a windowless cell.

Clytemnestra has a dream that her dead husband has returned and sends her daughter Chrysothemis to place offerings on Agamemnon's tomb. The queen lives in daily dread that her son will come to kill her. She prays to Apollo to deliver her from this terror that gives her no rest. The Tutor arrives and provides such a detailed account of Orestes' death in a chariot race that Clytemnestra believes him. She is touched with grief for a moment, then relieved. Her son is dead: her ordeal is over at last. Electra is plunged into despair: her only reason for living has now been taken away.

Chrysothemis returns from Agamemnon's tomb. She has found a lock of hair there and offerings to the dead. She is convinced that Orestes is alive. Electra tells her that this cannot be true: Orestes has been killed. She tries to enlist Chrysothemis' help in a desperate plan to kill Aegisthus. Now that the male heir is dead, the two women are the only ones left who can avenge their father.

Orestes and Pylades enter with an urn containing the supposed ashes of the 'dead' Orestes. Electra asks to hold the urn and utters a great lament for her lost brother and her wasted life. Orestes, touched to the heart, reveals himself. Brother and sister are reunited at last.

Orestes and Pylades enter the palace and kill the queen. Aegisthus arrives, having heard the news of Orestes' death. The two young men produce a body, which they say is that of Orestes. When Aegisthus uncovers the face, he sees that it is Clytemnestra. Orestes and Pylades take him inside to his death.

᠊ᢙ About the play

> What we thought
> Is not confirmed and what we thought not god
> Contrives. And so it happens in this story.
>
> Euripides, *Medea*, tr. Rex Warner

Electra is, with *The Cherry Orchard*, perhaps the most formally perfect play ever written and, like *The Cherry Orchard*, it is the product of a profoundly religious sensibility. Its themes are hope, steadfastness, transience – unexpected fulfilment and unexpected disaster. Like Sophocles' *Oedipus*, the play dramatizes the terror and magnificence of life, and its uncertainty. Oedipus begins the day the confident and much loved ruler of a kingdom; he ends it blind, powerless and reviled. Setting out to track down a murderer, he finds the criminal is himself. Electra has lost Orestes, hopes for his return, loses him once more to death . . . and finds him again when she least expects it. The passage from Euripides quoted above sits at the end of *Medea* as a comment on the action. In Sophocles, this feeling of unpredictability cannot be separated out: it is part of the most intimate movement of the play. *Electra* shows us the miraculous strangeness of life as 'an event rather than a fact – a verb (as Martha Graham liked to say) rather than a noun'.

Rescue, false rescue, real hope, false hope – the pattern runs right through the play. Clytemnestra prays for deliverance from her terror and immediately her wish is granted. The Tutor appears to announce Orestes' death. It is a strange moment.

CLYTEMNESTRA: Oh God! What am I to say of these things?
Am I to call them fortunate or . . . terrible but beneficial?
I am in a sad state if I have to save my life by the sufferings of my own flesh and blood . . . It's a queer thing to be a mother. Even when you suffer at their hands you cannot hate those you bore.
    tr. J. H. Kells

The Tutor's lies have provoked a true emotion – relief and regret both mixed together. The regret is all the stronger in that the Tutor's portrait of the young Orestes as a courageous and skilful athlete so closely corresponds to all the hopes that Clytemnestra might once have had for her son. Yet the story is a trap which will deliver the queen, unsuspecting, to her death.

There is a parallel in the way in which Aegisthus comes hurrying home, buoyed up with false hope, full of excitement that the threat of Orestes' vengeance has finally been removed. His moment of triumph reveals his nature as surely as Clytemnestra had revealed hers earlier.

AEGISTHUS: Where are these strangers from Phocis?
   The ones who brought news of Orestes' death
   In a shipwreck of chariots. Answer me.
   You! Yes, you Electra. Where are they?
   What? Silent? You had so much to say before.
   Tell me. He was your brother; you must know.
      tr. Kenneth McLeish

All his arrogance and excitement come pouring out. Yet within twenty lines he is lost for ever.

AEGISTHUS: Oh gods! What sight is this?
ORESTES: Look and see. Are you afraid?
AEGISTHUS: Who are you? Answer. What trap is this?
ORESTES: You called me dead. I am alive again.
      tr. Kenneth McLeish

In a piece of bravura construction, the play's central theme of reversed expectations is recapitulated sharply just before the end.

The play is structured in such a way as to get characters to show their inmost nature. Euripides, when he writes a plot, is interested in creating situations that are exciting, strange or memorable. Sophocles has a different interest. He wants to create a way in which his characters can reveal the deepest truth about themselves – moments which are like snapshots taken from the viewpoint of eternity. This was what Virginia Woolf meant when she wrote of *Electra*: 'Sophocles chose a design which, if it failed, would show its failure in gashes and ruin, not in the gentle blurring of some insignificant detail; which, if it succeeded, would cut each stroke to the bone, would stamp each fingerprint in marble.'

Electra's moment of self-revelation comes when she is most lost, grieving over the ashes of Orestes.

ELECTRA: Oh, all there is for memory of my love,
my most loved in the world, all that is left
of live Orestes, oh, how differently
from how I sent you forth, how differently
from what I hoped, do I receive you home.
Now all I hold is nothingness,
but you were brilliant when I sent you forth.
[. . .]
The hands of strangers
gave you due rites, and so you come again,
a tiny weight enclosed in a tiny vessel.
Alas for all my nursing of old days,
so constant – all for nothing – which I gave you;
my joy was in the trouble of it. For never
were you your mother's love as much as mine.
[. . .]
Therefore receive me to your habitation,
nothing to nothing that with you below
I may dwell from now on. When you were on earth,
I shared all with you equally. Now I claim
in death no less to share a grave with you.
    tr. David Grene

The paradox is that when she considers herself deserted, cut off from all help, she has never been less alone. Her speech reaches out towards the dead Orestes but it is not a soliloquy: the person it is addressed to is present to receive it. Electra's solitude is already over at the moment she feels it most keenly. The combination here of abandonment and security, the fact that she is lost and found all in an instant, make this scene perhaps the most moving in all Greek tragedy.

TUTOR: Orestes is dead. There it is, in one short word.

ELECTRA: O God, O God. This is the day I die.

CLYTEMNESTRA: What is it you say sir, what? Don't listen to her.

TUTOR: What I said and say now is 'Orestes is dead.'

ELECTRA: God help me, I am dead – I cannot live now.

CLYTEMNESTRA: Leave her to herself. Sir, will you tell me the truth?

tr. David Grene

The Tutor's recounting of Orestes' death is placed in the exact centre of the play. Everything leads up to and away from this moment. Each half of the play has a parallel construction: each contains a lament from Electra, a scene between Electra and her sister, and a scene with Clytemnestra. As the pattern repeats itself, all the relationships are subtly charged and altered by the fake account of Orestes' death.

Sophocles' structural mastery is shown in his handling of Orestes' story. Orestes' presence is vital to the plot, since his revenge is the trigger for the action, but Sophocles carefully makes use of it for his own purposes. Orestes, Pylades and the Tutor are the first characters to enter; they set up what will happen next – and then it's as if they vanish from the play. What happens is that the dry, practical, rather laconic men we meet in the first scene are displaced by waves of female emotion. Orestes, from being a person, becomes a memory, a cause, an object of yearning. The actual man in all his prosaic there-ness is replaced by his image in the desires and fears of the chorus, of Electra and Clytemnestra, and this image is more vivid than the real thing. The man is replaced by a dream of his presence.

This is why the Tutor's speech produces such an extraordinary effect. Sophocles has made it enormously detailed and circumstantial, partly so that Clytemnestra and Electra will believe it, but more importantly so that the audience will believe it too. The fantasy Orestes, who has been constantly invoked through the first half of the play, is now killed off in fantasy and his death feels as real as his life has done. When Electra embarks on her great lament, we don't look at her from the outside as some poor dupe, we feel along with her in fullest sympathy. When Orestes reappears, it comes as a surprise not just to Electra but to the audience as well.

The pattern of vacillating emotion also holds good for Chrysothemis. She comes running joyfully from Agamemnon's tomb, convinced that Orestes is alive, only to be told bluntly by Electra that he is dead. Here is another instance of Sophocles swiftly recapitulating his theme and the emotions associated with it. He cleverly uses the minor characters, Aegisthus and Chrysothemis, to shadow and amplify the reversals of the major characters, Clytemnestra and Electra.

Critics who approach the play by attempting to determine Sophocles' attitude to matricide – is he for it or against it? – are trying to grasp a mirage. Matricide is a fact in the story: it is not the point of the story. Since the whole play has been about impermanence, since every feeling and situation in it has been shown to be subject to the laws of change, the triumph of Electra and Orestes will also not be lasting. Whether or not Orestes will suffer remorse or be pursued by the Furies are questions that Sophocles is not interested in addressing directly. He has already answered them.

Like Aeschylus, but in a different way, the retribution visited by Clytemnestra on Agamemnon, and by Orestes on Clytemnestra, is shown to be part of something larger. Sophocles struggled for years to make the Aeschylean tragic action work itself out within the confines of a single play. It is fitting that an episode from Aeschylus' *Oresteia* should mark his total mastery of the problem he had set himself. It is in *Electra* above all that the Sophoclean world view is most perfectly expressed.

The play draws all the characters into its pattern of lost and found, certain and uncertain, safe and unsafe, threatened and secure, and the pattern can be imagined extending indefinitely beyond the confines of the play to embrace the whole of life. The work seems to have no horizon. Chekhov is the only other European dramatist to achieve this effect. What he shares with Sophocles is a feeling for time and change and hope and disappointment, and an ability to give his characters their full human individuality while at the same time holding them steady in a pattern which is itself a feeling.

ELECTRA: Is he alive then?
ORESTES:　　　　　　　　Yes, if I am living.
ELECTRA:　　　　And you are he?
ORESTES:　　　　　　　　Look at this signet ring
　　that was our father's, and know if I speak true.
ELECTRA:　　　　O happiest light!
ORESTES:　　　　　　　　Happiest I say, too.
　　　tr. David Grene

∾ Translations

The Chicago translation by David Grene provides a good guide to the play, though a certain stiffness in the diction makes it unsuitable for use in performance. The best text for the theatre is by Kenneth McLeish (Methuen). There is a strong, clear version from Michael Ewans (Everyman). The Frank McGuinness (Faber) is fluent but has a tendency to smooth over the sharpness of the original. There is also an eccentric and thought-provoking version by Ezra Pound and Rudd Fleming (New Directions).

∾ In performance

The year of the first performance is unknown; a range of dates between 420 and 410 BC is possible. There is an opera by Richard Strauss (1909) and a play by Jean Giraudoux (1937). Recent productions have included those at the Old Vic (1951), the Théâtre National de Chaillot (1986), the RSC

(1989), the Donmar Warehouse (1997) and the Citizens' Theatre, Glasgow (2000).

Philoctetes (Philoktetes)

∾ The legend

Heracles was half-human, half-divine, son of Zeus and a mortal woman Alcmene. He was gifted with more than human strength and his twelve labours rid the earth of various monsters and helped to civilize the world. Many of these labours were accomplished with the help of his famous bow, which never missed, and arrows dipped in the Hydra's venom, which were invariably fatal. Heracles was unwittingly given a poisoned robe by his wife Deianeira: the garment stuck to his flesh and caused him terrible pain. He had a funeral pyre built and offered his bow and arrow to the man who would light it for him so he could be burnt alive. Philoctetes, son of the king of the country where Heracles was living, lit the pyre and received the hero's weapons as his reward.

Some time later Philoctetes sailed with seven ships to join the Greek expedition to capture Troy. He was bitten by a snake while sacrificing on the island of Chryse. The smell from his suppurating wound and his cries of agony led the Greeks to put him ashore on the island of Lemnos and sail to Troy without him.

∾ The story

Ten years have passed since Philoctetes was marooned on his desert island. He has spent the time living in a cave, sleeping on a bed of leaves, shooting sea birds and wild animals to eat. The terrible wound in his foot has never healed and is still tormenting him. The Greeks who are besieging Troy discover that they can only take the city with the help of two men: one of them is Philoctetes and the other is Achilles' son Neoptolemus.

The Greeks send Odysseus to collect Neoptolemus from his home in Skyros and Odysseus and the young man travel together to fetch Philoctetes from his island. But there is a difficulty. Philoctetes hates the Greeks and Odysseus in particular for having abandoned him: he has no desire to help them out. If he sees Odysseus he will try to kill him. Ten years ago Neoptolemus was only a boy and so was not implicated in the earlier betrayal. Odysseus persuades him to try to trick Philoctetes into parting with the bow.

Neoptolemus pretends to have quarrelled with the Greek commanders and be sailing home. He offers to take Philoctetes with him, meaning to kidnap him as soon as he's aboard and take him to Troy by force. Philoctetes is ready to leave the island but Neoptolemus starts to have second thoughts. He has come to pity the crippled Philoctetes and feels that in carrying out Odysseus' plan he is acting against his own true nature.

The sore on Philoctetes' foot bursts open and he passes out with the pain, leaving Neoptolemus holding the bow. Odysseus appears and makes Neoptolemus leave with him, abandoning Philoctetes to his solitude. Philoctetes is in despair. Without his bow he will starve to death and the new friend he trusted has betrayed him.

Neoptolemus finds he can't abandon the wounded man. He returns to give Philoctetes back the bow, hoping that by doing so he can persuade him to leave the island and come to Troy. But Neoptolemus' treachery, however brief, has confirmed Philoctetes in his hatred for the Greeks and his desire to do everything he can to thwart their plans. He refuses point blank to go to Troy and demands that Neoptolemus take him home. Neoptolemus accepts defeat and the two of them are heading for the ship when Heracles appears and orders Philoctetes to abandon his resistance. His resentments, though justified, must in the end give way to history: Troy must fall and the honour of its capture go to two men working together, the archer Philoctetes and the warrior Neoptolemus who protects him.

∿ About the play

Let us say before I go any further that I forgive nobody. I wish them all an atrocious life in the fires of icy hell and in the execrable generations to come.

Samuel Beckett, *Malone Dies*

History says, 'Don't hope
On this side of the grave.'
But then once in a lifetime
The longed-for tidal wave
Of justice can rise up
And hope and history rhyme.

Seamus Heaney, *The Cure at Troy*

Philoctetes is perhaps the greatest play ever written about power and vulnerability. The battle lines are clearly drawn. Odysseus and Neoptolemus are well-fed, rested and physically whole. They have the resources of the whole Greek army at their back. Their opponent is weak and isolated and alone. Yet he has a power that is uniquely his which the others cannot do without. The first half of the play is about subterfuge – how the powerful approach the weak to take advantage. The second half of the play is about stubbornness and refusal – how an individual can use power uncreatively to block and thwart.

Aeschylus and Euripides had both written earlier plays about the story. Both feature a chorus of Lemnians and revolve around a confrontation between Odysseus and Philoctetes. In Aeschylus, Odysseus pretends that Agamemnon has died, the Greek army has been destroyed and that he himself has been executed, before stealing the bow by force. In Euripides, Athena disguises Odysseus so that Philoctetes does not recognize him. The action gains added suspense from the arrival of a Trojan embassy, who have also come to secure the bow. One ancient commentator described Euripides' work as 'a masterpiece of declamation' and 'a model of ingenious debate'.

Sophocles does a number of things differently. Firstly, he makes Lemnos uninhabited, increasing Philoctetes' loneliness and isolation. Secondly, instead of bringing Odysseus and his victim into direct confrontation, he introduces a third character, Achilles' son Neoptolemus (the name means New-to-the-War). The antagonism between the two former rivals flows through the young man, whose sensitive nature becomes a focus for much of the play's feeling.

The moral debate begins straightaway in the opening scene. Neoptolemus reacts with disgust to Odysseus' plan to take the bow by stealth:

> I am Achilles' son, noblest of Greeks –
> How can I cheat and steal to get my way?
> I'll conquer by force, not treachery.
> The man's outnumbered, a poor cripple –
> If he fights, he'll lose. I know
> I was sent to help you, to obey you;
> But with respect, my lord, I'd rather
> Fight fair and lose than cheat and win.
>   tr. Kenneth McLeish

Neoptolemus has to come to terms with the fact that if he wants the renown of capturing Troy he will have to accept certain compromises in order to bring it about. Odysseus confronts the younger man with a tempting bargain:

> ODYSSEUS: For one little day, for one dishonest hour
>   Do as I say. When it is done, your life
>   Can be the noblest the world has ever seen.

Neoptolemus comes to accept that deceit is the only way forward. But it remains to be seen whether this decision will survive an encounter with the living, suffering Philoctetes. The theory of treachery is one thing, but to cheat a vulnerable human being face to face is something else again. 'Must I look him the face and lie to him?' Neoptolemus asks Odysseus nervously.

At first everything goes according to plan, but when it comes to the moment to get Philoctetes on board ship, Neoptolemus hesitates. The tension is built up with great skill. Three times departure becomes a possibility and three times it is delayed. As Neoptolemus starts to have second thoughts, a messenger sent by Odysseus arrives. He tells a string of lies designed to hurry things up, but the time it takes to tell them slows things down. Neoptolemus is given time to think and, before anything more can happen, Philoctetes' wound breaks open. The pain of it makes him faint. Neoptolemus' resolve does not survive this encounter with utter helplessness. When Philoctetes has recovered and, leaning on the young man's shoulder, is making his way painfully towards the harbour, Neoptolemus finally bursts out with the truth.

The picture of Philoctetes' suffering and isolation is carefully built up. In the opening scene the cave where he lives is described with its bed of leaves, its crudely carved wooden cup, a few twigs to light a fire, and outside some scraps of old rag used as bandages, drying in the sun. Before we see him, we hear Philoctetes howling with pain, like an animal.

> He must have stumbled on the path
> and his moaning carried all the way here.
> Or perhaps he stopped to look at the empty harbour
> for it was a bitter cry.
>   tr. David Grene

Aristotle said, 'Man is by nature a political animal', meaning that to live in society was an essential part of being human. Hard as the physical conditions are, the worst part of Philoctetes' predicament for the Greeks would have been his isolation. The appearance of Robinson Crusoe as the ideal self-sufficient capitalist individual lies some two thousand years in the future.

One of the most painful deprivations has been the lack of language. Philoctetes is pathetically grateful when he realises that the newly arrived strangers speak Greek. Yet language, which brings with it the possibility of deceit, is very nearly his undoing. The natural world, which appeared so inhospitable when he was alone, comes to seem kindly and welcoming compared to his fellow human beings.

PHILOCTETES: Caverns and headlands, dens of wild creatures
    you jutting broken crags, to you I raise my cry –
    there is no one else that I can speak to –
    and you have always been there, have always heard me.
    Let me tell you what he has done to me, this boy,
    Achilles' son.
        tr. David Grene

Odysseus has trapped Philoctetes physically by marooning him on a desert island. Neoptolemus traps him psychologically by playing on his isolation and his desire for human contact.

Where are the chorus in all of this? They are Achilles' men, warriors who sailed with him to Troy, so they are fifteen or twenty years older than Neoptolemus, whom they refer to at one point as 'boy'. But Neoptolemus is their commander and they are under his orders just as he is under the orders of Odysseus. They sympathize with Philoctetes but take an active part in the deception, returning equivocal assurances when straight speaking would give the game away. In doing this they place a question mark over the conduct of Neoptolemus. It's one thing to take on an opponent man to man, but when a group gangs up together against a single victim, the whole event begins to look less savoury.

In *Electra* Sophocles had already created a monumental study in loneliness and endurance; in *Philoctetes* he goes one step further. First there is the continual presence of physical pain.

PHILOCTETES: By God if you have a sword ready to hand
    use it.

> Strike the end of my foot. Strike it off, I tell you now.
> Do not spare my life. Quick, boy, quick.

Then there is the sense of time gone by and the wasted years.

> PHILOCTETES: O stop! Tell me no more. Let me understand
>   this first. Is he dead, Achilles dead? . . .
> NEOPTOLEMUS: God help you, I would have thought that
>   your own sufferings
> were quite enough without mourning for those of others.
>   tr. David Grene

And beyond the pain there is the worry about the pain – the fear that the wound and the suffering it causes will repel those people to whom he must turn for help. Yet it is Philoctetes' helplessness that makes it impossible for Neoptolemus to act against him.

> Come! One day, hardly one whole day's space
> that I shall trouble you. Endure this much.
> Take me and put me where you will,
> in the hold, in the prow or poop, anywhere
> where I shall least offend those that I sail with.
> By Zeus himself, God of the Suppliants,
> I beg you, boy, say 'yes', say you will do it.
> Here I am on my knees to you, poor cripple,
> for all my lameness. Do not cast me away
> so utterly alone, where no one even walks by.
>   tr. David Grene

Neoptolemus' moral education is not complete without a last and final twist to the story. The young man defies Odysseus and returns the bow to Philoctetes. He thinks that because he has changed and done the right and difficult thing that Philoctetes will undergo a similar change. But the world does not work like that. What has sustained Philoctetes through years of loneliness has been hoping for justice and for revenge on his enemies – and the treatment to which he has been subject earlier at the hands of Neoptolemus has increased his resentment. Now that his bow has been given back to him the only use he can think to make of it is to withhold it. The freedom of choice has been restored to him and with that freedom comes the freedom to misuse it.

Even when Philoctetes is offered a cure and the promise of undying fame he prefers to cling to his resentment. His anger has kept him going through the years and he is unable at the last to give it up. Neoptolemus is forced to recognize that there are some things that can't be solved by behaving decently (which of course was Odysseus' point in the first place). He finally consents to live up to his promise and take Philoctetes home, giving up his own hopes of glory and earning the enmity of the Greek commanders.

The play is full of fathers. The shade of great Achilles haunts Neoptolemus who in the action stands between two other fathers – the worldly Odysseus and the suffering Philoctetes. It takes the appearance of one last father figure, Heracles, to force Philoctetes to surrender his anger and give way to the tide of history. Heracles is not merely the owner of the bow: the agonizing nature of his own death is a guarantee that Philoctetes' pain has been acknowledged. Philoctetes in turn is forced to accept that he is not the centre of the universe but part of something bigger. The single Sophoclean hero finally becomes a couple: it is Neoptolemus and Philoctetes together working hand in hand that will bring about Troy's downfall.

∾ Translations

There are two fine modern translations – by Kenneth McLeish (Methuen), and by Judith Affleck (Cambridge Translations from Greek Drama). The latter comes with excellent notes. The Everyman translation by Graham Ley is good and David Grene (Chicago) is still perfectly acceptable; there is also a version by Keith Dewhurst (Oberon Books). Seamus Heaney's translation called *The Cure at Troy* is beautiful but rather softens the flintiness of the original.

✌ In performance

The play was first performed in 409 BC. It won first prize. An eighteenth-century adaptation by the French playwright Chateaubrun (1755) gave Philoctetes a daughter called Sophie to provide Neoptolemus with a love interest. The play inspired one of the great works of German Romantic criticism, *Laocoon* by Gotthold Ephraim Lessing (1766). André Gide wrote a *Philoctète* (1898) and Heiner Mueller a *Philoktet* (1958–64). *Philoctetes* was performed at the National Theatre (1964), at Manchester Royal Exchange (1982), by Cheek by Jowl at the Donmar Warehouse (1989) and by Field Day (1990).

Oedipus at Colonus (*Oidipous epi Kolonoi*)

✌ The legend

Laius, king of Thebes, was warned that if he had a son, that son would grow up to kill his father.

When Oedipus was born Laius pierced the child's ankles, bound them together and gave him to a servant to abandon on the mountain outside the city. The servant spared the baby's life and gave him to a passing shepherd to look after.

The shepherd took the boy to Corinth where he was adopted by the king and queen, Polybus and Merope, who had no children of their own. They brought him up to be their heir. When Oedipus grew to manhood he was taunted by a drunk with not being the true son of his parents. He went to Delphi to consult the oracle and learned that his fate was to kill his father and sleep with his mother.

Oedipus was horrified and resolved never to go back to Corinth. Making his way north, he encountered an older man in a chariot who tried to push him off the road. There was a fight and Oedipus killed the man and his attendants.

Without knowing it he had just struck his father Laius dead.

Later in his wanderings he came to Thebes which was being attacked by a strange monster, part woman and part animal, called the Sphinx. Oedipus overcame the monster by answering the riddle it posed: 'What goes on four feet in the morning, two feet at noon and three feet in the evening?' The answer is man.

The grateful Thebans made Oedipus king of their city. He married Laius' widow Queen Jocasta – and so the second part of the prophecy was fulfilled. They had four children together – two boys, Eteocles and Polyneices, and two daughters, Antigone and Ismene. When after many years Oedipus came to discover what he had done, he put out his eyes. Queen Jocasta hanged herself.

After the disaster Oedipus went on living at Thebes for a time but the feeling grew that he was a source of pollution to the city and it was decided to expel him. His two sons, now grown to manhood, did nothing to defend their father. His two daughters were more loyal. Antigone accompanied her blind father on his wanderings. Ismene remained behind to warn her father and her sister of any development in Thebes which might threaten them.

The name Oidipous in Greek means Swell-Foot but it also incorporates the Greek word *oida* which means 'I know'.

~ The story

Oedipus is an old man, poor and destitute. He and his daughter Antigone arrive at Colonus, a small village in Athenian territory, about a mile and half northwest of the city.

When Oedipus learns that the grove in which he is resting is sacred to the Furies, who avenge all crimes within the family, he refuses to go any further. Apollo prophesied that this would be his final resting place. The local inhabitants try to make him leave but Oedipus will not go. He tells them to summon Theseus, king of Athens: he, Oedipus, has a precious gift to give him.

Ismene arrives from Thebes with news of an oracle. Apollo has foretold that when Oedipus dies his grave will bring blessings on the people in whose land he is buried. The Thebans who had driven Oedipus out now want to reclaim him: but they don't intend to readmit him to the city, merely to bury him at the frontier.

Theseus is full of pity for the blind old man and promises to protect him. Oedipus reveals that in death his presence will protect Athens against future harm.

Creon, Jocasta's brother, now an old man himself, comes with soldiers to kidnap Oedipus and take him back to Thebes by force. His men capture Ismene and, when Oedipus refuses to move, they seize Antigone as well. Theseus, true to his word, drives off the intruders and keeps Oedipus safe.

Oedipus' sons have quarrelled over who should rule the kingdom. The younger son, Eteocles, has seized power and driven out Polyneices, the rightful heir. Polyneices comes to beg his father for support in regaining the kingdom but Oedipus curses his son for having abandoned him. Polyneices realizing that he faces the certainty of death in battle nevertheless sets out for Thebes at the head of his army.

A clap of thunder signals that Oedipus' time has come. The blind man stands and, swiftly and unaided, he sets out, followed by Theseus and his daughters.

A messenger describes his death. The god's voice could be heard summoning Oedipus, then the old man disappeared. Theseus alone knows where he is buried: not even Antigone and Ismene can be told. The secret of the hero's last resting place will be passed down from generation to generation and protect Athens against future calamity. Antigone and Ismene set out to return to Thebes, hoping against hope that they might be able to prevent their brothers from killing each other.

ᴄ᷉ About the play

> . . . and then a voice to make the hair stand on end.
> And the god called him again, in many ways.
> This man, this man Oedipus, why delay?
> You've stayed too long.
>
> tr. Timberlake Wertenbaker

Oedipus at Colonus is Sophocles' last play, written when he was nearly ninety. There is a story that the playwright's sons tried to sue their father for control of his estate on the grounds of mental incompetence. Sophocles appeared in court. He made no defence other than to read from the play he was working on, which was *Oedipus at Colonus*. The jury not only acquitted him but gave him an ovation.

In *Oedipus Tyrannus* we see the dismantling of a hero. Oedipus is brave and clever, a wise ruler, yet his bravery and intelligence bring about his downfall. His uncompromising drive to discover the truth wrenches his whole life apart. The play charts his journey from hero to outcast. *Oedipus at Colonus* charts the journey back.

Oedipus starts the play a beggar and ends it as something close to a god. The transformation begins at that moment when he realises that the grove of the Furies is the place foretold by the oracle. There was a time when he struggled to avoid his fate: now he knows that he must accept what has been ordained for him. The knowledge that his existence is somehow precious to the gods gives him strength. He may be destitute but he can deal with Theseus as an equal. His death has a value that his life no longer possesses, and his grave will protect the city against future harm.

He has also come to terms with past events. When challenged by the chorus about his father's murder, he mounts a robust defence.

> And yet how was I evil in myself?
> I had been wronged: I retaliated; even had I

Known what I was doing, was that evil?
Then knowing nothing I went on. Went on.
    tr. Robert Fitzgerald

The frenzy of shame that had seized him at the end of the previous play has been put behind him.

I was caught in ruin.
I am pure before the law.
I came to this without knowing.
    tr. Timberlake Wertenbaker

This acceptance is very far from being Christian resignation. Oedipus is a hero in the Greek mould whose values are helping friends and harming enemies: there is no injunction to turn the other cheek. Restored to his old self, Oedipus is restored to his pride, his anger and his sense of what is owed him. Electra, Philoctetes – Sophocles' characters are marked by an uncompromising sense of their own worth which renders them magnificent but undoubtedly awkward to deal with.

Antigone pleads with her father to listen to his son Polyneices.

You are his father, so even if he wronged you,
Was disrespectful, you should not wrong him in return.
. . . Remember
All you suffered because of your mother and father
And the wild anger that blazed then in you.
That led you to your endless darkness, you should think
    of it.
    tr. C. A. Trypanis

But Oedipus cannot forget old wrongs, and curses his son with terrifying force.

                  Never conquer Thebes,
Never return to Argos, but be killed
By your own brother's hand, and you kill him,
Who drove you from your city and your throne.
And let the bitter darkness of Black Tartarus

Lead you like a father to his home,
And may the Goddesses whose ground we tread,
And the god of Strife, who kindles your dreadful hate,
See that your father's curses are fulfilled.

tr. C. A. Trypanis

Violence, bitterness, sensitivity and righteousness all here speak at once. But while Oedipus is finally able to achieve a kind of rest, the new generation rushes to destruction with renewed vigour. The foolhardy, rash, despairing Polyneices is a bitter study in political folly, while Creon is Sophocles' most unsparing portrait of a corrupt politician. Ajax when he dies is torn away from a world of honour and military glory; Antigone's death tears her away from her family and hopes for the future. These are the plays of a younger man. The perspective of the ninety-year-old Sophocles is different. Oedipus' death marks an escape from restlessness, violent self-seeking and blind ambition.

In this play Sophocles is working within an established genre, which he is adapting for his own ends. It is the genre of the suppliant play (or as we would say, the play about asylum seekers), of which the first example is Aeschylus' *Suppliants*, written nearly sixty years before. Euripides wrote two further plays in this line, *The Children of Heracles* and *The Suppliant Women*, both of which glorified Athens as protector and champion of the weak. These works share a common outline. A group of refugees arrives seeking protection; they pose a problem for the city to which they come for help; their pursuers follow them threatening violence; there are long speeches leading up to the ruler's decision to take them in; finally the city extends its protection and sees off the intruders. Each play raises the question of where justice lies.

Elements of this pattern are present in *Oedipus at Colonus* but significantly changed. Oedipus is a suppliant but not a desperate one. His arrival has been willed by the gods. The advantages he confers are equal to the benefits he receives. He comes to Athens as a wanderer not a fugitive. It is not until the middle of the play that the Thebans realise that there is something at stake and set out to capture him. Theseus for his part is never in doubt as to what justice and his affections require.

> You would have to describe the most terrible deeds for me to withdraw. I was once brought up an exile, like you, and I faced all the dangers that beset a foreigner and because of this I would never turn away a foreigner like you now, but would always help him.

> I know I am only a man and have no greater security in the morrow than you do.
>   tr. Timberlake Wertenbaker

This magnanimous speech is a reminder that Sophocles was a close friend of the great Athenian statesman Pericles. There is an echo here of the famous funeral oration which according to Thucydides Pericles delivered in celebration of Athens' achievements.

> Again in questions of general good feeling there is a great contrast between us and most other people. We make friends by doing good to others, not by receiving good from them. This makes our friendship all the more reliable, since we want to keep alive the gratitude of those who are in our debt by showing continued good will to them . . . We are unique in this. When we do kindnesses to others we do not do them out of any calculations of profit and loss: we do them without afterthought, relying on our free liberality. Taking everything together then, I declare that our city is an education to Greece . . .
>   Thucydides, tr. Rex Warner

Oedipus at Colonus is Sophocles' last play: it marks an ending in other ways as well. It was written in 406/5 BC but not performed until 401, and those five years saw the end of the great period of Athenian democracy, as the city finally surrendered to its Spartan and Theban enemies. The long-drawn-out Peloponnesian war that had lasted for more than twenty-five years ended with the defeat of Athens and its unconditional surrender. The Athenian fleet was disbanded, their fortifications dismantled, and their democratic institutions that had lasted almost a century were dissolved to be replaced by a reactionary dictatorship, the Thirty Tyrants, who instituted a reign of terror. But bad as it was, it could have been worse. The Thebans and Corinthians pressed for the total destruction of the city and the enslavement of the population, but the Spartans refused to go that far. The excesses of the Thirty Tyrants soon led to a popular uprising and the return of democracy, albeit in a weakened form. Right at the last gasp, as it were, Sophocles composed a celebration of his native city – its physical beauty, its generosity to strangers, and offered a hope that it would be shielded against disaster in the future. Today Colonus is 'a bus station in an industrial suburb' but as long as language lasts Sophocles' vision of his birthplace will endure.

> Heavy with the drink of morning dew,
> day after day the narcissus flowers,
> crown of sorrow for the two goddesses,
> and the crocus opens petals like sunset.
> Every day sleepless springs
> sprinkle streams, spread rivers, feed
> plains, swell the contours of the land . . .
> land where the muses are not silent,
> land loved by Aphrodite,
> light goddess hands on golden reins.
> tr. Timberlake Wertenbaker

∾ Translations

The play has been lucky in its translations. The best performing versions are by Timberlake Wertenbaker (Faber) and C. A. Trypanis (Aris and Philips) but there are excellent translations by Robert Fagles (Penguin), Robert Fitzgerald

(Chicago), and Gregory McCart (Everyman). The McCart has useful notes and the Fagles has the benefit of an outstanding short introduction by Bernard Knox. David Thomson (Methuen) is serviceable but rather pedestrian and there is short-breathed version by Kenneth McLeish (Nick Hern Books). The Ranjit Bolt translation (into rhyming couplets) is to be avoided.

∾ In performance

The play was first performed in 401 BC some years after the playwright's death, directed by his grandson, also called Sophocles. In recent times the play was staged at the Abbey Theatre Dublin in 1927 in a translation by W. B. Yeats, by the Royal Shakespeare Company in 1991, by the National Theatre in 1996, and at the Burgtheater Vienna in 2003 in a translation by Peter Handke. A black American version *Gospel at Colonus* by Lee Breuer was staged in New York in 1983. It was revived on Broadway for a limited run in 1988.

Euripides (Euripides) 485/4–406 BC

EURIPIDES: In *my* plays . . .
  Everyone gets a say: wife, daughter-in-law,
  Slaves, even old Granny in the corner.
    Aristophanes, *Frogs*, tr. Kenneth McLeish

Life

Euripides' father was a landowner called Mnesarchos; his mother was called Cleitho; they lived in the Athenian deme of Phyla. Euripides was born on the island of Salamis, where the family also had property. That is more or less the sum total of our knowledge. The ancient sources are full of gossip of one kind and another – all of it unreliable. Euripides was comparatively unsuccessful in his lifetime. He wrote somewhere in the region of ninety plays (he was given a chorus to stage twenty-two tetralogies) yet he won first prize on only four occasions. His first production, in 455 BC, came third.

Eighteen of his plays have come down to us – more than the surviving works of Aeschylus and Sophocles put together. Eight of them come from a single alphabetically arranged volume in his collected works: *Helen, The Children of Heracles, Electra, The Suppliants (Hiketides), Iphigeneia in Aulis, Iphigeneia Among the Taurians, Ion* and *Cyclops*. The titles of the other surviving works are *Alcestis, Medea, Hippolytus, Hecuba, Andromache, The Trojan Women, The Phoenician Women, Orestes* and *The Bacchae*. Another play, *Rhesus*, is attributed to Euripides but is almost certainly by someone else. Aeschylus died the year before Euripides' first play was performed but Sophocles and Euripides competed against each other for the next half-century.

The great war between Athens and Sparta broke out when Euripides had just turned fifty and the remaining years of his life were shaped by this bitter struggle for mastery between the two leading powers of the Greek world. Euripides' career coincided with the arrival of the sophists in Athens and their impact on the intellectual life of the city. The sophists were important because they brought to the centre of the Greek world the habits of scientific enquiry and unprejudiced questioning that had been developed in the East Greek cities of Ionia. Their most celebrated representative was Protagoras who famously remarked: 'Man is the measure of all things, of things that exist that they are, of things that do not exist that they are not.'

The chronology of Euripides' works is comparatively clear and we can trace the way in which, like Shakespeare, he gradually loosened the pattern of his verse as he grew older to bring it closer to ordinary speech. Euripides' reputation as a realist should not obscure the beauty of much of his poetry – particularly the choral lyrics. Plutarch in his *Life of Nikias* tells the story of how when the miserable survivors of the Athenian expedition to Sicily were starving to death in captivity, anyone who could recite some verses by Euripides was allowed to go free – so highly did the guards value any contact with the playwright's work.

If tragedy explores the relationship

- between man and his own death and other men
- between man and the immortal gods and things that do not change
- between man and the passions that live inside him,

then each of the three great dramatists approached these problems in his own particular way. Euripides' special interest lies in how people relate to their emotions (Medea, Phaedra, Hecuba, Creusa) and how they relate to each other. Towards the end of his life he wrote a series of fascinating studies of political life and the passions that underpin it – *Orestes, The Phoenician Women, Iphigeneia in Aulis, The Bacchae*.

A large number of fragments of the 'lost' plays have come down to us and many of these fragments are quite substantial. Euripides gives a fascinating slant to the well-known stories of Oedipus and Antigone. His Oedipus is the victim of a palace coup, blinded not by his own hand but by Creon's soldiers. In Euripides' *Antigone*, Antigone and Haemon are saved by the intervention of the god Dionysus, get married and live happily ever after. In *Bellerophon* the central character goes up to heaven to confront the gods with their mismanagement of the world and is punished for his presumption. *Antiope* contains a debate on the contrasting merits of the active and the contemplative life that was famous in late antiquity. In *The Cretans* the heroine Pasiphae who gave birth to the Minotaur defends her passion for a bull, the beast's father, saying she could not help herself. In its rhetorical power and its liking for paradox the passage is typical Euripides.

Why should you think I would choose a bull?
It is improbable, it is preposterous!
Why should the thought of him gnaw at my heart like that?
To love a bull – is that something to be proud of?
Do you think he was such a handsome sight in his fine
    clothes, with red hair and shining eyes and a dark beard?
Do you think his body was so graceful, so beautiful, so
    different from your own that I could not resist it?
You think these things would be enough to draw me to him,
to be a Queen who puts off her clothes to wear an animal
    skin,
to stand before him in the field, so utterly confused, consumed, driven only by the need of him?
You think I wanted to bear his children – you think for
    this I would risk being torn apart by him?
I was out of my mind. I was not myself. I was possessed.
    tr. Deborah Gearing

Euripides spent the last years of his life at the court of Archelaos, King of Macedonia. He was part of a group of artists there which included the painter Zeuxis, the tragedian Agathon, and perhaps even the historian Thucydides. His death in a foreign country should not be seen as evidence of estrangement from his native city but more as proof of the popularity of tragedy in the Greek world outside Athens.

When Sophocles learned of his death, he dressed his chorus in mourning as a mark of respect.

Alcestis (*Alkestis*)

∿ The legend

The god Apollo had a son, Asclepius, a healer whose powers were so great that he could bring the dead to life. Zeus, king of the gods, saw this as an infringement of his power and killed Asclepius with a thunderbolt. Apollo was furious and in revenge he killed the Cyclopes, who made Zeus' weapons for him. Zeus punished Apollo by sentencing him to work for a year as a slave to a mortal man.

Apollo was fortunate in his master, Admetus, king of Pherai in Thessaly, who treated him honourably. Apollo resolved to reward him as best he could. Admetus was doomed to die and Apollo arranged that if someone could be found to die for him, Admetus could live on. Admetus' elderly parents and his other relatives all refused to help. Finally his wife Alcestis agreed to sacrifice herself to save her husband's life.

Alcestis (the name means Strong Helper) had already been involved in another resurrection story in her youth. She was one of three daughters of Pelias, king of Iolchos. Medea, who wanted to kill Pelias in the cruellest way possible, showed his daughters a ram, which she cut up and put in a cauldron of boiling water. The ram emerged rejuvenated. Medea persuaded Pelias' daughters to try the same trick on their father. Alcestis alone refused to take part – wisely, for the device proved to be a trick and Pelias died in agony. This story was the subject of Euripides' first play, *The Daughters of Pelias*, written seventeen years previously.

～ The story

Alcestis has agreed to die in her husband's place and this is now her last day on earth. Apollo is leaving Admetus' house to avoid the taint of mortality and meets Death at the threshold, ready to go in. The god tries to persuade Death to let Alcestis go, and when Death refuses, Apollo tells him that a human being will later come and wrest her from his power.

The dying woman is brought into the open air for the last time. She says farewell to her children and makes Admetus swear that he will never marry again, so that there will be no stepmother to make things hard for her son and daughter. Admetus, heartbroken, vows not only that he will not remarry but that he will remain celibate for the rest of his life and have a statue of Alcestis made to share his bed.

The palace is in mourning for the dead queen when Heracles appears on his way to Thrace to capture the horses of Diomedes. Admetus, always a good host, offers him hospitality. He presses Heracles to accept, pretending that the person who died was not his wife but a stranger. Admetus' father, Pheres, brings funeral gifts for Alcestis, which Admetus furiously rejects. There is an ugly scene between father and son in which Admetus disowns his parents, while Pheres points out that his son is a coward for allowing a woman to die in his place.

Heracles, innocent of the true situation, has been drinking and feasting with abandon. When the disgruntled servants point out the true state of affairs, Heracles goes off to wrestle Alcestis from the power of Death. He comes back leading a veiled woman whom he pretends to have won in an athletic contest and persuades Admetus to break the vows he made so recently and take the veiled woman into his house. Admetus lifts the veil and finds his wife. Alcestis says nothing: she may not speak for three days until the stain of death has disappeared.

∾ About the play

> It's not that I'm afraid to die. I just don't want to be there
> when it happens.
> Woody Allen

> I see the black water and the dead
> lake   the boat beached on the sand
> and look
>   Charon
>   there at the rudder
> calling me.
> tr. William Arrowsmith

Everyone knows that death is certain. As Shakespeare says,
'We owe God a death'. *Alcestis* looks at what would happen if
the natural order were interfered with. What would it mean
if human beings could become masters of life and death?
What would the implications be if mortality came under
human control?

Euripides gave the traditional story a particular inflection
of his own. Two earlier tragedians, Phrynichus and Aeschylus,
who had written plays on the subject, seem to have confined
the action to Alcestis' wedding day. Euripides places the
exchange of one life for another in the past, several years
before the play begins. Since then there has been a long and
happy marriage, which has produced two children. The
deadly promise has become part of everyday life; no one
thinks about it any more; so when the debt is suddenly called
in, it comes as a terrible surprise. Alcestis is the only character in Greek tragedy who dies non-violently, yet the playwright makes us feel that her death is an outrage.

A sense of the couple's shared life together is carefully built
up. *Alcestis* has more domestic detail than any other Greek
tragedy except Euripides' *Electra*. Here is Alcestis saying
goodbye to her marriage bed:

> But there in her room
> she threw herself on the great bed, and the sobs
> broke from her. 'Dear bed', she cried,
> 'it was here I offered my maiden body and my love
> to Admetos. Now I offer him my life . . .
> Sweet bed I love you still . . . even now. So much
> that I would rather die than live without you
> both. And now it is good bye.
> Some other girl will sleep here in my place
> perhaps – not more loving, not more loyal than me,
> but happier, much happier, I think.
>   tr. William Arrowsmith

Later in the play, Admetus describes what it is like coming back to the deserted house.

> The empty rooms, the empty bed, the chair she used
> to sit on, and the shining floor all dark with dust,
> and the children sobbing, huddling at my knees,
> wherever I go, crying for their mother . . .
>   tr. William Arrowsmith

Alcestis makes Admetus promise that he will not remarry and put her children at the mercy of a stepmother. Admetus goes well beyond what she asks and renounces all sexual pleasure for the remainder of his life. He goes on to renounce his parents, too. The scene with Pheres has an uncommon brutality of tone.

> Go and be damned to you,
> you and that woman I used to call my mother.
> You have no son.
> Grow old, both of you, as you deserve –
> childless, heirless, alone.
> Never let me see you in this house again.

Pheres rightly points out that life is precious even to the old and that accusations of cowardice are likely to rebound on Admetus' own head.

> You dare to call
> me coward, when you let your woman outdare you,
> and die for her magnificent young man . . .
> You have found a clever scheme by which you will *never*
> die.
> You will always persuade the wife you have at the time
> to die for you instead.
>
> tr. Richmond Lattimore

The paradox is that Alcestis has accepted death to save Admetus' life, but the life she has given him is not worth living, since it is stripped of parents, honour and all erotic pleasure. Admetus is caught in a bind. In order to be properly grateful for his wife's death he must behave as if the life she has given him is worthless. The ungrateful thing would be to go on as normal and forget her.

The play falls into two halves. The first half reduces Admetus to a painful state of death in life; the second brings about a double resurrection – Alcestis brought back from the underworld and Admetus restored to a sense of living connection that once again includes his own imminent death. The agent of this miracle is Heracles, half human, half divine, whom, both here and in the play named after him, where he is called the 'civilizer of the world', Euripides uses as an exemplar of human powers at their most godlike. Part of what makes Heracles a hero is his frank embrace of transience and his appetite for life.

> Enjoy yourself, drink, call the life you have today
> your own, but only that, the rest belongs to chance.
>
> tr. Richmond Lattimore

This unabashed enjoyment of his own vigour leads Heracles not only to overpower death and bring Alcestis back but also to restore Admetus to a sense of what life is for and how it should be lived. That is the significance of the veiled figure. Admetus must accept life on its own terms and accept it trustingly, not knowing where it will lead, before Alcestis can be restored to him. This involves coming to terms with Necessity. The chorus sing:

> Necessity is stone,
> implacable she has no face
> but rock; no human shape or likeness owns,
> no cult, nor shrine. She heeds no sacrifice.
> She is force, and flint; no feeling has, no
> pity. None.
>   tr. William Arrowsmith

Necessity in Euripides takes many forms. In *Alcestis* it is death; in *Hippolytus* and *Heracles* it is the enmity of the gods; in *Hecuba* and *The Trojan Women* it is war. Each of these plays involves characters coming to terms with something that is stronger than they are. In *The Bacchae*, Pentheus, who recognizes no reality outside his delusions, is destroyed utterly.

Heracles is present and able to help because of Admetus' own largeness of spirit. It was Admetus' qualities as a good master that led Apollo to strike a bargain with Death in the first place; his determination to fulfil his obligations as a host by taking Heracles into his house rescues him a second time. The well-meaning intervention of the god leads to disaster and the steady efforts of the mortal actors restore things to their rightful place. 'Man is the measure of all things,' said Euripides' contemporary Protagoras. This belief in the restorative power of human agency is far removed from the mighty vision of Aeschylus, which dramatized the balance between the powers under the earth, the powers in the heavens, the natural world and Zeus the bringer of Justice. With Euripides, the scale of what is being contemplated has shrunk, with the consequence that human beings have grown bigger in proportion.

The story also has a political dimension. Admetus is able to escape his fate because of a special dispensation from Apollo, granted by one *grand seigneur* to another. Death is quick to pick up the implications when Apollo suggests that he let Alcestis go.

DEATH: My privileges mean more to me when they die
   young.
APOLLO: If she dies old, she will have a lavish funeral.
DEATH: What you propose Apollo is to favour the rich.
   tr. Richmond Lattimore

The action of the play shows that privilege brings unhappiness and that equality before the law of death is the best and most humane arrangement.

Alcestis was performed in the spot usually reserved for the satyr play; that is to say, it was presented in fourth place after a sequence of three tragedies. This has led some critics to exaggerate the comic and burlesque elements in the play. Others, faced with explaining the serious treatment of the story, have gone so far as to invent a special genre – 'prosatyric' – of which *Alcestis* is the sole example. By the middle of the fifth century, the impulse that had produced the original satyr plays was beginning to fade. In the same decade as *Alcestis*, for example, a new tragic festival was instituted in the Lenaia, in which satyric drama played no part at all; in the fourth century the genre began to be used for topical plots involving contemporary characters. Euripides' work is part of this trend. It is certainly a mistake to overstress the comic elements in the belief that doing so is true to the play's supposed genre.

Euripides was seventeen years into his career when he wrote *Alcestis* and it is his first surviving play. It is fascinating to see here themes and motifs that were to be taken up again throughout his *œuvre*. In particular, the theme of voluntary sacrifice stands out. Alcestis is the first in a line which embraces the king's daughter in *Erechteus*, sacrificed by her father to save Athens from Thracian invasion; Macaria in *The Children of Heracles*, who dies to save her brothers; Polyxena in *Hecuba*, killed as an offering to Achilles' ghost; Menoeceus in *The Phoenician Women*, who commits suicide offering his life for his city's safety; and Iphigeneia in *Iphigeneia in Aulis*, sacrificed for a wind so that the Greek fleet can sail. It is also characteristic of Euripides that children should play an important part in the play. He often uses them as a way of emphasizng vulnerability and making the situation even more unbearable by showing his heroes as members of a family. Alcestis' son and daughter are the predecessors of Medea's slaughtered children; of the drowned Polydorus in *Hecuba*; of Heracles' three murdered sons; of baby Orestes nestling in his mother's arms in *Iphigenia in Aulis*; and, perhaps most poignantly of all, little Astyanax in the *The Trojan Women*, killed by being hurled headlong from the battlements.

Vulnerability is offset by the figure of Heracles, who possesses the strength to confront things as they are. The healing power of human agency is explored further in the strange trio of plays *Iphigeneia Among the Taurians*, *Ion* and *Helen*, which Euripides wrote twenty-five years later, after the failure of the Sicilian expedition. The play also shows Euripides' interest in realistic detail. *Alcestis* is the only Greek tragedy in which a character is worried about a dusty floor.

∾ Translations

The best modern translation is by William Arrowsmith (Oxford), though he goes overboard dealing with Heracles' drunkenness. There is another useful version by Richmond Lattimore (Chicago) and a slightly less good one by J. Michael Walton (Methuen). Ted Hughes's adaptation (Faber), made while he was dying of cancer, powerfully brings out the struggle between life and death in the play. Those seeking a literal translation should consult the Penguin edition.

∾ In performance

Alcestis was first performed in 438 BC as part of a tetralogy in which the other plays were *The Cretans*, *Alcmeon in Psophis* and *Telephus*. There is an opera by Gluck (1762). The play was staged by Robert Wilson at the American Repertory Theater in 1986 and by Northern Broadsides in 2000.

Medea (*Medeia*)

∾ The legend

Medea was the daughter of Aeetes, king of Colchis, which lay at the far eastern end of the Black Sea. When Jason arrived there on his quest for the Golden Fleece, Medea fell in love with him and helped him. In doing so, she betrayed her father and murdered her brother. Jason swore her an oath that in return for her assistance he would never leave her.

Medea and Jason returned to Greece, to Jason's home town of Iolchos. There Jason had to redeem his inheritance from his uncle Pelias, who had usurped the throne. It was Pelias that had sent Jason to steal the Golden Fleece. The task was thought to be impossible and Pelias hoped that Jason would be killed in the attempt, so that he could keep the kingdom for himself.

Medea used a trick to get rid of Pelias, who was too powerful to overthrow by force. She took his daughters to one side and showed them an old ram, which she cut up and put into a cauldron full of boiling water. The ram emerged rejuvenated as a young lamb. Medea persuaded the girls to try a similar experiment on their elderly father. They duly cut Pelias up and boiled him but the simple result was that he died. Jason and Medea had to flee into exile to escape the bloodguilt and came to live in Corinth.

∾ The story

Jason and Medea and their two children are living in exile in Corinth. Jason plans to establish himself in this new city by marrying the daughter of King Creon and starting a new family.

When the play begins Medea (whose name means Cunning) is planning her revenge. Creon announces that she is to be banished; he is afraid of what she might do. Medea succeeds in persuading him to allow her a day's delay – a day which will prove fatal to Creon and his daughter.

Jason tries to persuade Medea that what he is doing is the best thing under the circumstances both for her and for their children. She scornfully rejects his arguments but is frightened to take action till she knows that she has a safe line of retreat. King Aegeus of Athens is passing through on his way home from the oracle at Delphi where he has been to seek a cure for his childlessness. Medea offers to help him in exchange for the promise of a safe refuge in Athens if she should need it.

Medea's way is now clear. She summons Jason back and pretends to be contrite. She sends her children with wedding gifts for the new bride – a beautiful dress and a gold crown. But the gifts have been smeared with poison and when the princess puts them on they eat into her flesh. Her father, who tries to rescue her, becomes stuck to her and dies in agony.

Medea completes her revenge by killing her two children. When Jason comes to look for her she appears hovering in the air in a chariot sent by her grandfather the Sun, the dead bodies of her sons beside her. She is triumphant, out of reach, while Jason is left childless and alone amid the wreckage of his new life.

JASON: In god's name let me touch the soft skin of my sons.
MEDEA: I will not. Your words are wasted.

∾ About the play

You feel like a woman but talk like a man talks.
    Aeschylus, *Agamemnon*, tr. Tony Harrison

MEDEA: They say our life at home is free
    From danger while they go off to war.
    The fools! I would rather fight three times
    In war, than go through childbirth once.
       tr. John Harrison

> Marriage is to a girl what war is to a boy.
>
> J.-P. Vernant, *Myth and Society in Ancient Greece*

Achilles was prepared to destroy the Greek army because he felt Agamemnon had insulted him; Odysseus massacred his wife's suitors to avenge his honour; Ajax set out to murder the other Greek commanders who had refused him the armour of Achilles, and when his plan failed killed himself. Medea takes her place in the company of these great heroes. She knows that an insult must be avenged if it is to be survived. Her values are the heroic ones of helping friends and harming enemies and she is as fierce in defence of her honour as any warrior. Roman authors – Ovid and Seneca – tried to explain Medea's power by making her a witch. Euripides' character is neither sub-human nor superhuman: she represents a set of human possibilities carried to the utmost limits.

Medea, like Oedipus, stands at the centre of her play; like Electra and Antigone her fixity of purpose drives the action. Euripides never wrote like this again: it's as if his extraordinary creation needed plenty of room and no distractions. The concentration on a single figure gives the narrative a tremendous force and power.

Euripides builds up his portrait with great finesse. Already in the first scene the Nurse is frightened about what her mistress is capable of.

NURSE: I fear she's plotting something
  And she is a woman to fear: if you arouse
  The hatred of Medea, don't expect
  An easy victory, and to go home singing.
    tr. Alistair Elliot

Next we hear Medea howling with grief and rage inside the house. Suddenly the children begin to look vulnerable.

NURSE: Poor children I'm sick with fear for you.
  I know something is going to happen.
    tr. Alistair Elliot

Before we see her, Medea is twice compared to an angry bull, her eyes rolling with uncontrollable fury, but when she comes out to speak to the chorus not a trace of this remains. The wildness is all buried inside – yet the audience knows it's there. A woman who can have such strong emotions and then apparently master them is someone to beware of.

This is clearly brought out in the next scene with Creon, where Medea turns the tables on him. Creon arrives quite clear about what he wants to accomplish.

> CREON: You sour-faced woman, squalling at your husband,
> Medea, I give you notice: you are banished.
> You must leave now. Now! Take your children with you.
> Don't make me wait. I shall not leave
> Until I've seen you off Corinthian land . . .
> I'm afraid of you; no need to wrap
> The fact in phrases. I'm afraid that
> You might do my daughter some irreparable harm.
>> tr. Alistair Elliot

Yet his will is not in the end strong enough to withstand Medea's arguments: at the end of the scene he makes a fatal concession.

> CREON: Remain then, if you must, this one day more:
> Too short a time to do us harm.
>> tr. Alistair Elliot

Creon may be a man but he lacks the true heroic obduracy – and daring. As Medea enters the play's central scene, her argument with Jason, she has the chorus on her side and she has triumphed over the immediate threat.

Medea is not Jason's possession: she is his equal. When she saved his life in Colchis, she did so of her own free choice, independently. The pact they made was between equals and the oath they swore was as binding as an oath taken on the battlefield or a treaty between two heads of state. When Medea married Jason she was not given away by her father; she chose her husband freely. She wasn't part of an exchange between two men and she brought no dowry except her bravery and intelligence.

It is the violation of his oath as much as anything else that Jason does that puts him in the wrong.

NURSE: And now my princess, scorned, invokes the oath
That Jason swore to her, recalls the pledge
Given by his strong right hand
And bids all heaven to witness.
   tr. Jeremy Brooks

Medea is a paradox. As a female she has no power, yet as a person her heroic qualities – her anger, her daring, her resourcefulness, her sense of entitlement – make her her formidable. And she has an advantage not available to other Greek women: she entered on her marriage as an equal so that there are gods she can call on to punish a man who violates his oath – and these gods stand squarely behind her.

Sophocles contrasts his heroic women Antigone and Electra with their more conventional sisters Ismene and Chrysothemis, who argue the case for submissiveness and a womanly acceptance of the status quo. Here Medea does this for herself. The conventional housewife is another of the possibilities she contains.

MEDEA: I have begun to take myself to task:
'Obstinate, silly woman, you must be mad
Why are you so opposed to good advice?'
Why make an enemy of the king
And of my husband who is acting only
In our best interest, marrying a princess
To give my children brothers? Will I never
Curb my temper? What's wrong with me? The gods
Provide so well for everything I need.
   tr. Alistair Elliot

Jason, a prisoner of his own conventional outlook, takes these protestations at face value. But it's all pretence: Medea is at her most dangerous when she seems most compliant. As she says:

I'm a woman: so, although disbarred
By nature from the noble deeds of man
I have mastered all the arts of cowardice.

Medea is alone: there is no one who can deflect her from her purpose, except her own weakness, so when it comes to killing the children she is forced to debate the issue with herself. This led Euripides to invent the modern soliloquy – an invention so startling that some critics have thought the speech must be an interpolation from a later period.

My hand's not going to weaken.
No! No!
No raging heart, don't drive yourself to do this.
Not this. Not the children's lives: let them alone.
They'll live there with us – they will bring us joy.
No by the vengeful spirits that live in Hades,
I shall not leave my children, I cannot leave them
To suffer the violence of my enemies.
    tr. Alistair Elliot

There is a direct line here through Seneca to *Hamlet* and *Macbeth*.

Euripides was obviously fascinated by the Medea story. He made three attempts at it. His very first trilogy contained a play, *The Daughters of Pelias*, which dealt with Medea's killing of Jason's uncle. In *Aegeus* (date uncertain) she appears as a jealous stepmother who tries to get rid of her stepson Theseus. The legend has many variants and it's interesting to see what Euripides includes and what he leaves out. There are alternative versions of the story in which Medea killed her children accidentally while trying to make them immortal, or in which the Corinthians killed them in revenge for the murder of Creon and his daughter. There is even a variant in which Medea was queen of Corinth and the children were killed in a popular uprising. In choosing to make Medea murderer of her own offspring Euripides is creating something new and different and more shocking than anything that had gone before.

Not only does Medea kill her children but she escapes unpunished. Her final ascent in the Sun god's chariot is extraordinary in its implications. There is nothing like it in the rest of Greek tragedy. This position – high up and out of reach – is traditionally reserved for the gods. This is where Apollo appears at the end of *Orestes*, Athena at the end of *Ion*, Artemis at the end of *Hippolytus*. Medea began the play as a hero and she finishes it as a god. The ending is an acknowledgement that Medea stands for something more than the personal – some permanent human force like that represented by Dionysus in *The Bacchae* or by Aphrodite.

EURIPIDES: In my plays the woman spoke . . . and the young girl and the old woman.

  Aristophanes, *Frogs*, tr. Bernard Knox

Medea is exceptional. As a foreigner and a hero she has a licence to express herself but the frustrations she gives voice to are familiar and everyday:

Of all earth's creatures
We women are the most unfortunate.
First we must secure a husband
At an exorbitant price
And then to make a bad deal worse
We set him up as tyrant over our bodies
And only then we discover
Whether we've made a good choice or a bad one.
Divorce is not respectable for a woman;
Nor can she, having wed, repel the man.
Next must the wife learn new ways and new customs,
Lessons not taught at home.
If with good luck we manage to perform
Our tasks with thoroughness and tact
So that our man stays with us without struggling
Against the marriage yoke, then all is well.
If not it were best to die.

  tr. Jeremy Brooks

ᕽ Translations

The Chicago version by Rex Warner is stiff and now best treated as a literal, though its formality sometimes catches the tone better than more unbuttoned modern translations. The Alistair Elliot version (Oberon) is excellent and Jeremy Brooks (Methuen), Frederic Raphael/Kenneth McLeish (Nick Hern Books), and John Harrison (Cambridge) all have their points. The Harrison comes with useful notes. The Penguin (John Davie) is pedestrian.

ᕽ In performance

Medea was first performed in 431 BC in a tetralogy with *Philoctetes*, *Dictys* and the satyr play *Theristae*. It won third prize. The figure of Medea has exercised a powerful fascination on succeeding ages. There are plays by Seneca (see page 358), Corneille, Grillparzer, Anouilh, Maxwell Anderson, Robinson Jeffers, Dario Fo and Franca Rame, Heiner Mueller, Marina Carr and Liz Lochhead among others; operas by Charpentier and Cherubini; a ballet by Martha Graham and an unsettling novel by Christa Wolf. There is a film by Pier Paolo Pasolini and a performance art piece *Deafman Glance* by Robert Wilson. The first performance in the modern world was staged at Westminster School in the 1540s in a Latin translation by George Buchanan. More recent Medeas have included Sybil Thorndike (1919), Eileen Atkins (1982), Diana Rigg (1992), Isabelle Huppert and Fiona Shaw (both 2000). A Japanese version directed by Yukio Ninagawa was seen in Tokyo in 1978 and in London 1987 and on tour world-wide.

Hippolytus (*Hippolytos*)

∿ The legend

Theseus, king of Athens, had two fathers – one human, one divine. His divine father Poseidon gave him the gift of three fatal curses that could be used against his enemies.

Theseus had an illegitimate child called Hippolytus by the conquered Amazon Antiope. Later he married Phaedra, sister of King Deucalion of Crete and daughter of Pasiphae, who had famously been consumed with lust for a bull and given birth to the half-human Minotaur.

Phaedra had two children by Theseus but fell desperately in love with her stepson Hippolytus. He was a devotee of the virgin goddess Artemis and rejected his stepmother's advances. She hung herself in despair but left a note accusing Hippolytus of having raped her. Theseus in anger used one of Poseidon's curses against Hippolytus. As the young man was driving his chariot along the beach a gigantic bull appeared in a tidal wave to stampede his horses. Hippolytus was dragged from his chariot and smashed to death against the rocks. The name Hippolytus means He-Who-Lets-His-Horses-Loose.

∿ The story

The play presents itself as a struggle between two goddesses – Aphrodite, the goddess of love, and Artemis, the goddess of chastity and the hunt.

Aphrodite, angered by Hippolytus' devotion to Artemis and his neglect of her own power, resolves to destroy him. The instrument of her revenge is Phaedra. She infects the queen with a consuming passion for her stepson.

Phaedra struggles to overcome her feelings and is resolved to die rather than say anything. She is slowly starving herself to death. The Nurse, desperate to save her mistress, wheedles the true story out of her and goes to tell Hippolytus, having first made him swear to keep the matter a secret. Hippolytus is outraged by the Nurse's approach and denounces Phaedra with such violence that she becomes convinced that he will tell her husband. In despair Phaedra hangs herself but leaves a note which incriminates Hippolytus.

Theseus, who had been away consulting the oracle, returns. He believes Phaedra's last words and not Hippolytus who, bound by his oath, is unable to defend himself. Hippolytus is struck down by his father's curse and as he lies dying the goddess Artemis appears to give him what comfort she can. She promises to destroy some favourite of Aphrodite's in revenge.

Theseus learns from Artemis the true story of what occurred and father and son are reconciled at last.

∾ About the play

This is in outline a terrifyingly straightforward story. The goddess of sexuality sets out to destroy a young man who is impervious to her power. She cannot touch him directly, so she makes a woman fall desperately in love with him. This woman is so tormented by her feelings that when she is rebuffed, she hangs herself. She leaves a note accusing the young man of having raped her. He is too honourable to tell the truth, is cursed and dies.

Three gods are present in the play: Aphrodite, whose vendetta drives the action; Artemis, who could rescue her worshipper but chooses not to; and Poseidon, who sends the bull from the sea to smash Hippolytus' chariot. Each god wields a power before which human beings are helpless. The gods that destroyed Oedipus were somewhere in the background, inscrutable; here the destructive forces are placed squarely in view and their frightening ability to do harm openly acknowledged.

Aphrodite in the first speech of the play is quite clear about what she wants.

APHRODITE: Alone
  of all men Hippolytos hates me.
  Sex, to his mind, stinks. To him
  the greatest of goddesses is Artemis. Each day
  he bathes his body according to her rituals
  and, purified, romps with her in the forest
  hunting – no, exterminating every living thing.
  Well let him and his darling, if death delights them,
  slice the life out of a thousand deer
  a day. That doesn't bother me. What does
  is his bizarre belief: because he honours
  Artemis he needn't honour Aphrodite
  too! For that I'll break him. Gods,
  like men, demand their crumb of recognition.
     tr. David Lan

Aphrodite's quarrel with Hippolytus is straightforward
enough: in one sense he has brought it on himself by his open
disregard of her powers. What is really frightening is that
Aphrodite casually destroys Phaedra who is quite innocent
because this is the most direct way to advance her plan.

APHRODITE: Phaidra will die too.
  She's innocent but her death I need.
  Compassion's not my hallmark. What is? Satiety.
     tr. David Lan

Aphrodite's vengeance is like great tidal wave that surges
through the play, dashing to pieces the human beings in its
path.

The gods are simple and direct – it is the human beings that
are complicated. *Hippolytus* occupies a special place among
Greek tragedies because it represents the author's second
thoughts. Euripides had written an earlier version of the story
known as *Hippolytus Kalyptomenos* (Hippolytus Who Covered
His Face) – as opposed to the present play, which was known in
antiquity by the title *Hippolytus Stephanepheros* (Hippolytus
Who Offered the Wreath). In the first play Phaedra's character

is comparatively all-of-a-piece. She lusted after Hippolytus, tried openly to seduce him, and when he turned her down, took revenge by complaining to her husband that she had been raped by her stepson. She killed herself only after Hippolytus' death, when her treachery came to light. The Athenians were shocked by the play, which met with an unfavourable reception. Several years later Euripides tried again.

In *Hippolytus II* the playwright's second thoughts have become the second thoughts of the characters as well. Phaedra is a woman divided against herself.

NURSE: Your every word has been to bring you out,
 but when you're here, you hurry in again.
 You find no constant pleasure anywhere
 for when your joy is upon you, suddenly
 you're foiled and cheated.
 There's no content for you in what you have
 for you're forever finding something dearer,
 some other thing – because you have it not.
  tr. David Grene

Phaedra does everything in her power to resist the forces that are attacking her. Although she is in the grip of passion, her dreams are all of purity.

PHAEDRA: O,
 if only I could draw from the dewy spring
 a draught of fresh spring water!
 If only I could lie beneath the poplars
 in the tufted meadow and find my rest there!
  tr. David Grene

She would sooner die than surrender.

CHORUS: She's wasting away. Nothing left of her –
NURSE: She refuses to eat. Three days now.
CHORUS: God's snatched her wits? She wants to die?
NURSE: To starve herself, yes. Make an end of it.
  tr. Frederic Raphael and Kenneth McLeish

Her determination to exercise a moral choice and not to give in to her impulses contrasts favourably with the behaviour of the gods, whose conduct is both selfish and lethal.

This sense of a consciousness divided against itself is something that Euripides is particularly interested in. He is fascinated by the struggle between reason and unreason, which becomes one of the great themes in his work.

PHAEDRA: We know
   always what we should do, we just won't do it.
   Either we're too afraid or we're tempted
   by other pleasures than that of being virtuous.
     tr. David Lan

Already in *Medea* he had invented a soliloquy for his heroine in which she is in two minds as to whether or not to kill her children. His last play *Iphigeneia in Aulis* is entirely given over to various attempts to go back on a decision that has already been made.

The scene in which the Nurse manages to wheedle out of her mistress the secret of her passion strikes a new note in Greek tragedy.

NURSE: Theseus! How can His Majesty hurt you?
PHAIDRA: He can't. He doesn't. And I won't hurt him.
NURSE: You're terrified. You want to die. What is it?
PHAIDRA: Let me do it. I won't hurt *you*.
NURSE: Tell me. I insist. I can help you.
PHAIDRA: If I tell you, you'll share the pain.
NURSE: More pain than if I lose you?
PHAIDRA: You'll die of it. My honour too.
[. . .]
PHAIDRA: Why must I say it? Why can't you guess?
NURSE: What am I, a prophet? Must I read your mind?
PHAIDRA: When people talk of love, what do they mean?
NURSE: The best thing, child, and the worst thing.
PHAIDRA: Worst thing! I know that worst.
NURSE: Ah. You're in love. Sweetheart, who's the man?

PHAIDRA: What's his name . . . *her* son . . . the Amazon's son.
NURSE: Hippolytos!
PHAIDRA: *You* said. *I* never said.

> tr. Frederic Raphael and Kenneth McLeish

Nothing like this had been written before – except perhaps for the brief exchange in Aeschylus' *Agamemnon* when Clytemnestra tries to persuade her husband to walk on the red carpet. The psychological subtlety and suspense of the writing here look forward to Euripides' supreme achievements in this line – the great bravura dialogue scenes in *Electra*, *Ion*, *Iphigeneia Among the Taurians*, *Orestes* and *The Bacchae*.

Nowadays with the shortage of parts for older women Phaedra is usually played by an actress in her forties. It's doubtful whether Euripides intended this. Phaedra is Theseus' second wife, a young woman of childbearing age, so it's likely that she and Hippolytus are contemporaries – he might even be a little bit older than her. At all events they are well matched. Hippolytus is a seeker after that elusive Greek quality *sophrosune*, which is sometimes translated as moderation or prudence, but which might also be rendered as self-control. It is one of the paradoxes of the play that Phaedra struggles so hard to achieve this self-control that Hippolytus represents *par excellence*. The more she loves this quality in him the less she is able to achieve it in herself.

Hippolytus too is not without complexity. He might at first sight appear rather priggish and aloof but like his stepmother he would rather die than go back on a promise that he has made. The Nurse swears him to secrecy before revealing the truth about her mistress's passion. Hippolytus's first reaction is full of horror.

HIPPOLYTOS: You should be hung for what you've told me!
NURSE: Sh! You'll be overheard.
HIPPOLYTOS: Overheard?
   I'll shout it in the streets.
NURSE: One word will ruin me.
HIPPOLYTOS: Oh it will? Why?

What she feels is 'ordinary'. Didn't you say that?

NURSE: What I said was for your ears, not the whole city's.

HIPPOLYTOS: 'A natural affection'. So why can't I talk about it?

NURSE: Because you swore not to! Will you break your word?

HIPPOLYTOS: My tongue swore, not my heart.

tr. David Lan

But in the last resort Hippolytus keeps his oath and is con-demned to death by his own silence. When his father accuses him of rape he refuses to say the one thing that would excul-pate him.

HIPPOLYTOS: Is that what I am? Is that what you think I am?

THESEUS: You should have thought of it before,

When you risked all you had to have your father's wife.

HIPPOLYTOS: If these walls could speak,

They'd speak for me –

THESEUS: Dumb witnesses: the best you'll find.

What you did is voiceless, and it shrieks your guilt.

tr. Frederic Raphael and Kenneth McLeish

It is Theseus, who, unlike his wife and son, makes no attempt to check his impulses, that brings about the final catastrophe.

The play is criss-crossed by skeins of images. The most important of these is water, or perhaps first and foremost, the sea – from which Aphrodite is born and out of which the deadly bull comes surging at the end. But it's not just Hippolytus that is overwhelmed. The Nurse says to Phaedra:

You've fallen into the great sea of love

and with your puny swimming would escape.

tr. David Grene

And Theseus confronted with his wife's suicide exclaims:

I am like a swimmer that falls into a giant sea:
I cannot cross this towering wave I see before me.
   tr. David Grene

The unbridgeable gap between the human and divine is touchingly portrayed in the final scene.

ARTEMIS: What you feel, I feel. Poor boy, brave heart, born to suffer.

HIPPOLYTOS: Her scent. The divine perfume. She's here. Oh, everything is easier. Artemis!

ARTEMIS: I'm here.

HIPPOLYTOS: Look, look what they've done to me.

ARTEMIS: I've seen. I pity you. I do.

HIPPOLYTOS: Where is your huntsman? He's gone. You've lost him.

ARTEMIS: How I'll miss you.

[. . .]

THESEUS: I was mad. Aphrodite made me mad.

HIPPOLYTOS: Curse her! Curse Aphrodite! See what damage you can do her.

ARTEMIS: Revenge you leave to me. She broke you because you loved me only. Someone she loves I'll kill.
  Take him hold him. Now you can't hurt him.

THESEUS: I didn't mean to.

ARTEMIS: Hippolytos, a last command. You must not hate your father. This crime must end. Forgive him.

HIPPOLYTOS: I always obey you.

ARTEMIS: I'll go. I may not see corpses. That's what you almost are. Farewell.
   tr. David Lan

As in *Ion*, *Heracles* and *The Trojan Women* the gods withdraw, leaving the devastated human beings to pick up the pieces as best they can. The closing of this tragedy is the opening of another tragedy, somewhere else.

∾ Translations

The best translation is by David Lan (Almeida Theatre Company). It catches the play's savagery and ballad-like quality, though it is occasionally altered to fit the needs of a particular production. Frederic Raphael and Kenneth McLeish (Methuen) and David Grene (Chicago) are also serviceable. There is an eccentric, clotted version by David Rudkin (Heinemann). The Oxford translation by Robert Bagg is disappointing.

∾ In performance

The play was first performed in 428 BC. Euripides won first prize. Seneca took up the story in *Phaedra* (c.AD 50), as did Jean Racine with *Phèdre* (1677) and Sarah Kane in *Phaedra's Love* (1996). Benjamin Britten wrote a dramatic cantata *Phaedra* in 1975. There is also a film by Jules Dassin (1962). The play was staged in 1904 by Harley Granville Barker. Recent productions include the RSC (1978) and the Almeida Theatre (1991).

Hecuba (*Hekabe*)

∾ The legend

The play brings together two separate stories. The first was handed down as part of the cycle of epic poems called *Nostoi* or *The Returns* which describes what became of the Greek expedition after the fall of Troy. It tells how the fleet was becalmed in Thrace on the journey home and how the ghost of Achilles appeared to demand a human sacrifice before the ships could sail.

The second story, for which Euripides is the only source, goes as follows. Priam and Hecuba, king and queen of Troy, were afraid of what might happen to their family if the city fell.

They sent their youngest son, still a little boy, to safekeeping abroad at the court of King Polymestor of Thrace. With him they sent a sum of gold which was to prove his undoing. When Troy was captured, Polymestor killed the child, kept the money for himself and threw the body into the sea.

∽ The story

After the sack of Troy, Queen Hecuba and her daughters Cassandra and Polyxena are enslaved by the conquering Greeks, along with the rest of Troy's female population. The Greek fleet has crossed the Bosphorus, taking the captives to the coast of Thrace, where they are waiting for a favourable wind before they can set sail. The ghost of Achilles appears, demanding that Polyxena be sacrificed in his honour. Hecuba pleads with Odysseus to spare the girl's life but to no avail. Unless Polyxena dies, the fleet cannot sail. Polyxena disdains to beg for her life and goes bravely to her death.

Hecuba is waiting to prepare the body for burial but the corpse that is brought in is that of her youngest son, Polydorus, who has been murdered by the Thracian king. Hecuba intuits what has happened and begs Agamemnon for justice. Agamemnon promises to do no more than stand aside while Hecuba takes her revenge, which she does in a strikingly gruesome fashion. She lures Polymestor and his two sons into her tent where a mass of women swarm all over him, kill his children and put out his eyes with their brooches. The blind Polymestor reveals the manner of Hecuba's death: she will be transformed into a bitch and drown at sea. The place where she dies will thereafter be known as The Bitch's Grave.

∽ About the play

Might is that which makes a thing out of anybody who comes under its sway. When exercised to the full, it makes a thing of man in the most literal sense, for it makes him a corpse. There where someone stood a minute ago, stands no one.

Simone Weil, *Intimations of Christianity*

Revenge is a kind of wild justice.

Francis Bacon, *Essays*

Hecuba is one of Euripides' grimmest and most unsparing works, and rises to a climax of horrifying violence in which both victim and perpetrator are reduced to the level of animals.

The Peloponnesian War, which was to the Greek world what the two world wars were to the twentieth century, had broken out some six years before *Hecuba* was written. The play comes comparatively early in the conflict (some of the later plays are bleaker still), but this short period had already provided instances of massacre and depopulation. Here is Thucydides' account of the fall of Plataea in 427 BC:

> They [the Spartans] brought the Plataeans before them one by one and asked each of them the same question. 'Have you done anything to help the Spartans or their allies in this war?' As each man answered 'No' he was taken away and put to death; no exceptions being made. Not less than 200 of the Plataeans were killed in this way, together with twenty-five Athenians who had been with them in the siege. The women were made slaves. As for the city . . . they razed it to the ground. This was the end of Plataea in the ninety-third year after she became an ally of Athens.
>
> It was largely, or entirely, because of Thebes that the Spartans acted so mercilessly towards the Plataeans; they considered at this stage in the war the Thebans were useful to them.
>
> tr. Rex Warner

The understanding of motive here and the insight that cruelty can be calculated for political advantage are something that the historian shares with the playwright. The twenty-seven-year span of the war overlaps almost completely with Euripides' surviving output and his work is shaped by it far more than that of his older contemporary Sophocles. *Hecuba*, *The Trojan Women*, *Andromache*, *The Suppliants*, *The Children of Heracles* and *Iphigeneia in Aulis* are all concerned in one way or another with the victims of war; and Euripides' interest in political process and how events emerge from a maelstrom of competing demands, which shows in plays like *Electra*, *Orestes* and *The Phoenician Women*, was undoubtedly provoked by the turbulence that the fighting produced on the home front. The particular tone that we think of as being Euripidean is also in large part a *wartime* tone.

Like Aeschylus' *Persians*, *Hecuba* is a portrait of a defeated foreign community. Unlike the Aeschylus it is written not in the aftermath of victory but in the middle of a savage struggle for survival and it shows a renewed feeling for people who are exposed, defenceless, at the mercy of the powerful. The play begins with two ghosts, who make their demands on the living. One ghost, Achilles, is powerful and unseen: he demands human sacrifice as a token of honour and respect. The ghost we do see is the helpless one, the submerged child Polydorus. The play's opening is a parade of the defenceless. First the drowned boy, then the elderly mother, accompanied – doubled – by her equally frail handmaiden, then the chorus of newly enslaved women and lastly the sacrificial victim herself, another vulnerable innocent.

Euripides is good at depicting the humiliations of the defenceless; he also provides an enduring portrait of the insolence of power – though perhaps carelessness would be a better word. The powerful are only required to consult their own interests and have no need to take anyone else into account. Odysseus arrives bringing the army's decision that Polyxena is to be killed but he is under an obligation to Hecuba for having saved his life.

HECUBA: Do you remember how

You came to Troy, a spy, dressed as a beggar,
Smeared with filth, in rags and tears of blood
Were streaming down your beard?
ODYSSEUS: I remember. It's written in my heart.
HECUBA: And Helen recognised you and told
me who you were. Told me alone.
ODYSSEUS: I remember I was in deadly danger.
HECUBA: And how humble you were. How you
fell at my knees and begged.
ODYSSEUS: And my hand almost froze on your dress.
HECUBA: And you were at my mercy, *my* slave then.
Do you remember what you said?
ODYSSEUS: Anything I could. Anything to stay alive.
HECUBA: And I let you have your life. I sent you home.
ODYSSEUS: Because of what you did, I am alive today.

> tr. Janet Lembke and Kenneth J. Reckford

It's a strong claim and undeniable. It's instructive to watch
how Euripides lets Odysseus wriggle out of it.

ODYSSEUS: Everything I am today I owe to you
and in return stand ready and willing
to honour my debt and save your life. Indeed
I have never suggested otherwise.
But note
I said *your* life not your daughter's life
a very different matter altogether.

> tr. William Arrowsmith

This brings to mind Brecht's remark about injustice: 'the
degradation of those who feel it, the degradation of those
who cause it'.

The Trojans are all women and powerless. The powerful
are all men: Euripides provides us with a little gallery of
contrasting types – unyielding (Odysseus), sympathetic
(Talthybius), judicious (Agamemnon) and treacherous and
greedy (Polymestor). It is left to Polyxena to step outside the
world of power. She refuses to beg for her life:

I shall go with you because I must
And because I want to die. If I did not
I should appear a weakling and a coward.
What have I to live for?
   tr. Peter D. Arnott

She has a sense of royal pride. She would rather die than be a slave. In this she is different from Menoeceus (*The Phoenician Women*) and Iphigeneia, who offer their lives for the general good. It needs to be remembered that until a few days before the action of the play begins, Hecuba and Polyxena were Odysseus' equals: now they are possessions. The suddenness of the change has left them raw. It's also worth remembering that in the *Odyssey*, Book XI, when the ghost of Achilles is begging to return to life even if it means the poorest life imaginable, the example he chooses is not that of a slave but that of a 'landless labourer, toiling beside another landless man'. A labourer may have been free but he was at everyone's mercy: a slave at least had a protector of a kind.

The first half of the play contains enough grief and suffering for a whole tragedy but the discovery of the corpse of Polydorus propels the story to a new plane of agony. The Greeks would have had no comprehension of our sentimental post-Christian view that suffering ennobles. They knew that it did not. They understood that the point of degradation was that it degrades people and that those who are cornered and robbed of hope are capable of behaving very badly indeed. Euripides' defenceless characters, such as Medea and Orestes, always have a dangerous quality: the more vulnerable they become, the more explosive the violence when they strike back.

The anonymous muffled corpse is the pivotal image. Hecuba doesn't know at first who it is. Is it Polyxena or perhaps Cassandra? The last thing she can imagine is that it is her youngest child, Polydorus. She only knows that it belongs to her. And once she has made her terrible discovery, the inescapable fact is that her only means of redress is through

Agamemnon – until a few days ago her mortal enemy. She depends on him absolutely, but the combination of her need and her hatred makes it impossible for her to look him in the face. The weight of what is at stake leads Euripides to an unusual formal invention; no other scene in Greek tragedy has so many asides – a device common enough in comedy but unusual in the context of serious drama.

'Euripides maligns us whenever there are theatres, tragedies, choral songs . . . so that as soon as our husbands come back from the auditorium they look at us suspiciously.' This is the chorus of women in Aristophanes' play *Thesmosphoriazusae*: the kind of thing they had in mind was a passage like the following.

HECUBA: As for the rest, don't worry. I'll take care of that.
AGAMEMNON: You? How? Will you take a sword in your old hand
　　and kill the barbarian yourself, or poison him?
　　Who'll help you? Where do you have friends?
HECUBA: There are a lot of Trojan women in that tent.
AGAMEMNON: You mean the slaves, the spear-spoil of the Greeks?
HECUBA: They'll help me to avenge my slaughtered son.
AGAMEMNON: How can you women overpower a man?
HECUBA: Enough of them would scare you soon enough
　　and with cunning they're a force hard to resist.
　　　tr. Tony Harrison

Hecuba's asides have given her scene with Agamemnon a grim sardonic quality but with the entry of Polymestor the writing acquires a new suppleness and shimmer. The intimate colloquial tone has its own sense of dancing horror.

HECUBA: I smuggled some jewels away from Troy.
　　Could you keep them for me?
POLYMESTOR:　　　　　　You have them with you?
　　Where are they hidden?
HECUBA:　　　　　　　　There, inside the tent . . .
　　　tr. William Arrowsmith

Once again, Hecuba refuses to look at the man she is talking to – not, as with Agamemnon, out of pride, but in case Polymestor might be able to read in her eyes her knowledge of his crime and her deadly intentions. The murder itself is one of the grimmest in Greek tragedy (matched only by the massacre of the children in *Heracles*): the sound of the trapped and blinded Polymestor battering on the walls of the tent as he tries to get out is a peculiarly horrifying detail. The chorus have just before reminded us in images of drowning about the fate of the submerged child: Polymestor could be said to be another one who has 'gone under' as he plays a grim game of blind man's buff, running on all fours around the stage with the blood streaming from his eyes, snatching at his tormentors.

In *The Trojan Women*, Hecuba finds that, when everything else has been stripped away, language itself can provide a kind of shelter: her suffering and the fall of Troy would be remembered and talked about in times to come. In this play, language has a more utilitarian purpose and even that frail weapon breaks in her hand.

> Why do we study other sciences,
> We mortals, and pursue them with such pains
> Instead of spending labour mastering
> Persuasion, which alone is lord of men?
> And hiring teachers in that art, so man
> Might set his wish to words and move his hearers?
> For there's our only hope of victory.
>   tr. Peter D. Arnott

Where words lack power, only violence speaks.

The end of the play is unrelenting in its savagery. Hecuba and Polymestor snarl at each other:

POLYMESTOR: But the pain I'm in. My children! And my eyes!

HECUBA: You feel pain as I do for my son.

POLYMESTOR: You love insulting me, you cruel bitch!

HECUBA: Why shouldn't I enjoy my sweet revenge?
    tr. Tony Harrison

Polymestor prophesies Hecuba's death. Then, still unsatisfied, he goes on to include the bystanders, foretelling the
death of Agamemnon and Cassandra too, till the Greek
general orders him to be silenced.

POLYMESTOR: Can't you bear to hear?
AGAMEMNON: Stop his drivelling mouth.
POLYMESTOR: Gag me. All's said anyway.
    tr. Tony Harrison

∾ Translations

William Arrowsmith (Chicago) and Janet Lembke and
Kenneth J. Reckford (Oxford) provide the best introduction
to the play. There are racy performing versions from Frank
McGuinness (Faber), Kenneth McLeish (Absolute Classics)
and Timberlake Wertenbaker (The Dramatic Publishing
Company) – the last is technically speaking an adaptation.
Peter D. Arnott's translation (Methuen) is fine as far as it goes
but the blank-verse form gives it a slightly pedestrian feel.
Tony Harrison's fine new translation (Faber) is set to appear
in 2005.

∾ In performance

There is no firm date for the original performance, but the
play can be dated on internal evidence to around 423 BC.
Some parts of the story are incorporated into Seneca's version
of *The Trojan Women*, written around the middle of the first
century AD. Recent productions include the Mermaid
Theatre (1966), Théâtre de Gennevilliers (1988), the Gate
Theatre London (1992), ACT San Francisco 1997, the
Donmar Warehouse (2004) and the RSC (2005).

Heracles (*Herakles*)

❧ The legend

Zeus, king of the gods, slept with Alcmene, a mortal woman, wife of Amphitryon. She bore him a son Heracles, who was half human and half divine. Hera, Zeus' wife, was furiously jealous and persecuted the child almost from the day it was born. She sent a serpent to kill it in its cradle but Heracles, who had superhuman strength, strangled the snake and survived.

Heracles grew to manhood and married Megara, daughter of the king of Thebes. Amphitryon, his mortal father, was forced into exile from Argos because he had killed his cousin in an accident. Heracles set out to recover his father's birthright by carrying out twelve labours for the new king, Eurystheus. The last of these labours involved going to the underworld to capture the three-headed dog Cerberus.

Heracles was absent for a long time in the land of the dead and people were afraid he would never return. In the meantime a usurper, Lycos, had come to power in Thebes where Heracles' family were awaiting his return. Lycos had killed Megara's father Creon and planned to follow this up by murdering Megara and with her Heracles' children in case they should grow up and take revenge on him.

❧ The story

The usurper Lycos is threatening to murder Heracles' father Amphitryon, his wife Megara and his two children. They have taken refuge at the altar of Zeus the Rescuer but cannot hold out indefinitely without food or water. Megara prepares her children to face their death but at the very last minute Heracles appears, returning against all expectation from the land of the dead. Amphitryon lures Lycos into the palace where Heracles kills him. It seems that the family has been saved and all is well. But at this moment of triumph, two gods appear: Iris, Hera's messenger, and Madness, sent by Hera to drive Heracles out of his mind.

Madness does her duty under protest. The deranged Heracles murders his wife and children and is only prevented by Athena's intervention from murdering his father too. When he comes to his senses he finds himself surrounded by the dead bodies of his family. Theseus arrives with an army from Athens. He has come too late to save Megara and the children but just as Heracles has rescued him from the under-world, now it is his task to rescue Heracles and to rekindle his desire to live.

∾ About the play

Heracles is one of Euripides' most shocking and unrelenting plays; only *Hecuba* has a more shattering effect. Reading it one can understand how the playwright was thought by Aristotle to be 'the most tragic' of the three great dramatists. But where *Hecuba* ends with two of its principal characters reduced to the level of animals, *Heracles* concludes with an affirmation of human solidarity and mutual help.

Amphitryon in his first speech refers to Heracles as 'clear-ing the land of monsters' or in another translation 'civilizing the earth'. The extent of Heracles' power is made clear by the catalogue of his labours. His achievements encompass the whole known world from North Africa to the Black Sea and from Thessaly to the Peloponnese. He defends the farmers by killing the Centaurs who were ravaging their fields; he protects travellers by disposing of Cycnus who murdered pilgrims on their way to Delphi; he helps mariners by killing the sea-monster Triton; he works cooperatively with others when he leads a pan-Hellenic expedition to sub-due the Amazons; and he is capable by himself of holding up the sky, making the stability of the world depend on a single man.

Euripides has altered the traditional story here. In most versions Heracles undertakes his labours as a penance for the murder for his children, so that the killing is where it all begins. As Euripides tells it, the work is done, not out of necessity, but as an act of family piety, to regain the kingship of Argos for his father. This means that Hera strikes down Heracles at the high point of his life, with his civilizing mission now complete. There is something in all this that recalls Sophocles' great celebration of human achievement in *Antigone*:

> The world is rich with wonders
> Yet none more baffling than man.
> Driven by the stormy South he crosses the ocean white
> with rage . . .
> His cunning controls the animals
> That nest in the wilderness
> Or roam across the hills.
> He has tamed the rich-maned horse
> Putting a yoke on its neck
> The wild mountain-bull he has conquered.
>   tr. C. A. Trypanis

Heracles resembles that other Sophoclean hero Oedipus. Both have cleared the land of monsters; both are struck down at the height of their power; with both it is their particular strength that brings about their downfall – with Oedipus it is his restless intelligence, with Heracles it's his physical prowess, and skill with the bow. For both of them the reason for their fate remains inscrutable. Both plays pose the question of man's relationship to the gods: what is the dividing line between divine and human? Can the behaviour of the gods be interpreted and judged by human standards? The Sophoclean sense of the precariousness of life, that those who are lost are found, and those who are found are lost, which runs through *Oedipus Tyrannus* and *Electra*, is also strongly present here.

What is different from Sophocles is the emphasis on solidarity. In Euripides' vision, if human beings work together they can repair some of the damage caused by the gods. In

Euripides' retelling of the Oedipus story, whatever curse the gods have laid on her son/husband, Jocasta stands by him to the last. The power of human agency to change things for the better is one of *Heracles'* central topics.

As the play opens Euripides shows us – not for the first time – the predicament of people who have crossed the line that separates the powerful from the powerless. Amphitryon was once a great warrior and famous general; Megara, a king's daughter and wife of a great hero. Now they are homeless, starving, huddled at the altar in just the clothes they stand up in. The chorus at their entry intensify the atmosphere of vulnerability; they too have fallen from power to powerlessness, from youth to age.

Confronted with adversity Amphitryon and Megara each adopt a different attitude. Amphitryon wants to hold on for as long as possible: he believes that in the end justice will prevail. Megara prefers to die rather than put things off. She believes that death bravely faced is what Heracles would wish for his family.

MEGARA: Must we live on, like this?
Is that what you want?
AMPHITRYON: I want to live.
While there's life there's hope.
MEGARA: In sensible plans
Not in impossible dreams there's hope.
[. . .]
AMPHITRYON: Bad luck can't last forever. Storm winds of fate
Will blow themselves out one day.
Everything changes: one day we're down
The next we're up. To despair is spineless.
Hope, always hope. Be brave.
tr. Kenneth McLeish

Another way in which *Heracles* is like the work of Sophocles is that it shares a preoccupation with suicide. It asks which choice is better when confronted with a situation seemingly beyond hope – endurance or death embraced with noble courage? This is the dilemna Megara and Amphitryon face at the beginning of the play. This is the choice confronting Heracles after the murder of his family. The presence of Heracles' three children adds to the pathos:

MEGARA: First one then the other bursts in tears
 and asks: 'Mother where has Father gone?
 What is he doing? When will he come back?'
 Then, too small to understand, they ask again
 for 'Father'. I put them off with stories;
 but when the hinges creak, they all leap up
 and run to throw themselves at father's feet.
  tr. William Arrowsmith

Euripides with his special feeling for the exposed and defenceless is particularly good with children; they feature in many of his plays – *Alcestis, Andromache, The Trojan Women, Iphigeneia in Aulis*. In this play we feel their loss the more because they are so vividly created.

HERACLES: They will not let me go but clutch my clothes
 more tightly. How close you came to death!
 Here I'll take your hands and lead you in my wake,
 like a ship that tows its little boats behind,
 for I accept this care and service
 of my sons. Here all mankind is equal:
 rich and poor alike, they love their children.
 With wealth distinctions come: some possess it,
 some do not. All mankind loves their children.
  tr. William Arrowsmith

The children have another function too. The way that human beings cherish their offspring is contrasted with Zeus' failure to protect his son.

The accumulating tension of the first third of the play releases itself in an outburst of joy when Heracles finally appears and Lycos is lured to his death. Earlier Amphitryon had been outspoken in his criticism of Zeus.

AMPHITRYON: For nothing then O Zeus you shared my wife!
  In vain we called you partner in my son!
  Your love is even less than you pretended;
  and I a mere man, am nobler than you, great god.
  I did not betray the sons of Heracles.
      tr. William Arrowsmith

Heracles' return against all the odds seems to show that Zeus has been watching over his son after all. The chorus's song of triumph includes an assumption that the world is just.

CHORUS: The gods of heaven do prevail;
  they raise the good and scourge the bad.
      tr. William Arrowsmith

But their rejoicing is broken into by the sudden appearance of Madness and Iris on the palace roof.

CHORUS: This cruel vengeance will show
  Whether the gods approve of justice.
  Ah, ah,
  What is this appearing over the house?
      tr. William Arrowsmith

The line change 'justice/Ah, ah' is the pivot of the play, where the miracle of deliverance is transformed into a violent nightmare. Generally the gods appear at the beginning or the end of the dramatic action: their intervention here around the halfway point is doubly startling. Athena appears to Odysseus in the middle of the satyr play *Rhesus* but other than that this is the only example in the corpus of Greek tragedy.

It is clear that the violence of Hera's anger against Heracles is unprovoked by anything he has done. Her vindictiveness has followed him since birth: once his labours are completed he is now fair game. Previously Zeus and Necessity protected him: now he is delivered over to Chance and Hera. Just as Hippolytus is literally torn apart by the rivalry between Aphrodite and Artemis, the quarrel between Hera and her husband tears Heracles' life apart. The fact that he is an innocent victim is underlined by Madness herself, who is appalled at what she has to do and undertakes to do it only under duress.

The murder scene itself is one of Euripides' rhythmic tours de force. As Madness fixes on her prey, the beat of the verse accelerates and the tone becomes wilder and more violent. The chorus cap this with a welter of impressionistic images which are punctuated by the cries of Amphitryon from inside the house. The climax is a messenger speech of unusual gruesomeness. Under the influence of Madness, Heracles commits the crime that he killed Lycos to prevent – the murder of his family. Suddenly the hero and the tyrant, the saviour and the executioner, the great and the low-born are on a level. All Heracles' superhuman qualities, his power and his confidence, are seen to count for nothing. The remainder of the play shows how he comes to terms with his common humanity and is one of the most affecting scenes in Greek drama.

When he returns to his senses, Heracles immediately wants to kill himself. Like Megara earlier in the play his first choice is for a noble death. But Megara is dead and Amphitryon, who stood for endurance, has survived, thanks to the intervention of Athena.

Once again Amphitryon speaks up for life and he is seconded in this by Theseus, whom Heracles had rescued from the underworld. The Athenian king now rescues his rescuer in return.

Heracles has to be persuaded that true heroism does not lie in the code of toughness and self-reliance which has shaped his life so far, but in something else entirely. Theseus suggests that suicide would be 'ordinary'; the noble thing to do is to go on living. In making this choice for life Heracles accepts the legacy of Amphitryon his mortal father and renounces the part of him that comes from Zeus. From now on he will be fully human, and that means accepting help and allowing himself to be cared for by his friends. This is what marks men off from gods. The human solidarity and kindness shown by

Theseus and Amphitryon are in stark contrast to the savagery of Hera and Zeus' failure to protect his son.

HERACLES: One thing you say, I accept.
I'll not kill myself, slink out of life,
'He faced every danger,
But he couldn't face himself' –
They won't say that. I'll endure to live.
For your city, for your kindness,
I'm grateful. I'll go with you.
Oh Theseus! I gorged on suffering!
Pain, torment, I faced them all dry-eyed,
And now tears. Is this what weeping is?
I'm floundering. Fate does what it likes with us,
And we must bear it; we're slaves, we're slaves.
    tr. Kenneth McLeish

Athens of course is Theseus' city and it is fitting that Athens should become the home of this reconfigured heroism, made up of endurance, empathy and mutual help.

⟜ Translations

There are fine translations by Kenneth McLeish (Methuen) and William Arrowsmith (Chicago). There is an interesting and moving modern adaptation *Mister Heracles* by Simon Armitage (Faber).

⟜ In performance

There is no firm date for the first performance. The play can be dated on internal evidence to around 421–416 BC. There are plays by Seneca, *Hercules Furens* (*c.*AD 50) and Heiner Mueller (1966) and a short film by Werner Herzog (1962). The play was staged at the Gate Theatre in 1998 and as *Mister Heracles* at the West Yorkshire Playhouse in 2001.

Electra (Elektra)

∾ The legend

While Agamemnon was away at Troy commanding the Greek army, his wife Clytemnestra took a lover. She hated her husband because he had sacrificed their eldest daughter Iphigeneia to Artemis to secure a fair wind for the expedition. When Agamemnon returned from the war, Clytemnestra murdered him in his bath. Their son Orestes was saved by his tutor and smuggled into exile; their daughter Electra remained in the palace, disinherited. When Orestes grew to manhood he returned home. With the help of his sister, and in obedience to the command of the god Apollo, he avenged his father by killing his mother and her lover Aegisthus.

∾ The story

Orestes and his friend Pylades arrive at the remote mountain farm where Electra is living. Her mother, afraid that her daughter might marry a nobleman and bear a child who would avenge Agamemnon's murder, has married her off to a peasant farmer. Electra's husband welcomes the strangers into his cottage but there is not much food in the house and supplies have to be brought in by a neighbour who turns out to be Orestes' old tutor. He recognizes Orestes when Electra did not.

Brother and sister plot their revenge. Aegisthus is leaving the city to sacrifice at a country shrine. Orestes strikes him down at the altar. Electra sends word to her mother that she had just given birth. Clytemnestra hurries to be present at the lying-in. She is lured into the cottage where she is killed. Castor and Polydeuces arrive *ex machina* to tie up the plot. Orestes is to go to Athens to seek absolution for his crime: brother and sister will never see each other again. Electra (still a virgin) is to marry Pylades and her peasant husband is to be rewarded for his tact.

CASTOR: We watched you kill
  Our sister, your mother. She deserved to die.
  But the guilt is yours. Apollo spoke –
  Our Lord, we don't blame Apollo –
  But what he said was wrong.
  It's happened. It can't be changed. Now hear
  What Zeus and the Fates ordain for you.
    tr. Kenneth McLeish

∽ About the play

Electra opens with a series of shocks. The first shock is the setting – a remote mountain farm. *The Libation Bearers*, Aeschylus' version of the story, begins at Agamemnon's tomb. Sophocles' version is set in front of the seat of power, the royal palace where Clytemnestra murdered her husband and now lives with Aegisthus. Euripides places the action at the margins of the kingdom – and at the margins of the heroic world, whose grand exploits reach this rural backwater only in the form of a distant echo. Everything is on a different scale here, more ordinary and down to earth, which suits the playwright's particular take on the story. Assassinate your mother – what would that really be like?

The first character to appear looks like a menial. He is a peasant farmer, from a good family fallen on hard times. The shock here is that he turns out not to be a menial at all, like the Nurse in *Medea* or the Watchman in *Agamemnon*, but Electra's husband. This encompasses a secondary shock – the notion of Electra as a sexual being, who poses a threat to the ruling dynasty as soon as she becomes of marriageable age. Sophocles' *Electra* is about endurance, and the playwright made the character older as a way of underlining this. It is important for Euripides that his Electra is young.

The final shock in this opening sequence is the appearance of a girl with her hair cropped short like a slave, carrying a pitcher on her head, as if she were a member of the chorus in Aeschylus' *The Libation Bearers*. But this is not a slave; this is

Electra, who wears her hair short in mourning for her murdered father. The play has been going for about five minutes and has announced as clearly as possible that the story may be familiar but the treatment will be radically new.

This new realism is apparent in the scene between Electra and the Tutor. He has just found a lock of hair placed on Agamemnon's tomb and thinks it might belong to Orestes:

OLD MAN: Go there. Try the hair against your own.
See if the colour matches.
Brother: sister. It might, it happens.
ELEKTRA: How could they match?
His hair's an athlete's, a gentleman's
Hard and strong; mine a woman's.
Soft with combing . . . .
OLD MAN: The footprints in the dust, beside the grave:
Go there, match them against yours.
ELEKTRA: There's no dust there. It's rock.
And how could our footprints match –
A man's, a woman's? His feet would be bigger.
OLD MAN: You're right. We'll not recognize him that way.
I know! He'll be wearing some garment
You made for him years ago,
I smuggled him to safety in.
ELEKTRA: When Orestes went into exile I was a little girl.
Even if I had made him a garment
He was a child then. It'd hardly fit him now . . . .
    tr. Kenneth McLeish

This may be a satire on Aeschylus' way of handling the encounter between brother and sister in *The Libation Bearers* but it functions in another way as well. The rejection of the 'poetic solution' acts as a guarantee that the scene we are watching is really happening.

The play is deeply rooted in the particular. Electra sets out to fetch water from the well, her husband goes to put the cows to pasture and start the spring sowing. Aegisthus leaves the city to visit his stud farm. The use of props also helps to ground the action – the concern with clothes, Electra's pitcher, the young lamb and cheeses, the garlands and flowers and the jug of wine that the old man brings to entertain the strangers. These realistic touches are thought to be particular to Euripides, but they might not seem so unusual if more of Aeschylus' work had survived, especially the satyr plays. In *The Bone Gatherers*, for example, a stinking chamber pot is shied at someone's head, and the Nurse in *The Libation Bearers* gives a memorable account of dealing with baby Orestes' dirty nappies. And behind Aeschylus stands Homer. Sophocles characteristically took his tone from the *Iliad*, but Euripides is far closer to the *Odyssey*, with its special feel for everyday life – the odour of roast meat, the armour that is put in the store room to protect it from the smoke, the swineherd who gives Odysseus refuge in his hut.

This celebration of the ordinary which runs through the play extends from things to people. There is a sense in which the humble must make good what the haughty have destroyed. The unhappiness of the ruling class characters is contrasted with the quiet decency of the villagers and of Electra's husband, which gives Orestes pause for thought.

ORESTES: This man, for example.
  He's nobody, a man in the street,
  And when need arises
  Look what a prince he is.
  There's a lesson here for us all:
  Stop philosophising,
  Making maps and charts of virtue;
  Start with a clean slate with everyone you meet,
  See what they do, and what they say, then judge.
    tr. Kenneth McLeish

There would be no point in enumerating the play's features – its realistic detail, its unusual setting, the sharpness of its psychological insight – without saying the most obvious thing about it, namely that it's an extremely gripping narrative, so full of twists and shifts of sympathy that it's difficult to find one's feet. *Electra* is remarkable for the invention of the modern dialogue scene, which occurs here for the first time in the history of world drama. Aeschylus and Sophocles had limited their dialogue to ten or fifteen lines at a time and the exchanges usually take the form of an argument. Euripides vastly expanded the scope of these encounters – the two big dialogue scenes in this play are each seventy lines long – and in doing so, he changed their nature. The extra space allows the characters to interact in different ways, to probe each other's minds, to show sympathy and revulsion, to be seen thinking. With their rapid rhythm and strong forward movement these scenes mark a big step forward in the dramatic presentation of developing action.

Euripides' new invention was particularly suitable for conspiracy scenes and scenes of recognition, both of which feature in *Electra*. Here is Orestes plotting how to kill Aegisthus.

OLD MAN: I just now thought of something. Listen to this.

ORESTES: Go ahead. I'll listen if it's worthwhile.

OLD MAN: Aigisthos – I saw him as I came here.

ORESTES: You have my attention. Where?

OLD MAN: Over in the meadows where his horses graze.

ORESTES: Doing what? I begin to see hope.

OLD MAN: Preparing a feast, I think, for the Nymphs.

ORESTES: In thanks for living children or for one not born?

OLD MAN: I know only that he was making ready for sacrifice.

ORESTES: Were free men there? Or was he alone with is slaves?

OLD MAN: No citizens, just his household staff.

ORESTES: Was there anyone there who'd recognize me?

OLD MAN: No, only slaves who never saw you as a boy.

    tr. Janet Lembke and Kenneth J. Reckford

Some critics seem to have it in for Electra. One calls her 'implacable, self-centred, fantastic in hatred, callous to the verge of insanity, a woman in whom it is hardly possible to find a virtue'. Another labels her as 'a bitter self-pitying, sharp-tongued virago'. All this is considerably in excess of the facts. The playwright's first emphasis is on her youth and fertility, and the difficulties these pose for the royal house. Her husband refers to her as 'a young virgin'. Her youth brings her closer in age to Orestes – she was only a child when he went into exile. In Sophocles she is already old enough at the time of Agamemnon's murder to be instrumental in helping to spirit her brother away to safety.

There is a pride to Electra that befits her royal lineage, but also a softness and uncertainty that go with her youth. She makes a display of going to the well in order to shame the people who have degraded her, but at the same time she is determined to play her part in the household and not be a burden to her hard-working husband. Euripides is at pains to show her accommodation to her new life. The first glimpse of Sophocles' Electra shows her in grip of grief and rage; Euripides' Electra is first seen going about her household chores. She is careful not to give full vent to her grief until her husband has gone to work. And when Orestes invites her to gloat over Aegisthus' corpse her first response is not to exult but to turn away: 'I am ashamed'.

The reason some commentators have had such difficulty with Electra's character is that in reading the play they neglect its temporal element – the way the narrative unfolds in time. Euripides first enlists our sympathy with the avengers and then, as the play proceeds, he makes us feel for the victims. He walks us round the story letting us look at it from different aspects. First we encounter Orestes and Electra, hardly more than teenagers, as they nerve themselves to take on their father's killers. Then the balance of the play shifts. Aegisthus is not as monstrous as we might expect. He is pious, hospitable, trusting, which is why Orestes finds it easy to murder him.

MESSENGER: We found Aigisthos
In a grove of trees, cutting myrtle leaves.
He saw us. 'Morning', he called.
'Good to see you. Where are you from?'

Lord Orestes answered, 'Thessaly.
And we're on our way to Olympia; we're pilgrims.'
'Stay here tonight', Aigisthos said.
'No excuses: you're welcome.
I'm making a sacrifice, holding a banquet.
Be my guests, get up early tomorrow –
One day on your journey
Won't make all that difference.'
    tr. Kenneth McLeish

The confrontation between mother and daughter comes right at the end of the play. Clytemnestra enters on a magnificent chariot – an irruption of moneyed splendour made all the more powerful by the humble setting. She is surrounded by slave girls from Troy who have become sort of surrogate daughters to her, replacing Iphigeneia who died and Electra who has been cast out. She asks them to help her down.

CLYTEMNESTRA: Get out of the chariot, Trojan maidens;
   hold my hand
  tight so I can step down safely to the ground.
  Mostly we give the houses of our gods the spoils
  from Phrygia, but these girls, the best in Troy, I chose
  to ornament my house and replace the child
  I lost, my loved daughter. The compensation is small.
ELECTRA: Then may not I, who am a slave and also tossed
  far from my father's home to live in misery,
  may not I mother hold your most distinguished hand?
CLYTEMNESTRA: These slaves are here to help me. Do not
   trouble yourself.
ELECTRA: Why not? You rooted me up, a casualty of war;
  my home was overpowered, I am in your power
  as they are too – left dark, lonely, and fatherless.
    tr. Emily Townsend Vermeule

Clytemnestra is very far from being a hate figure: she is harassed, lonely and uncertain. She tries to turn aside her daughter's threats.

CLYTEMNESTRA: My child from birth you have always
   adored your father.
This is part of life. Some, children always love
the male, some turn more closely to their mother than him.
I know you and forgive you. I am not so happy
either, child, with what I have done or with myself.
How poorly you look. Have you not washed? Your clothes
   are bad.
I suppose you have just got up from bed and giving birth?
O god how miserably my plans have turned out.
    tr. Emily Townsend Vermeule

The sense of pain on both sides is overwhelming and driven
home by the stage picture – the imposing vehicle, the Queen
in her finery surrounded by her palace slaves, who have
cropped hair like her daughter, but are much better dressed. It
is typical of Euripides to defer this climactic encounter to the
last possible moment, just before Clytemnestra goes to her
death. The irony is that if she had not been so tender-hearted
and in such a hurry to see her daughter's new baby she would
have escaped alive. As one commentator put it: 'It is difficult
to hate someone who has just become a grandmother.'

∾ Translations

The best two translations are Kenneth McLeish (Methuen)
and Janet Lembke and Kenneth J. Reckford (Oxford). Emily
Townsend Vermeule (Chicago) is also useful.

∾ In performance

It's impossible to pinpoint an exact date for the first performance. The present consensus places the play in the period 422
–417 BC. *Electra* is part of a series of works dealing with the
Trojan War and its aftermath which preoccupied Euripides in
the last dozen years of his life. *Electra* was staged in 1906 at
the Court Theatre by Harley Granville Barker. There is a

film version by Michael Cacoyannis (1960). Other productions include Stratford East (1964), the Mermaid Theatre (1966), La Mama New York (1974/78/86) and the Gate Theatre London (1995).

The Trojan Women (Troiades)

∾ The legend

When Hecuba, Queen of Troy, was pregnant with her son Paris, she dreamt that she gave birth to a blazing torch. The dream was interpreted to mean that her newborn would grow up to destroy his native city. Hecuba arranged for the baby to be exposed on the mountains, but the child was rescued by a shepherd and brought up as part of his family.

When Paris grew to manhood, three goddesses came to seek him out to settle a dispute as to which of them was the most beautiful. A golden apple was the prize. Hera promised him power if he gave it to her; Athena promised him wisdom if he gave it to her; Aphrodite promised him the love of the most beautiful woman in the world. Paris gave the prize to Aphrodite.

Still ignorant of his parentage, Paris went to Troy to compete in the funeral games that were held every year in memory of his supposed death. He won three victories and made the other royal princes jealous. One of them, Deiphobus, plotted with Hecuba to kill the newcomer. But Paris' true identity was revealed and he was welcomed back into the royal family.

Paris went on an embassy to Sparta where he met Helen, the most beautiful woman in the world. She ran away with him to Troy leaving behind her husband Menelaus – and so the Trojan War broke out, when a Greek expeditionary force under the command of Menelaus' brother Agamemnon sailed to Troy to bring Helen back home.

The war lasted ten years but eventually the Greeks proved victorious by smuggling a band of armed men into the city hidden inside a gigantic wooden horse.

∾ The story

The action takes place amid the smoking ruins of Troy. The men have all been killed and the women and children are to be distributed as slaves to the victorious Greeks. Among them are the surviving members of the Trojan royal family – Hecuba and her daughters Cassandra and Polyxena, Andromache, the wife of Hecuba's dead son Hector, and Hector's son Astyanax, the last male survivor of the dynasty. The Greeks, afraid that the child might pose a threat to them sometime in the future, execute him by throwing him from the battlements.

Helen, cause of all the conflict, is among the prisoners. The assembly have voted that she be handed over to her husband Menelaus to do with as he sees fit. Hecuba demands that she be executed but it is clear that Menelaus has once more fallen under her spell and she will escape scot-free.

The body of Astyanax is laid in his father's shield and prepared for burial. The Greeks torch what remains of the city. Hecuba tries to throw herself into the flames but is prevented by the soldiers. The Trojan women board the ships as the blazing citadel collapses.

∾ About the play

> and lastly
> I think of the slaves.
>   Louis MacNeice, *Autumn Journal*

> Vanished are your sacrifices and the auspicious strains of choral song and the night-long festivals under the dark sky . . . It troubles me, it does trouble me, lord, to wonder if you think of all this as you sit enthroned in heaven – of the ruined city, undone by the fire's flaming onrush.
>   tr. Justina Gregory

> It is a universal and eternal law that in a city taken during a war, everything, including persons and property, belongs to the victor.
>
> Xenophon, *Cyropaedia*, VII.5.73

The Trojan Women is about community, hope, and memory and what it means to live on after a catastrophe. It was the Greek tragedy that spoke most directly to the twentieth century, as *Antigone* had to the nineteenth. The play's emotional power was acknowledged early on. Plutarch tells a story about a bloodthirsty fourth-century tyrant, Alexander of Pherae: 'Once, seeing a tragedian act *The Trojan Women* of Euripides, he hurriedly left the theatre. He sent a message to the performer telling him not to be afraid but to go on acting to the best of his ability. He had not left because he disliked the performance but because, having killed so many men and never felt pity, he was ashamed to be seen by the citizens weeping over the suffering of Hecuba and Andromache.'

As the play begins the god Poseidon stands among the ruins of Troy, the city he had helped to found. He is getting ready to leave.

POSEIDON: So I must leave my altars and great Ilium
  since once a city sinks into sad desolation
  the gods' state sickens also and their worship fades.
    tr. Richmond Lattimore

There is no permanence and no loyalty. When a city is destroyed the gods move on. Even Zeus, whose beloved cup-bearer Ganymede was a Trojan, has refused to take an interest.

CHORUS: And you,
  Ganymede, go in grace by the thrones of God
  with your young calm smile even now
  as Priam's kingdom
  falls to the Greek spear . . .
  For the gods loved Troy once.
  Now they have forgotten.
    tr. Richmond Lattimore

The Greeks will be no better off. Athene is angry with them for having violated her altars and she enlists Poseidon's help to shatter their fleet on the way home. The gods retire and leave the humans to pick up the pieces.

Aristotle wrote: 'A slave is a property with a soul.' In becoming a slave, a person gives up their country, their family, control over their body. This is the situation in which the Trojan women find themselves. If children are born to a new relationship in exile, they do not constitute a new family, since they can be taken from their mothers at any time, in the same way that slaves were sold down river in the American South. As one historian put it: 'The slave was always a deracinated outsider – first in the sense that he originated from outside the society into which he was introduced as a slave, second in that he was denied the most elementary of social bonds, kinship' (M. I. Finley). Documents of sale recorded in Egypt show no instances of male slaves and their families being sold together: of twenty-nine cases where women were recorded as being sold, only two had children with them. According to a modern calculation a slave stood a 50/50 chance of being sold at least once in their life. It is taken for granted that the women in the play will never see each other again. Cassandra is to go with Agamemnon to Argos, Andromache to Skyros with Neoptolemus: both are expected to sleep with their new masters.

Each of the four principal characters represents a different quality. Hecuba is all endurance. Three times in the play we see her lying prostrate on the ground – once crushed with despair at the opening of the play; a second time when she faints after the scene with Cassandra; and a third time when she hammers her fists on the earth so that her dead children will hear her underground. Three times she picks herself up to face life once again.

HECUBA: Up, wretch. Cursed of the gods,
  Look up. Troy's gone.
  No city now. No queen. All's changed.

God's changed. Endure.
Sail with the current, sail with god.
Life's stormy now. Sail with the current.
Don't butt the waves.
  tr. Kenneth McLeish

Cassandra stands for the freedom of the mind, even in the darkest circumstances. Apollo gave her the gift of prophecy in an attempt to seduce her. When she decided to resist him it was too late to recall the gift but Apollo punished her by making sure she would never be believed. Her insight enables her to see into the future, so she is able to understand how transitory her unhappiness is, and how terrible her oppressors' end will be.

CASSANDRA: Trust Apollo. If God is god
  This marriage will ruin His Lordship.
  Agamemnon, grand Admiral of Greece!
  I'll hurt him more than Helen did.
  I'll kill him, strip all his house
  Till the price is paid
  For my father and my brothers dead.
  Cassandra, hush! Don't tell it all:
  Don't sing of knives, necks chopped,
  Mine and those others',
  Blood-feud, the mother dead,
  The dynasty destroyed,
  My marriage price!
    tr. Kenneth McLeish

Andromache has been the perfect faithful wife.

ANDROMACHE: I was Hector's wife. I kept my place,
  Did my duty, stayed indoors
  As women should. No loose talk,
  No market chatter. All I knew
  I learned from my own quiet thoughts,
  At home. When Hector spoke,
  I listened.

Conventionality has been her pride. When her way of life is shattered, she longs for death. She envies her dead sister Polyxena, sacrificed by the Greeks to appease Achilles' ghost.

ANDROMACHE: She's dead. It's done. She's lucky now.
Far luckier than me. They make me live.
tr. Kenneth McLeish

Hecuba persuades her to go on living for the sake of her son Astyanax, in the hope that one day, through him, the royal dynasty will rise again.

The execution of Astyanax is appalling because it is so unnecessary. 'Here lies a little child, killed because they were afraid of him.' Even the herald Talthybius considers the killing monstrous and can hardly bring himself to break the news. Euripides is always good with children. He gives a vivid sketch of them clinging to their mothers in terror the night that Troy was sacked and the innocence and frailty of the little prince – 'O child's sweet fragrant body' – are powerfully evoked.

A brilliant stroke of dramatic construction places Helen's entry between the taking of Astyanax away to execution and the announcement of his death. Helen is the cause of the whole sorry mess: the dead child is the result of her selfishness and vanity. A sort of trial takes place with Hecuba as counsel for the prosecution. Hecuba wins the debate but Helen's beauty exerts a pull that reasoned argument can't match – which of course was how the war came about in the first place. Menelaus begins the scene determined to take revenge on Helen but ends by agreeing to let her come back to Greece with him and even offers to take her in his ship.

The Trojan Women was originally part of a trilogy. The other two plays are lost but we have enough fragments to piece together what went on in them and trace the way in which they are linked thematically. The first play *Alexander* (the Trojan name for Paris) tells the story of how Paris returned to Troy as an unknown shepherd to take part in his own funeral games; how his true identity was discovered; and how he was welcomed back into the royal family, with fatal consequences. The second play, *Palamedes*, is set in the Greek camp. Palamedes was the inventor of writing. Odysseus, jealous of his accomplishment, arranged to have some gold buried in his tent and framed him as a Trojan spy. Palamedes was executed but his son made use of his father's invention to write the truth of what had happened on the blades of oars, which he launched into the sea. The oars were carried by the tides to Greece, where Palamedes' relations took revenge by lighting false beacons and luring the Greek fleet on to the rocks.

Palamedes is linked to *The Trojan Women* because it is about memory: it also contains an unjust execution. *Alexander* and *The Trojan Women*, which deal with Priam's family, have even more in common. In both plays Cassandra makes prophecies that are ignored. In *Alexander* Hecuba dreams of the firebrand that will destroy the city; in *The Trojan Women* we see the citadel go up in flames. Hector, Astyanax's father, has an important role to play in *Alexander*; this makes his absence in *The Trojan Women* even more telling. Finally both plays revolve around the death of children. In *Alexander* Hecuba tries twice to kill her son Paris – once when he is born and then a second time when he returns to Troy. The direct result of these two failed attempts is the death of all her other children and of little Astyanax, the last survivor of the royal line.

Euripides punctuates his narrative with a series of unforgettable images. Andromache and her son are brought on in a cart, surrounded by the rest of Neoptolemus' loot. They are chattels just like the other goods heaped up around them. Astyanax is buried in his father's shield because there is no time to make a coffin for him before the ships sail. The smashed infant with a shield for a cradle is a brutal summation of what the war has brought. And there is fire. Hecuba had famously dreamed of giving birth to a fire-brand. Cassandra enters waving a burning torch in parody of a wedding – repeating an action she performs in *Alexander*. At the end of the play the Greeks torch the citadel, the whole stage goes red and we see the Trojan women silhouetted against flames.

Hecuba tries to throw herself into the fire but is prevented by the soldiers. She is Odysseus' property now and cannot be allowed to harm herself. But there is one consolation the Greeks cannot take away, a consolation for the defeated in any struggle – the consolation of language, and the hope that the story of their suffering will endure.

HEKABE: BUT if they hadn't brought us down so low,
   face down in the dust, we'd disappear for ever.
   Whereas now we are stories everyone will tell.
     tr. Tony Harrison

Every time an audience watches the play, Hecuba's prophecy is fulfilled.

∾ Translations

The Chicago version (Richmond Lattimore) gives the big speeches a fine rhetorical energy. Kenneth McLeish (Absolute Classics) is terse and vivid, sometimes to the point of self-parody. Don Taylor (Methuen) is verbose and full of anachronisms – 'commando', 'war-machine', 'payload' – which give the effect of trying too hard. There is also an Irish version by Brendan Kennelly (Bloodaxe) and an adaptation by Tony Harrison which forms part of his play *The Common Chorus* – a double bill of *The Trojan Women* and *Lysistrata* set at Greenham Common.

∾ In performance.

The play was first performed in 415 BC as part of a trilogy with *Alexander* and *Palamedes*. Seneca wrote a version *Troades* c.AD 50. The play was staged in 1905 at the Court Theatre by Harley Granville Barker and at the Théâtre National Populaire in 1965 in a translation by Jean-Paul Sartre. Recent productions include Stratford East (1964), La Mama New

York, (1974/78/86/96), the Gate Theatre London (1991), the National Theatre (1995) and the Shakespeare Theatre Washington (1999). There is an opera by Aribert Reimann (1986).

Iphigeneia Among the Taurians
(Iphigeneia he en Taurois)

∾ The legend

The story of Iphigeneia's sacrifice at Aulis and her rescue by the goddess Artemis occurs in the *Cypria*, an epic poem (now lost) which told the story of the lead-up to the Trojan War. A summary of the poem survives from the fifth century AD:

> When the expedition had gathered for the second time at Aulis, Agamemnon shot a deer while hunting and claimed to be excelling Artemis. The goddess took offence and held them back from sailing by sending storms. Calchas explained the goddess's wrath and told them to sacrifice Iphigeneia to Artemis, so they sent for her on pretext of marriage with Achilles and set about sacrificing her. But Artemis snatched her away to the Taurians and made her immortal, setting a deer on the altar instead of the girl.
>
> tr. M. J. Cropp

Iphigeneia means Strong Born, and besides being the name of Agamemnon's daughter is also an epithet of the goddess Artemis. The Taurians lived the southeast of the Crimean peninsula and would have been known to the Greeks who had colonized the richer agricultural areas to the northwest and east. The play is often referred to by its Latin title, *Iphigenia in Tauris*.

∾ The story

Iphigeneia, the daughter of Agamemnon, is living in exile on the Crimean coast, where she is the priestess of Artemis, charged with the ritual killing of any shipwrecked sailors washed up on the shore.

Her brother Orestes and his friend Pylades travel to the Crimea, sent by Apollo to seize the statue of Artemis from the temple there and bring it back to Greece. They are arrested by the local people and brought to Iphigeneia to be sacrificed. When she learns that the two young men come from Greece, she promises to spare Pylades' life if he will take a letter to her family. In case it should go astray, she tells him the contents and so reveals her identity to her astonished brother.

Iphigeneia tells Thoas, the Taurian king, that the goddess has been polluted by the presence of the matricide Orestes, and that she must take her brother and the statue to the sea to wash them clean. Meanwhile the inhabitants of the city are told to stay indoors to avoid being tainted. When the Greeks reach the shore they embark on their waiting ship, which is held by winds in the harbour mouth, unable to escape. It looks as if the fugitives will be caught and killed until Athena intervenes to secure a favourable wind and arranges for the chorus of Greek slaves to return home safely.

∾ About the play

THOAS: O great Apollo what barbarian
  Would do the things these Greeks have done?
    tr. Witter Bynner

If we go on to take the whole corpus [of Greek tragedy] into account, we can note that there is not a single play in which the opposition between Greeks and barbarians, or between citizens and aliens, does not play a significant role.
    Pierre Vidal-Naquet in *Greek Tragedy and the Historian*,
    ed. Christopher Pelling

IPHIGENEIA: Ah, I shall never forget the horror of that day.

It is a paradox that tragedy, the Athenian art form *par excellence*, is hardly ever set in Athens. Of the thirty-three surviving plays, only four take place partly (*Eumenides*) or wholly (*Oedipus at Colonus*, *The Children of Heracles* and Euripides' *Suppliants*) in Athenian territory. This is partly to be expected: the world of heroes cannot be contained within a single city. But the foreign settings also have an expressive purpose. Troy is a place of vulnerability, of death and bereavement; Thebes is a city divided against itself; Argos is more malleable, a city in the process of becoming. There are nearly three hundred Greek tragedies that we know at least something about and of these nearly half portray barbarian characters or are set in non-Greek locations. The very first tragedy to survive, *The Persians* by Aeschylus, is set at the court of the Persian king. Aeschylus' work ranges across the whole of the known world from Crete to the Caucasus, from Libya to Thrace. Euripides wrote plays that took place in Ethiopia, on the shores of the Black Sea, in Egypt, and southern Italy and North Africa.

This interest in things foreign comes partly from the old legends on which the tragedies were based, was partly a liking for the exotic, and partly a way of defining what it meant to be Greek. The great period of classical Greece was shaped in its beginning by conflict with the Persian Empire. The victories of Marathon (490 BC) and Salamis (480 BC), in which the invaders from the East were beaten back, underpin the remarkable flowering of fifth-century BC Greek culture. The epitaph on the tomb of Aeschylus makes no mention of his plays but records simply that he fought at Marathon. Distant locations also provided a way of talking about concerns that might otherwise have seemed too close to home – much as Shakespeare set plays in Vienna, Messina, Venice, Verona and ancient Rome. The Trojan women may be Trojan but they're also Greek; Oedipus and Antigone may be Theban but they're Athenian too.

There are not many plays in the world repertoire where the central character has been a human sacrifice. The land of the Taurians is grim and dark, with its bloodstained altar and the skulls of former victims hanging on the wall, yet it is not altogether foreign. It seems in many ways the logical place for the children of the house of Atreus to end up – Iphigeneia murdered by her father, Orestes the murderer of his mother. The whole unhappy family history which took so long in the telling in the opening chorus of *Agamemnon* is here condensed into a single nightmare image. The altar stained red with human blood, which occupies a central place on the stage, is a permanent reminder of past savagery and the threat of savagery to come.

ORESTES: And is this the altar dripping with Hellenic blood?
PYLADES: At least the top of it is brown with bloodstains.
ORESTES: And hanging underneath, do you see the spoils?
PYLADES: Yes, skulls of slaughtered strangers, as an offering.
    tr. Richmond Lattimore

The first part of the play is an ascending curve of grimness – the apparent hopelessness of the young men's mission, the loneliness of Iphigeneia, her dream of Orestes' death, which removes the hope of rescue and seems to make all her endurance pointless, the final hardening of her heart and her abandonment of any feeling of pity for her victims. The sense of gathering violence makes it seem possible that the murder of a brother might well be added to the other crimes of the house of Atreus. In Aeschylus' *Agamemnon*, Orestes and Electra encounter each other at their father's tomb. Here Iphigeneia enters with funeral offerings, as Electra did, but the siblings are not meeting at the grave of a hero to be avenged but at an altar on which the brother is to be sacrificed.

The recognition scene is one of the master narratives of Greek tragedy. It expressed something very powerful about the Greek attitude to life. Over and over they liked to dramatise and watch the moment when what had seemed lost for ever was suddenly restored. These scenes captured perfectly the sense of life's uncertainty, its sheer unpredictability – the fact that when you get up in the morning you have no idea what might happen to you before nightfall. The recognition scene interpreted this uncertainty in a positive way to show how it was possible for sorrow to be healed; it worked as a counterpoise to those other moments when people suddenly plunged from security into unexpected horror. The whole of *Oedipus Tyrannus* can be read as one long recognition scene, ending in disaster.

Iphigeneia Among the Taurians provides the longest and most elaborate example of the genre. There is something self-delighting in Euripides' virtuosity here. The scene divides into five movements. In the first Iphigeneia interrogates her two captives. The messenger has already told her that one of the two is called Pylades but Orestes refuses to give his name.

ORESTES: You don't need my name to kill me.
IPHIGENEIA: It's too big a name to tell?
ORESTES: You're killing a body, not a name.
IPHIGENEIA: Where in Greece do you come from?
ORESTES: What does it matter? I'm a corpse.
    tr. Kenneth McLeish

If Orestes gave away his identity the scene would be over – but he doesn't. In the same way Iphigeneia comes close to revealing herself, but stops just short.

IPHIGENEIA: And Achilles, the sea-nymph's son. What of Achilles?
ORESTES: He's dead. That marriage of his in Aulis: nothing.
IPHIGENEIA: As I should know.
ORESTES: You're well informed on Greece. Who are you?
IPHIGENEIA: Years ago, I was a child in Greece.
    tr. Kenneth McLeish

Iphigeneia makes the proposal that she will spare one of the young men if he will carry a letter from her back to Greece. The scene between Orestes and Pylades in which they debate which one of them is going to survive comes at the midpoint of the play and is as full of emotion as the scenes between brother and sister. It became a legend in later times for its portrayal of male tenderness.

PYLADES: I would be shamed to see the daylight while you die.
I shared your voyage. I must also share your death.
[. . .]
ORESTES: It is not really bad for me
to end my life, since the gods make it what it is,
You are a happy man, you hold a house that's clean,
not sick, like mine; my house is cursed and evil-starred.
If you survive, and beget children from my sister
whom I have given you to have and hold as wife,
our name might be continued, and my father's house
not be obliterated with no children born.
Go on your way and live and hold your father's house.
    tr. Richmond Lattimore

It's easy to see why the two of them belong together. The nervy, sensitive Orestes is matched by the more stolid, phlegmatic Pylades – the brilliance of the one, the reliability of the other. It is because Pylades is so meticulous that he manages to save Orestes' life. His insistence on making quite sure that he will be able to deliver Iphigeneia's message, even if the letter is lost, leads at last to the recognition.

PYLADES: Wait a minute. There is one thing.
IPHIGENEIA: Say it. If it's reasonable, let's hear it.
PYLADES: Suppose my ship sinks, and the letter's gone
And I've nothing left except what I stand up in?
What happens then?
IPHIGENEIA: It's easy. I'll tell you what's in the letter.
Then, if it's lost, you can tell
My friends in person.
    tr. Kenneth McLeish

Iphigeneia Among the Taurians shares a number of features with Euripides' *Helen*, which was written about the same time. In both plays a Greek princess is living in a foreign land, attended by a chorus of Greek slaves. In both she believes that all hope of rescue has been lost. Both heroines have a recognition scene in which they find a long lost relative and both finally manage to make their escape by sea. It is remarkable that two plays with such similarities of structure should be so different in tone. This arises from the different way in which the elements of the story are distributed. *Helen* is by far the sunnier piece. Helen and Menelaus find each other and are out of danger by the halfway mark, leaving the second part of the play for the development of their plan of escape. In *Iphigeneia Among the Taurians* by contrast Iphigeneia and the two young men only turn to plotting their getaway when the action is three-quarters over. The time before that has been taken up not just with the characters in jeopardy but also with the revisiting of past sorrows; these things combine to give *Iphigeneia Among the Taurians* its darker colouring.

The climax of the play is an impressive ritual of purgation. The matricide Orestes and his accomplice Pylades are led from the temple; their heads are covered in thick cloth so that the sun will not be polluted by shining on them. The whole population of the city are shut in their houses to avoid the sight; smoking torches are used to fumigate the temple.

IPHIGENEIA: Now I see the strangers coming from the
    shrine. I see as well
holy properties of the goddess, young lambs, so that,
    blood by blood
I can wash away the stain; I see the lighted torches, all
that I ordered for the cleansing of the strangers and the god.
Now I warn the citizens: avoid infection and stand clear,
all who come to serve the temple, clean of hands before
    the gods,
all who come to join in marriage, or relief in giving birth:
stand back all; take flight; begone, lest this pollution fall
    on you.
    tr. Richmond Lattimore

As a stage spectacle this is as elaborate as anything in Aeschylus and it functions on a number of different levels. The matricide that has brought Orestes to this dangerous place also provides a means of escape: the worst thing about him comes to his rescue.

In one sense the ritual is bogus, part of a conspiracy to hoodwink Thoas: but it is also painfully real. The reason that Orestes has come to the Crimea is that his bloodguilt is still not properly discharged. What might have seemed sacrilegious to a Greek audience if portrayed directly becomes allowed as part of a play within a play. The slow procession, the attendants, the torches, the two Greeks with their muffled heads would all have made an imposing and memorable stage picture.

The chorus are Greek slaves and their longing for home amplifies Iphigeneia's yearning – and of course they are bound in fellow-feeling to the newcomers as well. They have it in their power to betray Iphigeneia and her brother to the Taurians and so perhaps help themselves. Iphigeneia goes to each of them in turn begging them not to give her up.

IPHIGENEIA: I'll come back.
  You know I'll come back.
  I'll fetch you home to Greece.
  Hold my hand. Kiss me. Your cheek.
  Think of them waiting for news.
  Your mother, your father, your children . . .
     tr. Kenneth McLeish

In the end Thoas falls victim to a Hellenic conspiracy when the chorus accept to take part in the ritual purification knowing it to be false. The cheated king is clear where the blames lies and it is only Athena's intervention that finally saves the day.

∾ Translations

The three most useful translations are Richmond Lattimore (Oxford), Kenneth McLeish (Methuen) and Witter Bynner

(Chicago). The Lattimore and the Bynner are both rather stiff and the McLeish adopts a deliberately slangy tone. None of them really manages to catch the play's special atmosphere – its strangeness, its realistic detail, its lyric beauty and its emotional power.

∾ In performance

The first performance can be dated on internal evidence to around 417–412 BC. There are operas by Scarlatti (1713) and Gluck (1779). In 1673–6 Jean Racine outlined a version of the story which he never completed. Goethe wrote an *Iphigenie auf Tauris* in prose (1779) and in verse (1787). The play was staged in London in 1912 by Harley Granville Barker. Recent productions include Stratford East (1964) and Chicago (1997). There is dance piece by Pina Bausch (1974).

Ion (*Ion*)

∾ The legend

Creusa was the daughter of the king of Athens. The god Apollo raped her. She kept her pregnancy secret and when the baby was born she exposed him in the cave where the seduction had taken place. Apollo sent Hermes to spirit the child away to Delphi, where the priestess of the shrine took him in and brought him up. When Creusa went back to the cave the baby was gone and she thought that some wild animal had eaten it.

Athens was at war with Euboea and was victorious under the leadership of Xuthus, a foreigner from Achaea. His reward was marriage to Creusa, the only surviving child of the royal dynasty. The marriage was childless and the royal family in danger of dying out. Creusa and Xuthus went to Delphi to consult Apollo about their difficulty.

ᕽ The story

Ion, child of Creusa and Apollo has grown up at Delphi, ignorant of his true parentage. He meets his mother when she comes to consult the oracle about her childless marriage. They have a long conversation in which each is sympathetic to the other's pain – the young man pities the older woman's childlessness, while she feels for the boy who has grown up without a mother. Neither is aware of the other's true identity.

Xuthus, Creusa's husband, is delighted when it is prophesied that he will not leave Delphi without a child. The oracle tells him that the first person he meets after leaving the temple will be his son. He encounters the astonished Ion, whom he claims as his and orders a feast to be prepared in celebration.

The chorus bring Creusa the news that Xuthus has found a son and she must remain forever childless. Creusa determines that the royal house of Athens should not descend to a former temple slave who has been fathered by a foreigner. She resolves to poison Ion. The plot is discovered and Creusa is condemned to death by stoning. She takes refuge at Apollo's altar. Ion, now furious in his turn, can hardly be restrained from dragging her from the holy place by force.

The High Priestess, who has brought Ion up, learns that he is leaving for a new life and brings out the cradle, the baby clothes and the jewellery which are his sole link with his past to give to him. Creusa recognizes them and immediately runs from the altar.

> I will desert the altar even though
> I have to die.
>> tr. R. F. Willetts

Mother and son are reconciled. Ion insists that Apollo should confirm his parentage but Athena appears instead to resolve the action. Ion is to found the Ionian nation, which will populate Attica and the Greek cities of Asia Minor. Xuthus is to go on believing that he is Ion's true father. He will have two sons by Creusa, Dorus and Achaeus, whose descendants will in turn populate the Peloponnese and Western Greece.

∽ About the play

CHORUS: You will never have a child
      To hold or take on to your breast.
CREUSA: I wish I were dead.
   tr. R. F. Willetts

Ion is about a rape and its consequences. A baby is abandoned; a woman spends her life mourning her lost child and wondering what happened to him; a young man grows up not knowing if he has a family, and is left to fill the place where they might have been with his imagination. The play is also the story of how the damage is repaired and made good by gods and humans working together, often at cross purposes and with some narrow escapes along the way.

Euripides was always an innovator and in this play he seems to have invented modern comedy. Ion is the first of a line which runs through the work of Menander and Plautus to *Twelfth Night*, *Cymbeline* and *The Winter's Tale* and beyond them to *The Importance of Being Earnest*. Satyrus, a Greek critic writing in the third century BC, hit the nail on the head when he remarked; 'The whole business of vicissitudes, raping of young women, substitution of children, recognition by means of rings and necklaces, these are of course the main elements of New Comedy and Euripides brought them to perfection.'

The elements that come together here had been present in Euripides' work for years but had never combined in this particular way. There is his often-noted fondness for realistic detail – one ancient source says that he trained as a painter. *Alcestis* takes place almost entirely in the domestic sphere and shows what happens to a household when the woman around whom it centred is no longer there. *Electra* makes a grand dynastic story play itself out in the humble setting of a mountain farm. The homeliness of the everyday activities – the spring sowing, the fetching of water from the well – as well as the ordinary objects that figure in the action – the water pitcher, the cheeses, the garlands of flowers – act as a sort of guarantor of the truth of the events depicted.

The precipitating factor that made *Ion* possible was Euripides' invention of the modern scene. In Aeschylus and Sophocles dialogue exchanges (*stichomythia*) were generally brief – usually about ten lines, never more than twenty – and came at the end of long speeches in which the two characters had set out their positions. The dialogue recapitulated and condensed the main points of opposition and the overall effect of the scene was to function as a sort of poster for the narrative. Euripides expanded these dialogue exchanges tenfold. *Electra*, which precedes *Ion* by about five years, has a dialogue scene which goes on for nearly 70 lines. Creusa's opening encounter with Ion, which comes in at 105 lines, is the longest passage of dialogue in Euripides, followed by Creusa's 94-line dialogue with the Old Man later in the play. This huge expansion of spoken exchanges allows a quite different and more flexible interaction between the characters to occur, which is open to the ebb and flow of feeling and to the more detailed portraiture of psychological states. The scenes between Pentheus and Dionysus in *The Bacchae* represent Euripides' supreme achievement in this line, producing a dual portrait of compelling sexual intimacy and threat.

Another way of defining *Ion* is to look at what it leaves out. There is no ideological confrontation between family and state as in *Antigone*; there is no resolution of a blood feud reaching back into the distant past as in the *Oresteia*; man is not confronted by elemental forces as in *Hippolytus* or *The Bacchae*; the fall of Troy is not at stake, as in *Philoctetes*; the action does not, like *The Persians*, present the ruin of a mighty empire. The play is domestic in scale, and the space that in other Greek plays is taken up by politics is filled instead with plot and intrigue. Here, for the first time in the history of drama, we meet that old standby the poisoned chalice that will crop up in countless future plays including *Hamlet*. For the first time too we meet the tokens and the baby clothes which become the standard way of identifying children separated at birth and were still doing useful service in Joe Orton's *What the Butler Saw* in 1971. The handbag that so scandalised Lady Bracknell is a direct descendant of Ion's cradle.

> When the suffering involves those who are near and dear to one another, when for example brother kills brother, son father, mother son, or son mother, or if such a deed is contemplated, or something else of the kind is actually done, then we have a situation of the kind to be aimed at.
>
> Aristotle, *Poetics*, tr. T. S. Dorsch

It is interesting how many elements of this tragic recipe are present, though transmuted. Ion tries to kill Creusa as Orestes did his mother; Creusa tries to kill Ion as Medea did her sons. And the play has a striking number of things in common with Sophocles' *Oedipus*. In both there is a mother who abandoned her child and thinks he's dead; in both Apollo's oracle has an important part to play; in both the hero fears his unknown mother may be a slave. Oedipus kills his father Laius after a misunderstanding; Ion has a misunderstanding with his supposed father Xuthus and draws his bow on him. But Ion, unlike Oedipus, stays his hand. Sophocles' play is about the limitations of human power, while that of Euripides is a celebration of human resilience. Oedipus' recognition of the truth about himself leads him to despair; Ion's discovery of who he is leads to a happy ending.

If Sophocles could be said to be the first to have uncovered the grand outlines of the human psyche – the male child's rivalry with the father and love for the mother, paralleled by the daughter's love of her father and fraught relations with her mother – it was left to Euripides to write the world's first case history. In this sense the line of descent from *Ion* includes plays such as *Rosmersholm*, *Hedda Gabler* and *Little Eyolf*.

Ion has a special note of yearning which sounds throughout the play. Here is Creusa regretting that she gave up her child.

I am cheated of home, cheated of children,
Hopes are gone which I could not achieve.
　　tr. R. F. Willetts

Ion finds his supposed father but is full of regrets for the mother he has never known.

Mother. Where are you? My longing
to find you, to see you is greater
than ever, more powerful. Wherever
you are. Wherever you've got to.
My arms ache to hold you.
　　tr. David Lan

It is left to the chorus to celebrate the joys of family life – ironically enough, for they are slaves, and their children can be taken from them at any time and sold.

For myself I would choose, rather than wealth
Or place of kings, to rear
And love my own children.
　　tr. R. F. Willetts

In this same period Euripides wrote another 'case history' play, *Phaethon*, which is also about a family entanglement and a young man uncertain of his paternity. Phaethon's worries are brought to a head by the prospect of marriage. How can he marry when he doesn't know who he is? At his mother's suggestion he goes to find his true father Helios (the Sun). Helios has said that he will acknowledge his son by granting him a wish. Phaethon asks to drive the Sun god's chariot, fails to control the horses and is destroyed by a thunderbolt. His search for identity ends in death.

Phaethon at least has a mother and a stepfather, though he is destroyed by the secrets in his past. Ion literally knows nothing about who he is: he has no parents, no family, not even a name until Xuthus gives him one. Creusa is also uncertain of her identity. She was a mother once – but what is she now? In her first scene she refers to her child's conception as having happened to 'a friend'. Xuthus thinks he is not a father, discovers to his delight that he is one after all and goes on believing it, although Creusa and the audience know he's been deceived. Even Apollo doesn't have things entirely his own way. His plan, announced by Hermes in the prologue, is to get Ion safely installed in Athens before he tells Creusa what he's done. This scheme is first derailed by the chorus and then called into jeopardy by Creusa's furious reaction. Only the intervention of the High Priestess gets things moving in the right direction once again; in the end it is Creusa's courage in leaving the altar and taking her life in her hands which saves the day. Apollo is not just fallible, he is wilfully obscurantist. Ion warns Creusa that it is pointless to press the oracle for answers about the rape.

> No one will give this oracle to you.
> Convicted of evil here inside his own temple,
> Apollo would justly take vengeance on
> His prophet. Think no more of it; avoid
> A question which the god himself opposes.
>   tr. R. F. Willetts

At the play's climax Ion is led to challenge the god directly.

> Don't you see? If the gods lie
> how can we ever know the truth?
> I have to hear from his own mouth
> whose son I am.
>   tr. David Lan

Ion's father never gives a straight answer because Athena arrives to tie up the story.

Solon, the great Athenian lawgiver, used to refer to Athens as 'the eldest land of Ionia' and there is a sense in which the play presents an Athenian foundation myth. But *Ion* is about confusion. It would be hard to base an ideology of blood and soil on a story whose essence is uncertainty; and Euripides is careful to give the immigrant Xuthus a place of honour in the final settlement.

∾ Translations

The Chicago version by R. F. Willetts is reliable as ever, giving a sense of how the Greek moves in clear modern English. There are two recent versions – a good one by Kenneth McLeish and an outstanding one by David Lan, both published by Methuen. The poet HD, who was a patient of Freud's, made a translation in 1937 which is still worth looking at. The Penguin functions as a painstaking literal but can hardly be read with any pleasure.

∾ In performance

Ion was first performed c.413/12 BC. Recent productions have included the RSC and the Actors' Touring Company (both 1994) and the Gate Theatre (2002). There is an opera by Param Vir (2003).

Helen (*Helene*)

∾ The legend

Paris was the son of King Priam of Troy and Queen Hecuba. Three goddesses, Aphrodite, Hera and Athene, asked him to judge which of them was the most beautiful. Each goddess promised him a different reward. Hera promised him power, Athene promised him wisdom and Aphrodite promised him the love of the most beautiful woman in the world, who was Helen, wife of Menelaus king of Sparta. Paris judged in Aphrodite's favour. He sailed to Sparta and stole Menelaus' wife away from him. The Greeks sent an expedition to reclaim her and so the Trojan War began.

But Hera did not give in easily and was unwilling to see her rival victorious. She made a cloud that had the shape of Helen and this was what Paris took with him to Troy. The real Helen was spirited away by Hermes and set down at the court of Proteus, king of Egypt. In all the years when the Greeks and Trojans were slaughtering each other for the sake of a phantom, the real Helen was living quietly in exile.

This version of the legend was not traditional but seems to have been put together by Euripides from a variety of different sources.

∿ The story

It is seventeen years since the Trojan War began and Helen is still stranded in her Egyptian exile. King Proteus has died and his son Theoclymenus has come to the throne. Theoclymenus wants to marry Helen and has decreed that any Greeks who land in his kingdom are to be put to death in case they try to rescue her.

A Greek warrior cast up on the shore brings Helen news from home. She learns that her mother committed suicide out of shame at her behaviour, that Troy has fallen and, worst of all, that her husband Menelaus has been lost at sea. This means that she will never get home and has no choice but to marry Theoclymenus

Theoclymenus has a sister Theonoe (Mind of God) who has an infallible insight into the future. Helen goes to her to ask if it is really true that Menelaus is dead and all hope of rescue gone. Meanwhile Menelaus arrives in a desperate state, having been shipwrecked with his crew. He has left the sailors guarding the phantom Helen in a cave by the seashore and has come to look for help.

Helen recognizes the castaway as her long lost husband: Menelaus gradually realizes that the woman standing in front of him is his long lost wife. Their reunion is confirmed when one of Menelaus' sailors announces that the phantom has suddenly dissolved into thin air. Menelaus and Helen are now in deadly danger because of Theoclymenus' decree. How are they to make their escape?

Two powerful goddesses have an interest in the outcome. Aphrodite wants Helen dead so that the news of how she has been tricked will never come to light. Hera wants Helen alive so that her revenge will be clear to everyone. The final decision is left in Theonoe's hands. Helen and Menelaus plead for their lives and Theonoe agrees to keep Menelaus' presence a secret from her brother.

Helen and Menelaus make a plan. Helen promises to marry Theoclymenus but only after she has performed the funeral rites for her husband. Because he died at sea he must bury an effigy of him out of sight of land. She will need a ship and sailors to man it. Theoclymenus agrees to provide these. Once they are safely away from the coast, Menelaus' sailors overpower the Egyptian crew and set their course for home.

Theoclymenus is furious with his sister for not warning him and is determined to kill her. Castor and Polydeuces, who are Helen's brothers and share her semi-divine nature, appear high in the air to stop the murder and resolve the play.

∾ About the play

> Every man I have known has fallen in love with Gilda and woken up with me.
> Rita Hayworth

> What is honour? A word. What is that word, honour? Air.
> Shakespeare, *Henry IV, Part I*

Helen is about the most beautiful woman in the world – but her beauty doesn't seem to have done her much good. She has been living celibate, alone, in exile for seventeen years. Her mother committed suicide in shame over her supposed behaviour; her daughter has grown up without a mother and now can't find anyone to marry her. And the disaster is on a wider scale than this. The image of her beauty has led to a bloody ten years' war in which a great city has been destroyed and thousands of people have died. This image, over which men have fought so fiercely, has nothing to do with her but has led to her being hated and reviled by both sides. It is no wonder that she would like the gift of her good looks to be revoked:

HELEN: I wish that like a picture I had been rubbed out
　　and done again, made plain, without this loveliness.
　　　tr. Richmond Lattimore

Euripides liked to explore the gap between the heroic world of legend and how things were likely to have happened in reality. He exploits the difference to shocking effect in *Electra* and again in *Orestes*. In this case the solution is more radical. It's not a question of cutting a heroic figure down to size: the heroic figure never existed in the first place. The portrayal of the havoc brought about by the pursuit of an illusion and the personal grief caused to someone whose image is appropriated for political ends gives the play a very modern feel. And this is still unmistakably the same playwright who wrote *The Trojan Women* only three years before.

Countless mothers mourn a son,
and countless Trojan girls,
sisters of corpses, have shaved off their curls
in grief by swirling Skamander's side.
Greece too wails inconsolably for her Greeks;
a river of tears runs for her dead;
she has beaten her fists against her head
and scored her fingernails
in stripes across her cheeks
till the soft skin bled.
　　tr. James Michie and Colin Leach

If 'Helen of Troy' turns out to have been empty air and a whole ten years' war fought for nothing, what else might prove to be an illusion? Menelaus comes close for a minute to thinking that he has strayed into an alternate universe.

                              Can it be
there is some other man who bears the name of Zeus and
     lives
beside the banks of the Nile? There is one Zeus: in
     heaven.
And where on earth is Sparta except only there where
Eurotas' waters ripple by the lovely reeds?
Tyndareus is a famous name. There is only one.
And where is there another land called Lacedaemon
or Troy either? I do not know what to make of it.
I suppose it must be that in the great world a great many
have the same name, men named like other men, cities
like cities, women like women.

    tr. Richmond Lattimore

Some thirty years later, in Book VII of *The Republic*, Plato
was to make philosophy of such bewilderment. The famous
myth of the cave likens human perception to the situation of
men sitting with their backs to a light source, with their heads
fixed so that they can't look round, staring at the shadows of
objects thrown on to a wall in front of them.

> 'Do you think that such men would have seen anything of
>   themselves or of each other except the shadows thrown
>   by the fire on the wall of the cave opposite them?'
> 'How could they,' he said, 'if all their life they had been
>   forced to keep their heads motionless?'
> 'What would they have seen of some of the things carried
>   along the wall? Would it not be the same?'
> 'Surely.'
> 'Then if they were able to talk with one another, do you
>   not think that they would suppose what they saw to be
>   the real things?'
> 'Necessarily.'
> 'Then what if there were in their prison an echo from the
>   opposite wall? When any of those passing by spoke, do
>   you imagine that they could help thinking that the
>   voices came from the shadow passing before them?'

'No, certainly not,' he said
  tr. A. D. Lindsay

Internal evidence suggests that *Helen* is the last of three so-called 'romances' – the others being *Iphigeneia Among the Taurians* and *Ion* – which Euripides wrote in fairly quick succession around the time of the Sicilian expedition – the Athenian equivalent of Passchendaele or the Somme. *Helen* shares with *Ion* a sense of the importance of simple human decency and the feeling that, whatever the gods hold in store, resourcefulness, fellow feeling and conjugal love are important things that will endure.

At the centre of the play stands a character, Theonoe, invented by Euripides. Her name means Divine Mind but in spite of this she is a human being and Euripides makes her the pivot of the story. In *Hippolytus* the rivalry of Aphrodite and Artemis destroys three human lives. Here too there is a struggle between two goddesses: Hera wants Helen alive so that the trick she played on her rival will be obvious to all; Aphrodite wants Helen dead so that her secret will be safe for ever. But there is a difference: this time the arbiter is a human being and the outcome is happier because of it.

THEONOE: It's up to me, they've left it to me.
  If I tell my brother you're here, you're dead,
  Aphrodite wins. If I hide it, Hera wins, you live.
    tr. Kenneth McLeish

It is human agency that here has the capacity to make things right. Unlike the gods, a human being has a place in time and is situated in a web of obligations. What swings the argument is that Theonoe is Proteus' daughter and she does not want to dishonour his name. 'I have myself to think of and my father's name is not to be defiled.' Unlike the eternal present of the gods, human beings also have a future:

THEONOE: We're human:
  What we do stands for us or against us
  In the afterlife. Our bodies die,

But our souls live on:
Our essence, that never dies.
All right. I'll say nothing.
  tr. Kenneth McLeish

In keeping with the emphasis on human agency, the chorus have an unusually vivid role in the play. They are Helen's fellow Greeks but more disadvantaged and more vulnerable. She is a princess; they are slaves. She still hopes for rescue; their exile can have no end. Just as much as Theonoe they have it in their power to betray Helen and her husband to Theoclymenus. Helen promises to come back and rescue them if she escapes.

HELEN: Keep our secret safe – and one day soon
  When we're away from here we'll save you too.
    tr. Kenneth McLeish

But the effect of her flight is to put them in jeopardy. When Theoclymenus discovers Helen's plot, the chorus have to be very quick to cover themselves.

CHORUS: Menelaus here! And no one noticed, lord:
  No one noticed, not you, not us.

They also have an unusually active part to play towards the end when they intervene as individuals to stop Theoclymenus from entering the palace to murder Theonoe. This follows a novel chorus entry in *Ion* where the women are portrayed as individual tourists visiting Delphi before they coalesce into a group later in the play. In *Helen*, the final settlement saves Helen, Menelaus and Theonoe but leaves the chorus stranded. Castor is quite blunt about it.

CASTOR: Heaven never hates the noble in the end.
  It is for the nameless multitude that life is hard.
    tr. Richmond Lattimore

The priestess will keep Menelaus' identity safe but he and Helen still need to escape. The second half of the play is given over to an adventure story of the kind that Euripides had invented a few years previously in *Iphigeneia Among the Taurians*. One of Euripides' innovations in dramatic technique was the scene of extended dialogue. He first used it to great effect in *Electra* (*c.*419 BC) and then carried it to new heights of virtuosity in *Ion* (413/12 BC). This involved the creation of a new dramatic rhythm, which involved not just the clash of opposing viewpoints but something subtler – an openness, a curiosity and a developing personal exchange. This new kind of dialogue was well suited to the recognition scene, a process of slow natural discovery. But it was also good at showing two people thinking together, developing a plan, plotting in short – both preparing a plot and then carrying out the deception.

In *Helen* the recognition and the plotting are part of the same pattern. The first half of the play involves the dispelling of a divinely made illusion, carried out on a grand scale that has gripped the world for nearly two decades and brought many men to their deaths. The second half of the play involves two human beings creating with courage and ingenuity a more modest illusion, which they have to sustain just long enough to save their lives. What *Helen* shares with *Ion* is that it shows human beings engaged against all the odds in the active contrivance of happiness.

Who knows where honour lies?
Spear points, battle lines –
Will you find it there
End mortal pain?
Blood drowns out argument.
Helen, Helen for example:
They could have talked for her,
They chose to fight for her.
    tr. Kenneth McLeish

∿ Translations

The Chicago translation by Richmond Lattimore is not particularly successful, though it can usefully be consulted by anyone wanting to know how the thought moves in the original. This leaves the field clear for Kenneth McLeish's sprightly speakable version (Methuen). The Oxford translation by James Michie and Colin Leach steers a middle course.

∿ In performance

Helen was first performed in 412 BC in a trilogy with *Andromeda* and perhaps with *Ion*. It would have been linked to *Andromeda* by its African setting and by the theme of rescue and to *Ion* by its emphasis on the healing power of human agency. Despite its charm and emotional power the play has not had a rich performance history. There is an opera by Richard Strauss *Die aegyptische Helena* (1928). *Helen* was staged at the Mermaid Theatre in 1967 and elements from the play were incorporated in the Royal Shakespeare Company's *The Greeks* by John Barton and Kenneth Cavander in 1979. The most recent London production was at the National Theatre Studio in 1995. The Public Theatre New York staged the play in 2002 in a version by Ellen McLaughlin, directed by Tony Kushner.

Orestes (*Orestes*)

∿ The legend

Tantalus was the son of Zeus; when he asked to have everything the gods have he was punished by having a huge rock suspended over his head.

His son Pelops fathered two boys Atreus and Thyestes. The brothers quarrelled over the succession. Atreus found a lamb with a golden fleece among his flock and claimed the throne on the strength of it. Some say that Thyestes stole the sheep and usurped the throne, others that he committed adultery with his brother's wife. Atreus took revenge by killing Thyestes' children and serving them up to their father at a banquet.

The family misfortunes carried over into the next generation. Agamemnon, Atreus' eldest son, was forced to sacrifice his daughter Iphigeneia to secure a wind for the Greek fleet to sail to Troy. Menelaus, Atreus' younger son, was married to Helen, whose adultery caused the Trojan War.

When Agamemnon returned at the war's end he was murdered by his wife Clytemnestra. Orestes, Agamemnon's son, avenged his father by killing his mother with the help of his sister Electra.

∾ The story

Six days have passed since the killing of Clytemnestra. Orestes and Electra are imprisoned in the palace. The citizens of Argos plan to put them on trial for murder. If they are found guilty they will be stoned to death.

Orestes has been driven mad by the vengeful Furies and has fallen into an exhausted sleep, watched over by his sister. Their only hope is to throw themselves on the mercy of their uncle Menelaus, who has just landed with his soldiers on his way home from Troy. He has sent his wife Helen on ahead under cover of darkness. She is afraid of being attacked by the citizens who blame her for starting the Trojan War.

Tyndareus, Orestes' grandfather, grimly demands he pay the penalty for his crimes. Menelaus also refuses to intervene and brother and sister are condemned to execution. Rather than face the ignominy of being stoned to death Orestes and Electra decide to kill themselves.

Orestes' friend Pylades suggests that if they are to die they might as well take revenge by killing Helen. Electra comes up with a refinement of the plan: if they take Helen's daughter Hermione hostage they might even stand a chance of escaping afterwards.

Orestes and Pylades kill Helen. Menelaus arrives with his soldiers and the Argive mob is on the point of storming the palace. Orestes, Electra and Pylades appear on the roof; they threaten to kill Hermione and set fire to the building. At the last moment the god Apollo appears to resolve the action. Helen has not been killed but spirited away and turned into a star; Electra is to marry Pylades; Orestes is to marry Hermione. Menelaus is to take a new wife and go back to his home in Sparta. Apollo undertakes to make peace between Orestes and the citizens.

∽ About the play

> The plurality of independent and unmerged voices and consciousnesses and the genuine polyphony of fully val-
> ued voices . . .
>
> Mikhail Bakhtin, *Problems of Dostoevsky's Poetics*

Orestes has had a mixed reception. It was one of the most popular plays of late antiquity. It is quoted more often in the surviving sources than the works of all the other Greek trage-dians put together. Modern commentators, by contrast, have not hesitated to condemn the play in the most robust terms. It has been called febrile, outrageous, melodramatic, a vicious play full of vicious characters.

The reasons for its popularity are not far to seek. *Orestes* is a virtuoso piece of playwriting – a gripping and suspenseful narrative full of memorable characters. It was written almost twenty years after Euripides, in his *Electra*, had invented the modern dialogue scene. Sophocles and Aeschylus typically kept their dialogue exchanges short – about ten or fifteen lines on average. Euripides expanded this to five times the length and so opened up a whole new set of dramatic possi-bilities. This invention, which he refined and extended in *Ion*, *Iphigeneia Among the Taurians* and *Helen*, enabled him to chart the psychological development of his characters in more realistic detail and to create passages of mounting excitement and sustained suspense in ways that had not been done before.

A superb example of this is the scene between Pylades and Orestes as they nerve themselves to face the Argive assembly.

ORESTES: Let's go then. Not die like dogs.
PYLADES: Well said.
ORESTES: Shall we tell Electra?
PYLADES: Good God, no.
ORESTES: She'd cry.
PYLADES: Bad luck for certain.
ORESTES: There's just one thing –
PYLADES: What?
ORESTES: If the goddesses come . . . another fit . . .
PYLADES: I'll see to you.
ORESTES: It's horrible.
PYLADES: I'll do it.
ORESTES: You could catch . . . what I've got.
PYLADES: For heaven's sake!
ORESTES: You don't mind?
PYLADES: I'm supposed to be your friend.
ORESTES: All right, let's go.
    tr. Kenneth McLeish

Exciting as this is, it is capped by the conspiracy scene in which the two young men plot to get their revenge on Menelaus by killing his wife.

PYLADES: Well then. Break Menelaus' heart. Kill Helen –
ORESTES: How? I'm ready, eager – but how?
PYLADES: Cut her throat. Is she there inside?
ORESTES: She's making lists – of my father's treasures.
PYLADES: Not any more. She has a date, in hell.
ORESTES: But how? She has servants. Trojans.
PYLADES: Foreign riffraff? They don't scare me.
ORESTES: Mirror-bearers, perfume-dabbers –
PYLADES: She's brought them with her?
ORESTES: She finds us Greeks 'provincial'.

PYLADES: They're slaves. Won't fight free men.

ORESTES: If we bring this off, they can kill me twice.

PYLADES: If I die at your side, they can kill me too.

ORESTES: How shall we do it?

    tr. Kenneth McLeish

Orestes and Pylades plan to kill Helen and set fire to the palace but Electra has a better idea. If they take Helen's daughter hostage there may be a chance they can escape alive.

ELEKTRA: Orestes, I know a way: to kill and to escape alive.

    You, me, Pylades, all three of us.

ORESTES: God's helping us, you mean? Or what?

    You've got some plan, some cunning plan?

ELEKTRA: Listen. Pylades, you too.

ORESTES: Tell me. Good news to make me smile.

ELEKTRA: You know she has a daughter?

    Of course you do.

ORESTES: Hermione, yes.

    Our mother brought her up.

ELEKTRA: She's gone to our mother's grave.

ORESTES: What for? What's that to us?

ELEKTRA: When she comes back, grab her. Hostage.

ORESTES: I still don't understand.

ELEKTRA: When Helen's dead, if Menelaos tries anything –

    Against you, me, Pylades, any of us –

    Tell him we'll kill Hermione.

    Hold your knife to her throat.

    tr. Kenneth McLeish

There are few passages in Greek tragedy to rival this for cumulative excitement. The scene develops from despair through vindictiveness to hope and a giddy (and perhaps illusory) feeling that it might be possible to escape scot-free. The writing is remarkable for the sharpness of its psychological insight. We see virtues corrupted by their context. The tenderness Electra and Orestes feel for each other, the loyalty of Pylades, are twisted into something cruel and very dangerous

– and we can observe the process as it happens, step by step. In the opening speech of the play Electra evokes the crimes of her ancestors with a sort of bewilderment that such terrible things could happen. Here we have demonstrated for us how such things come about, and it is Euripides' invention of this new supple dialogue that makes the demonstration possible.

It is this sense of movement that makes *Orestes* so unsettling: the characters don't stay the same. The exhausted tenderness of Orestes and Electra in the opening scene renders them intensely sympathetic:

ELEKTRA: How happy it made me to see you fall asleep
    at last.
    Should I raise your head, dear?
ORESTES: Yes, please. Help me up.
                          Now wipe away
    this crust of froth from around my mouth and eyes.
ELEKTRA: This service is sweet and I do it gladly,
    nursing my brother with a sister's love.
ORESTES: Sit here
    beside me. Now brush this matted hair
    from my eyes so I can see . . .
      tr. William Arrowsmith

The frailty of brother and sister is contrasted with the horrible confidence of the other characters. Helen is a wonderful portrait of an ageing sex-goddess, done with the lightest of touches. The first thing she asks her dishevelled and exhausted niece is why she hasn't got a husband yet. Helen can't imagine life without a man. And how nervously she approaches the matricides: 'They say you can't pollute me. Apollo was at fault.' When she's required to cut a lock of hair to lay on her sister's grave, she just trims the ends a bit – something Electra is very quick to notice. 'Still the same old Helen.' She has dynastic ambitions too. She and her husband will inherit the kingdom on Orestes' death – a fact that is not lost on him. 'She's putting seals on everything we own.'

Helen's father Tyndareus is scarcely more engaging.

TYNDAREUS: Is *he* here?
If I had known that he was here,
I would never have come. Look at him,
Menelaus: the man who murdered his mother,
coiled like a snake at the door, those sick eyes
glowing like coals –

                What a loathsome sight.
How can you bear to speak to a *thing* like this?

    tr. William Arrowsmith

Tyndareus' Spartan bluntness is contrasted with Menelaus'
politic shiftiness.

MENELAUS: Believe me, Orestes
I sympathize from the bottom of my heart.
And nothing in the world would please me more
than to honor that touching appeal for help.
We are joined, besides, by a common bond of blood,
and I am honor bound to come to your defense
against your enemies even at the cost
of my life – obliged in short to do everything
it lies in my power to do.

                    God knows
I only wish I could.

    tr. William Arrowsmith

Menelaus has a lot at stake. If he plays his cards right he
will be the next king of Argos. His interrogation of Orestes,
though kind-seeming, draws out every detail of his nephew's
weakness. His first entry is a brilliant effect. Triumphant,
healthy, surrounded by his soldiers, he is a sharp contrast to
the haggard, defenceless and half-mad Orestes. His vitality
has something sinister about it and it's clear that a man like
him will always side with the powerful against the weak. But
Euripides gives him at the last the genuine accent of helplessness. Orestes has his sword at Hermione's throat and Pylades
has the torch ready to set the palace on fire. 'You've got me,'
Menelaus says simply, confessing defeat.

It is this shifting sympathy that accounts for the play's bad press. The characters simply won't stay still. Euripides first makes us identify with Orestes and Electra, then, in what feels like a betrayal, he begins to push the characters away and distance them. Brother and sister, driven by despair, become steadily more monstrous. It's an uncomfortable process: as with the 'polyphonic' narratives of Dostoevsky, the spectators are denied any standpoint from which they can judge the action. *The Bacchae* presents a similar reversal – only this time it works the other way round. Pentheus begins the play wholly unsympathetic, yet, by the end, the punishment meted out to him has been so extreme that it is difficult not to feel sorry for him.

'Having taken an event, I tried only to clarify its probability in our society' (Fyodor Dostoevsky). The action of *Orestes* is made more immediate by its contemporary setting. Aeschylus' *Oresteia* shows how the murder of Clytemnestra sets in train a process which leads directly from the world of blood feud to the establishment of the rule of law. In Euripides' play the rule of law is seen as having been established long ago. Orestes is persecuted by the Furies as tradition demands, but the immediate danger comes from the citizens of Argos. It is their patrols that roam the streets making it impossible for him to escape. They plan to put him on trial for matricide. He is free to plead his case but if he is found guilty he will be stoned to death. It is possible to see here echoes of the oligarchic coup that had taken place at Athens three years before the play was written: when democracy was restored many desperate young aristocrats must have gone in fear of their lives. The messenger speech gives a memorable account of the assembly debating the issue.

The appearance of Apollo at the end of the play has come in for a good deal of criticism. Some commentators have suggested that his intervention is supposed to be comic or satirical. But Euripides' treatment of the gods is unabashedly Homeric in its acknowledgement of their capriciousness. His deities do not possess the moral grandeur they have in

Aeschylus or the inscrutability they have in Sophocles. They relate to an older tradition, stemming from *The Iliad*, where the gods appear simply as human beings writ large, with all their selfishness and unpredictability. To imagine that such a thrilling narrative as *Orestes* could end simply in a joke is to mistake the whole nature of Euripides' bravura.

Orestes is the one Greek tragedy for which a fragment of the music survives. We don't know whether this fragment was composed for the original production or whether it was written for a later revival , but either way it is an important reminder of a lost dimension. Euripides was continually on the lookout for ways to make his writing more expressive and he made more – and more inventive – use of music as his career progressed. In this play Electra is an important singing role and in an extraordinary coup de théâtre the messenger speech is not spoken but sung – a brilliant stroke which increases the feeling of hysteria and the sense of things running out of control.

∼ Translations

There are three fine translations – by William Arrowsmith (Chicago), Kenneth McLeish (Methuen), and John Peck and Frank Nisetich (Oxford). The Arrowsmith is good for reading but the McLeish is probably best for performing. The edition of M. L. West (Aris and Philips) comes complete with a literal.

∼ In performance

The first performance was in 408 BC. We know there was a revival in 341 BC and the play was enormously popular in late antiquity. It fell out of favour after the Renaissance and, despite a spirited defence by the great nineteenth-century scholar Jacob Burckhardt, remains one of Euripides' least regarded works. It was staged at the Mermaid Theatre in 1966 and at Gate Theatre London in 1995.

The Phoenician Women (*Phoinissai*)

∾ The legend

Cadmus came to Greece from Tyre on the Phoenician coast. Guided by Apollo, he arrived at the site where the city of Thebes was to be built and killed the dragon that was living there.

Athena told him to sow the teeth of the dead dragon in the ground and when he did so a race of armed men sprang up. Cadmus threw a stone into their midst and the men began to fight each other. They continued until there were only five of them left and the earth was soaked with blood. On this spot Cadmus and the five survivors, known as the Spartoi or Sown Men, proceeded to build the city of Thebes.

The manner of its founding haunted the city. Cadmus had Apollo and Athena on his side but he had angered the goddess Earth and Ares, god of war, whose dragon he had killed.

Cadmus had a grandson called Laius. Apollo told Laius that if he had a male child, that son would kill him. When his wife gave birth, the boy was exposed and left for dead.

A shepherd rescued the child, whose name was Oedipus. When he was grown to manhood Oedipus met his father on the road. The older man was in his chariot, arrogant: the younger man would not give way. The two men fought and Laius was killed.

An earth-born monster, the Sphinx, was ravaging the countryside round Thebes. It was proclaimed that whoever destroyed the monster would become king and marry the widow of King Laius, Queen Jocasta. Oedipus travelled to Thebes and overcame the Sphinx. He married his mother and became king of the city. The marriage produced four children – two boys, Eteocles and Polyneices and two girls, Antigone and Ismene.

When Oedipus learned the truth he put out his eyes. His two sons, fearing a public scandal, imprisoned their father in the palace and were cursed by him for doing so.

∾ The story

Eteocles and Polyneices, the two sons of Oedipus, made a pact to take it in turns to govern the city of Thebes. They were afraid that if they both stayed at home they would quarrel and kill one another.

Eteocles had first turn but when it came time to hand over the kingdom he changed his mind. Polyneices, who in the meantime had married the daughter of the king of Argos, came with an army to claim his share and laid siege to the city. Jocasta arranged a truce and tried to reconcile her sons but Eteocles refused to give way.

Polyneices and his army attack the city walls. The defenders consult the prophet Teiresias to see if he can advise them. Teiresias prophesies that if Creon, Oedipus' uncle, sacrifices his son Menoeceus, Thebes will be saved. Creon decides to put family before fatherland and spare the boy. Menoeceus overhears Teiresias' prediction. He considers it shameful to live, if by dying he could save the city, and commits suicide by jumping off the battlements.

With Menoeceus dead, the Argive armies fail in their attack. Polyneices and Eteocles arrange to fight each other in single combat. Both are killed and Jocasta commits suicide over their bodies. The blind Oedipus emerges from the palace and lays his hands on the corpses of his sons, who have been destroyed by his curse. His daughter Antigone leads him into exile. Creon, the sole survivor of the ruling house, is left to govern the city. He decrees that Polyneices should be denied burial for the crime of having brought a foreign army to attack his country.

∾ About the play

The flogged warriors on the battlefields, the tortured nations, were the victims of quarrelsome, selfish, self-righteous and completely hopeless thinkers, unable to get clarity into their poor warped brains and incapable,

furthermore, of understanding, or of getting along with
one another.

Wolfgang Koeppen *The Hothouse*, tr. Michael Hofmann

Anyone familiar with the works of Shakespeare or the 'epic'
plays of Bertholt Brecht will feel instantly at home with *The
Phoenician Women*. Not only is it one of the longest of the surviving tragedies, it also has a larger number of principal characters and a more complex and wide-ranging action than any
other Greek play. It is a portrait not of a single figure like
Oedipus or Electra but of a general condition. Its themes are
blindness and mutual slaughter.

The story of the two fratricidal brothers was a well-known
one: Aeschylus had dealt with it in his *Seven Against Thebes*
and Sophocles in his *Antigone*. Euripides gives the story a new
and darker inflection. Here is Thucydides describing some of
the changes that took place in Greek society as the
Peloponnesian war dragged on:

> To fit in with the change of events, words, too, had to
> change their usual meanings. What used to be described
> as a thoughtless act of aggression was now regarded as the
> courage one would expect to find in a party member; to
> think of the future and wait was merely another way of
> saying one was a coward; any attempt at moderation was
> an attempt to disguise one's unmanly character; ability to
> understand a question from all sides meant that one was
> totally unfitted for action. Fanatical enthusiasm was the
> mark of a real man, and to plot against an enemy behind
> his back was perfectly legitimate self-defence. Anyone
> who held violent opinions could always be trusted, and
> anyone who objected to them became suspect. To plot
> successfully was a sign of intelligence, but it was still
> cleverer to see that a plot was hatching . . . It was equally
> praiseworthy to get one's blow in first against someone
> who was going to do wrong, and to denounce someone
> who had no intention of doing any wrong at all.

Thucydides Book 3.82, tr. Rex Warner

This evokes, better than any commentary, the particular climate of the play.

Early in his career Euripides had developed a special feeling for the power of the irrational, for sudden surges of passion that erupted seemingly out of nowhere; so when Athenian society began tearing itself apart under the stress of a long war, or when the oligarchic putsch of 411 BC briefly ran its course, he was well placed to understand and describe the passionate and blinkered selfishness that suddenly came to the fore. Each of the characters in *The Phoenician Women* is in the grip of a delusion or thinks that the rules which govern other people somehow don't apply to them. Eteocles imagines that he is a great commander when he is nothing of the kind. Polyneices thinks that the justice of his cause will do all the work for him and doesn't see that the Thebans may not take kindly to being invaded by a foreign army. Creon is given a prophecy about what needs to be done to save the city but since it involves the life of his son keeps it to himself and hopes that everything will come out all right. Jocasta thinks that despite their father's curse and their own bitter rivalry she nonetheless has the power to reconcile her sons. And omnipresent but unseen is the deposed king Oedipus, hidden in the palace, physically sightless as the others are morally blind.

The only characters who are not part of this pattern are the very young – Menoeceus and Antigone. Menoeceus knows that he must die to save the city and acts directly and unselfishly on this knowledge. Antigone is fierce in defence of her father and her dead brother. Her power may be slight but she is direct enough in wielding it.

ANTIGONE: Do you think I would live to marry your son?
CREON: You must. What else can you do? Where will you go?
ANTIGONE: If you force me to it, I'll kill him.
CREON: Do you hear that, Oedipus? She'll say anything. She shames us all.
ANTIGONE: I swear it. By this sword of my brother's, I swear it.

Euripides at various times in his career wrote other plays based on the Theban legend – a *Cadmus*, an *Antigone* and an *Oedipus*, none of which have come down to us, except in fragments. *The Phoenician Women* introduces several new twists to the familiar story. First, there is the survival of Jocasta, who does not, as in Sophocles, hang herself when the truth about her incestuous relationship is revealed, but lives on to witness the death of her sons. Then there is Oedipus: instead of banishing him from the city his sons have attempted to conceal his crime by keeping him perpetually sealed inside the palace. Oedipus remains unseen for most of the play but the palace walls which form a backdrop to the action are a continual reminder of the blind criminal concealed inside. As Teiresias points out, Thebes is being polluted by his presence. Lastly, there is the sacrifice of Menoeceus, which seems to be a wholly Euripidean invention. His death occurs halfway through the play and marks a turning point in the action. It brings about a separation between the fate of the city, which is saved, and the fate of its ruling class, which continues working out its ruin.

The play presents a brilliant portrait of the two warring brothers. Polyneices (the name means Very Quarrelsome) is shown as the more attractive of the two; he loves his sister, is fond of his mother, respects the gods and is willing to compromise – up to a point. Here he is talking to Jocasta about the pains of exile:

JOCASTA: Is it a great evil to be exiled from your homeland?
POLYNEICES: The greatest of all evils. Worse in fact than people say it is.
JOCASTA: What about it is so hard to bear?
POLYNEICES: The worst thing is you can't speak freely.
JOCASTA: That's the mark of a slave, to have to watch your mouth.
POLYNEICES: And you have to put up with the ignorance of the powerful.
JOCASTA: Colluding in stupidity – that must be difficult.

The dialogue here cuts both ways. While Jocasta is trying to remind her son how much his country means to him she is also reminding him how much he hates the humiliations of exile and would do anything to avoid them.

JOCASTA: How did you live before you were married?
POLYNEICES: Some days I had food and some days I didn't.
JOCASTA: Your father's friends, couldn't they help you?
POLYNEICES: You need good fortune. If you don't have it,
    then you have no friends.

Because Euripides is interested in politics, he's also interested in class (not just here, with Polyneices' loss of status, but also in *Electra*, where a princess is married to a commoner), and money (Helen putting her seal on the palace property in *Orestes*). For Polyneices money and the power to lead an independent life are inseparable, so that for all his willingness to compromise there is a point beyond which he will not yield.

Money is the most valuable thing of all.
It's what people respect.
That's why I've come here with ten thousand soldiers.
A well-born man is nothing if he's impoverished.

Eteocles' reply is even more chilling.

I would travel to the place where the stars of heaven arise
Or underneath the earth if I could do
One thing – seize power – the greatest of all gods.
This is the prize, mother. I will not give it up
To someone else when I could keep it for myself.
It would be unmanly to let the better go
And settle for the worse . . . If one must do wrong,
It's best to do it for the sake of power.

It's no wonder that this naked defence of might so impressed one Nazi critic that he took Eteocles for the hero of the play. The use of language here links Eteocles with those clever young men who used the teachings of the Sophists to justify their selfishness and aggression. Part of the pose is an affectation of moral relativism. When Polyneices reasonably points out that there was a pact which his brother has violated, Eteocles dismisses his claim by arguing that there can be no such thing as an agreed morality.

> If everyone meant the same thing when they
> Call things hurtful or useful there would be
> No argument. But fairness or equality
> Are only words: reality is something else.

The point to which the action is heading is the mutual slaughter of Eteocles and Polyneices but Euripides makes the journey as complicated as possible. The play's length allows room for the characters to develop over time. Antigone who begins as a timid young girl is transformed into someone willing to kill to get her way. Creon, who seems so sensible when set against Eteocles, proves sadly wanting when he is personally affected. Despite his appearance of gravitas he is prepared to sacrifice the city to save his son. There is room too for gestures that lodge in the memory: Jocasta's little dance of joy at the sight of Polyneices; Oedipus bending down to touch the bodies of his dead sons so that he can 'see' them; Antigone stretching out her hand to lead her father into exile.

Who are the Phoenician women and what are they doing in the play? Like Cadmus they have come to Thebes from Tyre. They are young women on their way to Delphi, where they are to become temple servants to Apollo. The outbreak of war has trapped them in the city, so that they both belong and don't belong. In Aeschylus' *Seven Against Thebes*, which deals with the same story, the chorus were native Thebans and much of the action is driven by their panic fear of what might happen to them if the city falls. Euripides' chorus are more detached (whatever the outcome they are safe) but because of their connection with Cadmus they know the city's history and are one of the ways the past is kept present in the action.

Euripides uses a wide array of verse forms to pace the narrative and drive it forward on a mounting rhythmic wave.

He is continually searching for maximum expressiveness through the pursuit of musical and metrical variety. It is not always apparent in modern translation or performance that the last quarter of the play resembles that miracle of dramatic pacing that is the finale to Act 2 of *The Marriage of Figaro*, where the developing flow of incident and emotion is borne along by a series of different metres that both carry and create the action. This is not as surprising as it might seem, since the invention of opera at the Renaissance was an attempt to reach back and recreate something of the lost musical and dramatic whole that was Greek tragic drama.

∾ Translations

The two most readily available versions, Elizabeth Wyckoff (Chicago) and David Thompson (Methuen), are both beginning to show their age, though the latter formed the basis for a very successful recent production at the RSC. The 1981 Oxford version by Peter Burian and Brian Swann is worth looking at, if only because it manages to give a good account of the play's rhythmic variety. Anyone contemplating a production should consult the magisterial edition by Donald J. Mastronarde (Cambridge).

∾ In performance

The play was first performed sometime between 412 and 409 BC. Like *Orestes*, it was especially popular with audiences in late antiquity. Seneca left a version unfinished at his death. *La Thébaïde* (1664) is Racine's treatment of the story. In modern times it was performed at Greenwich Theatre in 1977 under the title *The Children of Oedipus*, and by the Royal Shakespeare Company in 1994.

Iphigeneia in Aulis (*Iphigeneia epi Aulide*)

∿ The legend

Tyndareus, King of Sparta, and his wife Leda had three daughters. The youngest of them, Helen, was the most beautiful woman in the world. Tyndareus made her suitors swear an oath that they would all rally to defend the man who eventually married her. That man was Menelaus, and when Paris came from Troy and seduced his wife, the Greek princes, faithful to their oath, formed a mighty expedition to cross the sea and bring her home.

The Trojan side of the story goes as follows. Paris was the son of Priam, King of Troy. One day three goddesses appeared before him naked and asked him to judge which of them was the most beautiful. They were Hera (Power), Athene (Wisdom) and Aphrodite (Love). Hera promised she would make him a great king. Athene promised that she would make him wise. Aphrodite promised him the love of the most beautiful woman in the world. Paris gave the prize to Aphrodite and his reward was Helen, Menelaus' wife.

∿ The story

The Greek expeditionary force is becalmed at Aulis. The prophet Calchas tells Agamemnon, the commander in chief, that he must sacrifice his daughter Iphigeneia to secure a wind. Without the sacrifice the fleet will stay becalmed and Troy will not fall.

Agamemnon sends for his daughter on the pretext that she is to be married to Achilles. Then he changes his mind and tries to stop her coming – but it is already too late. Iphigeneia and her mother Clytemnestra arrive to find the proposed marriage is a sham. Agamemnon is too terrified to back down. He fears that if he refuses to go through with the

sacrifice the army will turn on him. Achilles, when he understands the full truth of the situation, offers to defend
Iphigeneia with his life. She decides to accept her fate and
offers her life so that the fleet can sail.

Aulis is a city on the coast of Greece opposite the island of
Euboea, at the very northern end of the channel that separates it from the mainland. It is famous for the fickleness of
the winds.

ᴄᴜ About the play

She was certain that the Vicario brothers were not as
anxious to fulfil the sentence as to find someone who
would do them the favour of stopping them.
  Gabriel Garcia Márquez, *Chronicle of a Death Foretold*

Oh call back yesterday, bid time return . . .
  Shakespeare, *Richard II*, Act III, Scene 2

This is another of Euripides' gripping late-period narratives.
The action begins – like so many Greek tragedies – before
dawn. Agamemnon is sitting outside his tent drafting and
redrafting the letter that will stop his daughter on the road.
The scene is full of atmosphere – the stars, the sea, the sen-
tries on the fort, the lamp, the table with its writing materials.
The story will end badly because we know that the fleet sailed
and the Trojan War took place but right from the outset
Agamemnon is trying to prevent what is about to happen.

The letter is despatched and it seems – for the first time in
the play though not the last – that the catastrophe will be
averted. But Menelaus intercepts the letter and accuses his
brother of irresponsibility. He threatens to tell the army what
Agamemnon has been planning.

MENELAUS: Do you see this letter? It was meant
    to betray all of us.
AGAMEMNON: That letter – in the first place
    give it back to me.

MENELAUS: Not until I have told the Greeks what it says.

AGAMEMNON: You mean you broke the seal. So you know
    what you have no business knowing.

MENELAUS: Yes, I broke the seal. And it's you
   who will suffer as a result, for acting
   behind our backs.

    tr. W. S. Merwin and George E. Dimock, Jr

Agamemnon claims the right to change his mind.

AGAMEMNON: If yesterday
   I was without wit or wisdom but today
   Have counselled with myself well and wisely –
   Does that make me mad?
               I will not kill my children.

    tr. Charles R. Walker

While the two brothers debate, Iphigeneia arrives in the
camp, accompanied by her mother Clytemnestra, and this
arrival changes everything. The presence of the girl alters the
situation making it both more urgent and harder to unravel.
Confronted with the reality of murder, Menelaus suddenly
relents.

MENELAUS: All the words spoken I now withdraw and
   From them I retreat. I stand in your place
   And beseech you do not slay the child.
   It is against all justice that you should
   Groan from the same cause that makes me
   Fortunate or that your daughter die while
   All my children live and face the sun.

    tr. Charles R. Walker

Now it's Agamemnon's turn to be in difficulty. One obstacle
has been removed: Menelaus is longer threatening to expose
him; but he remains afraid of what the army might do under
the influence of a demagogue like Odysseus.

AGAMEMNON: He'll stand up in front
   Of the whole army, and explain every detail

Of Calchas' prophecy, line by line!
He'll tell them I promised to go along with it
And make the sacrifice, and then retracted
My promise. With that sort of speech
In our situation, he could stage a coup,
Take command of the army, and have us both killed,
As well as the girl.

    tr. Don Taylor

We are now one third of the way through the play and the trap has closed. As the second movement of the action begins, the focus shifts to Clytemnestra and Iphigeneia. The playwright invites the audience to watch the process of betrayal step by step. When we think of Euripides' female characters, we think first of those who, like Medea, Phaedra, Hecuba, Electra, stand outside the norms of everyday life – so it's particularly interesting in this play to see women acting in conformity with male expectations.

Clytemnestra's first entrance in her carriage, surrounded by her attendants, is carefully contrived to alter the play's atmosphere. She is shown first with the baby Orestes in her arms, emphasizing her fertility, her femininity and her continued sex life with her husband – so unlike the usual portrait of the hard-faced adulteress who welcomes her Agamemnon on his return from Troy. She has come from Argos bringing her daughter to be married but is still ignorant of the bridegroom's name and parentage. She receives her husband's instructions obediently.

CLYTEMNESTRA: And where do *I* make the women's feast?
AGAMEMNON: Here, by these proud sterns of our ships.
CLYTEMNESTRA: By the anchors and hawsers? Well,
  May good fortune come of it?
AGAMEMNON: My lady
  This you must do – Obey!
CLYTEMNESTRA: That is no revelation –
  I am accustomed to it.

    tr. Charles R. Walker

But when Agamemnon tries to send her home before the wedding on the pretext of looking after her other daughters, that is where she draws the line. Men and women exist in separate spheres. Agamemnon is lord in his but just as surely Clytemnestra is sovereign in hers.

AGAMEMNON: Before the Greek army . . . I shall give away
my daughter.
CLYTEMNESTRA: And where, pray, shall I be, while all this is
going on?
AGAMEMNON: Back in Argos. Looking after your other girls.
CLYTEMNESTRA: Leaving my daughter? I must light her
wedding torches . . .
AGAMEMNON: I shall light the flames myself . . . for the
marriage, I mean . . .
CLYTEMNESTRA: That's unheard of, an outrage to all
decency.
tr. Don Taylor

There follows a celebrated scene which dramatizes the division of realms. Achilles arrives at Agamemnon's tent to speak to the commander in chief. He has no idea that he is supposed to be Iphigeneia's bridegroom and has been made the pretext for bringing her to Aulis. Clytemnestra comes out and seeks to congratulate him on his forthcoming marriage. He cannot understand what she is talking about and starts to think she has gone mad. This is brilliantly done. The shock of the young man left unchaperoned with a married woman, and his confusion when she treats him in a familiar way, underline the powerful charge surrounding relations between the sexes and how women are simultaneously disregarded and made important. It is this rigid gender division that makes Agamemnon's deception possible and the scene slides from what is almost a comedy of manners – almost, but not quite; the encounter has an edge that is altogether too disquieting – to horror and outrage, as Achilles and the Queen work out at last how they have been used.

Aeschylus and Sophocles both wrote plays about the story

of Iphigeneia and in the Sophocles Odysseus the intriguer played a major role. Whatever these plays may have been like, we can be certain that Euripides' *Iphigeneia in Aulis* was very different. Like *The Phoenician Women*, Euripides' play has a large number of principal parts – Menelaus, Agamemnon, Clytemnestra, Achilles and Iphigeneia. It is a portrait of a group, where competing egoisms mesh together to create an atrocity. Euripides is interested in the process which goes into making such an event. As his career developed he became steadily more adept at dramatizing change, showing people at the actual moment of making up their minds, pulled this way and that by conflicting demands. Already his early plays *Medea* and *Hippolytus* take us into the mind of characters who are having second thoughts, and it is fitting that his last work should contain the fullest exploration of this theme. The whole of *Iphigeneia in Aulis* is about attempting to retrieve a situation that is running dangerously out of control.

Iphigeneia is a delightful and affecting character. Those historians who theorize that there was no such thing as the loving nuclear family before the early modern period are plainly not familiar with Greek tragedy. At her first appearance, she runs impulsively into her father's arms.

IPHIGENEIA: But I must be first, Father, to hold you
In my arms after so long, just to look at you.
I've missed you so much! Mother, don't be angry!
CLYTEMNESTRA: No. This is just as it should be. Of all
My children, you've always loved your father most.
IPHIGENEIA: I'm so happy, Father, it's been such a long
time . . .
tr. Don Taylor

The scene where she realizes her father's true intentions is one of those moments that led Aristotle to call Euripides 'the most tragic of poets'.

IPHIGENEIA: O Father,

My body is a suppliant's, tight clinging
To your knees. Do not take away this life
Of mine before its dying time. Nor make me
Go down under the earth to see the world
Of darkness, for it is sweet to look on
The day's light.
I was the first to call you father,
You to call me child. And of your children
First to sit upon your knees . . .

tr. Charles R. Walker

In the end it is Iphigeneia who resolves the impasse at which the situation has arrived. On the one hand there is the implacable demand of the army for the sacrifice and a fair wind; on the other is Achilles' offer to die for her, her father's anguish and the collapse of the expedition. Iphigeneia cuts through the tangle by deciding freely to offer herself to the slaughter. Aeschylus in *Agamemnon* offers a gruesome picture of Iphigeneia dragged struggling by armed men to the altar. Euripides makes the drama of sacrifice into a story about self-sacrifice, Iphigeneia's sudden change of heart provoking Aristotle to cite the character as an example of inconsistency. But then Aristotle with his philosopher's liking for the plausible was not best placed to understand Euripides, a dramatist who always valued surprise and the unexpected. Iphigeneia is not the first Euripidean heroine to offer herself up to death – there is also famously Alcestis, and Macaria in *The Children of Heracles* and Polyxena in *Hecuba*. In *The Phoenician Women* it is Creon's son Menoeceus who offers himself up to save the city in defiance of his father's wishes.

Iphigeneia in Aulis comes right at the end of Euripides' life. It is, with *The Bacchae*, his last surviving work and there are indications that the play was left unfinished at his death. There are some odd repetitions in the opening scene that scholars think might be due to different drafts being put together – though there is nothing rough or unpolished about the opening lyrics which, on the contrary, are extremely beautiful. The main problems come with the ending. It is generally agreed that the section of the play after Iphigeneia's exit is by someone else. The writing is clumsy and the messenger's narration of how at the last minute Artemis substituted a deer to be sacrificed instead of the girl feels perfunctory and lacking gravitas. It seems Euripides intended some such resolution as fragments of a speech by Artemis herself which evidently belong in the play are quoted by an ancient author. Perhaps the original was lost and what we have here is a substitution by another hand.

Strange as it may seem, these divine interventions that conclude so many of Euripides' plays are part and parcel of his realism. From the outset Euripides was interested in how events came about. Is their causation supernatural or can it be attributed to ordinary human motives? In pursuit of this interest he developed to a very high degree various ways of dramatising change. His supple dialogue was good at plans, motives, feelings, intentions, at the way thought carries over into action, and that strange borderline where the logical and illogical come together. The appearance of the *deus ex machina* is something that came naturally to Euripides. It's not a mark of an impasse so much as the point at which the playwright's investigation of causes is brought to a close. As one great scholar put it:

> More and more, as the human takes the place of the
> divine in the causation of suffering, so the divine becomes
> something which stoops down to man from above, at the
> last moment, to guide and reconcile.
> Karl Reinhardt

The chorus in the play are sightseers – women who have come over to the mainland from their home in Chalcis in Euboea to see the famous warriors of the Greek army. They have no stake in the action they observe. Their first song is a paean to the military might of the expeditionary force and the glamour of its arms. Their admiration for their heroes – these troubled, imperfect, unheroic figures – adds another layer to the play's ironies.

∾ Translations

The two most modern versions are by Don Taylor (Methuen) and W. S. Merwin and George E. Dimock, Jr (Oxford) but the Charles R. Walker (Chicago) is still useful.

∾ In performance

The play was first performed in 405 BC, the year after Euripides' death as part of a trilogy with *The Bacchae* and *Alcmaeon* (now lost). There are operas by Scarlatti (1713), Gluck (1765) and Cherubini (1782), plays by Jean Racine (1674), Friedrich Schiller (1790) and Gerhardt Hauptmann (1943), and a film by Michael Cacoyannis (1977). Recent productions have included the Mermaid Theatre (1966), the Court Theater Chicago (1997), Southwark Playhouse (1999) and the Crucible Theatre Sheffield (2003), in an adaptation by Edna O'Brien. *Iphigeneia in Aulis* formed the prologue to *Les Atrides*, Ariane Mnouchkine's 1993 production of the *Oresteia* trilogy. The play was staged at the National Theatre, London, in 2004.

The Bacchae (*Bakchai*)

∾ The legend

Cadmus founded the city of Thebes. He had four daughters, Semele, Agave, Antinoe and Ino.

Zeus, king of the gods, fell in love with Semele and made her pregnant. Hera, Zeus' wife, was jealous and caused Semele to doubt the identity of her lover. Semele made Zeus promise to grant her a wish. When he agreed, she asked him to reveal to her who he truly was. Zeus did as she asked and Semele was destroyed by the lightning flash of his divine power. Zeus took her unborn child and sewed it in his thigh, where he carried it to term. Dionysus, god of Ecstasy, was born.

Two of Cadmus' grandchildren came to a bad end, destroyed by the gods for disrespecting their power. Actaeon, Antinoe's son, boasted that he was a better huntsman than Artemis: she turned him into a stag and he was devoured by his own hounds. Pentheus (the name derives from the Greek word for sorrow) denied the divinity of his cousin Dionysus and sought to banish him from Thebes. For this blasphemy Dionysus arranged for Pentheus to be torn to pieces by maenads, among them Agave, Pentheus' own mother.

∾ The story

Dionysus, god of Ecstasy, arrives with his followers in Thebes. Pentheus, the young ruler of the city, refuses to acknowledge his power. But he is not the only blasphemer. Agave and her sisters have always denied that Semele's lover was king of the gods. They said he was just some ordinary man, whom their sister lied about from shame. Dionysus causes all the women of Thebes to be possessed by his spirit. They abandon the city and seek refuge on Mount Cithaeron. When they are disturbed they go berserk, tearing cattle to pieces with their bare hands.

Cadmus and the old prophet Teiresias acknowledge the power of the god and set off to join the women. Pentheus orders his guards to seize Dionysus, who has disguised himself as a human, and lock him in a stable. An earthquake destroys the building and the god is free once more.

Pentheus is curious about what the women are doing: he has let his sexual fantasy run riot. Dionysus suggests that he might like to go and spy on them. He also suggests that Pentheus will need to dress as a woman to disguise himself. The god and Pentheus, now in women's clothing, set off for the mountain. But Pentheus' disguise proves no protection. The women recognize him and, led by his mother, tear him to pieces.

Agave returns to the city cradling her son's head in her arms: she thinks it is the head of a young lion, not of a human being. Cadmus collects the rest of the scattered limbs and brings them back to the city for burial. Agave returns to her senses. Both she and her son have been heavily punished for their unbelief. Agave and her sisters must leave the city, which they have polluted. Cadmus is sent into exile and the destruction of the royal house is complete.

∾ About the play

> The soil of delusion brings forth the harvest of death.
> Aeschylus, *Seven Against Thebes*

> You do not know what your life is, or what you are doing, or who
> you are.
> *The Bacchae*, tr. David Franklin

The Bacchae is a dazzling and enigmatic work. 'To this day scholars are trying to figure it out' (Karl Reinhardt). More than most Greek tragedies it resists explanation, because more than any other it is the account of a process – the process of infatuation.

Right from the beginning Euripides had a special interest in the workings of the mind. In Phaedra and Medea he created characters torn between conflicting impulses. As his career went on he became more and more skilled at depicting change and development – the way thoughts and desires carry over into action. The middle-period plays, *Electra*, *Ion*, *Iphigeneia Among the Taurians*, mark a step forward in this respect. And because he was interested in the irrational, he showed how much of what happens is brought about by self-delusion, by people in the grip of forces of which they are unaware.

These preoccupations are plainly visible in a remarkable trio of late-period works, studies in the politics of unreason. In *Orestes*, we see a group of terrified young people embarking on an act of terrorism; in *The Phoenician Women*, two self-centred young men destroy a dynasty and come close to destroying a city; in *Iphigeneia in Aulis*, selfishness, cowardice, and the inability to act decisively, bring about the death of a defenceless young girl. *The Bacchae* is a new departure. It strips away all subsidiary detail and presents the anatomy of a delusion in all its stark simplicity.

Formally the play is something of a throwback. The language is interspersed with Aeschylean and liturgical elements and Euripides has renounced some of the bold rhythmic innovations that are a feature of his late-period style. The use of music is more restrained and the chorus is fully integrated into the action. The story too goes back to Aeschylus, who wrote not only a Pentheus trilogy but also another set of plays about Lycurgus, a Thracian king who was driven mad by Dionysus, killed his own son and was shut up in a mountain cave. In these plays we find details of the earthquake, of Dionysus' imprisonment and escape, and a description of the god's effeminate appearance. All this gives *The Bacchae* a strange old-fashioned quality. At the same time Euripides has retained the looser and more colloquial rhythm of his verse. The play has a facing-both-ways feel – the modern rhythm of the dialogue and the equally modern preoccupation with psychic states are contrasted with the archaic subject matter and backward-looking vocabulary to create a tension that is central to the play.

At the outset Dionysus arrives determined to punish Thebes for the way his mother's sisters slandered her.

DIONYSUS: Like it or not this city must learn its lesson:
    it lacks initiation in my mysteries;
    that I shall vindicate my mother Semele
    and stand revealed to mortal eyes as the god
    she bore to Zeus.
      tr. William Arrowsmith

So far so conventional. In *Hippolytus*, where Aphrodite's anger drives the plot, she appears in the prologue in exactly the same way. But then she disappears never to be seen again. The singularity of *The Bacchae* is the presence of the god *within the action*.

'I have taken on mortal shape, exchanged my form for that of a man.' *The Bacchae* is unique in that it is the only Greek tragedy in which a god plays a leading part. Gods often appear in a prologue or epilogue to open or close a play and occasionally (as in *Heracles*) they intervene in the middle; but for a god to be the principal actor, to mingle with humans and engage with them over the full length of the action, is very unusual indeed. Part of the work's strange atmosphere derives from the tension between the divine nature of the god and the human form behind which it is concealed.

The play is structured round three encounters between man and god in which power shifts from one to the other. The first encounter is carefully prepared. The two old men Cadmus and Teiresias know that they must submit unquestioningly to the demands of Dionysus. Pentheus, however, makes clear his determination not to give in.

PENTHEUS: I hear too that some foreigner has turned up,
Some juggling charmer from Lydia,
All golden hair and perfume,
Flushed with drink and oh so beautiful.
When I get my hands on him
I'll stop him swinging his twig,
I'll part his head from his neck.
    tr. J. Michael Walton

The old prophet utters an ominous warning.

TEIRESIAS: Do not be so certain that power
is what matters in the life of man; do not mistake
for wisdom the fantasies of your sick mind.
    tr. William Arrowsmith

The stage is now set for the meeting between god and man. Dionysus at first offers no resistance. The guard who captured him is surprised. 'He refused to run or hide, held out his hands completely unafraid.' But this very passivity lures Pentheus on. The actor playing Dionysus wore a smiling mask, and this enigmatic and unchanging smile would have become more unsettling and hypnotic as the action progressed. It is one of the many paradoxes of the play that Dionysus, the god of abandonment, appears cool and reasonable throughout, whereas the supposedly rational Pentheus is the one who is out of control. In *Iphigeneia Among the Taurians* the heroine refuses to blame the gods for her predicament.

IPHIGENEIA: I also think these people, being murderous,
   put off the blame for their own vice upon the gods.
   I do not think any divinity is bad.
   tr. Richmond Lattimore

In *The Bacchae* the calmly smiling Dionysus encompasses all the frenzied projections that are put upon him.

Pentheus completely fails to grasp the phenomenon with which he is confronted. He is so caught up in his fantasies that he is incapable of seeing what is there.

PENTHEUS: You, we'll chain you up inside.
DIONYSUS: The god will free me whenever he wants.
PENTHEUS: Where exactly would he be, may I ask?
   He is not immediately apparent to my eyes.
DIONYSUS: With me. To a blasphemer invisible.
   tr. J. Michael Walton

Dionysus is led away to prison but the illusory nature of Pentheus' power is shown not just by the earthquake that come to free his prisoner but by what happens first.

DIONYSUS: He seemed to think that he was chaining me but never once
   So much as touched my hands. He fed on his desires,
   Inside the stable he intended as my jail, instead of me,
   He found a bull and tried to rope its knees and hooves.
   He was panting desperately, biting his lips with his teeth,

His whole body drenched with sweat, while I sat nearby,
watching quietly . . .

> tr. William Arrowsmith

'*He fed on his desires* . . .' In their second scene together,
Dionysus uses his opponent's prurient fantasies about the
maenads' sexual behaviour to lead him to destruction.

DIONYSUS: *Wait!*
  Would you like to see their revels – or not?
PENTHEUS: I would pay a great sum to see that sight.
DIONYSUS: Why, are you so passionately curious?
PENTHEUS: Of course
  I'd be sorry to see them drunk.
DIONYSUS: But for all your sorrow
  you'd very much like to see them?
PENTHEUS: Yes, very much.
  I could crouch behind the fir trees out of sight.
DIONYSUS: First however
  you must dress yourself in women's clothes.

> tr. William Arrowsmith

Euripides over his long career was responsible for an enormous development in the expressive powers of dialogue.
These scenes between Pentheus and Dionysus are among the
most remarkable things he ever wrote. This slow dance of
temptation, interest, withdrawal and renewed temptation,
both in its length and subtlety, marks something new in the
history of drama.

There had been something embarrassing about the two old
men Cadmus and Teiresias when we see them early in the
play dressed up as servants of the god; but the embarrassment
is the point. It is what the god demands and they have freely
chosen it. When Pentheus reappears from the palace wearing
a long wig and dressed as a woman a boundary has been
crossed between the embarrassing and the gruesome.

PENTHEUS: Do I look like anyone?
  Like Ino or my mother Agave?

DIONYSUS: So much alike
  I might almost be seeing one of them. But look;
  one of your curls has come loose from under the snood
  where I tucked it.
PENTHEUS: It must have worked loose
  when I was dancing for joy and shaking my head.
DIONYSUS: Then let me be your maid and tuck it back.
  Hold still . . .

   tr. William Arrowsmith

Eerie as this scene is it is topped by the image of Agave cradling her son's head in her lap.

CADMUS: And whose head are you holding in your hands?
AGAVE: A lion's head – or so the hunters told me.
CADMUS: Look directly at it. Just a quick glance.
AGAVE: What is it? What have I got in my hands?
CADMUS: Look more closely still. Study it carefully . . .

   tr. William Arrowsmith

This harrowing image is also part of a recurring Euripidean pattern – which is a feeling before it is an idea – the way the emotions shift as the play develops. At the outset we are 'for' Dionysus and 'against' Pentheus (as we are 'for' Medea and 'against' Jason or, in *Orestes*, we support Electra and her brother against Helen and Menelaus). Yet by the end the positions are reversed. The terribleness of the suffering seems to revoke all former judgements. The royal line has been destroyed utterly, as Dionysus said it would be at the outset of the play. Agave and her sisters are banished from the city and Cadmus and his wife turned into snakes. The savagery of divine power is as great here as in *Hippolytus*. But what remains in the memory is the story of how Pentheus walked step by step towards his own destruction.

The midpoint of the play is given over to a tantalizing vision of innocence – of harmony, community and plenty – before the destructive forces were let loose.

Rubbing the blur of soft sleep
from their eyes, they rose up lightly and straight,
a lovely sight to see: all as one
the old women and the young and the unmarried girls . . .
Breasts swollen with milk
new mothers who had left their babies behind at home
nestled gazelles and young wolves in their arms
suckling them . . . One woman
struck her wand against a rock and a fountain
of cool water came bubbling up. Another drove
her fennel in the ground and where it struck the earth,
at the touch of a god, a spring of wine poured out.
Those who wanted milk scratched at the soil
with bare fingers and the white milk came welling up.

tr. William Arrowsmith

∾ Translations

The two most useful translations are William Arrowsmith
(Chicago) and J. Michael Walton (Methuen). There is an
academically respectable version (with notes) from G. S. Kirk
(Cambridge) and also a translation from David Franklin in
the series Cambridge Translations from Greek Drama. The
version by Colin Teevan (Oberon) is fluent and modern but is
altered to suit the demands of a particular production and
includes annoying pieces of commentary spliced into the text.
There is also a version by Wole Soyinka (Methuen).

∾ In performance

The play was first performed in 405 BC, the year after
Euripides' death as part of a trilogy with *Iphigeneia in Aulis*
and *Alcmaeon* (now lost). Recent productions have included
Dionysus 69 directed by Richard Schechner (1968), the
Schaubuehne am Halleschen Ufer (1974), Shared Experience
(1988), the National Theatre, London (1973 and 2002), and
Syracuse (2002). There are operas by Egon Wellesz (1931)

and Hans Werner Henze (1966) and plays by Maureen Duffy (*Rites*, 1969) and Caryl Churchill and David Lan (*A Mouthful of Birds*, 1986).

Aristophanes (Aristophanes) *c.*447–388 BC

Old Comedy

> The early history of comedy . . . is obscure because it was not taken seriously.
>
> Aristotle, *Poetics*, tr. T. S. Dorsch

Comedy – in the form of the satyr play – had been part of Athenian drama from the beginning. The satyr play took its name from the chorus who were made up of satyrs, small rustic creatures, half goat, half human, earthy and grotesque and, like small children, full of uncensored appetites. The satyr play took the same mythological material as tragedy but approached it from the perspective of Papageno or Sancho Panza. The overall tone was playful, irreverent, sensual.

What we call Old Comedy was a comparative late-comer. The first official competition for comedies dates from 486 BC, nearly fifty years after the beginning of the competition for tragedies. Where comedy came from before that we don't know. In Aristotle's time there was a theory that it had first developed outside Athens in the Doric-speaking areas of Greece; but wherever it originated it was in Athens that it received its full development.

The first surviving example of comedy, *Acharnians* by Aristophanes, dates from 425 BC, just under sixty years after the competition for comedy was first instituted. All the other examples of the form that have come down to us are also by Aristophanes, so that it is difficult to generalize based on such a limited sample.

Old Comedy distinguishes itself from the satyr play in that its subject matter is original and not drawn from myth, and in the variety and strangeness of it choruses. This is reflected in the titles of the plays. Tragedies are often called after their leading characters – *Agamemnon, Hecuba, Heracles, Electra, Orestes, Niobe, Phaethon* and so on. Comedies (the word *komoidia* means 'party-song') are more often known by the names of the chorus – *Knights, Clouds, Babylonians, Banqueters, Acharnians*; often the names are those of animals – *Birds, Wasps, Frogs, Storks, Ants, Goats, Fishes, Nightingales*.

The plays seem to have shared a common structure. After a prologue there were four set pieces – the first entry of the chorus, a direct address to the audience, a battle or quarrel of some kind, and a grand finale. Like tragedy, the plays were composed in a variety of different metres which ranged from the lyric to the colloquial to the rhythmically overpowering. Old Comedy was an extraordinary creation – part drama, part revue sketch, part political lampoon, part Broadway musical.

The performers were all men and wore masks. The male characters had padded buttocks and paunches and wore drooping leather phalluses which could be seen dangling below their short tunics. There were three, sometimes four, principal actors who played all the parts between them. The chorus numbered twenty-four (as against twelve and later fifteen in tragedy) and obviously had an enormous visual impact, not just on their first entry, but whenever they danced and sang together.

Athenian Old Comedy was the creation of a particular time and place. It lasted roughly three generations. Chionides and Magnes are those whose names have come down to us as representatives of the first generation of comic playwrights. The second generation is represented by Crates and Cratinus, whom Aristophanes portrayed in *Knights* as a drunken old has-been. The third and last generation were Aristophanes and his contemporaries Eupolis and Ameipsias.

As the fifth century drew to a close and Athens stumbled towards defeat in her great war with Sparta, Old Comedy began to mutate into what is known as Middle Comedy and then finally into New Comedy (see p. 287).

Life

> Old Comedy, almost alone, retains the pristine charm of
> the Attic dialect, and is also distinguished by a most elo-
> quent freedom of expression . . . It possesses grandeur,
> elegance, attractiveness . . . There are numerous authors,
> of whom Aristophanes, Eupolis and Cratinus are the most
> outstanding.
>
> Quintilian, *Institutio Oratoria*, 10.1. 65–66, tr. Alan
> Sommerstein

We know that Aristophanes was an Athenian citizen, born in
the deme of Kydathenaion. His father's name was Phillipos.
We know he had thin hair because he tells us so in one of his
plays. And that is pretty much the sum total of our knowledge. The date of his birth is inferred from the fact that his
first play, *Banqueters*, was produced in 427 BC while he was
still very young. We don't know what his father did, whether
his family was rich or poor, or who his friends were. He is one
of the characters in Plato's *Symposium*, but that is more a work
of imagination than a biography.

Unlike his private life, Aristophanes' public career is comparatively well attested. At least forty plays were attributed to
him in antiquity, of which eleven have come down to us.
These are: *Acharnians* (425 BC), *Knights* (424 BC), *Clouds* (first
version 423 BC), *Wasps* (422 BC), *Peace* (421 BC), *Birds* (414 BC),
Lysistrata and *Women at the Thesmophoria* (both 411 BC), *Frogs*
(405 BC), *Women at the Assembly* (*c*.392 BC) and *Wealth* (388 BC).
Acharnians, *Knights* and *Frogs* all won first prize; *Wasps*, *Peace*
and *Birds* came second; the original version of *Clouds* came
third and last. How the remaining four were placed we do not
know. Other plays which have not survived include
Banqueters (427 BC), *Babylonians* (426 BC), *Amphiaraos* (414 BC)
and two comedies that were staged sometime after 388 BC,
Aiolosikon and *Kolakos*.

Because his plays are the only examples of Old Comedy
that survive intact and because the writing is so fresh and

vigorous, it's sometimes difficult to remember that Aristophanes comes at the end of a tradition, not at the beginning. He was not a pioneer but an inheritor. The first competition for comic dramatists took place at Athens in 486 BC (the winner was Chionides), thirty years before Aristophanes began work on his first play. In the meantime the form was taken forward and developed by writers such as Magnes, Cratinus, Crates and Eupolis, Aristophanes' contemporary – none of whose works have survived.

Aristophanes was also a latecomer to democracy, which was established at Athens sixty years before he was born. For Aristophanes, democracy was not something new and radical but simply a given. It was the politics of his parents' generation. He even missed the great period of Periclean ascendancy; Pericles died while he was still a teenager. Aristophanes' work was written against the background of the twenty-seven-year war between Athens and Sparta. Twice, as a consequence of defeat, he saw democracy at Athens overthrown and replaced by oligarchic rule: twice he saw it restored. He lived through the final collapse of Athenian power and the bitter conclusion to the war. The turn in his late work towards allegory and away from a direct engagement with politics is generally attributed to the difficult and changed circumstances of the time.

In the ancient world, a theatrical career often ran in families. Aeschylus and Sophocles both had sons who became tragedians. Aristophanes was no exception. His three sons, Araros, Phillipos and either Philetairos or Nikostratos (the ancient commentators differ about the name of the third son) took up their father's profession and became writers of comedy in their turn.

Acharnians (Acharneis)

∽ The story

Athens has been at war with Sparta for the last six years. Athens is a naval power and cannot be defeated as long as her fleet is safe: Sparta is a land power and cannot lose as long as her army is intact. The result is stalemate.

Every summer the Spartans invade Athenian territory to destroy the harvest and ravage the countryside. Even outside the campaigning season gangs of marauders make it dangerous for people to visit their farms. Countrymen find themselves having to live cooped up within the city walls.

The central character Dikaiopolis and his family are living as refugees in Athens. Dikaiopolis, seeing that the war is going nowhere and anxious to get back to his farm, goes to the Assembly to propose a truce. The Assembly however sees no urgency about the matter. The war is proving a useful source of jobs for the boys.

Dikaiopolis takes matters into his own hands. He decides to conclude his very own personal peace treaty with Sparta and arranges an individual ceasefire lasting thirty years. The inhabitants of Acharnia – an area seven miles north of Athens which had suffered particularly badly from the Spartan marauders – want revenge for their losses and are violently against any dealing with the enemy. These are the Acharnians of the title.

The Acharnians come looking for Dikaiopolis, whom they consider to be a traitor, and prepare to stone him to death. Dikaiopolis visits the playwright Euripides to borrow some beggar's rags from his costume store so that he can appear suitably humble as he pleads his case. He points out to the Acharnians that when the war broke out there was wrong on both sides – on the Athenian side just as much as the Spartan – and that the only people profiting from hostilities are the upper classes.

Dikaiopolis' opponents are now evenly divided. The war-party appeal for help to a general called Lamachos. Dikaiopolis is not impressed and dismisses the general as just another upper-class freeloader. This appeal to the class interest proves decisive: the Acharnians side with Dikaiopolis.

The treaty now begins to yield its benefits. Dikaiopolis opens his own personal market and is visited by two traders – a thin one and a fat one. The first is a Megarian whose city is being starved out by Athenian blockade. The man is so desperate that he sells Dikaiopolis his two daughters in exchange for a few cloves of garlic. The next man is a Boeotian, bringing all sorts of delicacies long unknown at Athens because of an embargo on trade with the enemy. Dikaiopolis doesn't part with money: he gives the Boeotian an informer in exchange for his goods. This benefits both parties: there's a scarcity of informers in Boeotia and a glut in Athens.

Word has now got out about Dikaiopolis and his personal treaty and other people begin to want a share. Dikaiopolis refuses them all, relenting only in the case of a new bride on the grounds that the war is after all not her fault.

Lamachos, the warrior, is summoned to the front, guarding the wintry passes in the mountains above Thebes. Dikaiopolis, the civilian, is summoned to a feast. Both parties make their preparations in parallel. Lamachos falls in a ditch and twists his ankle; he is brought back propped up by two soldiers. Dikaiopolis returns from the feast also finding it hard to stand but supported by two dancing girls. He has been victorious, not in battle but in a drinking contest, and he invites the chorus, and by extension the audience, to come and share the celebrations.

The name Dikaiopolis has a range of meanings which shade from Honest Citizen to Well-governed City and Lamachos means Great Fighter.

∾ About the play

Many are the joys of this world – women, fruit, ideas . . .
Nikos Kazantzakis, *Zorba the Greek*

Who am I? Mr Average, Man in the Street –
Or rather, thanks to this war, Man in a Mess.
What's your name, thanks to this war? Man in Clover?
　　tr. Kenneth McLeish

It is often said that tragedy could not have existed apart from
democracy. The same is true for comedy – only more so. It's
impossible to imagine Nero, say, or Tiberius, or Rameses II,
or Nebuchadnezzar, or the prophet Ezekiel, sitting in an
audience to watch the premiere of an Aristophanes play. So
it's fitting that *Acharnians* begins with a portrait of democracy
in action. Dikaiopolis has arrived at the Assembly early.

I'm always first. I find a seat –
No problem there – I wait here on my own,
I groan, I yawn, I stretch, I fart, I'm bored,
I scribble, scratch, do sums in my head,
I think about my farm, I long for peace . . .
Well, here I am. I'm ready. Start when you like.
I'll heckle and clap and shout
If anyone talks of anything but peace.
　　tr. Kenneth McLeish

When the councillors do arrive – late – they have no interest
in making peace. Instead they receive envoys newly returned
from Persia and from Thrace. Then as now foreign travel at
the state's expense was one of the privileges of the governing
class. It turns out the delegation to Persia has been away eleven
years with the ambassadors being paid two drachmas a day –
double the rate for an oarsman in the Athenian fleet – and they
have nothing to show for it except some ambiguous promises
of help. Yet when someone proposes to go to Sparta to open
peace talks the councillors refuse to pay his travel. Dikaiopolis
chips in with money of his own and asks the man to conclude a
private peace just for himself and his family.

As the messenger leaves, the other delegation arrives from
northern Greece. They haven't been away as long as their
colleagues but have been paid even more – at the outrageous

rate of three drachmas a day. All they have to show for it are a miserable group of limp-looking mercenaries who are prepared to fight only if paid over the odds and make themselves at home by stealing Dikaiopolis' lunch. He decides to put a stop to the proceedings and exercises his right to dissolve the Assembly on the grounds of an ill-omened drop of rain.

> Your Worships! Don't just sit there!
> Chair! I'm being mugged in my own backyard –
> And by northerners. Ah, the hell with it.
> I veto the Assembly. No more negotiations.
> I've had an omen. I felt a drop of rain.
>> tr. Kenneth McLeish

When orthodox channels fail, Dikaiopolis takes matters into his own hands. He has no doubt at all that he's completely within his rights to do so.

In next to no time (this is comedy) the messenger returns with three different types of treaty in three different bottles, like vintage wines, for Dikaiopolis to taste.

AMPHITHEOS: These are the five year: taste one?
DIKAIOPOLIS: (Splutters) Ugh!
AMPHITHEOS: What's the matter?
DIKAIOPOLIS: Don't like 'em.
  They smell of tar and caulking
  And the fitting out of warships.
AMPHITHEOS: Then try a ten-year one.
DIKAIOPOLIS: No . . . there's a whiff of embassies
  Very urgent, to all our allies,
  And all our allies stalling . . .
AMPHITHEOS: Then here are the thirty-year treaties
  Both for land and sea . . .
DIKAIOPOLIS: O Day of Dionysus! A sweet scent
  Of nectar and ambrosia,
  And never think of rationing any more,
  And in my mouth it says 'Go where you like'.
    tr. Patric Dickinson

But the Acharnians have caught wind of what is going on and arrive to stone Dikaiopolis to death as a traitor to his country. The average citizen is seen as caught in the middle between a political elite interested only in feathering its own nest and a popular war-party blinded by resentment.

One of the reasons that people fall in love with Aristophanes' work is that in it you can hear the Athenians talking. This makes the plays very difficult to translate. It's not just that they're colloquial, they're also in verse, and not just in verse, but in several different kinds of verse. The peasant earthiness of the speech, the way every sentence implies a gesture is particularly hard to carry over, since there hasn't been a peasantry in England for at least five hundred years. The closest parallels are with the language of mediaeval Mystery Plays (particularly the work of the York Realist) or of Shakespeare's Mrs Quickly or the city comedies of Middleton. 'She's got a tit like a turnip', exclaims Dikaiopolis as he grapples with one of the dancing girls. And then there are the puns and the contemporary allusions and the sexual innuendo and the parodies of other writers – Euripides is a particular favourite, though there's also Herodotus and (in other plays) Aeschylus, Euripides again, Socrates, and the Sophists – a whole running commentary on Athenian culture.

When Dikaiopolis is confronted with the wrath of the Acharnians it is parody that gets him out of it – a take-off of one of Euripides most famous early plays, *Telephos*. Telephos was king of Mysia in Asia Minor which a Greek expedition attacked thinking it was Troy. He was wounded by Achilles and was told by an oracle that he could only be healed by 'the one that had wounded him'. Telephos came to Agamemnon's court at Argos disguised as a beggar to seek help. In order to make Agamemnon listen to him he took his baby son Orestes hostage. Dikaiopolis, faced with the angry Acharnians, rushes into the house and comes out with a basket full of charcoal and a sword. The Acharnians, who were well known as charcoal burners, cannot bear to see their precious product threatened.

DIKAIOPOLIS: Keep your distance. Drop
  Those stones. One brick,
  The brazier gets it.
CHORUS: Stop!
  I'm feeling sick.
  Those coals are friends of mine.
  You wouldn't! Swine!
DIKAIOPOLIS: Ah, now you're on your knees.
    tr. Kenneth McLeish

Dikaiopolis has to plead for his life and in order to make himself seem as convincing as possible he goes to visit Euripides to ask for some rags, so that he can look properly like a beggar.

DIKAIOPOLIS: Give me some rags from that old play of
    yours,
  For I've got to make a long speech to the chorus
  And if I fail, I'm to die . . .
EURIPIDES: It depend what you mean by rags?
  Would it be the garb the poor dotard Oineus
  Wore when he entered?
DIKAIOPOLIS: No. Not Oineus.
EURIPIDES: What rags of time? What tattered outfit?
  Philoktetes?
DIKAIOPOLIS: No, much worse than that!
EURIPIDES: The squalid habit lame Bellerophon wore?
DIKAIOPOLIS: Bellerophon? No. But mine was lame, talked,
  (Like most of your characters) talked, talked, talked . . .
EURIPIDES: Ah, you mean Telephos.
    tr. Patric Dickinson

The reference to *Telephos* is more than just a parody of a well-loved and notorious drama: it feeds directly into the political message of *Acharnians*. As a Greek living in Asia Minor, Telephos stood between the two rival camps, the Greeks and the Trojans, and was able to see that there were rights and wrongs on both sides. Dressed in his beggar's rags, this is just the case that Dikaiopolis now proceeds to make.

> I detest the Spartans. They slashed my vines
> As well as yours. Day and night I pray for them
> To Poseidon, the Earthshaker: 'Oh god' I cry
> 'Make the earth move for them. Shake their houses down.'
> But the question remains – we're all friends here –
> Are they entirely to blame for everything?
>
> tr. Kenneth McLeish

He then launches into an exaggerated but nonetheless true account of the trade dispute that had started the war and points out that the Athenians had had several chances to back down.

> They [the Spartans] asked us more than once but we
> refused, and so the shields began to clash. I hear someone
> say they ought not to have declared war. Well, what ought
> they to have done? Tell me that. And tell me something
> else. Suppose a Spartan customs officer had confiscated
> and sold a puppy from Seriphos or some such spot on the
> map, alleging that it was being smuggled, would you have
> sat by and done nothing? Of course not.
>
> tr. Alan H. Sommerstein

The Acharnians are now in two minds. The pro-war faction appeals to General Lamachos for help. He comes swaggering on but is unmasked by Dikaiopolis as just another upper-class freeloader who gets well paid for doing very little.

> It makes me sick
> To see honest greybeards in the ranks,
> And tailor's dummies, men like you,
> Drawing wages for swanking behind the lines:
> Catering designers, protocol advisers,
> Accessory administrators, career consultants,
> Political spin-doctors; swankers all.
>
> tr. Kenneth McLeish

The chorus are now totally won over and embark on a speech of praise – not of Dikaiopolis, but of Aristophanes himself.

The fact is, he helps you.
You owe him. He tells you the truth,
Stops you falling for conmen and frauds . . .
He shows you true politics,
Shows you what life's really like
Here at home, how our allies behave –
And they swarm here to see him,
The risk-taker who Tells It Like It Is.
> tr. Kenneth McLeish

The second half of the play is taken up with the pleasures of life – food, drink, sex and driving a hard bargain – all the blessings that flow from that cannily concluded treaty.

DIKAIOPOLIS: Roast, grill, fry, boil, simmer, stew.
See to the rabbits. The party crowns!
Pass over those skewers. I'll start the thrush kebab.
CHORUS: What style! What art!
What panache! What ease!
DIKAIOPOLIS: Just wait till I start
Spit-roasting these.

The play's opposition between the advantages of peace and the disadvantages of war reaches its climax when Lamachos prepares to go on campaign and Dikaiopolis prepares for a feast.

LAMACHOS: Bring me the plumes for my helmet.
DIKAIOPOLIS: Bring me the pigeon and the thrush.
LAMACHOS: The ostrich feather is lovely and white.
DIKAIOPOLIS: This pigeon's meat is lovely and brown.
LAMACHOS: Boy! – bring me my spear off the peg.
DIKAIOPOLIS: Boy! – bring me my black pudding off the fire.
LAMACHOS: Better take the case off the spear.
DIKAIOPOLIS: Better take the pudding off the spit.
LAMACHOS: Now bring me my shield with the Gorgon's head.
DIKAIOPOLIS: Now bring me that nice round cheese-cake.
LAMACHOS: This mockery is absolutely disgusting.

DIKAIOPOLIS: This cheesecake is absolutely delicious.

    tr. Alan H. Sommerstein

Acharnians is the first Greek comedy to survive and it gives us a vivid and surprisingly complete picture of Athenian life. We see the Assembly at its work – ordinary, human, the opposite of grandiose – we see the different and conflicting class interests, the fascination with the theatre, the opposition between city and country, the dialects of foreigners, the native pleasure in getting a good bargain, the food, the drink, the frank relish of sexuality. There is even a picture of the fleet – the central pillar of Athenian power – as it prepares for war:

>   . . . wage paying, gilding
> Of figure-heads, uproar in the streets, allotment of
>   rations,
> Filling of wineskins, fixing of rowlock, bidding for water –
>   casks,
> Garlic, olives, garlands pilchards, flutegirls,
> And – black eyes!
> In the dockyards oarhandles planed, bolts hammered,
> Everything fitted out shipshape; flutes, pipes, and
>   boatswains' whistles.
>   tr. Patric Dickinson

∾ Translations

Kenneth McLeish's translation (Methuen) is by far the most vivid and actable. Patric Dickinson (Oxford) and Alan H. Sommerstein (Penguin) are both reliable and cleave slightly closer to the Greek. The notes to S. Douglas Olson's Oxford edition give a full and illuminating account of the physical life of the play.

∾ In performance

Acharnians was first produced in 425 BC. It won first prize.

Karolos Koun directed a production in 1976 and a version called *The Private Peace* was staged at Mecklenburg Staatstheater Schwerin in 1982.

Clouds (*Nephelai*)

∾ The story

Strepsiades is a well-to-do farmer who has married above himself – which is where his troubles begin. His son Pheidippides takes after his mother and has turned out to be an upper-class playboy only interested in horses and chariot racing. These are expensive pursuits and Strepsiades is now heavily in debt. The date is approaching when his creditors will come to claim their money and Strepsiades is at his wits' end.

Next door to Strepsiades' house is the 'Thinkery' or 'Pondertorium' – a private academy run by the philosopher Socrates. The school is famous for teaching the two arguments, the Right and the Wrong, and for making Wrong win. Strepsiades decides to enrol himself as a pupil in the hope of being able to swindle his creditors out of their money through fast-talking and equivocation. The students are an off-putting bunch, pallid, sickly and half-starved but Strepsiades suppresses his doubts and puts himself in Socrates' hands. The first action of the philosopher is to swindle him out of his coat and shoes.

Strepsiades is amazed to learn that the gods he has worshipped all his life do not exist; it turns out that the only divinities are Chaos, Clouds and Tongue. He is also astonished to see his first map. (He doesn't like the fact that the enemy city Sparta looks so close; he wants it moved further away.) Socrates introduces Strepsiades to the Clouds, the patron goddesses of thought and speculation.

In the end Strepsiades is too forgetful to retain what he has been taught, too simple-minded to grasp the nuances of the new thinking, and is unable to complete the course. There seems to be no way out until he has the bright idea of enrolling his son Pheidippides instead. Socrates, thinking of the money, is only too happy to try again.

The Right and Wrong Argument appear and have a set-piece debate. Right upholds the values of traditional education: pupils should be seen and not heard. He is obsessed with physical culture and the bodies of young boys. He is easily seen off by Wrong, who favours intellect, free enquiry and having a good time. Pheidippides goes off with Wrong eager to become his pupil. While Pheidippides is at his studies, Strepsiades uses some of his new skill at chop-logic to see off a couple of his creditors. It turns out that he has not been such a bad pupil after all.

Strepsiades' triumph is short-lived. He and Pheidippides quarrel over the respective merits of Aeschylus and Euripides and come to blows. Pheidippides gives his father a hearty beating and when challenged argues that he is only doing to Strepsiades what his father did to him when he was little. In fact he can see no reason why he shouldn't go on to beat his mother too. Dabbling in the new ways of thinking has led to the natural order of things being stood on its head. Strepsiades is appalled to see where his duplicity has landed him. In fury he turns on the Pondertorium and sets it on fire. The half-singed students are driven out and the Clouds sail gravely on their way.

The name Strepsiades derives from the Greek word 'to turn' and has connotations both of 'Twister' and 'Wits' End'.

ᛦ About the play

SOKRATES: These are the only gods there are. The rest are but figments.

STREPSIADES: Holy name of Earth! Olympian Zeus is a figment?

SOKRATES: Zeus?

What Zeus?

> Nonsense.
>
> There is no Zeus.

STREPSIADES: No Zeus?

Then who makes it rain? Answer me that.

SOKRATES: Why, the Clouds

of course.

tr. William Arrowsmith

How could any man or city that does not
nurture an element of fear inside the heart
still worship Justice?

Aeschylus, *Eumenides*, tr. Michael Ewans

The Athenians were prodigious innovators – 'quick to form
a resolution and quick to carry it out' – but they lacked a
theory of progress. When they looked back and took
account of all the changes that had taken place, a sort of
dizziness came over them. The two great dramatic expres-
sions of this dizziness are Sophocles' *Oedipus Tyrannus* and
Aristophanes' *Clouds*.

As free-ranging intelligence began to examine the workings of the universe, and as men began to see the benefits of
the civilization that they themselves had made, the gods
seemed to lose something of their former awe-inspiring
power. But if the gods do not exist and there is no such thing
as divine Justice, what is there to prevent society from col-
lapsing into a state of lawless savagery, where every man is
turned against his neighbour? Strepsiades sets out with the
perfectly reasonable ambition of cheating his creditors and
ends up staring into the abyss. We find this pattern again in
Molière, in works such as *Tartuffe*, *Don Juan*, and *The Miser*,
where the playwright takes an ordinary human quality – religious devotion, sexual desire, avarice – and follows it through
to the point of catastrophe.

The real-life Socrates was a moral philosopher who had no
interest in the natural sciences. The character as Aristophanes
draws him combines in one person the two forms of intellec-

tual enquiry that were seen as most threatening to the established order – the new fascination with rhetoric and an interest in the natural sciences. Strepsiades goes to the Thinkery to learn how to make the weaker argument prevail but finds himself confronted with students engaged in various (ludicrous) forms of scientific enquiry. *Clouds* contains the first ever description of a scientific experiment.

STUDENT: Just a minute ago Sokrates was questioning
    Chairephon
  about the number of feet a flea could broadjump.
  You see a flea happened to bite Chairephon on the eyebrow
  and then vaulted across and landed on Sokrates' head.
STREPSIADES: How did he measure it?
STUDENT: A stroke of absolute genius.
  First he melted some wax. Then he caught the flea,
  dipped its tiny feet in the melted wax,
  let it cool and lo! little Persian bootees.
  He slipped the bootees off and used them to measure the
    distance.
    tr. William Arrowsmith

The bewildered Strepsiades catches another group of students engaged in a mysterious activity.

STREPSIADES: Why are they staring at the ground?
STUDENT: They're engaged in geological research: a survey
  of the earth's strata.
STREPSIADES: Of course. Looking for truffles.
  – You there, don't strain yourself looking. I know where
    they grow big and beautiful. Hey, and look there:
  what are those fellows doing bent over like that?
STUDENT: Those are graduate students doing research on
  Hades.
STREPSIADES: On Hades? Then why are their asses scanning
  the sky?
STUDENT: Taking a minor in Astronomy.
    tr. William Arrowsmith

Socrates, who presides over all this, is presented as a plausible and greedy rogue – what Strepsiades himself might be if he didn't have his farm to back him up. He wastes no time in getting Strepsiades to give up his coat and footwear, which go straight down the pawnshop to pay for food, and he has invented an ingenious hook to filch people's clothes from the changing room at the gymnasium. He's also a coward. He threatens to beat Strepsiades for his ignorance but stops first to check what the reaction will be.

The chorus of Clouds – ethereal, majestic, shape-shifting and bounteous – are a brilliant invention. They provide a different perspective on the grubby dealings of the human beings.

STREPSIADES: I always thought they were just mist, and dew, and fog.
SOKRATES: No, no. They look after all of us; philosophers,
    Prophets, miracle-doctors, intellectuals,
    Quacks and poets. Especially poets . . .
    tr. Kenneth McLeish

Strepsiades wonders why they appear in the shape they do.

STREPSIADES: But look, if these are clouds, real clouds,
    Why do they look like women? Other clouds don't.
SOKRATES: Have you ever looked up and seen a cloud
    Shaped like a centaur? A leopard? A wolf? A bull?
STREPSIADES: Often. What of it?
SOKRATES: Well there you are. They look like what they
    look like.
    tr. Kenneth McLeish

Socrates claims the clouds as his patron saints but they have a wider power to give or withhold blessing.

CHORUS: There are certain advantages coming your way
    If you vote for the Clouds, if you give us first prize.
    When the season for ploughing begins you'll want rain.
    We'll water your fields first; the others can wait.

We'll keep a close eye on your vines as they grow:
They won't shrivel and die; they won't drown in a flood.
Any mortals who laugh at us gods that we are
Ought to know what the penalties are. Number One:
Barren acres. No harvest, no produce, no fruit.
All your olives ands vines when they blossom in spring
Will be battered to death by a torrent of rain . . .
. . . Number Three: family weddings? You want a nice day?
You won't get one. The choice is a simple one; move
To the deserts of Egypt or give us first prize.
   tr. Kenneth McLeish

The Thinkery in its first aspect is a hothouse of scientific experiment. This is a group of people to whom plainly nothing is sacred. But what Strepsiades has really gone there to learn is Argument, how to make Wrong (Inferior) triumph over Right (Superior). The confrontation of the two sides is postponed until the last third of the play. It takes the form of a debate about education which, because it concerns the shaping of the next generation, always becomes the focus of anxiety in times of social change. 'Right' stands for an old-fashioned training based on character.

SUPERIOR: Let me begin by explaining how education was
  run in the good old days . . .
First it was given that boys should be seen and not heard
and that students
should attend their district schools marching through the
streets in orderly pairs
behind the lyre master. Moreover they were never allowed
to wear cloaks
even if the snow was falling thick as porridge . . .
You'll be forever in the wrestling school, your bronzed body
glistening and hard. No wasting precious time twittering
away on absurd topics
in the marketplace, nor bickering in the courts, splitting
hairs, arguing the toss . . .
   tr. Peter Meineck

'Wrong' stands for the new curriculum, which encourages independence and freedom of thought.

INFERIOR: Why do you think the philosophers
named me the Inferior Argument? Because it was I who created
the concept of disputing entrenched ideals and ethics . . .
To be able to take up the Inferior Argument and win
is worth far more than any number of silver coins you
could care to count . . .
Suppose you've been indulging in an illicit love affair.
You are discovered!
A scandal! What will you do? You are finished because
you don't have the means
to argue your way out of trouble. But if you choose to
make my acquaintance,
your nature can run free . . . If the husband accuses you
of adultery, plead innocence and blame Zeus. Say that
clearly he can't resist his lust
for women, so how can you, a mere mortal, be expected to
have more strength than a god?
    tr. Peter Meineck

'Wrong' wins the contest through a mixture of flattery and up-to-date-ness. The way is now open for Strepsiades 'to live a life of luxury, licentiousness and liberty'. A new world opens up where the plausible man is king and the satisfaction of the passions is the only good. Fifty years later the philosopher Plato was to devote two of his great dialogues, *Gorgias* and *The Republic*, to proving this position wrong and establishing a new basis for morality. Aristophanes, the comic dramatist, has less time to spare; he solves the dilemma he has created on the principle of tit for tat. The chorus first begin to sound a note of warning.

Still crime doesn't pay
That's the lesson
That wicked old fraud

Will learn today
He's a clever old man:
Well, he'll soon wish he wasn't
And he thought up this plan
Well, he'll soon wish he hadn't.
　　tr. Kenneth McLeish

Payback begins within Strepsiades' own family. Father and son get into an argument and come to blows. Strepsiades complains he is easily out-argued and Pheidippides aspires to make his bad behaviour general. The Greeks, in a world without pensions or social security, set great store by the bond between parent and child, so Pheidippides' newfound lack of reverence is something truly shocking

PHEIDIPPIDES: Who made the law
　Back there in the good old days?
　Ordinary people like you and me.
　And how did they know they were right?
　They were persuaded, by argument.
　Well, now I want to change the law,
　By argument. I want to let sons beat fathers.
　　tr. Kenneth McLeish

The only remedy is to destroy the source of these subversive ideas. As the Thinkery burns Strepsiades celebrates the return of the status quo.

I'll teach you. I'll teach you to laugh at the gods,
And look at the Moon when she's gone to bed!
Bang! Wallop! Smash! Pay them back
For everything . . . but especially for mocking the gods.
　　tr. Kenneth McLeish

Aristophanes manages to bring his play to a suitably tidy conclusion but in real life things were more dangerous and less easily settled. The philosopher Anaxagoras, for example, escaped with his life only thanks to the intervention of his friend the great statesman Pericles.

Sotion, in his *Succession of Philosophers*, says that he (Anaxagoras) was prosecuted for impiety, because he maintained that the sun was a red-hot mass of metal, and that after Pericles, his pupil, made a speech in his defence, he was fined five talents and exiled. Satyrus in his *Lives*, on the other hand, says . . . that the charge was not only for impiety but also collaboration with the Persians; and he was condemned to death in his absence . . .

Diogenes Laertius, tr. J. E. Raven

And everyone knows that the real historical Socrates was condemned to death and executed for 'corrupting the youth of the city'. When the case came to trial, Aristophanes' caricature of him was remembered and helped to sway the jury against him. Here is Socrates speaking in his own defence.

What is the calumny which my enemies are spreading against me? It would run somewhat in this fashion: 'Socrates is an evil-doer, who meddles with inquiries into things beneath the earth, and in heaven, and who 'makes the worse appear the better reason' and who teaches others these same things. That is what they say; and in the Comedy of Aristophanes you yourself saw a man called Socrates swinging around in a basket and saying that he walked the air, and talking a great deal of nonsense about matter of which I understand nothing, either more or less . . . But the fact is, not one of these stories is true.

Plato, *Apology*, tr. F. J. Church

◆ Translations

The most vigourous and enjoyable translations are by William Arrowsmith (New American Library) and Kenneth McLeish (Methuen).

◆ In performance

Clouds was first performed in 423 BC and was a failure. The reasons for this are not clear but Aristophanes settled down to revise the play, which is the version that has come down to us. As far as is known, the play in its revised form was never staged in the author's lifetime.

Birds (Ornithes)

～ The story

Two men, Peisetairos and Euelpides, are tired of the taxes and the lawsuits at Athens. They want to find somewhere quiet to live. They go to see Tereus, who was once king of Thrace but was changed by Zeus into a bird. Not only can he speak their language but he might, on his travels, have seen a suitable place for them to settle.

Then Peisetairos has a bright idea. Why not found a brand new city in the sky? The birds occupy the space between heaven and earth. If they wall it off, they can hold the gods to ransom by refusing to allow the smoke of sacrificial offerings to reach the heavens. Once the old gods step down, the birds can take over and become rulers of the world.

Tereus calls a bird-assembly to listen Peisetairos' proposal. At first the birds are suspicious and seek to kill the two inter-lopers in revenge for all the destruction wrought on birds by humankind. Tereus persuades them to a truce. Peisetairos tells the birds that they were the first divinities, whose position was usurped by the Olympian gods. Now is the time to reclaim their powers and become once again the presiding deities of mankind. The assembly is won over by Peisetairos' eloquence.

Peisetairos and Euelpides become honorary birds and are kit-ted out with wings. They name the new city Cloudcuckooland and set about building fortifications and posting guards at the frontier. Heralds are despatched to heaven and earth demand-ing their submission. Peisetairos prepares a sacrifice to cele-brate the foundation of the new city. He repels various eager mortals who have heard what's going on and want to muscle in.

The birds' blockade of heaven begins to bite. Zeus sends his messenger Iris to demand that the siege be lifted. Peisetairos remains unimpressed by her threats. The herald sent to earth returns with a gold crown for Peisetairos to wear and the news that all things bird-like are the new fashion among men. Peisetairos now again prepares to sacrifice and is again interrupted by eager arrivals trying to get a foothold in the newly established kingdom: once again, he sees them off.

Prometheus comes to visit. Long ago, in the great war in heaven, he changed his allegiance from the Titans to Zeus because his prophetic powers enabled him to foresee which side was going to win. Now he is changing sides again. He tells Peisetairos that the gods are faint with hunger and on the point of surrender. Peisetairos will have the upper hand in any negotiations and should hold out mercilessly for what he wants. In particular he should refuse to settle until Zeus has agreed to let him marry Princess. Princess is Zeus' housekeeper and looks after the divine thunderbolts. With her as his consort, Peisetairos' power will be established for ever and unshakeable.

Poseidon, Heracles and a barbarian god arrive as an embassy from Zeus. Peisetairos follows Prometheus' advice and holds out for a settlement on his own terms. The famished Olympians, weakened by the smell of the meal that Peisetairos' chef is preparing for him, simply capitulate. Peisetairos is married to Princess and all the birds rejoice.

Peisetairos means Persuader of his Comrades and Euelpides means Optimist.

∾ About the play

MRS BUNDY: There are eight thousand, six hundred and fifty million species of birds in the world today, Mr Carter. It is estimated that five billion, seven hundred and fifty million birds live in the United States alone. The five continents of the world probably contain more than one hundred billion birds.

Town DRUNK: It's the end of the world.
    Alfred Hitchcock, *The Birds*

You can take the boy out of Essex but you can't take Essex
out of the boy.
    Popular saying

One of the special pleasures for the Athenian audience at a
comedy must have been the surprise factor. 'Nowadays,' says
Aristotle, 'the best tragedies are written about a handful of
families.' He was perhaps overstating things a little, but it
remains true that subjects for tragedy were drawn from an
existing fund of legends and stories. The treatment might
vary from play to play – Sophocles and Euripides handle the
story of Electra in very different ways, for instance – but the
basic legends remained the same.

Comedy was a different matter: there was no knowing
what might happen. The hero of Aristophanes' *Peace*, for
example, flies up to heaven on a dung beetle, while in *Frogs*
Dionysus and Heracles go down to the underworld to visit
the ghosts of Aeschylus and Euripides. Part of the excitement
of the form was its ability to take the audience on a kind of
magical mystery tour. *Birds* works by putting two different
ingredients together – heroic myth and ordinary Athenian
street life – and creating something extraordinary out of the
mixture.

The birds which Peisetairos and Euelpides are carrying on
their wrists when they enter have been bought in a shop or on
a market stall.

EUELPIDES: I was thinking of that birdseller.
    Nice service that was,
    swearing that these two specimens would lead us straight
    to Tereus, the king who turned into a Hoopoe;
    selling us a jackdaw for a penny, the damned jackass,
    and three pennies for that raven. What a pair!
    All they can do is peck.
        tr. Dudley Fitts

The street seller's patter refers to a well-known legend about Tereus, king of Thrace, who raped his wife's sister and cut out her tongue. The two women took revenge by killing his son and serving him up for dinner to his father. The gods turned all three into birds. Tereus became a hoopoe; his wife Prokne became a nightingale, endlessly lamenting her murdered child; the raped Philomela became a swallow. It's Aristophanes' genius that he can take this simple sales pitch, the kind of thing that might be overheard in the market every day, and use it to open the way into another world.

Guided by the raven and the jackdaw, Peisetairos and Euelpides leave ordinary reality behind and enter the realm of myth and magical transformation – which is also the world of the theatre. It is the way that the commonplace turns into the extraordinary and vice versa that gives the play its special atmosphere and exhilaration. The ordinary is enlarged and given wings (literally); the fabulous is domesticated and made familiar. Sophocles had written a tragedy, *Tereus*, a little while before. It is typical of Aristophanes that he should have taken the story and remade it in his own image.

The play is full of transformations. It is not just that Tereus and Prokne are changed into birds. Peisetairos sets out from Athens looking for somewhere peaceful to retire and ends up as ruler of the universe. At the beginning his only desire is for peace and quiet, yet he is soon hustling about, overseeing the foundation of a huge new empire. The birds themselves, trapped, harried and hunted, cooked and put in cages, are changed into powerful and resourceful creatures, capable of anything.

PEISETAIROS: Merciful Poseidon!
What workmen could build a wall as high as that?
MESSENGER: Birds, only birds . . .
                    Imagine thirty thousand Cranes
from Libya, each one with a belly full of stones
for the Rails to shape up with their beaks; ten
thousand Storks, at least,

all of them making bricks with clay and water
flown up by Curlews from the earth below.
PEISETAIROS: Mortar?
MESSENGER: Herons with hods.
PEISETAIROS: How did they manage it?
MESSENGER: *That* was a triumph of technology!
  The Geese shovelled it up with their big feet.
PEISETAIROS: Ah feet, to what use can ye not be put!
MESSENGER: Why, good Lord! There were ducks to set the
  bricks,
  and flights of little apprentice Swallows
  with trowel tails for the mortar in their bills.
PEISETAIROS: Who wants hired labour after this?
          But what about the joists and beams?
MESSENGER: All handled by the birds.
  When the Woodpeckers went to work on those portals
  it sounded like a shipyard!
     tr. Dudley Fitts

This magical world is made up of language and of spectacle. The first entry of the chorus in Aristophanes is always an
important moment, but here the playwright has surpassed
himself. The voices of the Hoopoe and the Nightingale can
be heard summoning the birds to the assembly. Then four
gorgeously costumed extras appear perched on the roof of
the *skene*. Lastly, the chorus themselves appear: for once, they
are not a uniform group. Twenty-four different birds enter in
groups of six in an accelerating rhythm.

PEISETAIROS: Look, there's a partridge.
EUELPIDES: Zeus above! And that's a francolin there.
PEISETAIROS: This one's a widgeon.
EUELPIDES: That one there must be a green kingfisher.
  But what's the bird behind it now?
HOOPOE: What that one? That's a snipper.
EUELPIDES: A snipper? *Is* there such a bird?
HOOPOE: Yes, Sporgilos the barber.
  Look, that's an owl.

PEISETAIROS: That can't be true. Who's brought an owl to
  Athens?
HOOPOE: A jay, a turtle-dove, a lark. A warbler, wheatear,
  pigeon.
  A vulture, falcon, ring-dove too. A cuckoo, redshank, shrike.
  A moorhen, kestrel, grebe and finch. Then lammergeyer,
  woodpecker.
PEISETAIROS: I've never seen so many birds!
  tr. Stephen Halliwell

The poetry for the bird chorus is some of the most brilliant
and enchanting in all Greek literature in its colour, its lyri-
cism and its rhythmic variety. The Greeks were often wary of
nature, seeing it as something that needed to be tamed and
subdued, but *Birds* is in one of its aspects a hymn to the
beauty of the world.

CHORUS: Joy of birds! In summer the long thick sunlight
  When the locust drones in the trance of noontime:
  Mad with sun we shout, and the forest dances
  Heavy with music.
    tr. Dudley Fitts

And the birds, these small intimate companions that are all
about us every day, are transformed into the presiding deities
of creation.

CHORUS: Listen, you men down there in the half-light!
  Shadowy, impalpable, dreamlike phantoms: feeble, wing-
  less, ephemeral creatures of clay, dragging out your
  painful lives till you wither like the leaves and crumble
  again to dust! Pay attention to us, the immortals; to us,
  the eternal, the airborne, the un-ageing, the imperishable;
  and hear from us the whole truth about lies round and
  above you! In the beginning there existed only Chaos,
  Night, Black Erebus and Dreamy Tartarus; there was no
  Earth, no Air, no Sky. It was in the boundless womb of
  Erebus that the first egg was laid by black-winged Night;
  and from this egg, in due season, sprang Eros the deeply

desired, Eros the bright, the golden-winged. And it was
he, mingling in Tartarus with murky Chaos, who begot
our race and hatched us and led us up to the light.

There was no race of immortal gods till Eros brought
the elements together in love; only then did the Sky, the
Ocean and the Earth come into being, and the deathless
race of all the blessed gods.

So you see we are much older than any of the gods.
And that we are the children of Eros is plain by many
tokens.

Like him, we fly.

Like him, we are associated with love

tr. David Barrett

Compared with this dream of power, the mortal spongers
who try to wheedle their way into the new kingdom are a
sorry lot – *littérateurs* who supply verse more clichéd and less
beautiful than the birds' own poetry, decree sellers who want
to cramp the freedom of the skies, town planners who want to
measure out the empty spaces of the air, informers who want
to abuse the gift of flight for their own ends. Even Peisetairos
and Euelpides, transformed by means of a magic potion, can
never have the grace of the authentic birds.

EUELPIDES: Sweet gods, in all my days,
I've never seen a sillier sight than you!
PEISETAIROS: Yeah,
what's so damn funny?
EUELPIDES: You and those baby wings.
They tickle me. You know what you look like, don't you?
PEISETAIROS: *You* look the abstraction of a Goose.
EUELPIDES: Yeah?
Well, if you're supposed to be a blackbird, boy,
somebody botched the job.

tr. William Arrowsmith

Several attempts have been made to interpret *Birds* as a
detailed allegory of the political situation at the time it was

written: none carry conviction. The irony, such as it is, is more general in scope and is aimed at the famous Athenian quality of *polypragmosune*. The word itself is double-edged: on the positive side it means energy, daring, ingenuity, enterprise; on the negative side it means restlessness, never being satisfied, meddling, being a busybody. It was acknowledged to be one of the defining characteristics of democratic Athens.

Peisetairos is an Athenian and, like his fellow countrymen, he is naturally full of *polypragmosune*. He says he wants a quiet life, but when the opportunity presents itself he throws himself headlong into founding a new empire. Just as Athens' allies in the war against Persia found themselves transformed into subjects of an Athenian empire without quite knowing how they'd got there, so the birds become conscripted into falling in with Peisetairos' proposals. He sees an opportunity, follows it up, persuades everyone to go along with him and the result is . . . world domination. In a tellingly Orwellian detail, the feast that Peisetairos is preparing when he receives the embassy of the gods is made up of the executed bodies of 'traitors' – birds that have gone against his power. This is only lightly touched on, for Aristophanes too is an Athenian. He understood very well that a certain discontent with the way things are, a desire to push back the boundaries, to test the limits and to live for ever were an important, indeed essential, part of being human.

ᕦ Translations

The play has called forth the best in its translators – there are excellent versions from William Arrowsmith (University of Michigan), Dudley Fitts (Faber), David Barrett (Penguin) and Kenneth McLeish (Methuen). Most recent of all is a verse translation by the poet Sean O'Brien (Methuen). There is an academically reliable version from Stephen Halliwell (Oxford), whose introduction is a valuable short guide to the work of Aristophanes as a whole.

∽ In performance

Birds was first performed in 414 BC. It won second prize.
Ameipsias won first prize with his play *Revellers* and Phrynichos
came third with *The Hermit*. An adaptation by Goethe was
staged at Weimar in 1780 and there was a famous Victorian
production by Planché in 1846. Karolos Koun's modern Greek
staging was seen in London as part of the World Theatre
Season in 1967 and the play was performed at the National
Theatre in 2002. There is an opera by Walter Braunfels.

Lysistrata (*Lysistrate*)

∽ The story

The Athenians and the Spartans have been at war for twenty
years. Advantage has lain now with one side, now with the
other. The Athenians had recently undergone a terrible setback when the great expedition they had sent to Sicily was
defeated and destroyed. Instead of seeking to negotiate, however, they drew on the financial reserves set aside for such
emergencies, fitted out a new fleet and pursued the conflict as
vigorously as ever.

Lysistrata, an Athenian housewife weary of the war, decides
to takes matters into her own hands. She gets women
together from Athens and all the other combatant nations
and persuades them to go on strike sexually until their husbands agree to make peace.

To make sure of success, Lysistrata develops a second line
of approach. She organizes a force of older women to occupy
the Acropolis: this is where the treasury, which provides
funds for the war, is housed. Lysistrata plans to cut off the
money supply which keeps the fighting going, while at the
same time forcing the combatants to the negotiating table by
means of sexual deprivation.

The Commissioner representing the Athenian government is easily seen off but Lysistrata has more difficulty quelling a mutiny in her own ranks. Her fellow conspirators are weaker willed than she is and keep trying to slip away to have sex with their husbands. They offer a variety of excuses but Lysistrata is adamant that the strike must remain solid.

An Athenian solider (Kinesias) turns up from the front looking for his wife (Myrrhine). Myrrhine, following Lysistrata's instruction to the letter, drives her husband into a frenzy of sexual desire by agreeing to go to bed with him and then inventing excuses – the need for a pillow, an extra blanket, some perfume – to get up and leave him unsatisfied. She makes him swear to give up fighting and then slips away at the very last moment leaving him in agony, desperate for peace to be concluded at the earliest possible opportunity.

The strike has now begun to hit home. The men are all going about bent double, nursing monstrous erections. A Spartan envoy arrives to sue for peace. His member is so big and stiff it looks at first as if he has a spear concealed beneath his cloak. Dizzy with desire, the representatives of the two great powers meet to conclude a truce. Lysistrata arrives accompanied by the naked figure of Reconciliation. The men are so mesmerized by the sight of her nude body, a ravishing reminder of what it is they have been missing, that negotiations are quickly concluded.

Spartan and Athenian take it in turns to entertain each other with song and dance and normal life and normal sexual relations are resumed among general rejoicing.

The name Lysistrata means Disbander of Armies.

∾ About the play

SHELLEY: Men start war.
GARY: Then why don't women stop 'em then?
  Peter Gill, *Friendly Fire*

A stiff prick has no conscience.
Popular saying

The ancients were convinced that women enjoyed sex more than men. There is a story that Zeus and Hera were arguing over who got more pleasure from the sexual act – men or women. They went to consult the prophet Teiresias who had in his time been both a man and a woman. His answer was that women had 90 per cent of the pleasure and men 10 per cent.

Women all over Greece are suffering because their men are away at the war.

LYSISTRATA: Just think of your husbands for a moment . . .
    The fathers of your children. Up at the front,
    Every one of them. Don't you miss them?
KALONIKE: Mine's been away in Thrace for months.
    Five months! Keeping an eye on that general . . .
    Whatsisname.
MYRRHINE: Mine's been in Pylos for . . . ooh, ages.
LAMPITO: Mine falls out, comes home, re-equips and runs.
LYSISTRATA: You see what I mean. No husbands, no lovers
    To blow on the embers.
MYRRHINE: No embers.
    tr. Kenneth McLeish

And as if they were not already frustrated enough, wartime restrictions have cut off the supply of dildoes too.

Lysistrata presents a sort of tit-for-tat solution to the problem of international conflict. War interferes with sex, so it seems only fair to use sex to interfere with war.

LYSISTRATA: All right, ladies. It's time to tell my plan.
    If we really want our men to end this war,
    All we have to do is give up . . .
MYRRHINE: What?
LYSISTRATA: I can't. It's too much too ask.
MYRRHINE: Of course you can. Give up what? Our lives?
LYSISTRATA: No. Sex.
    tr. Kenneth McLeish

Dikaiopolis in *Acharnians* and Peisetairos in *Birds* both escape the constraints of ordinary life by setting up private utopias where they are free to do as they like. Lysistrata is different. Her attempts to alter the status quo involve half the adult population of Greece and end up benefiting the whole community. It is Lysistrata's very lack of power that makes her solution so wide-reaching. Dikaiopolis and Peisetairos are men and as such have a far greater freedom of action. They can go out into the world as independent agents and conclude treaties and found new empires. Greek women by contrast were expected to confine themselves to the domestic sphere; public life affairs were men's work.

LYSISTRATA: Ever since this war began
  we women have been watching you men, agreeing with you,
  keeping our thoughts to ourselves. That doesn't mean
  we were happy: we weren't, for we saw how things were going;
  but we'd listen to you at dinner
  arguing this way and that.
                    – Oh you, and your big
  Top Secrets! –
                    And then we'd grin like little patriots
  (though goodness knows we didn't feel like grinning) and ask you:
  'Dear did the Armistice come up in Assembly today?'
  And you'd say, 'None of your business! Pipe down!', you'd say.
  And so we would.
OLD WOMAN: I wouldn't have by God!
MAGISTRATE: You'd have taken a beating then!
                    – Please go on.
LYSISTRATA: Well, we'd be quiet. But then you know, all at once
  you men would think up something worse than ever.
  Even *I* could see it was fatal. And 'Darling,' I'd say,

'have you gone completely mad?' And my husband would
    look at me
and say 'Wife you've got your weaving to attend to.
Mind your tongue if you don't want a slap. "War's
a man's affair."'

    tr. Dudley Fitts

It's only by banding together into a group that women can be
imagined as exerting any influence or taking independent
action.

The other women characters, with the exception of the
Spartan Lampito, are seen as stereotypically female, interested in clothes and sex and getting drunk.

KALONIKE: How can women end the war? Silk dresses,
    Flowers in the hair, fancy slippers,
    That dreamy new scent – that's all we know.
LYSISTRATA: That's all we need. Flower garlands,
    Fancy slippers, see-through silk . . .
KALONIKE: I don't understand.
LYSISTRATA: When I've finished
    No man will ever raise a spear again.
KALONIKE: I could wear that *daffodil* silk . . .
LYSISTRATA: Or swing a sword.
KALONIKE: That gorgeous negligee . . .
LYSISTRATA: Or wear a shield.
KALONIKE: I *must* buy some more shoes.

    tr. Kenneth McLeish

And when the going gets tough they are only too ready to
compromise with the enemy.

LYSISTRATA: I can't manage them any longer; they've gone
    man-crazy,
    they're all trying to get out. Why, look:
    One of them was sneaking out of the back door
    over there by Pan's cave; another
    was sliding down the walls with rope and tackle . . .

    tr. Dudley Fitts

Lysistrata, though, is extraordinary. She is the first female heroine in Greek comedy and her courage, resourcefulness and intelligence drive the play. When challenged about her competence, she responds by viewing the city as a larger version of her household.

LYSISTRATA: The first thing you do with wool is wash the grease out of it; you can do the same with the City. Then you stretch out the citizen body on a bench and pick out the burrs – that is, the parasites. After that you prise apart the club-members who form themselves into knots and clots to get into power, and when you've separated them, pick them out one by one. Then you're ready for the carding; they can all go into the basket of Civic Goodwill – including the resident aliens and any foreigners who are in debt to the Treasury! Not only that. Athens has many colonies. At the moment they are lying around all over the place, like stray bits and pieces of the fleece. You should pick them up and bring them here, put them all together and then out of this make an enormous ball of wool – and from that you can make the People a coat.

    tr. Alan Sommerstein

Aristophanes had a love-hate relationship with Euripides. He parodied his plays, made fun of him, and boasted that he was the better writer of the two:

I use the rounded polish of his style
But make my heroes' minds somewhat less . . . vulgar.

    tr. Alan Sommerstein

It took him a while however to meet the challenge presented by Euripides' heroines. When *Lysistrata* was written it was twenty years since Medea had complained that she would rather go into battle three times than give birth once. Lysistrata takes up where Medea left off.

LYSISTRATA: Two agonies are ours:
  We bear you sons, we wave goodbye when they march off to die.

COMMISSIONER: Don't mention dying.

LYSISTRATA: We're young, in the prime of life
  And what does the war bring us? Single beds.
  Bad enough for wives – but what about
  Young girls, unmarried, doomed to die old maids?
  A woman's bloom is short, and when it fades,
  No magician can conjure her a husband.

  tr. Kenneth McLeish

A sex comedy would be nothing without erections and the second half of the play is a procession of frustrated men more or less incapacitated by their rampant pricks. The penis of the Spartan ambassador is so large and stiff that the Athenians think it must be a concealed weapon.

HERALD: I've come to ask for peace negotiations.

KINESIAS: I suppose that's why you've brought your spear
  along.

  tr. Stephen Halliwell

The usual costume for a male actor in Greek comedy included an erect leather phallus, signifying an unrestrained appetite for life. In *Lysistrata* the men, driven wild by sexual deprivation, are more engorged than ever.

MYRRHINE: I'll just fetch a bed.

KINESIAS: What? On the ground, the ground.

MYRRHINE: No darling. You may be a pig
  But I won't let you wallow on the ground.

She goes in.

KINESIAS: She loves me. She loves me. You can always tell.

Myrrhine returns with a folding bed.

MYRRHINE: You set it up. I'll get undressed.
  No, silly me, I forgot the mattress.

KINESIAS: *Forget* the mattress.

MYRRHINE: I can't have you having me on sacking.

KINESIAS: Give me a kiss before you go.

MYRRHINE: Mmmmmmmmm.

She goes in.

KINESIAS: Hoo-hoo-hoo. For god's sake hurry
Myrrhine returns with a mattress.
MYRRHINE: There. You lie down. I'll get undressed.
   Oh no. No pillow now
KINESIAS: I don't *want* a pillow.
MYRRHINE: But I do
She goes
    tr. Kenneth McLeish

Some commentators complain that the playwright is cheating here because he makes no mention of other forms of relief – brothels, for example, or slave girls, or masturbation: but Aristophanes is not writing about the sex industry, he's writing about married love.

The final negotiations take place in a haze of hormones. The spokesmen for both sides are spellbound by the naked figure of Reconciliation. The exchange of territory is worked out in purely sexual terms – with the Athenians ceding control over the girl's arse to the Spartans while keeping the rights over her vagina for themselves. The peace settlement is achieved by sleight-of-hand. The men are forced to surrender by their own biological needs and by Lysistrata's control over the money supply. They listen to her arguments but are spared the necessity of having to be convinced by them. Aristophanes is also careful to show that the Spartans are the first to crack.

As Lysistrata presents it, the long war is nothing more than a kind of family quarrel.

LYSISTRATA: We are all Greeks.
   Must I remind you of Thermopylai? of Olympia?
   of Delphoi? Names deep in all our hearts?
   And yet you men go raiding through the country,
   Greek killing Greek, storming down Greek cities –
   and all the time the Barbarian across the sea
   is waiting for his chance – That's my first point.
AN ATHENIAN: Lord! I can hardly contain myself!
LYSISTRATA: And you Spartans:

Was it so long ago that Perikleides
came here to beg our help? I can see him still,
his white face his sombre gown. And what did he want?
An army from Athens! Messenia
was at your heels, and the sea-god splitting your shores.
Well, Kimon and his men,
four thousand infantry, marched out of here to save you.
What thanks do we get? You come back to murder us.

> tr. Dudley Fitts

The real grounds of contention – what Thucydides described as 'the growth of Athenian power and the fear that this caused in Sparta' – are cleverly passed over.

As with *Acharnians* and *Birds* the utopia with which the play concludes is a restoration of the 'good life' – food and drink, plenty of sex, the pleasures of family life and peace in which to enjoy them. Their object achieved, Lysistrata and her fellow conspirators return to barracks. Their brief assumption of power is at an end. Lysistrata herself, like a fairy godmother, drops from sight before the final celebrations. It is not until *Women in Power*, which Aristophanes wrote five years later, that women are seen taking over the state on a permanent basis:

We're going to stand up, take over the state
And run it like it's never been run before.
Women in power! We can't do worse than men.

> *Women in Power*, tr. Kenneth McLeish

∾ Translations

There is a racy, actable version from Kenneth McLeish (Methuen) and an academically scrupulous one from Stephen Halliwell (Oxford). Dudley Fitts (Faber) and Alan Sommerstein (Penguin) are both serviceable, though they both go a bit mad with the funny accents.

∾ In performance

The play was first performed in 411 BC. *Lysistrata* was staged
at the Royal Court Theatre (1957), at the Old Vic (1993) and
at Battersea Arts Centre (1999) in a version by Germaine
Greer. A musical version with Melina Mercouri was seen on
Broadway in 1972.

Menander (Menander), 342/1–c.293/89 BC

New Comedy

> The whole business of vicissitudes, raping of young women, substitution of children, recognition by means of rings and necklaces, these are of course the main elements of New Comedy and Euripides brought them to perfection.
>
> Satyrus, *Life of Euripides*, tr. Bernard Knox

Old Comedy lasted about eighty years from the time the first competition for comedy was instituted at Athens in 486 BC. Towards the end of the century it began to change into what is known as Middle Comedy, which in turn became New Comedy around 321 BC.

In Middle Comedy the role of the chorus was greatly reduced. There were fewer topical references and a general turning away from politics towards subject matter that was more abstract and allegorical. In Aristophanes' play *Wealth*, for example, first produced in 388 BC, two of the principal characters are Wealth and Poverty. Poverty argues that without the fear that she inspires no one would ever do anything. Wealth is represented as blind, which is why the distribution of his blessings is so unequal. Wealth has his sight restored and a new age of plenty is inaugurated.

A character in Athenaeus' *Banquet of the Learned* (written *c.*200 AD) boasts, 'I have read more than eight hundred plays of so-called Middle Comedy.' Only two examples of the genre survive, both by Aristophanes.

With New Comedy we enter a world that is recognisably modern. This is the start of a line that leads through Plautus to *commedia dell'arte* and on to Molière and Goldoni.

The Roman poet Ovid wrote:

So long as fathers bully, servants lie,
And women smile, Menander cannot die.

(*Amores*, 1, XV. 17)

This is a little unfair to Menander – it underrates his elegance
and inventiveness – but is a useful summary of New Comedy
as a whole. The chorus has now disappeared almost entirely
(it is confined to a series of quite unrelated musical interludes
between the scenes) and the characters are a collection of
stock types – the young lover, the wily slave, the father, the
mistress, and so on. The actors still wear masks but the
extravagant paddling and leather phalluses that were such a
notable feature of Old Comedy have disappeared. The performers now look more naturalistic.

What brought about these changes? It seems that the predominant factor was political. Perhaps the greatest achievement of Athenian democracy in its earliest manifestation was
the creation of a public sphere into which all the city's ener-
gies could be channelled. The sense of rivalry and competition that in an aristocracy had gone into war or sport was
harnessed instead for the benefit of the whole community.
Citizens strove to outdo each other in the contribution they
could make to public life. But as Athens stumbled towards
humiliating defeat in her great war with Sparta, the institutions of democracy came under enormous stress, and the
public sphere began to shrink. There was a vicious oligarchic
coup followed by a restoration of democracy, followed by
another oligarchy installed at sword point by a Spartan army,
followed again by a popular revolt and a return to democracy.
In times like these Old Comedy stood on dangerous ground.
Its democratic outspokenness attracted the hostility of the
oligarchs while its irreverent criticism of the foibles of
democracy made it unwelcome to the democrats.

This change is particularly clear when we reach the world
of New Comedy, from which any sense of a public sphere is
completely absent. A political culture where generosity,
engagement and a sense of adventure were shared by a whole

community has ceased to be a reality. It survives only as a theatrical dream, shrunk to a cosy neighbourhood world, where all disputes manage in the end to find a resolution.

The fourth century BC saw an enormous expansion of dramatic activity across the whole Greek world. It was thought for a long time that pressure from these non-Athenian audiences for plays that were more 'universal', less tied to a particular place, less full of political jokes and references, helped influence the transformation from Middle to New Comedy. Recent archaeological evidence from southern Italy, however, shows that the Old Comedy of Aristophanes formed a recognized part of the repertoire there, so audiences were obviously more sophisticated that had been assumed.

New Comedy's focus on the everyday did not spring up suddenly out of the blue. There are links that go right back to the *Odyssey*, and descend (probably) through the satyr plays of Aeschylus to the tragedies of Euripides, in which the portrayal of the details of domestic life often bulks so large.

Reversal (*peripeteia*), which Aristotle singled out as one of the distinguishing marks of tragedy, began in Euripides to lose the majesty and terror it had possessed in the work of Aeschylus and Sophocles, and declined into something that at times was perilously close to a 'plot twist'. In New Comedy we can see this process reach its logical conclusion. The legacy of high tragedy is transmuted into something where 'reversals of fortune' become simply the vicissitudes of everyday life, and what had once been the fall of great dynasties is transformed into the ups and downs of young men in love, or the comic comeuppance of an elderly miser.

Life

Menander and Life,
Which of them was copying the other?
   Aristophanes of Byzantium

The vicissitudes of Menander's work make up a curious chapter in the history of taste. Menander was one of the most celebrated authors of antiquity. Aristophanes of Byzantium (*c.*257–180 BC) rated him second only to Homer among the Greek poets. The Roman critic Quintilian in his survey of Greek and Latin literature devoted four paragraphs to him; only the author of the *Iliad* had more space. Then he disappeared. His plays failed to survive the dark ages of the eighth and ninth centuries. For over a thousand years all that was left were fragments, a few lines here and there quoted in the works of other writers.

It was not until 1897 that eighty consecutive verses from his play *Georgos* surfaced at last and in 1905 substantial portions of five more plays were discovered at Aphroditopolis in Egypt in what had been the house of Flavius Dioskoros, a Roman lawyer who lived there in the sixth century AD. Then nothing except fragments again for another half century until finally in 1959 a complete play *Dyskolos* was published for the first time, followed in 1965 by a substantial portion of another play *Sikyonios* and in 1969 by the almost complete *Samia* and a long fragment of *Aspis*. Menander the playwright is a modern discovery and more of his work may turn up at any moment.

Menander was born in Athens into a well-to-do family. His parents were Diopeithes and Hegestrate. He is alleged to have drowned while swimming in the Piraeus. He wrote 105 plays in a comparatively short life. His first was said to have been performed before he was twenty. He won first prize on only eight occasions. Seventeen works have come down to us that can be identified more or less securely: *Aspis* (The Shield), *Georgos* (The Farmer), *Dis Exapaton* (The Double Deceiver), *Dyskolos* (The Misanthrope), *Epitrepontes* (The Arbitration), *Heros* (The Hero), *Theophorumene* (The Madwoman), *Karchedonios* (The Carthaginian), *Kitharistes* (The Lyre Player), *Kolax* (The Flatterer), *Konmeiazomenai* (The Women Who Take Hemlock), *Misumenos* (The Man She Hated), *Perikeiromene* (The Girl Who Had Her Hair Cut), *Perinthia* (The Girl from Perinthos), *Samia* (The Girl from Samos),

Sikyonios (The Man from Sikyon), *Phasma* (The Apparition). *Dyskolos* is complete, *The Girl from Samos* almost complete, and we have about two thirds of *The Shield*.

If Menander's comedy no longer takes its material from contemporary politics like the plays of Aristophanes, it's because politics had become much more dangerous since Aristophanes' time. The great period of Athenian power was over. The city was divided into those who wished to pursue some kind of independent policy and those who thought that Athens' interests were best served by accepting the protection of the King of Macedon. These divisions corresponded roughly (but not exactly) to the divisions between poor and rich, democrats and oligarchs. Power shifted to and fro between the two groups and each shift brought purges and executions. Menander himself only just escaped with his life when the oligarchy was overthrown in 307 BC and replaced with a short-lived democracy. With the world of politics so unstable and so dangerous it is not surprising that theatre found something else to talk about.

Plutarch tells a celebrated anecdote about Menander, which goes as follows. The deadline is getting near and a friend says to the playwright, 'I wonder if you've managed to finish your new play yet?' 'Finished my play?' says Menander. 'Oh absolutely. I've got the plot worked out – I just have to fill in the dialogue.' The soul of Menander's comedies lies in their construction: that is not to say that the dialogue is not lively and full of feeling (it is both) but the particular airy and graceful quality of the action derives from the way the plays are put together. The emotion is generated by the structure, as the twists and turns of the plot lead gradually but inexorably towards the happy ending. It is as if the generosity and openness that in Aristophanes' day was a general political culture shared by the citizens of Athens as a whole can now exist only within the confines of the stage – nowhere else can good intentions and a happy outcome be guaranteed.

The scholar A. W. Gomme writes as follows of Menander's virtues:

He was a wonderful observer of mankind, with a gift for
clear portraiture in language exactly suited to his purpose;
a language of just the right range, full of charm, never
sublime, never 'pure' poetry, seldom rhetorical; an instrument of which he was complete master. An easy mastery,
both of his material and his language, is his most notable
characteristic; how apt, in fact is the story that 'he only
had to add the verses' . . . Within his chosen range, even
in the little that is left of him, he shows wonderful variety
of character and situation. He seldom or never strikes a
false note; and it is remarkable how high a standard he
maintains, not only in the three plays best preserved, but
whenever enough is left, a scene or part of a scene, to
enable us to form a judgement.

Essays on Greek History and Literature

The Girl from Samos (Samia)

∾ The story

In Athens a rich man (Demeas) and a poor man (Nikeratos)
live next door to each other. Demeas has a young mistress,
Chrysis – the girl from Samos of the title – and an adopted
son Moschion, both of whom he loves very much.

Chrysis becomes pregnant with Demeas' baby. The old
man doesn't want any more children, so he tells Chrysis to
abort the child or else give it away. He and Nikeratos leave
for a long business trip to the Black Sea.

While the two men are away, several things happen. First,
Chrysis miscarries: Demeas' child is born dead. Second,
Moschion seduces Nikeratos' daughter Plangon and gets
her pregnant. Before Demeas and Nikeratos return
Plangon gives birth to a baby boy. Moschion intends to
marry Plangon but is afraid of what his father might say.
Meanwhile Chrysis has taken the baby into her house and is
looking after it as if it were her own.

Demeas and Nikeratos return from abroad having cooked up a plan to marry Moschion off to Plangon. Plangon and her mother are frightened by the news at first because Nikeratos simply tells his daughter that she is to be married but hasn't said to whom. There is delight all round when the misapprehension is cleared up: Moschion is relieved to find that the obstacles he thought would stand in his way simply don't exist.

Demeas discovers that Chrysis has, as he thinks, disobeyed him and kept her child. Moschion defends the girl and Demeas agrees that perhaps he has been too quick to condemn her.

Preparations for the marriage are in full swing when Demeas overhears one of the servants talking to the baby and saying he looks just like his father Moschion. Demeas immediately concludes that his adopted son has seduced his mistress. He puts all the blame on Chrysis and throws her and the baby out of his house. The kindly Nikeratos takes her in, hoping that the row will soon blow over.

Moschion returns from the city, where he has been whiling away the time before the marriage ceremony, to find the household in crisis. He thinks that his father has discovered about Plangon's illegitimate baby and that he has thrown Chrysis out because she helped conceal what had happened. He bravely tells his father that the child is his, thus confirming Demeas' worst fears. Nikeratos joins in the quarrel by refusing to marry his daughter to a young man who has betrayed his father's trust in such a shameless manner.

Moschion confesses the truth to Demeas. Nikeratos is so furious with Chrysis for having seduced his best friend's son that he threatens to kill her and the baby too. Demeas takes Chrysis back into his house to keep her out of harm's way.

The neighbours patch up their quarrel and everything is now ready for the wedding. Moschion however is in a sulk. He feels it was wrong of Demeas to suspect him so readily and, to punish the old man, he pretends to be leaving home to enlist as a mercenary. Demeas points out to Moschion that is unfair to set a solitary misunderstanding above years of care and devotion. When Nikeratos threatens to have Moschion arrested if he tries to leave, Moschion is glad of a chance to give in. The wedding procession forms up and the play comes to an end with a general celebration.

Moschion means Bull Calf. Samos is an island in the eastern Mediterranean, near the coast of Ionia. The Ionians were felt to be more hot-blooded and sensual than the mainland Greeks.

∾ About the play

What gives *The Girl from Samos* its special charm is its benevolence – not just the benevolence of the central character Demeas but also the benevolence of the author, who ensures that every setback is temporary and every complication speedily resolved. Difficulties arise only to be disposed of almost immediately, and are followed by more difficulties, which are also quickly resolved – and so on. The play presents itself from the outset as a succession of happy endings.

The first happy ending takes place before the action begins. The orphan Moschion is adopted by the wealthy Demeas.

MOSCHION: He was kind to me when I was too young to appreciate it. I was treated like every other boy of good family, 'one of the crowd' as the saying goes, though I certainly wasn't born with a silver spoon in my mouth . . . I made my mark when I backed a dramatic production and gave generous contributions to charity. I had horses and hounds too – at my father's expense. I was a dashing officer in the Brigade, sufficiently in funds to give a bit of help to a friend in need. Thanks to my father I was a civilized human being . . .

    tr. Norma Miller

Menander is constantly toying with the audience's expectations. When Demeas falls in love with the much younger Chrysis, it's possible to imagine, as Demeas himself does later in the play, that Moschion might try to steal the girl for himself. Not a bit of it. In fact it is Moschion who urges his father to bring Chrysis into his home to discourage the attention of younger rivals.

MOSCHION: Then father fell for a girl from Samos. Well, it could happen to anyone. He tried to keep it quiet, being a bit embarrassed. But I found out for all his precautions, and I reckoned that if he didn't establish himself as the girl's protector, he'd have trouble with younger rivals for her favours. He felt a bit awkward about doing this (probably because of me) but I persuaded him to take her into the house.

   tr. Norma Miller

Real life turns out to be more generous and surprising than convention might suggest.

When Moschion wants to marry Plangon, we expect (and so does he) that Demeas will put obstacles in his way. The girl's family are after all much poorer and less distinguished: the well-to-do Moschion is something of a catch and might be expected to marry well. Countless dramas have been written about young lovers struggling to get married in the face of parental disapproval. Menander however disposes of the issue with typical panache.

MOSCHION: Now. That other little matter we were talking about. What do you want to do?
NIKERATOS: Marrying my daughter to your boy, you mean?
DEMEAS: Yes.
NIKERATOS: I still feel the same. Let's take the bull by the horns and name the day.
DEMEAS: You really think so?
NIKERATOS: Absolutely.
DEMEAS: Splendid. It's what I've been hoping for all along.

   tr. J. Michael Walton

Where Moschion feared the worst, all has turned out for the best. The wedding that will end the play has already been arranged before the end of the first act.

We might expect that Plangon's illegitimate baby will prove a problem too but Chrysis and Plangon's mother, who have long been friends, work together to keep the birth a secret. Chrysis takes the baby under her protection and nurses it instead of her child that died. Moschion's bastard, far from proving an embarrassment, turns out to be a way of uniting the two households and drawing people closer together. In a pattern typical of Menander, what might have been a source of difficulty turns out instead to be a source of satisfaction. Not the least part of the play's charm is that it's about making a good home for Plangon's child and arranging for it to be in the care of two loving parents.

It is the presence of the infant in Demeas' home in the midst of the wedding celebrations that brings about the play's biggest upset.

DEMEAS: Someone had put the baby down on a couch where it wouldn't be in the way. Of course it was yelling. And the women were all shouting at once 'Flour. Water over here. Fetch olive oil. More charcoal.' I joined in to give them a hand. Which is how I found myself in the store cupboard. I was quite a while in there, sorting things out and seeing what was what.

While I was in there this woman came downstairs into the room next door. It was Moschion's nurse, quite elderly now and a freewoman though she used to be a slave. Seeing the baby left to cry and nobody looking after it, and not realizing I was in the storeroom, she saw no reason to guard her tongue. She went up to the baby and said the sort of things they say to babies. 'Nice baby. What a good boy.' That sort of thing. 'Where's your mummy then?' Then she picked it up and gave it a cuddle. So it stopped crying and she said to it 'Oh dear, oh dear. It doesn't seem yesterday I was nursing Moschion – you've

got his eyes alright – now he's got a boy of his own'- until
some slip of a girl came rushing in. 'Here, the child needs
changing,' declares the old woman. 'You can't neglect a
baby just because its father is getting married.'
Immediately the girl hushes her up. 'Keep your voice
down, idiot. He's in there.' 'He's not is he? Where?' 'In
the store cupboard.' Then she says loudly, 'The mistress is
calling for you, Nurse. Run along, now.' And not so
loudly, 'He won't have heard. Don't worry.' 'Me and my
mouth,' the old woman mutters and off she trots, Lord
knows where.

> tr. J. Michael Walton

This discovery tests Demeas' loving kindness to its limits,
but even here he is reluctant to blame Moschion. Instead, he
takes out all his anger and disappointment on Chrysis.

DEMEAS: I simply cannot believe
That he, so well-behaved and self-controlled
Towards all others, would treat me like this,
Not if he were ten times adopted, not
My natural son. No, it's not his birth
I'm thinking of but his good character.
The woman's just a whore, a pestilence.
Why waste my breath on her? She'll not last long.
Now, Demeas, now you must be a man.
Forget you missed her, finish with your love,
And hide the trouble which has come on us
As far as may be for your dear son's sake,
And throw this wonder-girl from Samos out
Head first, out of the house to feed the crows.

> tr. Maurice Balme

Once again, however, the playwright is careful not to let his
characters suffer for too long. Demeas may put Chrysis on
the street but she is homeless only temporarily. Nikeratos
steps in to offer her shelter. The ground is clear for the climactic confrontation between Demeas and his son.

With Menander we arrive for the first time at a drama which is fully spoken. The range of verse forms is far narrower than in earlier comedy or in tragedy. The basic unit is the blank verse line, the iambic trimeter, and the only change is that the metre alters and intensifies as the play heads towards its point of maximum complication. Menander's comedies are also the first surviving plays to be divided into Acts, with a pattern that was to become familiar as it passed down through the centuries: Act I exposition, Act II rising action, Acts III and IV climax, and Act V resolution.

Menander is already able to exploit this new form to the full, using the Act break as a way of increasing tension, either by introducing new characters just at the last minute – Demeas and Nikeratos arrive back from the Black Sea just before the end of Act I – or by contriving a cliff-hanger of an ending, as with the expulsion of Chrysis in Act III. The chorus has not been done away with altogether but appears only between the Acts as a sort of divertissement. They were wholly separate from the action of the play and what they did and what they sang have not survived.

It is in Act IV that the play's misunderstandings reach their climax. Demeas is now convinced that Moschion has seduced Chrysis and made her pregnant; Moschion for his part is resolved to own up that the baby is his.

MOSCHION: What are you talking about?

DEMEAS: You really want me to tell you?

MOSCHION: Of course I do.

DEMEAS: Come here.

MOSCHION: Tell me.

DEMEAS: Oh, I'll tell you. The child is yours. I know. I was told by one of the servants. So stop playing games with me.

MOSCHION: But – what harm is Chrysis doing you if the child is mine?

DEMEAS: Who is to blame, then? Tell me that.

MOSCHION: But – how is she at fault?

DEMEAS: I don't believe it! Have you no conscience?

MOSCHION: What's all the shouting about?

DEMEAS: Shouting, is it, you scum? What a question. Listen: you take the blame on yourself, right? And you dare to look me in the face and ask this? Have you turned against me completely?

MOSCHION: Me? Against you? How?

DEMEAS: How? Need you ask?

MOSCHION: But father it isn't such a terrible crime. I'm sure thousands of men have done it before.

tr. Norma Miller

The scene is worth quoting not simply because it's funny in its own right but because it gives an idea of the suppleness and modernity of Menander's writing and its ability to convey a sense of people actually talking. What is not reproduced in the prose translation is the additional dancing quality to the dialogue which comes from the fact that is in verse, with (in the rapid passages) speech passing to and fro between the characters several times within a single line.

The Girl from Samos represents the creation of an Aristophanic utopia on a smaller and more domestic scale. Dikaiopolis in *Acharnians* establishing a private peace in the midst of a major conflict; Peisetairos in *Birds* founding a new empire of peace and plenty in Cloudcuckooland; these solutions have something dreamlike about them: they leave the world as it is while lifting the comic heroes out of it. Menander's approach is both more generous and more sentimental. He presents a world where jealousies between neighbours, economic necessity, difficulties of reconciling love with an arranged marriage, the ordinary asperities of male–female relationships, seem not to exist. What gives the play its airborne, euphoric quality is the sense that the only thing to fear is fear itself. When Demeas thinks the worst of Moschion he is proved wrong; when Moschion doubts Demeas' affection he is proved wrong as well. The characters are seen to suffer only because the good news hasn't reached them yet.

∾ Translations

The best translations are by Norma Miller (Penguin) and J. Michael Walton (Methuen). The Penguin has the benefit of an excellent introduction to Menander's work as a whole. The Maurice Balme translation (Oxford) is also useful.

∾ In performance

The play has generally been dated sometime within the period 315 to 309 BC. Its fluency and structural sophistication mean that it is more likely to be later rather than earlier.

Plautus (Titus Maccius Plautus), c.255/250–184 BC

Roman Comedy

The Greeks invented tragedy and comedy: the Romans had no need to repeat the process. The forms were there, ready to hand, waiting to be taken up. When the magistrates at Rome were looking for an entertainment to accompany the victory celebrations at the end of the First Punic War in 240 BC, they commissioned a Greek-speaking former slave, Livius Andronicus, to translate a tragedy for them. Andronicus, 'the first inventor' of Roman drama, tried his hand at comedies as well – though tragedies seem to have suited him better: Cicero thought his comic writing was notably unfunny.

Comedy was taken up by other dramatists who had more aptitude. A hundred and fifty years later a commentator called Volcacius Sedigitus drew up his 'ten best' list which went as follows: Caecilius, Plautus, Naevius, Licinius, Atilius, Terence, Turpilius, Trabea, Luscius and Ennius. The only complete plays to have survived are by Plautus and Terence. All that is left of the rest are lists of titles, together with odd lines and snatches of dialogue that pop up as quotations in the work of other writers.

When these dramatists set about adapting a Greek play, they were not trying to produce the perfect literary translation. Their aim was to come up with something that would entertain a Roman audience. To help them do this, they drew on previously existing forms of popular drama. There were lively *commedia*-style improvised farces associated with Campania in southern Italy, and in central and northern Italy the Etruscans had developed a form of rustic clowning which took place at harvest time. Recent study of painted pottery has shown that an Italian version of Greek New Comedy had already established itself around the Bay of Naples soon after

350 BC. The playwrights borrowed freely from anything they thought might prove useful, with the result that Roman comedy is brasher, cruder and more anarchic than the Greek plays on which it was based.

The first permanent theatre at Rome was built by Pompey in 55 BC. Before that performances took place in temporary wooden structures. The audience sat under an awning that shielded it from the sun and, as there was no chorus, the orchestra or dancing ground was filled with seats for the wealthier citizens, becoming what we now call 'the orchestra stalls'. Greek New Comedy had three actors; Roman comedy often had four, and sometimes more. Greek New Comedy was comparatively realistic and limited the use of music during the action; in Roman comedy at least half of the dialogue, and usually more, was either underscored or sung. The records of Roman performances regularly list the musicians alongside the writer. The Roman actors, like their Greek predecessors, wore masks.

Roman comedies were not set in Rome but in an imaginary Greek world. In recognition of this fact they were known as *palliatae* ('comedies with a cloak') because the actors were dressed as Greeks. A parallel set of comedies, where the action took place in the country towns of Italy, called *togatae* ('comedies with a toga') or *tabernariae* ('comedies in poor people's houses'), were developed later. They existed alongside the *palliatae* – we have a tantalizing list of titles – but they never enjoyed the same sort of popularity. It seems they were in every sense 'too close to home'. The outrageous behaviour of the characters in Plautus becomes acceptable because the action is seen to be taking place 'somewhere else'. The cry 'Let's Greek it up!' often prefaces some particularly heinous piece of intrigue.

Theatre at Rome worked in a recognizably modern way. Magistrates called aediles were responsible for providing the entertainment at the six great festivals that punctuated the Roman year – about fourteen performance days in total. An actor-manager would commission a play from a writer, take it to the magistrate and be given money to mount a production, which he would manage, direct and usually act in. Drama was only one of a variety of holiday attractions which included boxing, juggling, tightrope-walking and gladiators. Market forces soon came into play. A popular dramatist like Plautus would be able to sell his work for a higher price than a writer who had no track record, and magistrates anxious to make a splash might draw on their private funds to 'sponsor' some particularly lavish or costly set of performances.

The job of aedile was a step on the career path for young noblemen aspiring to hold the highest offices of state, so it is no surprise that Roman comedy kept its nose clean. It would have been foolish for either the writers, the actor-managers or the magistrates to have rocked the boat. Plautus' immediate predecessor Naevius got into trouble for being politically outspoken and there seems to have been no hurry to repeat the experiment.

Life

During the last few days I have read several plays of Plautus, whom I did not know, in the original. I was astonished at the vigour, effectiveness, terseness of the dialogue as well as its wit, imagination, colourfulness and rich variety. The *Asinaria* surprised me most of all. It combines demonic depravity with raging mockery of the upper crust, the middle class and the gentry, which sounds like the rumble of approaching social thunder and is prophetic of Spartacus. Nowhere else in ancient literature can I recall so acrid a smell of slaves' sweat and spleen.

Count Harry Kessler, *Diaries*

Time . . .
Worships language and forgives
Everyone by whom it lives.

W. H. Auden, 'Homage to W. B. Yeats'

We know very little about the lives of most ancient dramatists, and about Plautus we know even less than usual. Even his name is something of a puzzle. Maccius comes from the Latin word for clown and some scholars say that Plautus itself comes from the Latin word for actor. A celebrated comic playwright who goes by the name of Clown-Actor seems altogether too much of a coincidence. Other scholars says that his name derives from Plotus, an Umbrian word meaning flat-footed or big-eared, in which case he would more reasonably be known as Titus Big-Ears, the Comedian.

He was born in Sarsina in northern Italy, not far from Rimini. Like nearly every writer in the early republic, he was not himself of Roman origin and, perhaps more crucially, he came from a part of Italy that lay outside the immediate Greek sphere of influence. He is said – quite unreliably – to have made money 'in the service of the theatrical artists', lost it again through unwise investments, and turned to playwriting to restore his fortunes. What is indisputable is that he seems to have had an instinctive feeling for the theatre and it's not unreasonable to suppose that, like Shakespeare or Molière, he knew the business intimately from the inside.

Plautus' work met with extraordinary success, and not just in his lifetime. His plays continued to be revived after his death. In the second century AD there were as many as a hundred and thirty plays circulating under his name. A grammarian called Marcus Terentius Varro selected twenty-one of them as being genuine and these are the works that have come down to us. The full list of titles is as follows: *Amphitruo*, *Asinaria* (The Comedy of the Ass), *Aulularia* (The Pot of Gold), *Captivi* (The Prisoners), *Curculio*, *Casina*, *Cistellaria* (The Comedy of the Chest), *Epidicus*, *Bacchides*, *Mostellaria* (The Haunted House), *Menaechmi*, *Miles Gloriosus* (The Braggart Soldier), *Mercator* (The Merchant), *Pseudolus*, *Poenulus* (The Poor Carthaginian), *Persa* (The Persian), *Rudens* (The Rope), *Stichus*, *Trinummus* (The Three Coins), *Truculentus*, *Vidularia* (The Comedy of the Hamper).

Modern scholars have confirmed from internal evidence that all these are by the same hand. The remaining one hundred and nine, including nineteen that Varro thought were probably but not certainly genuine, were lost in late antiquity. We know that *Pseudolus* was first performed in 191 BC and *Casina* in 186 but we have no dates for the other plays.

When Plautus was born Rome had conquered her immediate neighbours in central Italy but did not yet bulk large in the general scheme of things. She was in the middle of the First Punic War (264–241 BC), fought against Carthage, a Phoenician colony on the coast of North Africa, for control of the eastern Mediterranean. This was followed by the conquest of northern Italy up to the Alps, the Second Punic War 218–201 BC (the famous war against Hannibal), the First and Second Macedonian Wars, and the War against Antiochus of Syria. By the time Plautus died Rome had extended her rule from one end of the Mediterranean to the other.

Plautus is the first commercial playwright to have come down to us – neither Aristophanes nor Menander wrote for a living – and this is an important shaping factor in his work. If the audience wasn't entertained, Plautus did not eat. His plays were based on Greek originals but these originals underwent a radical process of rewriting. Plautus tunnelled into the structures of Greek New Comedy, blew them up, and reassembled the fragments into something that might have looked like the original but was in fact a genuinely new creation.

He was helped in this work of transformation by the existence of a native Italian form of comedy called the Atellan farce, after the town of Atella in Campania where it is supposed to have originated. This was a lively kind of *commedia dell'arte*–style entertainment, improvised round stock characters such as the Foolish Old Man, the Glutton, the Braggart, the Swindler, the Clown and so on. Plautus may have owed his command of situation to these popular farces that he had seen, or even acted in, but his brilliant use of language with its gaudy vocabulary, its extravagant rhythms, its wall-to-wall inventiveness, was uniquely his own. There is also the music. It's worth remembering when we read these plays that well over half of each work was either sung or took the form of an accompanied recitative. In some ways Plautus stands as close to rap (and to Rossini) as he does to Shakespeare. So perhaps it's no surprise that his work has given birth to successful Broadway shows such as *Up Pompeii* and *A Funny Thing Happened on the Way to the Forum*.

The Swaggering Soldier (Miles Gloriosus)

∽ The story

A young Athenian Pleusicles (Famous Sailor) is in love with a courtesan called Philocomasium (Party Girl). While he is away on business, she is snatched by a mercenary called Pyrgopolynices (Tower Many Quarrels) who spirits her away to Ephesus.

Pleusicles has a slave called Palaestrio (Wrestler). He sets out to tell his master about the abduction but his ship is captured by pirates, who give him to the self-same Pyrgopolynices as a present. Finding himself in the same household as Philocomasium and finding that she still loves his master, Palaestrio writes Pleusicles a letter, telling him where to find the girl and summoning him to the rescue.

When the play begins Pleusicles has arrived in Ephesus and is living next door to Pyrgopolynices in a house belonging to a family friend Periplectomenus (Guardian). Palaestrio has tunnelled a hole in the wall between the two houses so that the lovers can see each other in secret.

One of Pyrgopolynices' other slaves Sceledrus (Rascal) catches sight of the two lovers kissing and cuddling: quick thinking is called for to prevent the master finding out. Palaestrio manages to convince his fellow slave that

Philocomasium's twin sister has arrived from Athens and has come to stay next door. Philocomasium dashes swiftly between the houses through the secret passage and manages to create the illusion that there are two of her. Sceledrus, convinced that he will be severely punished for slandering his mistress's honour, decides to make himself scarce.

The lovers' secret is still safe but how is Philocomasium ever to escape the clutches of the Swaggering Soldier? Palaestrio comes up with a scheme by which Pyrgopolynices will not only be glad to get rid of her, he will in fact pay for her to be taken off his hands. Palaestrio provides the know-how and Periplectomenus provides the personnel.

An up-market prostitute Acroteleutium (High End) is persuaded to pose as Periplectomenus' wife. She pretends that the Swaggering Soldier is so devastatingly handsome that she cannot help herself and has fallen passionately in love with him. Pyrgopolynices is so vain that he is readily persuaded that this is true. He becomes even more greedy when he realises that she is prepared to leave her husband and bring all her money with her.

Pyrgopolynices is desperate to remove any obstacles to what he sees as a very wealthy match and decides to pay Philocomasium off. Pleusicles poses as the captain of a ship about to leave for Athens and the soldier hurriedly sends the girl off with all the money, clothes and jewels he has given her. Palaestrio is sent along too as part of the package.

Finally everything seems set and Pyrgopolynices enters his neighbour's house to get to grips with his new admirer. But Periplectomenus has prepared an ambush for him. He is set on by the servants and beaten up for making advances to a married woman. Periplectomenus' cook even threatens to lop off his manhood with a carving knife. The mighty warrior turns out not be so mighty after all. He begs abjectly to be let off and retires bedraggled to his quarters

∾ About the play

> Shall we their fond pageant see?
> Lord, what fools these mortals be!
>> Shakespeare, *A Midsummer Night's Dream*

> We've just defied hot-iron tortures, crucifixion, chains,
> Strappadoes, fetters, dungeons, locking, stocking, manacles,
> And harsh persuasive whippers well acquainted with our
>> backs!
>> Plautus, *Asinaria*, tr. Erich Segal

The clever slave is a favourite Plautus character. In *The Swaggering Soldier* Pyrgopolynices may be the title part, but it's Palaestrio who drives the action. He not only carries out the various impostures, he invents them too: in this respect he is the playwright's proxy. In one of Plautus' last plays, *Pseudolus*, the slave who is running the intrigue has a speech which makes this relationship explicit.

PSEUDOLUS: No, Pseudolus, you haven't a clue, which end to start weaving or where to finish off. Well, after all, when a poet sits down to write he has to start by looking for something which doesn't exist on this earth and somehow or other he finds it; he makes a fiction look very much like fact. That's what I'll do; I'll be a poet.
>> tr. E. F. Watling

Working out a decent double-cross isn't easy though.

PERIPLECTOMENUS: Well, look at him!
Standing pensive, pondering profundities with wrinkled brow.
Now he knocks upon his head – he wants his brains to answer him.
Look – he turns. Now he supports himself with his left hand on his left thigh.
Now he's adding something with the fingers of his right hand. Now he

Slaps his right thigh – what a slap! What a to-do for what
    to do!
Look – he shakes his head. No, no, what he's invented
    doesn't please him
He'll cook up a plan that's well done – not half-baked –
    I'm sure of that.
    tr. Erich Segal

One of the ironies of the play is that Pyrgopolynices is supposed to be the great commander; the real strategist, however, is not the master but the slave.

PALAESTRIO: Then awake and beware the foeman is near;
He is laying an ambush to cut off your rear.
Look alive and take thought how to counter the host,
Do not sleep at your ease, there's no time to be lost,
Make a march, intercept him, get men up and doing,
Outflank the invader and save us from ruin,
Starve out the besiegers but save your supplies
And protect your own lines of defence from surprise.
    tr. E. F. Watling

As well as strategist, Palaestrio also doubles as field commander.

PALAESTRIO: Hey Periplectomenus and Pleusicles, produce
    yourselves.
PERIPLECTOMENUS: Here – at your command.
PALAESTRIO: Commanding's easy when your troops are
    good.
    tr. Erich Segal

The military metaphors would have had a particular reso-
nance because throughout the whole of Plautus' writing life
Rome was continuously at war. These were the campaigns
that turned her into a great Mediterranean power – the
Second Illyrian War (220–219 BC), the Second Punic War
(218–201 BC), the First Macedonian War (215–205 BC), the
Second Macedonian War (200–196 BC) and the War against
Antiochus III of Syria (192–189 BC).

Not only do the spectators see the intrigue put together before their eyes like an improvisation, and all the effort that goes into making it a success, there is also a real penalty to be paid if things don't work out. It's not just a question of having ideas; physical bravery comes into it as well. Palaestrio's campaign puts him in real danger of bodily harm: the threat of a good flogging or even crucifixion is constantly evoked. The cowardly Sceledrus makes his first entry already fearing the worst.

> SCELEDRUS: Today I fear we slaves are really leaping into
> Trouble and titanic tortures . . .
> If master learns of this
> Our whole household will be on the cross, by Hercules!
> Me as well!
> tr. Erich Segal

Palaestrio, though, is made of sterner stuff – and for the audience the danger he's in is part of the thrill: it's like watching an acrobat who works without a safety net. The risks he is taking are part of the pleasure.

The play's reversal of traditional values goes one step further when the warrior Pyrgopolynices is set upon by his neighbour's servants and threatened with castration: the military man turns out to be not so very brave after all.

> PYRGOPOLYNICES: Oh!! Enough, enough!
> COOK: When does the carving begin?
> PYRGOPOLYNICES: Mercy, mercy! Hear me before he cuts!
> PERIPLECTOMENUS: You may speak.
> PYRGOPOLYNICES: It wasn't my fault. I thought she was
> unmarried
> tr. E. F. Watling

This is a long way from the outrageous bragging that opens the play.

> ARTROTROGUS: How many? Yes, a hundred and fifty in
> Cilicia, a hundred in Scytholatronia, Sardians thirty,

Macedonians sixty – killed that is – in one day alone.
PYRGOPOLYNICES: How many does that make altogether?
ARTROTROGUS: Seven thousand
PYRGOPOLYNICES: Must be at least that.
ARTROTROGUS: And what about Cappadocia where you
    slaughtered five hundred at one fell swoop – or would
    have done if your sword hadn't been blunt at the time?
    tr. E. F Watling

Pyrgopolynices even claims to have taken on an elephant with his bare hands.

ARTROTROGUS: And then that elephant in India –
   The way your fist just broke his arm to smithereens.
PYRGOPOLYNICES: What's that – his *arm*?
ARTROTROGUS: I meant his leg of course.
PYRGOPOLYNICES: I just gave him an easy jab.
ARTROTROGUS: A jab, of course!
   If you had really tried you would have smashed his arm
   Right through his elephantine skin and guts and bone!
    tr. Erich Segal

The character is splendid, memorable, larger than life – but not much use dramatically. He's so self-satisfied that he's too inert to drive the plot. He's not a doer but only someone done-to, so he has to be tidied out of the way until the denouement, and the action handed over to Palaestrio.

The play divides into four. There are two intrigues, each prefaced by a character study. In the first intrigue Philocomasium scampers from house to house to convince the slave Sceledrus that she is her own twin. The prologue to this is Pyrgopolynices' unforgettable first entry and his monstrous boasting. The second intrigue is the gulling of Pyrgopolynices by Acroteleutium and her maid so that Philocomasium can go free. The preface to this is a portrait of the good life, as exemplified by all the anti-braggart virtues – true courage and intelligence (Palaestrio), affection (Pleusicles) and self-knowledge coupled with generosity (Periplectomenus).

PERIPLECTOMENUS: Thank the gods I can afford to entertain
 you as I'd like to.

 Eat! Drink up! Indulge yourself, let laughter overflow the
  brim!

 Mine's the house of freedom – I am free – I live my life
  for me.

 Thank the gods, I'm rich enough. I could've married very
  well,

 Could've led a wealthy wife to the altar.

 But I wouldn't want to lead a barking dog into my house.
  tr. Erich Segal

Pyrgopolynices' prodigious vanity is stoked by
Acroteleutium's little maidservant, just as Malvolio is fooled
by Maria 'the smallest wren of nine' in *Twelfth Night*. *The
Swaggering Soldier* is full of reminders of Shakespeare – not
just Ancient Pistol in *Henry IV Part II* but also Falstaff after
Gad's Hill.

PRINCE: What, fought ye with them all?
FALSTAFF: All! I know not what ye call all; but if I fought not
 with fifty of them, I am a bunch of radish; if there were
 not two or three and fifty upon poor old Jack, then I am
 no two–legged creature.
PRINCE: Pray God you have not murdered some of them.
FALSTAFF: Nay, that's past praying for.

There is also the empty and magniloquent Parolles in *All's
Well that Ends Well*, and Mistress Ford and Mistress Page
writing to entice their elderly beau in *The Merry Wives of
Windsor*; perhaps it's not too fanciful to see even the industri-
ous Puck as a distant descendant of one of Plautus' slaves.
The character of Captain Brazen in *The Recruiting Officer* by
George Farquhar shows that the joke about the soldier who is
both cowardly and boastful is still going strong as late as AD
1706.

 Pyrgopolynices' first entrance is centred round his military
exploits – his domination over other men. His second appear-

ance is about his personal vanity, his quite imaginary powers
over women, and his pathetic openness to flattery.

PYRGOPOLYNICES: Do you know the great honour I lavish
    upon her?
MAID: I know and I'll certainly tell her.
PALAESTRIO: The demand is so great I could ask for his
    weight in pure gold –
MAID: By the gods, you'd receive it!
PALAESTRIO: And the women he lies with he fecundifies with
    real heroes – and would you believe it –
  The children he rears live for eight hundred years.
MAID: Oh please stop it, you joker – I'm crying!
    tr. Erich Segal

A repeated joke is that Pyrgopolynices' attractions are so
powerful that women simply faint away at the sight of him.

ACROTELEUTIUM: Oh, hold me!
MAID: Why?
ACROTELEUTIUM: I'm falling.
MAID: Why?
ACROTELEUTIUM: Because I can't stand up!
MAID: By Pollux then you've seen the soldier!
ACROTELEUTIUM: Yes!
    tr. Erich Segal

Plautus is sometimes reproached with being a frankly male-
centred writer. It's certainly true that Philocomasium in this
play is more a trophy than a person, and that Periplectomenus
exhibits a conventional horror at the thought of being tied
down by a wife; but the sparky little maid, Milphidippa, and
Acroteleutium, fully aware of the power of her own beauty
and delighted to use her intelligence in the cause of mischief,
are splendid creations in their own right.

The Swaggering Soldier is thought to come early in Plautus'
career. It is his longest work and metrically one of the least
complex. The use of music is also comparatively restrained.
There are no big set-piece arias as in *The Menaechmus Twins*

(see below); yet what might seem strange to a modern audience is that in a play of 1,400 lines only 400 hundred or so are spoken without some form of musical accompaniment. The most lyrical passage comes when Milphidippa and Palaestrio, in an ecstasy of inventiveness, cook up their plot to hoodwink Pyrgopolynices. The music here gives the scene its special expansiveness and helps portray the couple's mounting delight at the success of their plan.

∼ Translations

The play is well served by Erich Segal (Oxford) and E. F. Watling (Penguin).

∼ In performance

The first performance cannot be dated securely. Scholars place the play early in Plautus' career and the year is generally given (on the basis of internal evidence) as 206 BC.

The Menaechmus Twins (*Menaechmi*)

∼ The story

A Syracusan merchant had two sons who were twins. When they were seven he took one of them with him on a business trip away from home. The boy's name was Menaechmus. Menaechmus became separated from his father in the crowd and was snatched by a merchant from Epidamnus. The merchant took the boy home, adopted him, saw him married to a wealthy wife, and left him his fortune when he died. The father meanwhile died of grief.

The grandfather brought up the other twin and changed the boy's name to Menaechmus to keep alive the memory of the brother who was lost. When this second Menaechmus

(Menaechmus 2) grew up he set off to find his missing brother.

The action of the play takes place in Epidamnus in the fifth year of the search. On this particular day Menaechmus 1, who is unhappily married to a shrewish wife, plans to spend the afternoon with his mistress, eating and having sex. He has stolen an expensive dress from his wife as a present for the girl. While lunch is being prepared he and his hanger-on Peniculus go to visit the forum.

Meanwhile Menaechmus 2 arrives in town with his slave Messenio. Their search has been going badly and their money is nearly exhausted. Menaechmus 2 can hardly believe his luck when suddenly a beautiful woman (his brother's mistress) appears and invites him into her house to eat and have sex with her. She also gives him an expensive dress, which she says she wants altered, and also a gold bracelet to take to the jeweller's.

Returning at the end of the meal, Peniculus, the hanger-on, is furious to find that his friend has apparently eaten lunch without him. He tells the wife that her husband is cheating on her. Menaechmus 1, back from the forum and looking forward to an afternoon of sexual dalliance, find himself confronted by a vengeful friend and an angry wife. To placate his wife he asks his mistress to give him back the dress. Thinking he already has it, she is furious and slams the door in his face.

Menaechmus 2 now appears carrying the dress, which Menaechmus 1's wife claims as hers. He has no idea who she is and tells her to get lost. The outraged wife sends for her father to back her up. The old man arrives and tries to reconcile the couple but without success. Menaechmus 2 pretends to be mad and puts the wife and the old man to flight. He sets off for the harbour to look for Messenio.

Thinking that his son-in-law is out of his mind the old man comes back with a doctor. As if Menaechmus 1's day had not been bad enough he is now taken for a lunatic. Four burly servants set upon him and begin to carry him off. Messenio, thinking that his master is being attacked, rescues him in the nick of time.

Eventually the two brothers meet and at Messenio's prompting work out that they are related. Menaechmus 1 decides to auction off his property (his wife too if anyone will have her) and return with his twin to Syracuse. Messenio is granted his freedom: his first job will be that of auctioneer.

Menaechmus was a celebrated mathematician of the period; in naming the twins after him Plautus is calling them the equivalent of Einstein.

⌒ About the play

Mon semblable! Mon frère!
  Charles Baudelaire, *Les fleurs du mal*

The first thing to say about *The Menaechmus Twins* is how vivid it is and how boldly drawn. This is Plautus' distinctive contribution to New Comedy. The first character we meet in Menander's *The Girl from Samos*, written a hundred years before, is a young man wondering how to tell his father that he has got their next-door neighbour pregnant. The first character we meet in Terence's *The Eunuch*, written fifty years later, is a young man worrying about his girlfriend and whether she really loves him or not. The opening of *The Menaechmus Twins* works in quite a different way. The first person we meet here is looking for a good meal – a sign that the play will be about appetites, not emotions. Then we are catapulted straight into the middle of a marital row. A man wearing a dress under his ordinary clothes comes out of his house and *sings*.

MENAECHMUS 1: If you weren't such a shrew, uncontrolled, ungrateful too

Whatever thing your husband hated, you'd find hateful too.

And if you act up once again, the way you've acted up today

I'll have you packed up – back to Daddy as a divorcée.
However often I try to go out you detain me, delay me,
    demand such details as
Where I'm going, what I'm doing, what's my business all
    about,
Deals I'm making, undertaking, what I did when I was
    out.
I don't have a wife, I have a customs office bureaucrat,
For I must declare the things I've done, I'm doing, and all
    that!
    tr. Erich Segal

Plautus is not interested in character but in situations. He
gives his people strong clear outlines and without wasting any
more time throws them together to see what happens. What
he likes best are three-handed scenes with two people going
at each other hammer and tongs and the third character
commenting, restraining the combatants, or egging them on.
Here is Menaechmus 1 offering the stolen dress tō his mistress while his hanger-on Peniculus chips in from the side-
lines.

MENAECHMUS 1: What risks I ran in stealing this!
    Hercules in labour number nine was not as brave as I,
    When he stole the girdle from that Amazon Hippolyta.
    Take it, darling, since you do your duties with such dili-
    gence.
MISTRESS: That's the spirit. Lovers ought to learn from you
    the way to love.
PENICULUS: Sure, that way to love's the perfect short cut to a
    bankruptcy.
MENAECHMUS 1: Just last year I bought my wife this dress. It
    cost two hundred drachmae.
PENICULUS: Well, there goes two hundred drachmae down
    the drain, by my accounts.
    tr. Erich Segal

This trio format is capable of enormous variation and its

unpredictability is part of its attraction. Here is another example from later in the play.

WIFE: Pulled a fast one on the sly, didn't you?
MENAECHMUS 1: What fast one are you talking about?
WIFE: You're asking me?
MENAECHMUS 1: Should I ask him instead?
WIFE: Take your paws off me.
PENICULUS: That's the way.
MENAECHMUS 1:   What are you so cross about?
WIFE: You ought to know.
PENICULUS: He knows all right, he's just faking.
MENAECHMUS 1:   With reference to what?
WIFE: That dress, that's what.
MENAECHMUS 1:   What dress that's what?
WIFE: A certain silk dress.
PENICULUS: Why is your face turning pale?
MENAECHMUS 1: It isn't.
PENICULUS: No, not much paler than a thin silk dress.
   That'll teach you to go off and eat dinner behind my back.
   Keep pitching into him.
      tr. Palmer Bovie

The presence of the third character keeps the audience on its toes. It switches the focus around and stops the scene from becoming predictable.

The second half of the play consists of a succession of trios in which the power balance varies. First Peniculus and the Wife ambush Menaechmus 1 when he returns from the forum: the scene ends with the discomfiture of Peniculus. Then Menaechmus 2 treats the Wife with such contempt that she calls her father to help her out. Thirdly the father and the doctor set upon Menaechmus 1 when they think he has taken leave of his senses. Last of all is the recognition scene in which Messenio flits between the two brothers as he teases out the facts of the situation.

The Menaechmus Twins begins with the pursuit of pleasure. Peniculus is looking for a good dinner and the solid citizen

Menaechmus 1 is looking to escape his wife and spend the day with his mistress at table and in bed. He has plenty of money – the dress he steals from his wife to give to his mistress, the dress he is wearing at the beginning of the play to smuggle it out of the house, is worth the price of a good ploughman – but his life is not rich in satisfaction. The day begins promisingly but soon veers towards disaster. First Menaechmus is delayed at the forum by an importunate client who not only makes him late for his rendezvous but then insists on ruining everything by not taking his advice. Next he returns to find that someone else has eaten his food and bedded his mistress. After that he is ambushed by his wife and set upon by the doctor's slaves. If Messenio had not stepped in to rescue him he would have ended in the madhouse. His day has been full of frustrations from beginning to end.

As if in a fairy-tale, the penniless Menaechmus 2 gets to enjoy all the pleasures that his twin had so painstakingly lined up for himself. Not only does he get free food and sex but he even gets paid for his enjoyment when Erotium gives him the valuable dress and the gold bracelet. Perhaps best of all, he gets to tell the harridan Wife a few home truths. In this respect he is his hen-pecked brother's unrestrained and uncensored alter ego.

MENAECHMUS 2: Good woman, did ye never hear why the Grecians termed Hecuba to be a bitch?

WIFE: Never.

MENAECHMUS 2: Because she did as you do now; on whomsoever she met withal she railed, and therefore well deserved that dogged name.

WIFE: These foul abuses and contumelies I can never endure; nay, rather will I live a widow's life till my dying day.

MENAECHMUS 2: Prithee for my part, live a widow till the world's end, if thou wilt.

tr. William Warner

This topsy-turvy holiday atmosphere is something common to all Plautus' plays, which take place not in Rome but in an imaginary place called Greece, where a different set of norms applies. This world – named Plautinopolis by one recent commentator – is internally coherent, but exists nowhere on earth. In Plautinopolis characters are free to behave in ways which in puritanical conservative Rome would get them arrested or even worse. This is a world where money matters less than love; where sons openly defy their fathers (who in real life exercised the power of life and death over their families); where wives are always shrewish, never dutiful; where gods are disrespected with impunity; where people eat rich food prohibited by law and where slaves cheat their masters and escape scot-free.

Another device that Plautus uses to keep the audience on their toes is direct address. These moments are not soliloquies, where characters are overheard talking to themselves, but direct appeals to the audience's complicity.

MENAECHMUS 1: My word barrage has put the wife in full retreat. It's victory!
   Now where are all the married 'lovers'? Pin your medals right on me.
   Come honour me en masse. Look how I've battled with such guts.
   And look this dress I stole inside – it will soon be my little slut's.
      tr. Erich Segal

Sometimes a character will have an entrance aria in which they introduce themselves through song. This is how Menaechmus 1's father-in-law first presents himself.

OLD MAN: Oh, my old age, my old age, I lack what I need,
   I'm stepping unlively, unfast is my speed,
   But it isn't so easy, I tell you, not easy indeed,
   For I've lost all my quickness, old age is a sickness.
   My body's a big heavy trunk . . .
      tr. Erich Segal

This device not only saves time, it also serves to lodge the character from the outset firmly in the audience's imagination. When Messenio, the slave who has only been a minor personage in the first half of the play, needs to be brought into focus shortly before the final denouement, Plautus gives him an aria of his own.

MESSENIO: If you should seek the proof of whether some-
    one's slave is good,
  See, does he honour his master's interest, serve right to
    the letter
  When Master is away – the way he should
  If Master were at hand – or even better.
  For if the slave is worthy, and he's well brought up,
  He'll care to keep his shoulders empty – not to fill his
    cup.
  His master will reward him.
    tr. Erich Segal

This oscillation between the (literally) show-stopping numbers and the accelerated rhythm of the three-handed scenes gives typical texture of a Plautus play. Singing is always a sympathetic thing to do; the Wife, who is the villain of the piece, only has a spoken part.

The Greek writers of New Comedy took music out of their plays in the interest of verisimilitude: the Romans put it back in the interest of entertainment. It was another way for them to make their characters appear larger than life. For three quarters of its length *The Menaechmus Twins* is half spoken and half sung, either as aria or recitative; the last quarter of the play is almost wholly sung. It could be said the play is closer to comic opera than it is to Shakespeare. It's impossible in translation to convey Plautus' mastery of rhythm – both long-range, as a way of structuring the story, and short-range, as way of creating the interaction between the characters. Plautus' language has a quite extraordinary exuberance and kick. It's full of puns and a bit of blasphemy and a bit of bawdy (not too much) and a lot of backchat and alliteration and new coinages – strange diminutives, extravagant superlatives, and loan-words from the Greek. When Menaechmus 1 has been turned away by both his wife and his mistress he speaks of himself as *exclusissimus* – 'absolutely, totally and completely shut out'. The vibrant antic quality of Plautinopolis exists at the level of language too.

∿ Translations

The best modern version is by Erich Segal (Oxford). There is a lively Elizabethan translation by William Warner, though it takes no account of the different registers (spoken/sung etc) of the original. It is most readily available as an appendix to the Signet edition of *The Comedy of Errors*. Also useful are Palmer Bovie (Johns Hopkins) and E. F. Watling (Penguin)

∿ In performance

There is no firm date for the first performance, which took place sometime roughly between 200 and 180 BC. *The Menaechmi* was presented at the ducal court of Ferrara in Italian translation in AD 1486. Shakespeare made an adaptation, *The Comedy of Errors*, *c.*1589, as did Goldoni – *I due gemelli Veneziani* – in 1746. Rodgers and Hart's musical version, *The Boys from Syracuse*, was written in 1938.

Terence (Quintus Terentius Afer), *c*.195–160 BC

Life

> O'erstep not the modesty of nature . . .
> Shakespeare, *Hamlet*, Act III, Scene 4

> I was exhilarated at finding that a Latin author could be
> read rather than solved like a quadratic equation . . .
> Edmund Wilson, *A Piece of My Mind*

Terence's life is far better documented than that of Plautus –
even if many of the supposed 'facts' are unreliable. The historian Suetonius wrote a biography of Terence about two hundred and fifty years after his death, which was transmitted to
us by a Christian writer called Donatus two hundred years
after that, as part of his commentary on Terence's plays.

According to Suetonius, Terence was born in the year 184
BC in Carthage in north Africa. He was brought to Rome as a
slave by the senator Terentius Lucanus who – 'on account of
his intelligence and good looks' – looked after his education
and later set him free. He enjoyed the friendship of many of
the nobility, especially Gnaeus Laelius and Scipio Aemilianus,
and it was rumoured that they were the true authors of his
work. (Much the same, of course, has been said about
Shakespeare.) He is reputed to have read his first play to the
famous comic dramatist Caecilius who was so impressed he
asked Terence to join him at dinner. He died young, apparently in a drowning accident on a trip to Athens, where he had
gone to track down copies of Menander's plays. In one version
of the story he is said to have dropped the precious manu-
scripts overboard and then been so distraught he jumped in
after them. He left a daughter, who married into the eques-
trian order, and a small estate near the temple of Mars.

There are several difficulties with this account – not least that Caecilius had died two years before Terence's first play was performed. The story of Terence's Carthaginian origin too may be no more than an inference from his cognomen Afer, 'The African' and the date of his birth is also suspect. It so happens that 184 BC is the year that Plautus died and ancient commentators liked to make the line of succession clear by matching the birth of a new writer to the death of an old one.

Terence wrote six comedies: *Andria* 166 BC, *Hecyra* (*The Mother-in-Law*) 165 BC, revived twice in 160, *Heautontimoroumenos* (*The Self-Punisher*) 163 BC, *Eunuchus* (*The Eunuch*) 161 BC, *Phormio* 161 BC and *Adelphoe* (*The Brothers*) 160 BC.

Perhaps the most trenchant and insightful criticism of his work comes from an unlikely quarter: Julius Caesar. Writing less than a century after Terence's death he went straight to the heart of the matter. He praised the unforced naturalness of the dialogue, calling Terence 'a lover of pure speech' (*puri sermonis amator*); he complained that the plays lacked force; and concluded by saying that Terence was a 'sort of watered-down Menander' (*dimidiate Menander*).

Terence's first play, *Andria*, was staged two years after the battle of Pydna in which Rome broke the power of the kings of Macedon. This began a new period when Greek influence at Rome was particularly strong. The spoils brought home by the conquerors included two hundred and fifty wagons full of paintings and sculpture and the whole of the defeated King Perseus' royal library. There had always been lively contact at a popular level – southern Italy was full of cities that were Greek colonies – but the sudden enthusiasm for things Greek among the aristocracy was something new. It became the fashion among the nobility to have your children educated by a Greek tutor – much as Tolstoy's aristocrats had a 'mademoiselle' as part of the household.

The plays of Terence reflect this altered climate. Like all the early Roman dramatists, Terence based his works on Greek originals; but where Plautus was quite ruthless, Romanizing what he wanted and jettisoning the rest, Terence made a particular effort to stay true to the spirit of his models. Where Plautus is radical and popular, Terence is conservative and of more limited appeal. He rejected the boisterousness of his Roman predecessors in favour of something quieter and more restrained, and his attempt to portray everyday life through the medium of observed speech was in many ways ahead of its time. Terence's struggles to humanize the dramatic stereotypes that he had inherited bring him curiously close to August Strindberg, who had his own difficulties in that area, as his *Preface to Miss Julie* testifies:

> Men have tried to create a new drama by pouring new ideas into the old forms. But this has failed, partly because the new thinkers have not yet had time to become popularised and thus educate the public to understand the issues involved . . . and partly also because we have not succeeded in adapting the old form to the new content, so that the new wine has burst the old bottles.
>
> tr. Michael Meyer

The Eunuch (*Eunuchus*)

∿ The story

The action of the play takes place in Athens and follows the adventures of two brothers. The older brother is called Phaedria and the younger is called Chaerea.

The older brother is in love with a courtesan and suffers agonies of jealousy because he has to share her with a soldier, who has more money than he does and can outspend him. Phaedria woos the girl by buying her an expensive eunuch and a slave girl from Ethiopia, but the soldier, Thraso, outdoes this by offering the services of a beautiful well-educated slave called Pamphila.

Pamphila, as it turns out, is not a slave at all, but a free citizen of Athens who was kidnapped as a child. The courtesan, Thais, hopes to restore the girl to her real family and in doing so stake her own claim to be admitted to full citizenship. She asks Phaedria to go off to the country for a few days until she can track down the girl's relatives: that way there can be no danger that the jealous Thraso will make a scene and take his gift back.

While Phaedria is away, the younger brother, who is something of a rake, passes Pamphila in the street and is completely smitten with her. He dresses up as a eunuch and pretends to be the elder brother's present in order to gain entry to the courtesan's house and see the girl again.

Thraso and Thais quarrel. He is overcome with jealousy when she invites Pamphila's last surviving relative to a party he is giving. He arrives at the head of a posse of his slaves and attempts to storm Thais' house and take back his present – but Thais and Pamphila's brother refuse to give the girl up.

Chaerea meanwhile has set the cat among the pigeons. Left alone in a house full of women and quite unable to control himself, he has flung himself on Pamphila and raped her. Delighted with his success he makes off to a friend's house to change out of his disguise.

Thais is furious with Phaedria because the eunuch he gave her has misbehaved in such a spectacular way. Now the girl has been dishonoured her family will be unable to take her back. Gradually the truth comes out and Chaerea, head over heels in love, agrees to marry Pamphila once he learns her status as a free citizen.

Chaerea and Pamphila are betrothed. Phaedria cannot marry Thais but Thraso is tricked into paying all the courtesan's expenses so that Phaedria can enjoy the girl cost-free.

∾ About the play

Terence has the unhappy distinction of being the author of the world's first resounding flop. His play *The Mother-in-Law* failed not once but twice. The first time it was put on the audience was under the impression that they were about to see some boxing and a display of tightrope-walking. There was a near riot and the play had to be called off. At the second performance everything was going well until the end of the first act when word went round that there was going to be a show of gladiators. A crowd burst into the theatre shouting and scrimmaging for places; the actors, unable to compete, were obliged to give up. *The Eunuch*, however, was an unqualified success. It is said to have been performed twice in one day and to have earned the highest fee ever paid for a comedy up to that time.

The kinds of things the playwright is interested in are clear from the very first speech.

PHAEDRIA: So what should I do? Should I not go, even now when she calls me? I ought to get a grip on myself, oughtn't I? Refuse to endure the insults of courtesans. She shut me out, she calls me back; shall I go? No, not if she begs me. If only I could leave her, that would be the best course, and the bravest. But suppose I start on it and haven't the strength to carry it off . . .

Terence likes emotion, ambivalence, complication. The passage quoted looks forward a hundred years to Catullus' famous love poem.

I hate and I love. And if you ask me how
I do not know: I only feel it and I'm torn in two.
tr. Peter Whigham

Like Plautus, Terence adapted his works from Greek originals. *The Eunuch* is based on two plays – *The Eunuch* and *The Flatterer* – by Menander, which have been put together to make something new. Plautus' plays are like comic fantasias on themes from Greek comedy and quickly start to take on a life of their own. Terence sticks more closely to his sources, although he brings his own particular sensibility to bear on them. His interest is not so much in what the characters do, as in what their emotions are while they are doing it. If the line of descent from Plautus ends in the modern musical then Terence's descendant is the soap opera.

The Eunuch opens with Phaedria talking about his feeling for his mistress; Act I ends with the mistress talking about her feelings for Phaedria.

THAIS: Ah me! I fear that he believes me not,
And judges of my heart from those of others.
I in my conscience know, that nothing false
I have deliver'd, nor to my true heart
Is any dearer than this Phaedria.
  tr. George Colman

Thais, it turns out, is very far from being the sort of girl who is interested principally in money. This technique of presenting traditional stock characters from the inside helps to blur their contours and make their behaviour appear less predictable. Parmeno, Phaedria's slave, in the first scene looks worldly and rather patronizing, leading the audience to think that perhaps he will be one of those skilled intriguers who knit the action of a play together. But then his judgement starts to seem questionable. He misinterprets Thais' motives, seeing her as no more than a conventional gold-digger. Finally his air of competence is exposed as simple bluster. Here he is trying to break the news to old man Laches that his younger son is about to be castrated for adultery.

PARMENO: I'm undone; my tongue
Cleaves to my mouth through fear.
LACHES: Ha! What's the matter?
Why do you tremble so? Is all right? Speak!
PARMENO: First be persuaded sir, – for that's the case
Whatever has befallen, has not befallen
Through any fault of mine.
LACHES: What is't?
PARMENO: That's true.
Your pardon, sir. I should have told that first
Phaedria lately bought a certain Eunuch
By way of present to this gentlewoman.
LACHES: What gentlewoman?

PARMENO: Madam Thais,
LACHES: Bought? I'm undone! at what price?
PARMENO: Twenty minae.
LACHES: I'm ruined.
PARMENO: And then Chaerea's fall'n in love
　　With a young musick-girl.
LACHES: How! what! in love!
　　Knows he already what a harlot is?
　　Is he in town? Misfortune on misfortune!
PARMENO: Nay sir! Don't look on me! It was not done
　　By my advice.

　　　tr. George Colman

Plutarch tells a celebrated anecdote about Menander, which goes as follows. The deadline is getting near and a friend says to the playwright, 'I wonder if you've managed to finish your new play yet?' 'Finished my play?' says Menander. 'Oh absolutely. I've got the plot worked out – I just have to put in the dialogue.' Working in this way, Menander put together plays which were all-of-a-piece; Terence's preoccupations often brought him into conflict with the plot that he'd inherited. He is the first, but by no means the last, playwright to be caught between the desire to stay close to his characters and the need to make something happen. What Terence achieves by dint of his alterations is a sort of privatizing of the emotions, which become the property of the individual characters, locked up inside them, instead of reaching out to make the action dance. The result of his tinkering is to create a series of small anecdotal truths, which are agreeable in themselves but impede the forward movement of the play.

The tension between the desire for realism – both of emotion and of physical detail – and the demands of the story shows itself in a strange uncertainty of tone. The rape of Pamphila is a good example. Here is Chaerea's account of what led up to it.

CHAEREA: She sat waiting in her room, looking at a picture
　　on the wall . . . it was the story of Jupiter pouring a

shower of gold into Danaë's lap. I looked at it too and it
got me all excited . . . to think he's played the same game,
disguising himself and coming down, through the sky-
light, to seduce a woman! I thought if he, a god, the
greatest of gods, could do that, why shouldn't I . . .
Anyway the girl went off and had her bath, and then they
brought her back and put her to bed. I stood there in case
she . . . wanted anything. One of the slave girls came up
and said, 'Hey Dorus take this fan and fan her gently
while we have a bath and then when we've finished, we'll
take over so you can have a bath.

tr. Kenneth McLeish

This has a lip-smacking, almost pornographic quality to it.
Later, in the interests of verisimilitude, the playwright gives
the girl's point of view, not once but twice. First from the
maid:

PYTHIAS: The girl's crying and doesn't dare say what happened when you ask her. And that fine fellow is nowhere
to be seen.

And then from the mistress.

THAIS: The girl's dress is torn, she's weeping, and she won't
say a word. The eunuch's gone. Why? What happened?

tr. John Barsby

It's clear that Terence wants to evoke action and reaction as
vividly as possible, yet he seems not to have taken into
account what effect this would have on the play as a whole,
where the marriage of rapist and victim is supposed to be part
of the happy ending. The discomfort arises not because of
modern sensibilities but because the playwright spends too
much time dwelling on things that would have been better
passed over in silence.

On the other hand Terence's delight in realistic detail
means that the play is full of incidental pleasures. There is
Parmeno on the home life of an escort girl.

PARMENO: So long as they're out in public, there's nothing
more refined, more composed, more elegant, as they pick
daintily at their food while dining with a lover. But to see
their filth, squalor, and poverty, and how repulsive they
are when they are alone at home and how greedy they are
for food, how they devour stale bread dipped in yesterday's soup . . .

And Chaerea on women's obsession with their teenage
daughters' looks.

CHAEREA: This girl is different from those local girls whose
mothers want them to round their shoulders and strap up
their chests to make them look slim. If one's a bit plump
they say she looks like a boxer and put her on a diet.
However well endowed she is by nature the treatment
makes her as thin as a reed.
   tr. John Barsby

And Gnatho on the birth of a sponger.

GNATHO: You saw what happened just now when we met
that beggar? He started life as I did: a gentleman, born
into a wealthy family with high social sanding. Then, just
like me, as soon as he inherited, he squandered all his
money. We both ended up bankrupt. But that's where the
resemblance ends . . .
   tr. Kenneth McLeish

And an unforgettable picture of an elderly eunuch, a 'shrivelled, lethargic, senile old man, the colour of a weasel'.

The Eunuch has fourteen speaking parts, more than any
other Roman comedy. This too is part of Terence's concern
for realism. He disliked Menander's practice of filling in the
narrative where necessary by means of direct address and was
always contriving situations where people could tell each
other things the audience needed to know, so that every plot
point could be ticked off. This often led him to go to absurd
lengths. Pamphila's wet-nurse, for example, is needed to

confirm the girl's identity. The action is already so crowded that the vital moment of her recognizing the tokens happens off stage. Nonetheless it's important that she come to bring the news. All we see of the character is as she shuffles slowly from the wings to Thais' house. She has one line, 'I'm coming as fast as I can' and is on stage for a total of about thirty seconds. It has to be one of the least rewarding roles in European drama. The parade of bit parts serves to create a sense of life going on outside and around the central intrigue but it is often quite exhausting for the audience when yet another new person is introduced never to be seen again.

Terence's great gift to the literature of the West was the simplicity and naturalness of his language. It is the polar opposite of Plautus' all-singing, all-dancing dialogue. Characters in Plautus don't express themselves so much as act themselves out; in Terence the audience feels as if it's eavesdropping. The quest for realism is reflected in the movement back towards spoken drama and in the comparatively restrained use of metre. The general relation of spoken to sung in Terence's work as a whole is 52 per cent to 48 per cent. The simplicity of his diction made him a set text for generations of schoolboys – including Shakespeare.

It seems fitting by way of conclusion to put in a word for Terence's director, Lucius Ambivius Turpio, who staged the first performances of all Terence's plays. Here he is speaking in his own behalf in the prologue to the third (and finally successful) production of *The Mother-in-Law*.

> Let me enjoy as an old man the same privilege as I did in my younger days, when I ensured that new plays which had been driven off the stage became established and that scripts did not vanish from sight along with the playwrights.
>
> tr. John Barsby

It seems to have been an exemplary life, devoted to the championing of the new.

∾ Translations

The clearest idea of the play is given by John Barsby's translation in the Loeb bilingual edition. George Colman's version from 1810 is full of charm and there is a racy adaptation by Kenneth McLeish/Malcolm Sargent (Methuen) – though it takes away some of the dignity of the original. The Penguin translation by Betty Radice is both stodgy and opaque.

∾ In performance

According to the records *The Eunuch* was first performed in 161 BC. The play was staged at Weimar in 1803 and broadcast by the BBC Third Programme in 1968. The most recent production was the Courtyard Theatre, London, in 2003.

Seneca (Lucius Annaeus Seneca), *c.* I BC–AD 65

Roman Tragedy

> Enslaved Greece enslaved her savage victor and brought
> The arts to rustic Latium.
>
> Horace, *Epistle*, 2.1

The 'first inventor' of Roman drama was Livius Andronicus, a Greek-speaking former slave form the south of Italy. A tragedy by him adapted from the Greek was presented at the Roman games (*ludi Romani*) in 240 BC at the end of the First Punic War.

Greek tragedy in its origins could draw on a literature and a variety of verse forms that had been developed over hundreds of years. The situation at Rome was quite different; Latin as a literary language was in its infancy. Andronicus himself was a key figure in its development. He translated *The Odyssey* for use in schools and his work for the theatre is the beginning of Latin literature. We have the titles of eight plays by Andronicus: *Achilles, Aegisthus, Ajax, The Trojan Horse, Hermiona, Andromeda, Danaë* and *Tereus*. The writers of Roman tragedy drew their subject matter from Greek myth and their plays were known as *cothurnatae* after the *cothurnus* or raised boot which the actors wore to make them seem more commanding.

As if to compensate for a certain lack of rhythmic sophistication, the language of Roman tragedy was from the start grander and more elevated than the work of the Greek dramatists. The simplicity and strength of Sophocles or the lyric beauty and closeness to ordinary speech which mark the writing of Euripides are left behind. Music too played a more important part than it did in Greece. It was as though the Roman dramatists were striving in every way possible to make their work 'impressive', to re-create the impact of the

Greek tragedians in a different context, using different means.

Italy in this period was a melting pot of theatrical forms.

One of the characteristics of early Roman drama was evidently an uninhibited attitude to generic boundaries. In fifth-century Athens, tragedy, comedy, satyr play and mime were kept carefully separate; the visual evidence suggests, however, that in the fourth- and third-century south-Italian theatre the distinctions were not observed in the same way.

T. P. Wiseman, *Roman Drama and Roman History*

A new, authentically Roman genre was the *fabula praetexta* or 'drama in the purple-bordered toga'. These plays took their subject matter from history, often from contemporary history. They seem to have been ceremonial in nature, perhaps like late mediaeval pageants. They were written to celebrate victories or extol a particular politician's ancestors. For example a *praetexta* called *Brutus*, about the overthrow of the tyrant Tarquin, was performed in 136 BC to mark the victory of one of Brutus' descendants over a Spanish tribe called the Callaeci. A correspondent of Cicero's relates how, at a provincial festival at Cordoba in 43 BC, L. Cornelius Balbus mounted a *praetexta* about his experiences in the Civil War and 'burst into tears during the performance at the poignant memory of his own adventures'. It has been argued that these *praetextae* were an important factor in shaping and transmitting Roman history. Not many titles have survived – but this may simply be because the plays were topical rather than because the audience disliked them.

Drama enjoyed enormous popularity in the early years of the Roman Republic – indeed it was for a while the pre-eminent form of Latin literature. Andronicus was followed by Naevius (who died *c.*200 BC), Ennius (239–*c.*169 BC), Pacuvius (220–130 BC), and Accius (170–*c.*85 BC). Andronicus and Naevius wrote comedies as well as tragedies; Ennius was an epic poet as well as a dramatist. It wasn't until Pacuvius that there was a writer who specialised solely in tragedy. The most successful and popular of the Roman tragedians was Accius. We know the titles of forty of his works, and roughly seven hundred lines survive. His plays included *Astyanax, Atreus, The Bacchae, The Battle on the Ships, Hecuba, Medea, The Myrmidons, Philocteta, Tereus, Thebes* and *The Trojan Women*. After Accius' death his work continued to be revived but no other dramatist of comparable stature arose to take his place.

In many ways Roman tragedy stands closer to the Elizabethans than it does to the Greeks. There is a liking for the lurid and the picturesque. Plots often featured ghosts, prodigies, shipwrecks, murders, treachery, and cruelty of every kind. Drama at Rome was a kind of entertainment not, as it had been for the Athenians, a communal meditation on power and responsibility. The audience must also have had its part to play. The population of Rome – estimated in its heyday at around 800,000 people, more than many modern cities – came from all over the Mediterranean basin. Many of them did not have Latin as their first language. (Slaves for example were granted citizenship on manumission and many were freed after ten years' service.) The diversity of cultures, expectations and languages among the spectators must have influenced the choice of subject matter and the way it was treated.

Accius was the last professional. From this point on tragedy began to separate itself from the theatre; playwrights now were men of independent means. Drama was no longer a way of earning a living but a chance to display one's literary accomplishment. Julius Caesar wrote an *Oedipus*, the Emperor Augustus wrote an *Ajax*, Cicero's brother wrote four tragedies in sixteen days. More impressive works were composed by Asinius Pollio (76 BC–AD 5) and Varius Rufus (75 BC–AD 14). The latter was a friend of Virgil; he helped prepare the *Aeneid* for publication after the poet's death and had one of his tragedies performed as part of the victory celebrations for the battle of Actium. The poet Ovid wrote a *Medea* that was highly praised and seems to have been a strong influence on the plays of Seneca.

In the early empire the theatre was mainly given over to dance, vaudeville and farce, although there were still tragic performances until at least the second century AD. It is a matter of debate as to how and in what context these tragic performances took place. We know for example that in Vespasian's reign (AD 69–79) a writer called Curiatius Maternus recited his tragedies in public. But equally the historian Tacitus tells us that Pomponius Secundus, a contemporary of Seneca's, had a fully staged production of one of his tragedies about AD 55. It seems that in the first century AD there were three ways that tragic drama was performed – as a recital given by a single speaker; as a fully mounted production in a private house; and on the public stage. There was also, of course, publication. But it is clear that in Seneca's time it was over fifty years since tragedy had been a regular part of the Roman theatre.

Life

Seneca's astonishing fusion of spectacle, bombast, paradox, epigram, brevity, plenitude, abstraction, grandeur, violence, disjunction, allusion, sensuousness is not simply a product of a baroque, postclassical sensibility but a means to articulate intellectual and moral urgencies of contemporary Roman life.

J. Boyle, Preface to Seneca's *Troades*

In almost all his tragedies he surpassed (in my opinion) in prudence, in gravity, in decorum, in majesty, in epigrams, all the Greeks who ever wrote.

Giraldi Cintio, *Discorsi*

Senecan tragedy, like Greek, is about power and those who exercise it, and it addresses the issues of power through the language of myth.

Frederick Ahl

Seneca was born into a literary family in Cordoba in southern Spain around the turn of the millennium, sometime between 4 and 1 BC. His father, Lucius Annaeus Seneca the Elder, was the author of a history of Rome (now lost) and two treatises on public speaking, *Controversiae* and *Suasoriae*. Seneca was the middle of three sons. His younger brother Mela was the father of the poet Lucan.

At Rome he was educated in rhetoric with a view to a political career and came into contact with the Stoic philosophy that was to have such a strong influence on his life and work. It seems that he suffered from some tubercular condition and spent part of his twenties in North Africa for his health. On his return to Rome in AD 31 he embarked on a career as a lawyer and politician. He survived the reign of Caligula (only just – it is said that Caligula wanted to have him killed but was talked out of it by a friend) but was exiled to Corsica by the Emperor Claudius for eight years AD 41–9.

Claudius' second wife Agrippina brought him back to court and made him tutor to her son Nero. When Nero became Emperor in AD 54, Seneca was one of his closest advisers, part of 'that tiny group of men on which there bore down, night and day, the concentric pressure of an enormous weight, the post-Augustan empire' (C. J. Herington). When Nero turned against his first wife and his mother and had them murdered, Seneca's power began to wane and he withdrew from political life. This did not save him, however, and in AD 65 Nero required his former tutor to commit suicide. The historian Tacitus describes what happened:

> He called for his will, and being deprived of that right of a Roman citizen by the centurion, he turned to his friends, and 'You see,' he said, 'that I am not at liberty to requite your services with the marks of my esteem. One thing, however, still remains. I leave you the example of my life, the best and most precious legacy now in my power. Cherish it in your memory and you will gain at once the applause due to virtue, and the fame of a

sincere and generous friendship . . .'

Then he directed his attention to his wife. He clasped her in his arms and in that fond embrace yielded for a while to the tenderness of his nature . . . Paulina was determined to die with her husband; she invoked the aid of the executioner and begged to end her wretched being. Seneca saw that she was animated by a love of glory and that generous principle he thought ought not to be restrained. The idea of leaving a beloved object exposed to the insults of the world, and the malice of her enemies, pierced him to the quick. 'It has been my care', he said 'to instruct you in that best philosophy, the art of mitigating the ills of life; but you prefer an honourable death. I will not envy you the vast renown that must attend your fall. Since you will have it so we will die together. We will leave behind us an example of equal constancy; but the glory will be all your own.'

These words were no sooner uttered, than the veins of both their arms were opened. At Seneca's time of life the blood was slow and languid. The decay of nature and the impoverishing diet to which he had used himself left him in a feeble condition. He ordered the vessels of his legs and joints to be punctured. After those operations, he began to labour with excruciating pains. Lest his suffering should overpower the constancy of his wife, or the sight of her afflictions prove too much for his own sensibility, he persuaded her to retire to another room. His eloquence still continued to flow with its usual purity. He called for his secretaries and dictated, while life was ebbing away, that farewell discourse, which has been published and is in everybody's hands. I will not injure his last words by giving the substance another form . . . .

Seneca lingered in pain. The approach of death was slow, and he longed for his dissolution. Fatigued with pain, worn out and exhausted, he requested his friend, Statius Annaeus, whose friendship and medical skill he had often experienced, to administer a draught of that swift-speeding poison, usually given at Athens to the criminals adjudged to death. He swallowed the poison but without any immediate effect. His limbs were chilled: the vessels of his body were closed, and the ingredients, though keen and subtle, could not arrest the principle of life. He desired to be placed in a warm bath. Being conveyed according to his desire, he sprinkled his slaves with the water and 'Thus, he said, 'I MAKE LIBATION TO JUPITER THE DELIVERER.' The vapour soon overpowered him and he breathed his last. His body without any funeral pomp was committed to the flames. He had given directions for that purpose in his last will, made at a time when he was in the zenith of power, and even then looked forward to the close of his days.

Annals XV 62–4, tr. Arthur Murphy

Seneca was a prolific author and letter writer. He was interested in science and wrote a book, *Naturales Quaestiones* (Researches into Nature). His philosophical works include *On Mercy, On The Good Life, On Providence, On the Tranquillity of the Soul* and that terrifying insight into the workings of absolute power, the treatise *On Anger*. Ten plays are attributed to him, of which he wrote eight – *Agamemnon, Phaedra, Oedipus, Medea, The Trojan Women, Hercules Furens, Thyestes* and *The Phoenician Women*. This last was left unfinished at his death. Another two plays, *Hercules Oetaeus* and *Octavia*, a history play about the death of Nero's first wife in which Seneca himself is a character, are of uncertain authorship.

No great literary artist has lived in closer proximity to absolute power – that place where politics becomes psychology. The Yugoslav writer Milovan Djilas has left an account – *Conversations with Stalin* – of the suffocating atmosphere at Stalin's court, but he was only a visitor and his position as a foreigner kept him on the margins. Seneca spent years in daily contact with the arbitrary exercise of personal power and witnessed its effects – both on the victim and the executioner – at first hand. His understanding of grievance, rage, resentment, envy and paranoia together with the abrupt, unorthodox structure of his plays make his work seem very modern.

We don't know how or where Seneca's plays were first performed. For years scholars held the view that they were intended solely for recitation. Experience of the work of Samuel Beckett, Sarah Kane, Caryl Churchill and Heiner Mueller (among others) has made people less certain than they once were that Seneca's writing is 'untheatrical' but there is no conclusive evidence either way. It's not hard to see how the recitation hypothesis has proved so tenacious: Seneca's plays lack the multi-vocal quality that distinguishes the work of his Greek predecessors. This is tragedy with the democracy left out.

Phaedra (*Phaedra*)

∾ The legend

Phaedra was the daughter of Minos and Pasiphae and sister to the half-human Minotaur. She was the second wife of Theseus, king of Athens.

Phaedra fell in love with her stepson Hippolytus. He was fanatically chaste and a devotee of Diana, goddess of the hunt. When Hippolytus rejected her advances, Phaedra pretended that he had raped her.

Theseus believed his wife and laid a curse on his son. Hippolytus was driving his chariot along the shore when a monstrous bull emerged from the sea. The horses stampeded, Hippolytus fell from his chariot and was dragged to his death.

Phaedra confessed what she had done and killed herself. Theseus was left alone amidst the wreckage of his family.

∾ The story

Theseus has been absent for four years on an expedition to the underworld. No one knows whether he will ever come back. Meanwhile his wife Phaedra, left alone, has fallen passionately in love with her stepson. He reminds her of what her husband used to look like when he was young.

Phaedra declares her love. Hippolytus is horrified and threatens to kill her. He runs off leaving his sword behind. Theseus returns unexpectedly from the world of the dead. Phaedra claims that Hippolytus has raped her. She shows Theseus the sword as evidence.

Theseus is quickly taken in and lays a terrible curse on his son. Hippolytus is thrown from his chariot and his body torn to pieces and strewn across the countryside. Phaedra confesses her lie and kills herself. Theseus is left trying to gather together the scattered fragments of his dead son so that he will have something to bury.

∾ About the play

> Pain and death . . . are the subjects of all Seneca's tragedies. It is in their way of presenting pain and death that the essential qualities of Seneca's tragedies are to be found, and from the consideration of this that evaluative judgements are to be made.
>
> D. and E. Henry, *The Mask of Power*

> Nature, red in tooth and claw . . .
>
> Tennyson, *In Memoriam*

The poet Martial in his collection *On the Games*, written to celebrate the opening of the Colosseum in AD 80 makes the point that Prometheus, who was chained to a rock and had his liver eaten by a vulture, was for the Greeks simply a character in a play; the Romans on the other hand had only to go down to the arena and see the flesh of a living man ripped to pieces by a bear. According to Juvenal, Messalina, wife to the

Emperor Claudius, used to sneak from the palace at night to prostitute herself in a stinking brothel.

> Here she graciously received all comers, asking from each
> his fee; and when at length the keeper dismissed his girls,
> she remained to the very last before closing her cell and
> with passion still raging hot within her went sorrowfully
> away.
>
> Juvenal, *Satire* VI, tr. G. G. Ramsay

The story of Phaedra, the lustful stepmother, could never look the same after this. A Roman Imperial tragedy may deal with the same legend as a Greek tragedy written five hundred years before but it does so in a very different manner.

In a world such as this, the dream of innocence becomes important. Almost exactly halfway through *Phaedra* Hippolytus imagines turning his back on civilization and going back to nature.

HIPPOLYTUS. There is no way of life so free and virtuous
    And which so cultivates our ancient ways
    As far from city walls to love the woods.
    No rage of avarice inflames the man
    Self-vowed to innocence on mountain heights;
    No people's breath, no base, dishonest mob,
    No poisonous spite or fickle favour.
    He serves no kingdom nor threatens kingship
    Pursuing vain honours and fleeting wealth,
    Liberated from hope and fear . . .
        tr. A. J. Boyle

This vision of rustic innocence is the first expression in drama of a feeling which will surface again in Shakespeare's *As You Like It* among the exiles in the Forest of Arden or with Karl and his band of brothers hiding in the greenwood in Schiller's *The Robbers*. The only place that is felt to be safe and truly human is somewhere far removed from civilization. This is of course the opposite of the Greek sense that man can only truly be himself as part of a community. Aristotle's famous saying 'Man is a political animal' defines human beings first and foremost as city dwellers and as citizens but the Romans experienced things differently.

The court, as Seneca portrays it, is a grim place: no wonder Hippolytus wishes to escape. Theseus, the king, is an unfeeling brute – a serial philanderer who murdered his first wife and neglected his second, disappearing with a male companion to try to rape Proserpina, queen of the underworld. He's not only a bad husband, he's cruel and tyrannical as well.

THESEUS: She still won't speak. We'll try fetters and whips
   on the old nurse who will betray what she
   refuses to admit. Clap her in chains;
   the lash has power to extract secrets
   from inside the mind.
     tr. Frederick Ahl

Phaedra, the queen, is restless, spoilt, unhappy and – as the nurse sees – reluctant to listen to anything disagreeable.

NURSE: It does not escape me, I should add,
   that royal vanity, unused to truth,
   hardens itself in swollen self-esteem,
   has no wish to be bent towards justice.
     tr. Frederick Ahl

The nurse can also see how wealth and ceaseless self-indulgence work together to make monsters.

NURSE: Now anyone who lives
   high in excessive affluence, wallows
   in constant streams of luxury, always
   hungers and hunts for the unusual.
   Then lust, ever the bad companion
   of great success, slips in. Banquets become
   routine and boring; so does ordinary
   wine, buildings of reasonable size.
     tr. Frederick Ahl

Phaedra makes overt a social criticism only implicit in the other plays. The world of the ruling family is closed, suffocating and without hope of change. Emotions fold in on themselves; there is no reciprocity of feeling. On the other hand Hippolytus' vision of a carefree life far from the city remains just that – a vision. His opening speech, when he calls his hunters together, shows that the countryside too is full of violence.

HIPPOLYTUS: Your job is to wait in ambush.
As the beasts run past, stampede them
with your loud cries. Then – it's all yours:
victory's won, so you can take your
crescent flaying-knife, releasing
innards as you slit the belly.

All nature is vulnerable to the hunter.

HIPPOLYTUS: No creature feeds in lonely fields
But fears, Diana, your bow.
tr. A. J. Boyle

The characters in the play are trapped twice over. As people they are trapped within the rigid confines of their world; as characters they are trapped in the framework of the traditional story. Their paths are prescribed from the outset. Phaedra is doomed by her ancestry – 'I recognize poor mother's fateful evil' – but also by the legend of which she is a part. Denied the freedom of any meaningful action, the people in Seneca's plays find the only way out is through feeling. Emotions – violent, exaggerated, all-engulfing – are the only things that authentically belong to them.

Each of the play's three principals has their own world of emotion that they live in. Seneca draws a powerful portrait of Phaedra burning with sexual desire.

NURSE: She has them prop her up then lay her down;
remove her ribbons, do her hair again.
Unable to endure the way she looks,

she changes her dress constantly. Her health
does not concern her; neither does her food.
Her feet move aimlessly, her strength is gone.
She now lacks her old energy. The bright
color that rouged her natural radiance
is gone.

Hippolytus, for his part, is eaten up with a hatred of women.

HIPPOLYTUS: Women lead us in evil. Engineers
of crime, they lay siege to our minds, leave us
obsessed. Because of them cities are burned
in thousands, nations engaged in countless wars,
kingdoms are depeopled and wiped out.
 tr. Frederick Ahl

Euripides makes the action of his play revolve round
Hippolytus' chastity. For Seneca chastity is hardly a value; the
focus instead is on the young man's beauty; and there is something gloating about the way that it is disfigured.

MESSENGER: Now far and wide he stains the fields with
 blood,
His head rebounding from the smitten rocks.
The bramble thickets pluck away his hair,
And that fair face is bruised upon the stones.
His fatal beauty that had been his bane
Is ruined now by many a wound . . .
At last his bleeding trunk upon a charred
And pointed stake is caught, pierced through the groin.
 tr. F. J. Miller

Theseus' defining characteristic is his rage which is violent,
impulsive, and brooks no interference. Like so many of
Seneca's characters, anger seems to give him a voluptuous
thrill.

THESEUS: Jaws of pallid death and you caverns of Taenarus,
 Balm of the damned, Lethe's stream, and you, stagnant
 pools,

Ravage this impious man, sink him in ceaseless pain.
Come savage monsters of the deep, come endless sea,
And all that Proteus hides in ocean's furthest womb,
For my evil triumph snatch me to your deep abyss . . .

The way *Phaedra* is put together is quite unlike that of a Greek tragedy. There is none of Euripides' care for logical development or for how the narrative unfolds from moment to moment. Seneca's manner of writing is more impressionistic; actions don't develop, they are juxtaposed. The play often feels as if it is made up of highlights.

The characters are seething with emotion; when they collide, the scenes have a lurid theatrical quality to them. The two great encounters in the play are Phaedra's attempted seduction of Hippolytus and her lying confession to Theseus that she's been raped. Hippolytus, horrified by Phaedra's advances, threatens to kill her before the altar of the goddess Diana.

HIPPOLYTUS: I'll draw my sword,
exact the price your whorish prayer demands.
I twist the hair upon your filthy head
with my left hand. O goddess of the hunt,
never was blood more justly offered you.
tr. Frederick Ahl

This kind of thing is familiar to modern audiences from the works of Webster, Ford and Tourneur – but the onstage presentation of violence is something that Roman tragedy invented. We are seeing it here for the first time in the surviving literature. The scene with Theseus produces an exchange that sums up the whole atmosphere of the play. The suicidal Phaedra is confronted by her husband.

THESEUS: Tell me what sin is to be purged by death.
PHAEDRA: That I live.
tr. A. J. Boyle

The play is bound together with chains of images. Hippolytus uses fierce Cretan hounds to hunt his prey;

Phaedra herself is a Cretan and her prey is Hippolytus. Phaedra's mother Pasiphae had sex with a bull and gave birth to the Minotaur and it is a huge bull from the sea, summoned by Theseus' curse, that destroys Hippolytus. Another set of important images is associated with Nature and her destructive powers – the ravages caused by sea and fire, the cold of winter and the heat of summer. The effect of these patterns, repeatedly underlined, is to make the play feel more claustrophobic than ever. The action has a dreadful circularity to it. The hunters who are dispatched by Hippolytus at the opening of the play to scour the Attic countryside for game end up tracking down the scattered pieces of their master's body.

MESSENGER: They search the places where Hippolytus,
　　as he was torn apart, left a long trail
　　marked with blood. His keening dogs now track
　　their master's limbs.
　　　　tr. Frederick Ahl

In Euripides the disaster that befalls the characters is something exceptional, brought about the intervention of an angry goddess. In Seneca the catastrophe, for all its horror, seems preordained, almost routine – the natural outcome of the way things are. The overall sense of suffocation and confinement is condensed into the final image of Phaedra's body tamped down for ever under the earth.

THESEUS: This one – earth press deep upon her
　　And soil lie heavy in her impious head.
　　　　tr. A. J. Boyle

∾ Translations

There is an Elizabethan translation by John Studley dating from the 1560s. The two best modern versions are by Frederick Ahl (Cornell) and A. J. Boyle (Francis Cairns Ltd). There is a sonorous blank verse translation by F. J. Miller. The Penguin (E. F. Watling) is also useful.

∾ In performance

We do not know when *Phaedra* was written and when (or how) it was first performed. A date *c.*50 AD seems most likely: internal evidence suggests it is one of Seneca's earlier plays. *Phaedra* was staged at Westminster School in the original Latin sometime in the 1540s. A more recent production was at the Théâtre des Quartiers d'Ivry as part of a season of all Seneca's plays in the winter of 1995–6.

Oedipus (*Oedipus*)

∾ The legend

Laius, king of Thebes, was warned that if he had a son, that son would grow up to kill his father.

When Oedipus was born Laius pierced the child's ankles, bound them together and gave him to a servant to abandon on the mountain outside the city. The servant spared the baby's life and gave him to a passing shepherd to look after.

The shepherd took the boy to Corinth where he was adopted by the king and queen, who had no children of their own. They brought him up to be their heir. When Oedipus grew to manhood he was taunted by a drunk with not being the true son of his parents. He went to Delphi to consult the oracle and learned that his fate was to kill his father and sleep with his mother.

Oedipus was horrified and resolved never to go back to Corinth. Making his way north he encountered an older man in a chariot who tried to push him off the road. There was a fight and Oedipus killed the man and his attendant. Without knowing it he had just struck his father Laius dead.

Later in his wanderings he came to Thebes which was being attacked by a strange monster, part woman and part animal, called the Sphinx. Oedipus overcame the monster by answering the riddle it posed: 'What goes on four feet in the morning, two feet at noon and three feet in the evening?' The answer is man.

The grateful Thebans made Oedipus king of their city. He married Laius' widow Queen Jocasta – and so the second part of the prophecy was fulfilled. When after many years Oedipus came to discover what he had done, he put out his eyes. Queen Jocasta killed herself.

ᗰ The story

Thebes has been stricken with a terrible plague; only King Oedipus remains untouched by it. Why? The prophet Teiresias sacrifices a bull and a heifer to find the answer. When the animals are opened up, their entrails are hideously deformed. The man who killed King Laius is polluting the city: but what is his name?

Teiresias raises Laius from the dead. The murdered king denounces his son. Oedipus feels that he is guilty but still believes that the King and Queen of Corinth are his true parents. When the truth is finally brought home to him he puts out his eyes and leaves the city taking the pollution with him. Queen Jocasta commits suicide by driving a sword into her womb.

ᗰ About the play

> The age's crime, the gods' odium, holy law's
> Devastation, since first I drank the virgin air,
> Already deserving death.
> *Oedipus*, tr. A. J. Boyle

THESEUS: Tell me what sin is to be purged by death.
PHAEDRA: That I live.
> *Phaedra*, tr. A. J. Boyle

The first three acts of *Oedipus* are three great panels of horror. In Act I there is Oedipus' description of Thebes ravaged by the plague.

OEDIPUS: our lungs scorch   we gulp for breath but there's no
air the heat never moves   the sun presses down on
us with its whole strength   the dog star the lion one
on top of the other a double madness every day closer
water has left us   the old river courses crack hard
greenness has left us grass bleaches and roasts it
powders underfoot   the corn should be ripe the
harvest stands but ruined shrivelled in the ear blasted
on the dry straws   the river Dirce our strong swift
Dirce it has been sealed off   springs dried up
a bed of hot stones   infernal   a string of stinking
puddles   what light there is stifles   under this
strange fog this hellish strange reek   thickening and
hanging   all day and all night the funeral pyres are
smouldering   stench of carcases burning   worse
stench of unburied carcases rotting   the stars
cannot pierce through to us   the moon crawls
through this fog too close hardly visible   heaven's
cut off we're buried away here between our walls
nothing can escape the plague it fastens on everybody
young old   men women children no distinction
young men in their strength old diseased men fathers
newborn sons the plague heaps everybody together
friend and enemy man and wife burn in the one flame
nobody weeps   there are no tears left   the groans
are for the living not the dead   screaming is not
mourning but torment or terror many die of terror
leap screaming from windows gulp down poison stab
themselves for terror   fathers with roasting eyes
stoke their sons' bodies in the flames mothers stagger
to and fro like madwomen between their children's
beds and the flames finally throw themselves into the
flames   mourners fall down besides the pyres and
are thrown into the same flames   survivors fight for
fuel even snatching burning sticks from pyres
even throw their families on top of other people's
fires   it's enough if the ones are scorched   there

isn't wood enough to turn everything to ashes   there
isn't ground enough to bury what's left   and prayers
are useless   medicine is useless   nurse and doctor
go into the flames   every hand that's stretched out
to help   the plague grips it.
    tr. Ted Hughes

In Act II there is Manto's description of the sacrifice that's
gone all wrong. The priestess stares into the entrails of the
slaughtered animal.

MANTO: something is wrong   no membrane to contain the
  entrails and the intestines quake   father what can
  this mean   usually they quiver a little but these are
  twisting   shuddering look how they shake my arm
  as if they had separate life   much seems to be
  missing   much of the intestines   the heart is
  missing no here is the heart shrivelled withered up
  diseased black buried down here far from its natural
  position what does it mean father   everything is
  reversed   the lungs are squeezed here far over to
  the right gorged with blood how did they breathe
  the liver is rotten breaks in my hand oozing black
  bitter gall   look   this liver is double headed
  the left wing swollen twice its proper size knotted with
  great veins the right wing is deathly white fungus
  rotten but the finger of it is enormous stiff black with
  blood   that is a fatal omen
    tr. Ted Hughes

And in Act III there is Creon's terrifying account of the
raising of King Laius from the underworld. The prophet
Teiresias has been trying to raise the dead.

CREON: he began to call for the ghosts
  and they came   a growing sound   a humming
  that seemed to silence everything   like a vast flock of
  autumn starlings a rushing gloomy wind of twitterings
  beating up at the light   swirling back and round and

round in the pit   grabbing at the earth the tree
roots our clothes   all crying in their thin bodiless
voices   till at last one of them laid hold of the roots
and clung there   his face pressed into the earth
Tiresias called to this creature commanding it to come
up   again and again he called   and as last it looked
up   it lifted its face and I recognized   Laius
our King   Laius   he pulled himself up   it was
him   his whole body was plastered with blood   his
hair beard face   all one terrible wound   a mash of
mud brains blood   his mouth lay open and the
tongue inside it began to move and quiver   he began
to speak

  — tr. Ted Hughes

With three quarters of the play gone, there has been hardly
any action as such, just a journey deeper into horror and
despair.

This is about as different as can be from the world of
Sophocles' *Oedipus Tyrannus*. But the two plays have one
thing in common: both are representative of the societies
from which they sprang. This appears first of all in the relationship between speech and action. Speech in fifth-century
Athens was something practical; it made things happen.
Speaking and doing were closely linked: debates in the council or the assembly formulated policy which the debaters then
had to carry out. In Imperial Rome, by contrast, power was
centred in the Emperor's hands; people could talk all they
liked, it was one man who decided things. At the same time
the art of public speaking became ever more elaborate; the
energy that in a democracy went into politics now got
diverted into language. *Oedipus* is genuinely an Imperial
tragedy in that for much of its length it is made up of brilliant
descriptions of things that the speaker is powerless to change.

Sophocles' Oedipus is proud, quick-witted, resourceful,
loved by his people. His energy drives the play. Seneca's
Oedipus is a haunted, guilty figure, unsure of himself and

equally unsure what to do. 'I fear all things and have no faith in me.' Sophocles' play captures the greatness and maturity of Periclean Athens: power and confidence are there but also the awareness that all things are subject to change and that any kind of power has its limits. The vision of Seneca's Oedipus is darker and more hopeless. The play portrays a fallen world, a whole kingdom tainted by the crimes of its ruler.

Oedipus Tyrannus unrolls in daylight under the clear impartial light of the sun. The light in Seneca's *Oedipus* is murky and uncertain. The smoke of the failed sacrifice gathers in an ominous wreath round Oedipus' head.

MANTO: oily heavy
   smoke   what does it mean   the smoke is reaching
   out towards the king   it is looping and thickening
   round the king's head   it's blotted the king's face out
   now it spreads   it's spreading over everything
      tr. Ted Hughes

Oedipus pollutes the atmosphere because he has killed his father and slept with his mother. Seneca's pupil Nero was guilty of crimes that rivalled those of Oedipus. He was responsible for the deaths of his half-brother, his wife and his mother – who was rumoured also to have been his lover. The historian Tacitus gives an account of the Emperor 'half dead with terror' on the night of his mother's murder.

But Caesar, when the crime was finally accomplished, understood its magnitude. For the rest of the night, sometimes dumb and stupefied, more often starting up in panic and out of his mind, he awaited daylight as if it would bring his doom.
      Tacitus, *Annals* XIV 7, tr. A. J. Boyle

This might also be a description of the play's opening scene. The killing of the real-life Empress Mother shares one gruesome detail with the suicide of the fictional Jocasta – a sword thrust into the womb.

The executioners surrounded the couch and the trierarch began by striking her on the head with a club. The centurion was drawing his sword to make an end, when she proffered her womb to the blow. 'Strike here,' she said and was despatched with repeated wounds.

Tacitus, *Annals* XIV 8, tr. John Jackson

JOCASTA: this point under my breast
or this long edge across my throat   don't you know
the place   it's here   this   the place the gods
hate   where everything began the son the husband
up here
       tr. Ted Hughes

Seneca wrote the speech the Emperor delivered to the Senate on the morning after his mother's murder. The edgy dialogues between Creon and Oedipus, adviser and autocrat, echo something of the uneasy relationship which ended when Seneca was ordered by his former pupil to kill himself.

CREON: a King cannot grant a man less than his silence
OEDIPUS: the silence in a kingdom can be deadlier than the speech.
CREON: if silence is forbidden   freedom is finished
OEDIPUS: power to command finished   the throne is finished
       the kingdom finished
              tr. Ted Hughes

The construction of Oedipus is idiosyncratic, but it is not untheatrical. Suddenly in Act IV the play receives a tremendous jolt of energy. The investigation into Oedipus' true parentage is compressed into a hundred lines of tense, fast-moving dialogue. All the energy that had been previously pent up is now let loose.

OEDIPUS: I am not a madman   you need only to speak
   who was that child   you are the only man who
   knows   who was its father   who was its mother
PHORBAS: its mother

OEDIPUS: who was its mother
PHORBAS: its mother was your wife.
   tr. Ted Hughes

The Roman Oedipus may for much of the play's length seem to lack the intellectual self-confidence of his Greek predecessor, but when it comes to physical courage he is his equal, perhaps even his superior. The option of suicide, which Sophocles passes over in silence, is here explicitly rejected as not punishment enough. There is something heroic about Oedipus' self-mutilation, the violence of it is so extreme. It seems that the only way to outdo the savagery of fate is to welcome that savagery into oneself. In taking the horror on to his own shoulders Oedipus sets his people free.

OEDIPUS: the contagion is leaving your land I am taking it with
  me   I am taking it away   fate   remorseless
  my enemy   you are the friend I choose   come with
  me
  pestilence   ulcerous agony   blasting consumption
  plague terror   plague blackness   despair
  welcome   come with me   you are my guides
  lead me
   tr. Ted Hughes

This deliberate assumption of the role of scapegoat is quite foreign to the Greek way of looking at things. But Seneca's portrait of a fallen world and a man who, taking the burden of sin upon himself, redeems a whole community, has something about it that meshes very well with the world-view of Christianity. It's no surprise to find that Seneca was taken up by the Christian commentators of late antiquity. A fourth-century writer went so far as to forge a whole correspondence between Seneca and St Paul which was taken to be genuine and became widely known in the Middle Ages. The celebrity of this fake exchange of letters is one of the reasons that so much of Seneca's authentic work has survived into the modern world.

∾ Translations

The Ted Hughes version (Faber) is outstanding in every way. It takes a few liberties over detail but these can easily be checked against the Loeb of F. J. Miller or the more conventional rendering of E. F. Watling (Penguin). The version by Rachel Hadas (Johns Hopkins) in – for some incomprehensible reason – rhyming couplets is more a hindrance than a help. There is an Elizabethan translation by Alexander Neville dating from the 1560s.

∾ In performance

Nothing is known about the year or the circumstances of the first performance. Scholars think the play was most likely written around AD 55–60. *Oedipus* was staged at the National Theatre in 1967, and at the Théâtre des Quartiers d'Ivry as part of a season of all Seneca's plays in the winter of 1995–6. Other productions include the Performance Group New York (1977), the RSC (1988) and the Sydney Theatre Company (2000).

Medea (*Medea*)

∾ The legend

Pelias was king of Iolcus. He stole the throne from Jason's father and drove him into exile. Fearing Jason might take revenge he sent him to fetch the Golden Fleece from Colchis on the Black Sea, hoping that he would die in the attempt.

Medea was the daughter of Aeëtes, king of Colchis. When Jason arrived at her father's court Medea fell head over heels in love with him and he with her.

Aeëtes set Jason a series of ordeals. He was required to yoke two fire-eating bulls and sow a field with a dragon's teeth. Medea gave Jason a magic to tame the bulls and told him to throw a stone among the warriors sprung from the dragon's teeth so that they would start fighting and kill each other. She also put to sleep the huge serpent that was guarding the Golden Fleece so that Jason could steal it.

Aeëtes pursued the Argonauts as they made off with their prize but Medea kidnapped her younger brother Apsyrtus, killed him and scattered the pieces of his body so that the pursuers had to stop and pick them up. In this way the expedition returned safe to Greece.

Back in Iolcus Medea took revenge on the usurper Pelias. She convinced his daughters that they could regenerate their ageing father by cutting him up and boiling him in a cauldron with some magic herbs. This was a trick and Pelias died in agony at the hands of his children.

Pelias' son Acastus swore to get revenge and once more Jason and Medea had to escape. They ended up in Corinth where Jason divorced Medea and married Creusa, daughter of King Creon. Medea took her revenge by killing Creon, Creusa and her own two children.

❧ The story

The play takes place on the day of Jason's wedding. Medea calls down curses on him and his new bride.

Creon wants to have Medea killed but Jason has persuaded him to exile her instead. Medea pleads with him to be allowed to stay in Corinth for one more day so she can say goodbye to her children.

When Medea sees that Jason will not take her back she decides to punish him. She concocts a magic potion, smears it on a dress and sends this to the new bride as a present. Anyone who touches the dress is consumed by fire. Creusa, her father and the royal palace go up in flames.

Medea completes her revenge by killing her two children – the second one before the eyes of his grief-stricken father. She makes her escape in a magic chariot given her by her grandfather the Sun.

ᴄ◡ About the play

> He [Seneca] is not trying to present the actions of human beings. His emphasis is on the action of Evil and the emotions which generate it.
>
> C. J. Herington

> *Here* I show you Hell.
>
> Seneca, Prologue to *The Madness of Hercules*

This is a suffocating and relentless play, about as far removed from Greek tragedy as it is possible to be. Euripides' Medea is a human being – an exceptional one, but human nonetheless. Seneca's Medea is a force of Nature, or rather becomes one over the course of the play. We witness her transformation from a person into something as merciless and implacable as a hurricane or a forest fire.

The play begins with Medea cursing Jason for his treachery. She asks the gods to punish him.

MEDEA: Now, now come to my aid, goddesses who punish crime,
　your hair foul with writhing snakes,
　grasping black torches in your bloody hands,
　come and help me now . . . Kill the new wife,
　kill the father-in-law, kill all his children.
　What can be worse? What evil for the bridegroom?
　Let him live! Through unknown cities let him wander, starving,
　exiled, frightened, hated, homeless.

It isn't long before she concludes that rather than wait for the gods it would be quicker and more satisfying to do the job herself.

MEDEA: My mind is plotting savage, unknown, dreadful
　things, which will make tremble heaven and earth –
　wounds and slaughter and death that creeps
　from limb to limb. But what I have spoken of is too feeble:

I did these things as a girl. Let my grief rise to more deadly
strength. Greater crimes suit me now that I am a mother.
Arm yourself with anger and ready yourself to wreak
     destruction
with the full force of madness.

Seneca had a special interest in anger. He knew Nero and
Caligula personally and had seen a lot of it, close-up. He
regarded it as one of the greatest of all evils and wrote a book
about it.

No plague has cost the human race more dear. You will
see bloodshed and poisoning, the downfall of cities, whole
nations given to destruction, princes sold at public auction, houses put to the torch, fires that do not stop within
the city walls but make great swathes of countryside glow
with hostile flame. Behold the most glorious cities whose
foundations can scarcely be traced – anger cast them
down. Behold deserts stretching for miles without a single
dweller – anger laid them waste. Behold the rulers who
have come down to posterity as examples of an evil fate –
anger stabbed this one in his bed, struck down this one at
table, forced this one to have his blood spilled by his son,
another to have his throat cut by a slave, another to have
his limbs stretched on the cross; what if, leaving aside
those who felt the force of anger's flame as individuals,
you should choose to view the populace butchered by soldiers let loose on them, whole peoples condemned to
death in common ruin . . .
     Seneca, *On Anger*, I, ii, 1–3, tr. John W. Basore

The terrible thing about anger from Seneca's point of view is
that it is an exclusively human quality. Animals are fierce or
savage but never angry.

No animal except for man is subject to anger: for while it
is the enemy of reason it is born only where reason
dwells. Wild beasts have impulses, madness, fierceness,
aggressiveness; but they no more have anger than they

have luxuriousness.

Seneca, *On Anger*, I, iii, 4, tr. John W. Basore.

How someone deals with their anger is a crucial test of who they truly are.

The opening of the play is so ferocious it's hard to see how it could develop, or even continue; but then there's a lull. When Medea enters for the second time she remembers her love for Jason.

MEDEA: But Jason had no power,
and surely did not plot this by himself:
he too was foreign under Corinth's laws.

He owed it you to steel himself for death
not steal away.

        Don't say that please, oh please,
raging voice of my pain. Jason must live,
be mine just as he was, if he has strength,
even if not. I still want him to live
and to remember me. I don't want him
to hurt the gift of life I gave him once.
    tr. Frederick Ahl

This slackening proves only temporary. Medea's resentment soon breaks again. This time the target is Creon. The Nurse tries to restrain her mistress by pointing out that she is all alone in the world. The reply when it comes is truly terrifying.

NURSE: The Colchians are gone, your husband is unfaithful,
    you have nothing left of your great wealth.
MEDEA: Medea is left. In her you see sea and land
    and steel and fire and gods and thunderbolts.
    tr. H. M. Hine

Medea retains enough control to argue her case in front of the king. Whatever crimes she has committed were all done for Jason's sake, so the beneficiary must surely share her guilt.

MEDEA: Why draw the line between two criminals?
　　Jason is why I went from home
　　and stole the fleece. For him I left father,
　　murdered my brother, mutilated him . . .

　　　　　　　　　　　　　　I've harmed
　　the many I have harmed not for myself but
　　because I have been made to harm.
　　　tr. Frederick Ahl

This scene of argument feels for a moment like something Euripides might have written. But the appearance is deceptive. Medea has opened her heart to rage and there is no going back. In yielding to her fury Medea becomes one with the engulfing sea or raging hurricane. Her destructiveness is as implacable as the laws of physics. A great American critic put it like this: 'Evil is something material, with consequences no less material than those of, say, fire. 'Is a napalm bomb a sin? Is sin a napalm bomb?' Seneca would have had difficulty in distinguishing between the two questions.'

The only thing that will satisfy such anger is omnipotence. Medea wants to control everything – even time. Nothing must alter, or if it does, it should change back into what it was before.

MEDEA: You order me to leave. Give me back my ship.
　　Give me back my companion. Why order me to leave
　　　alone?
　　I did not come alone.

For Medea the past is a comfort zone, full of certainties, free of challenge: that's why she wants to abolish the present. In this sense *Medea* is a study in noxious conservatism. Euripides' heroine makes sure her escape route is clear before she embarks on her killing spree. Seneca's Medea has no interest in the future: all she wants is to turn the clock back. The murder of the children has a triple function – it nullifies the marriage, restores her virginity and re-enacts the murder of her hapless brother Apsyrtus whose scattered limbs distracted the pursuers and allowed the Argonauts to escape.

Shakespeare's *Macbeth* is another play about what happens when evil makes itself at home within the human soul. Medea's opening soliloquy becomes Lady Macbeth's speech:

> Come you spirits
> That tend on mortal thoughts unsex me here
> And fill me from the crown to the toe top-full
> Of direst cruelty; make thick my blood
> Stop up the access and passage to remorse
> That no compunctious visitings of nature
> Shake my fell purpose, nor keep peace between
> The effect and it.
>
> *Macbeth*, Act I, Scene v

Lady Macbeth's threat to dash out her baby's brains is a memory of Medea's murdered children. The magic potion which Medea prepares surfaces again as Shakespeare's witches' cauldron.

> NURSE: The sickening galls
> of dying trees she mixed together, the rarest,
> most dangerous mosses, terrible molds, and powder
> she's made from the dried saps of noxious vines
> cut from their roots with a bloodied sickle . . .
> . . . She milks the serpents'
> venom for poisons to add to the stew. And birds,
> unclean carrion birds she submerges alive.
> The heart of a screech owl still beating she flings
> into her loathsome pot . . .
>
> tr. David R. Slavitt

What, most of all, Shakespeare has taken from his predecessor is the description of someone colluding with their own worst impulses to embark on a journey that will land them, and everyone about them, in a fresh-made hell. There is a common tripartite structure in Seneca's plays, which is also present in *Macbeth*. One modern commentator gave the three stages titles: first, there is 'The Cloud of Evil', that is to say the moment when anger or ambition are present, but only as temptations; then, 'The Defeat of Reason by Passion' in which the last checks of pity or morality are overthrown; and lastly, 'The Explosion of Evil', in which the horror and violence which have been pent up inside the individual are released into the world to become a general condition. The desolate music of Shakespeare's England scene has an authentically Senecan ring to it:

> Where sighs and groans and shrieks that rent the air
> Are made not mark'd; where violent sorrow seems
> A modern ecstasy; the dead man's knell
> Is there scarce asked for who; and good men's lives
> Expire before the flowers in their caps
> Dying or ere they sicken.
> *Macbeth*, Act IV, Scene iii

Roman society under the empire was like a series of performances. Everyone was at once actor and audience. It was not just a matter of the insincerities necessary under any tyranny, or the fact that Nero liked to appear in various roles, as actor, singer, charioteer and so on. The state itself was a form of theatre. The senate met as usual, consuls and other magistrates were appointed; everything appeared to be much as it had been under the republic. Yet it was all a sham. The forms of public life had all been hollowed out: real power lay with the emperor alone. This is what Caligula famously demonstrated when he had his horse appointed Consul.

Medea also acts herself out. 'Medea,' says the Nurse. 'I shall become her,' replies her mistress. As one German scholar puts it, 'This is a woman who has read Euripides.' Medea knows what is expected of her and is continually trying to live up to her reputation.

MEDEA: Be bold now, begin
whatever Medea is capable of, whatever she is *not* capable of!

Her murder of the children is only complete when she has Jason for an audience.

MEDEA: Come on now my soul; you must not waste your
   courage in secret. Have your handiwork applauded by the
      people . . .
      . . . Great pleasure is stealing over me against my will
   and, see, it is increasing. This is the one thing I lacked -
   to have him watching me . . .
      tr. H. M. Hine

Cruelty finds its fullest satisfaction only when it is performed in front of other people.

∿ Translations

H. M. Hine's literal version (Aris and Philips) gives as good
account as any of the play's grim music. David R. Slavitt
(Johns Hopkins) catches the headlong quality and the baleful
energy very well but is often at quite a distance from the original. The version by Fredrick Ahl (Cornell) is often beautiful
as well as accurate but is also rather tight and chilly, cramping
the work's demonic energy. There is an Elizabethan translation by John Studley dating from the 1560s.

∿ In performance

When the play was first performed, or how, we do not know.
The date of composition could be any time roughly AD
41–60. *Medea* was presented in the original Latin at Trinity
College Cambridge in 1560/61. There have been modern
productions at the Théâtre des Quartiers d'Ivry in 1995–6
and at the Citizens' Theatre Glasgow in 1998.

Thyestes (*Thyestes*)

∿ The legend

Tantalus wanted to impress the gods, so he killed his son Pelops and served the child up for them to eat. The gods were horrified. They restored Pelops to life and punished Tantalus by condemning him to eternal hunger and everlasting thirst.

Pelops had two sons, Atreus and Thyestes, who took it in turns to rule the kingdom. Thyestes stole his brother's wife and ousted him from power. Atreus took his revenge by killing Thyestes' children and serving them up to their father at a banquet.

⁓ The story

Tantalus is dragged back from hell to infect his grandchildren with the family evil. He tries to refuse the task but is tortured into submission by the Fury who accompanies him. His ravening and insatiable spirit enters the palace to wreak havoc there.

Atreus steels himself to take revenge on his adulterous brother. He tempts Thyestes back from exile with an offer of reconciliation. Thyestes for all his show of caution is easily taken in. He and his three children return to court.

Atreus sacrifices Thyestes' children at a dark altar hidden in the depths of the palace and serves them up to their father to eat. Thyestes is stuffed with the flesh of his offspring while Atreus remains unsatisfied, hungering for a revenge still more extreme.

⁓ About the play

When Hannibal saw a trench flowing with human blood, he is said to have exclaimed, 'O beauteous sight!' How much more beautiful would it have seemed to him if the blood had filled some river or lake!
    Seneca, *On Anger* II v. 4

Whatever terrifies must also tremble.
    Seneca, *On Anger* II xi 3–5

Perfection, of a kind, was what he was after,
And the poetry he invented was easy to understand . . .
    W. H. Auden, 'Epitaph on a Tyrant'

Internal evidence suggests that Thyestes is one of Seneca's last plays. It is certainly the fullest expression of the world he had made his own – a grim mixture of grievance, anger, resentment, paranoia, and the toxic conservatism of the central character. It is one of the most disturbing dramas ever written. It's not just the depiction of cruel events but the fact that the writer succeeds in creating something of the suffocating inner experience of cruelty that make Thyestes so uncomfortable.

The central theme is hunger, a sense of emptiness so profound that a person can eat, and go on eating for ever, and still not be satisfied. Tantalus, whose ghost opens the play, was condemned to a starvation that would never end. There was food in front of him he could not eat and water that he could not drink.

CHORUS: ripe apples with languid leaves mock him
   till hunger forces him to stretch out his hands –
         the fruit's snatched away.
Then thirst starts burning his blood, a cool stream flows
      at him then vanishes –
         he drinks deep from
      the whirling pool, deep dust.
   tr. Caryl Churchill

Tantalus has been brought back to earth to set in motion a chain of destruction that will swallow his descendants.

FURY: Let's have a wickedness
   competition, swords
   out in every street, no
   embarrassment at
   being very angry –
   blind fury. Then let
   rage harden and the long
   wrong go into the
   grandchildren. No time for
   anyone to hate

old crimes because here come
plenty of new ones
and the punishments are
even more wicked.
Whichever brother is
triumphant will lose
the kingdom, the exile
get back in. Fortune
will totter back and forth
between them, power
follow misery and
misery power
and waves of disaster
batter the kingdom.
    tr. Caryl Churchill

Even the former child-murderer quails at the Fury's picture of what is about to happen.

TANTALUS: I should be punished
    not be a punishment.

But the Fury tortures him until he acquiesces.

TANTALUS: What? why attack me
with whips and snakes? what? what's
this clawing hunger
you've thrust deep inside me?
My burnt chest blazes
with thirst, flame flickers
in my scorched belly.
I'm going
wherever
it takes me.
    tr. Caryl Churchill

Tantalus' terrible spirit enters the palace; the walls shake; and the action of the play can begin.

Atreus is tormented by a sense of emptiness every bit as

terrible as the one that afflicts his grandfather. He feels cheated, hollowed out, deprived – as if he hardly exists. The adultery of his brother Thyestes has unmanned him, taking away his wife, making him doubt the paternity of his children and his own virility. His anxieties are fuelled by a terrible paranoia – the fear that whatever he does his brother will do more of.

ATREUS: Is he
  ever beaten? Does he stop
  at anything when things go
  well, and when they go badly
  does he stop?
  Before he gets organised
  he must be attacked without
  warning or while I'm sitting
  quietly he'll attack.
     tr. Caryl Churchill

Like Dionysus in Euripides' *The Bacchae*, Atreus is not just the leading character in the play, he is also to a certain extent the director and the writer of it too. He dreams up what will happen and then performs it. His cruelty makes him a sort of perverted poet. He has the poet's attributes of originality, respect for tradition, and desire to create something that will be remembered through the ages. In planning his revenge he looks back to the example of how Procne punished Tereus by feeding him his own children. And, like Horace, who famously claimed that in his poems he had 'built a monument more lasting than bronze', he wants to do something that will bring its own kind of immortality.

ATREUS: Awake my heart,
  And do such deeds as in the time to come
  No tongue shall praise, but none refuse to tell.
     tr. E. F. Watling

Atreus shows too an artist's pride in a job well done. Horace wrote: 'If you include me among the lyric bards I

will hit the stars with my exalted head' (*Carmina* 1.1. 35/6).
When he has killed and cooked his brother's children, Atreus
exults:

ATREUS: I'm striding as high as the
   stars, I'm above everyone,
   my head's touching heaven.
      tr. Caryl Churchill

Twice in the play Atreus appears as his own impresario. He
stages an insincere welcome to greet his brother.

ATREUS: I see him, it's him
   and the children too.
   At last my hate's safe.
   When rage smells blood it
   doesn't know how to
   hide but still it must.
   How wonderful it is to
   see my brother. Give me the
   embraces I've longed for.
      tr. Caryl Churchill

And the deadly banquet is itself a form of theatre.

ATREUS: The hall's gleaming with torches.
   He's lying on purple and
   gold, head heavy on his hand.
   He belches. O wonderful
   me, I'm a god, I'm king of
   kings . . .
      tr. Caryl Churchill

Like any artist, Atreus derives his inspiration from the 'foul
rag and bone shop of the heart'. The place where he commits
the murders and sacrifices his brother's children at the altar
has its own uncanny quality. The rich and civilized façade
which the palace presents to the world conceals a space that is
darker and more primitive.

MESSENGER: But behind what everyone
   knows about and can visit
   the rich house divides into
   more and more spaces – the furthest
   in, a secret place, a deep
   hollow with old woods, the most
   inward bit of the kingdom.
   In the shadows there's a
   sad spring that seeps through
   black mud, like the ugly
   water of Styx that
   heaven swears by. They say
   gods who deal with death
   groan here in the blind night,
   chains clank and ghosts howl.
   Whatever you're frightened
   to hear of, you see.
   Wandering about, out of
   their graves, turbulent
   gangs who lived long ago,
   and monstrosities
   worse than you've ever seen
   jump out . . .
   Something keeps bellowing
   and the house is struck
   with terror at huge shapes.
   Day doesn't calm fear,
   the grove is its own night
   at noon you still feel
   this horror of spirits.
     tr. Caryl Churchill

At first Thyestes seems to stand for something more innocent and wholesome.

THYESTES: It is the height of happiness
   To stand in no man's way, to eat at ease
   Reclining on the ground. At humble tables

Food can be eaten without fear; assassins
Will not be found in poor men's cottages;
The poisoned drink is served in cups of gold.
My house is undefended but secure.
Great is my peace, as my estate is small.
> tr. E. F. Watling

But this love of the simple life is revealed to be more of an affectation than a true belief. Thyestes' protestations are undercut by his delight at returning to the city he has left and he caves in to his brother's requests with only a token show of resistance.

ATREUS: This throne can hold two.
THYESTES: Whatever's yours brother
I'll consider mine.
ATREUS: Who refuses gifts from
fortune when they flow?
THYESTES: Anyone who knows how
easily they ebb.
ATREUS: Can't I have my glory?
THYESTES: You've got your glory
already. Mine's waiting.
To refuse power
is my firm decision.
ATREUS: If you won't accept
your share, I'll give up mine.
THYESTES: I accept.
> tr. Caryl Churchill

He is not necessarily less ambitious than his brother, only less ruthless.

Thyestes, however deluded, and his children are the only characters who hope for change. Atreus' revenge is a form of radical conservatism which ensures that the future will be forever like the past. The cycle of vengeance will go on repeating itself, as the Fury had foreseen.

FURY: Driven out by their crimes
when god brings them home

they'll come home to more crimes,
everyone hate them,
just as they hate themselves . . .
     tr. Caryl Churchill

Time literally goes into reverse. The murder of the children plunges the world into darkness as the sun flees backwards into the preceding night. The chorus fear that human wickedness has brought about the end of the world.

CHORUS: Have we been chosen
  out of everyone
  somehow deserving
  to have the world smash up and
  fall on us? or have the last days come
  in our lifetime? It's
  a hard fate, whether we've lost the sun
  or driven it away.
     tr. Caryl Churchill

The fatal banquet takes place by torchlight because Atreus' crime has blotted out the sun – it is the ancient world's equivalent of nuclear winter.

There is no final chorus that concludes the play. Instead the two brothers are left face to face.

THYESTES: Avenging gods will come.
  I leave you to them
  for punishment.
ATREUS: For punishment
  I leave you to your children.
     tr. Caryl Churchill

Atreus has fed Thyestes his murdered children in an attempt to satisfy himself but he still feels empty. The thought he still has not had revenge enough torments him.

ATREUS: Even this is too
  little for me. Hot blood
  straight out of the wound

into your mouth while they
were still alive, yes,
my anger was cheated
because I hurried . . .
This pain is no use.
He tore his sons apart
but he didn't know
and they didn't know.
  tr. Caryl Churchill

Readers of Shakespeare will find an echo of Atreus' opening speech in one of Hamlet's soliloquies.

ATREUS: Am I a coward, sluggard, impotent,
  And – what I count the worst of weaknesses
  In a successful king – still unavenged?
  After so many crimes, so many sleights
  Committed on me by that miscreant brother
  In violation of all sacred law,
  Is there no more to do but make vain protests?
  Is this your anger Atreus?
    tr. E. F. Watling

This is familiar to us from *Hamlet*, Act II, Scene 2.

HAMLET: Yet I,
  A dull and muddy-mettled rascal, peak,
  Like John-a-dreams, unpregnant of my cause
  And can say nothing; no, not for a king,
  Upon whose property and most dear life
  A damn'd defeat was made. Am I a coward?

Behind Shakespeare's 'sweet Prince' there stands the blood-
boultered shadow of his Roman predecessor.

∾ Translations

There is an outstanding translation by Caryl Churchill
(Nick Hern Books) which captures the savagery and brilliant

oddness of the original. The Penguin (E. F. Watling) is also useful, if more conventional. The version by David R. Slavitt (Johns Hopkins) is too slapdash to be recommended. There is also a translation by Jasper Heywood, dating from 1560.

⌒ In performance

It is not known when *Thyestes* was composed. Some time after 55 AD is thought to be most likely. Vittorio Gassman directed the play in Italy in 1953. Other productions include the Citizens' Theatre Glasgow (1975), the Royal Court Theatre Upstairs (1994) and the Théâtre des Quartiers d'Ivry (1995–6.)

Further Reading

This makes no claims to be a comprehensive bibliography. It is simply a set of pointers for readers who want to know where to look next.

Origins: *Dithyramb, Tragedy and Comedy* by Sir Arthur Pickard-Cambridge, 2nd edition revised by T. B. L. Webster (Oxford) surveys the evidence but is rather dry. Gerald F. Else, *Origins and Early Form of Greek Tragedy* and John Herington, *Poetry into Drama: Early Tragedy and the Greek Poetic Tradition* are more approachable. Eric Csapo and William J. Slater, *The Context of Ancient Drama* provides a useful collection of background documents in translation. Anyone interested in the epic background should turn to Oliver Taplin's outstanding book *Homeric Soundings*.

Aeschylus: John Herington, *Aeschylus*; Christian Meier, *The Political Art of Greek Tragedy*; Thomas G. Rosenmeyer, *The Art of Aeschylus*; Oliver Taplin, *The Stagecraft of Aeschylus*; Anne Lebeck, *The Oresteia; a Study in Language and Structure*.

Sophocles: Karl Reinhardt, *Sophocles*; Bernard Knox, *Oedipus at Thebes* and *The Heroic Temper: Studies in Sophoclean Tragedy*. There is also a fine article by P. E. Easterling in *The Cambridge History of Classical Literature Volume 1*.

Euripides: There are excellent chapters on individual plays in *Word and Action: Essays on the Ancient Theatre* by Bernard Knox, who also contributes an overall survey of the writer's work to *The Cambridge History of Classical Literature, Volume 1*. *The Tragedies of Euripides* by T. B. L. Webster (Methuen) is a comprehensive account of Euripides' *oeuvre*, including fascinating chapters on the fragmentary works. There is also a useful study, *Euripides and the Education of the Athenians*, by Justina Gregory. There isn't the depth of interesting writing about Euripides that there is about the two other tragedians. A new overall study of the dramatist is badly needed.

Aristophanes: Readers need look no further than K. J. Dover's brilliant *Aristophanic Comedy*.

Plautus and Terence: Erich Segal's *Roman Laughter* is the best short introduction to the work of Plautus. The background is described in *The Roman Theatre and its Audience* by Richard C. Beacham. There are good chapters on both authors in *The Cambridge History of Classical Literature, Volume 2* and in Gian Biagio Conte's magisterial *Latin Literature*. *Roman Drama and Roman History* by T. P. Wiseman and *Comic Angels* by Oliver Taplin, though slightly more specialist, throw fascinating light on the origins of Roman tragedy and comedy respectively.

Seneca: There is an outstandingly good article by John Herington in *The Cambridge History of Classical Literature, Volume 2*. Also useful are D. and E. Henry, *The Mask of Power* and Alessandro Schiesaro, *The Passions in Play: Thyestes and the Dynamics of Senecan Drama*.

Stage History: *Medea in performance 1500–2000*, edited by Edith Hall, Fiona Mackintosh and Oliver Taplin and *Dionysus since 69: Greek Tragedy at the Dawn of the Third Millennium*, edited by Edith Hall, Fiona Macintosh and Amanda Wrigley, both published by Oxford, are part of an ongoing series examining the performance of Greek drama through the ages. Related articles and information can be found at www.apgrd.ox.ac.uk

Other: The religious background is provided by *Religion and the Ancient Greek City* by Louise Bruit Zaidman and Pauline Schmitt Pantel. Useful general surveys are Albin Lesky, *Greek Tragedy*; Bernhard Zimmermann, *Greek Tragedy: an Introduction*; and Alan H. Sommerstein, *Greek Drama and Dramatists*. *The Cambridge History of Classical Literature, Volume 1, Greek Literature* and *Volume 2, Latin Literature* may sound rather off-putting but have wide-ranging and reliable chapters on individual authors. Good general guides to the historical background are J. K. Davies, *Democracy and Classical Greece* and Christian Meier, *Athens: A Portrait of the City in its Golden Age*.

Acknowledgements

We are grateful to all the publishers and translators of texts quoted in this book and in particular to the following for the extracts from the translations indicated:

Aeschylus:
Agamemnon translated by Louis McNeice (1936), reprinted by permission of the publishers, Faber and Faber Ltd.
The Eumenides translated by Tony Harrison in *Plays 4* (Faber, 2002), reprinted by permission of the author.

The Eumenides translated by Robert Fagles in *The Oresteia* (Penguin, 1977), translation copyright © Robert Fagles 1975, reprinted by permission of Sheil Land Associates Ltd. and of Viking Penguin, a division of Penguin Group (USA) Inc.

The Eumenides and *The Libation Bearers* translated by Peter Meineck in *The Oresteia* (Hackett, 1998), translation copyright © Peter Meineck 1998, reprinted by permission of Hackett Publishing Company, Inc. All rights reserved.

The Libation Bearers translated by Ted Hughes in *The Oresteia* (1999), reprinted by permission of the publishers, Faber and Faber Ltd.

The Persians translated by Janet Lembke and C. J. Herington (OUP, 1981), copyright © Janet Lembke and C. J. Herington 1981, reprinted by permission of Oxford University Press, Inc, and Janet Lembke.

Prometheus Bound translated by Frederic Raphael and Kenneth McLeish in *Aeschylus Plays 1* (1991), reprinted by permission of the publishers, Methuen Publishing Ltd.
Seven against Thebes translated by Anthony Hecht and Helen Bacon (OUP, 1999), copyright © Anthony Hecht and Helen Bacon 1999, reprinted by permission of Oxford University Press, Inc.

Seven against Thebes and *Suppliants* translated by Michael Ewans in *Suppliants and Other Dramas* (Everyman Paperbacks, a division of the Orion Publishing Group, 1996), reprinted by permission of the publishers.

Aristophanes:

Acharnians translated by Kenneth McLeish in *Aristophanes Plays I* (1993), reprinted by permission of the publishers, Methuen Publishing Ltd.

Acharnians translated by Alan H. Sommerstein in *Aristophanes: Lysistrata and Other Plays* (Penguin Classics, 1973, revised edition 2002), copyright © Alan H. Sommerstein 1973, 2002, reprinted by permission of Penguin Books Ltd.

Birds translated by Dudley Fitts (1958), reprinted by permission of the publishers, Faber and Faber Ltd.

Clouds translated by Kenneth McLeish in *Aristophanes Plays II* (1993), reprinted by permission of the publishers, Methuen Publishing Ltd.

Clouds translated by Peter Meineck in *Aristophanes Plays I* (Hackett, 1998), translation copyright © Peter Meineck 1998, reprinted by permission of Hackett Publishing Company, Inc. All rights reserved.

Clouds translated by William Arrowsmith in *Aristophanes: Three Comedies* (Ann Arbor, University of Michigan Press, 1969), reprinted by permission of the publishers.

Lysistrata translated by Kenneth McLeish in *Aristophanes Plays I* (1993), reprinted by permission of the publishers, Methuen Publishing Ltd.

Lysistrata translated by Dudley Fitts (1960), reprinted by permission of the publishers, Faber and Faber Ltd.

Euripides:

Alcestis translated by William Arrowsmith (OUP, 1974), copyright © William Arrowsmith 1974, 1990, reprinted by permission of Oxford University Press, Inc.

The Bacchae translated by William Arrowsmith from *The Complete Greek Tragedies* edited by David Grene and Richard Lattimore (Chicago University Press), copyright © 1959 by the University of Chicago, reprinted by permission of the publisher.

Electra translated by Emily Townsend Mermeule from *The Complete Greek Tragedies* edited by David Grene and Richard Lattimore (Chicago University Press), copyright © 1959 by the University of Chicago, reprinted by permission of the publisher.

Electra translated by Kenneth McLeish in *Euripides Plays IV* (1997), reprinted by permission of the publishers, Methuen Publishing Ltd.

Hecuba translated by Tony Harrison (Faber and Faber, 2005), reprinted by permission of the author.

Helen translated by Kenneth McLeish in *Euripides Plays III* (1997), reprinted by permission of the publishers, Methuen Publishing Ltd.

Heracles translated by William Arrowsmith from *The Complete Greek Tragedies* edited by David Grene and Richard Lattimore (Chicago University Press), copyright © 1956 by the University of Chicago, reprinted by permission of the publisher.

Heracles translated by Kenneth McLeish in *Euripides Plays V* (1997), reprinted by permission of the publishers, Methuen Publishing Ltd.

Hippolytus translated by David Grene from *The Complete Greek Tragedies* edited by David Grene and Richard Lattimore (Chicago University Press), copyright © 1942 by the University of Chicago, reprinted by permission of the publisher.

Hippolytos translated by David Lan (Almeida Theatre Company, 1991), reproduced by permission of David Lan.

Hippolytus translated by Frederic Raphael and Kenneth McLeish in *Euripides Plays* (1997), reprinted by permission of the publishers, Methuen Publishing Ltd.

Iphigeneia in Aulis translated by Charles R. Walker from *The Complete Greek Tragedies* edited by David Grene and Richard Lattimore (Chicago University Press), copyright © 1958 by the University of Chicago, reprinted by permission of the publisher.

Iphigeneia in Aulis translated by Don Taylor in *Euripides Plays II* (1991), reprinted by permission of the publishers, Methuen Publishing Ltd.

382 ACKNOWLEDGEMENTS

Iphigeneia in Tauris translated by Kenneth McLeish in *Euripides Plays IV* (1997), reprinted by permission of the publishers, Methuen Publishing Ltd.

Iphigeneia in Tauris translated by Richard Lattimore (OUP, 1973), copyright © Richard Lattimore 1973, reprinted by permission of Oxford University Press, Inc.

Medea translated by Jeremy Brooks in *Euripides Plays I* (1988), reprinted by permission of the publishers, Methuen Publishing Ltd.

Medea translated by Alistair Elliot (Oberon Books, 1993), reprinted by permission of the publisher (*www.oberonbooks.com*).

Orestes translated by William Arrowsmith from *The Complete Greek Tragedies* edited by David Grene and Richard Lattimore (Chicago University Press), copyright © 1959 by the University of Chicago, reprinted by permission of the publisher.

Orestes translated by Kenneth McLeish in *Euripides Plays IV* (1997), reprinted by permission of the publishers, Methuen Publishing Ltd.

The Trojan Women translated by Kenneth McLeish (Absolute Classics, 1995), copyright © Kenneth McLeish 1995, reprinted by permission of Oberon Books (*www.oberonbooks.com*).

Homer:
The Iliad of Homer translated by Richard Lattimore (Chicago University Press, 1951) copyright © 1951 by The University of Chicago, reprinted by permission of the publisher.

Menander:
The Girl from Samos translated by Norma Miller in *Menander: Plays and Fragments* (Penguin Classics, 1987), copyright © Norma Miller 1987, reprinted by permission of Penguin Books Ltd.

Plautus:
Brothers Menaechmus and *The Braggart Soldier* translated by Erich Segal in *Plautus: Four Comedies* (Oxford World Classics,

1996), reprinted by permission of Oxford University Press.
The Swaggering Soldier translated by E F Watling in *The Pot of Gold and Other Plays* (Penguin Classics, 1965), copyright © E. F. Watling 1965, 2002, reprinted by permission of Penguin Books Ltd.

Seneca:
Oedipus translated by Ted Hughes (1969), reprinted by permission of the publishers, Faber and Faber Ltd.

Phaedra translated by Frederick Ahl in *Three Tragedies - Trojan Women, Medea, Phaedra* (Cornell University Press, 1986), reprinted by permission of Frederick Ahl.

Phaedra translated by A J Boyle (Francis Cairns, 1994), reprinted by permission of Francis Cairns (Publications) Ltd.

Thyestes translated by Caryl Churchill in *Plays 3* (Nick Hern Books, 1998), copyright © Caryl Churchill 1995, reprinted by permission of the publishers: www.nickhern-books.co.uk.

Sophocles:
Ajax translated by Herbert Golder and Richard Pevear (OUP, 1999), copyright © Herbert Golder and Richard Pevear 1999, reprinted by permission of Oxford University Press, Inc.

Antigone and *King Oedipus* translated by C. A. Trypanis from *Three Theban Plays* (Aris & Philips, 1986), reprinted by permission of Oxbow Books.

Electra translated by David Grene from *The Complete Greek Tragedies* edited by David Grene and Richard Lattimore (Chicago University Press), copyright © 1957, 1959 by the University of Chicago, reprinted by permission of the publisher.

Oedipus at Colonnus translated by Timberlake Wertenbaker (1992), reprinted by permission of the publishers, Faber and Faber Ltd.

Philoctetes translated by David Grene from *The Complete Greek Tragedies* edited by David Grene and Richard

Lattimore (Chicago University Press), copyright © 1957 by the University of Chicago, reprinted by permission of the publisher.

Women of Trachis translated by C K Williams and Gregory W Dickerson (OUP, 1978), copyright © C. K. Williams and Gregory W. Dickerson 1978, 1991, reprinted by permission of Oxford University Press, Inc and the Joan Davies Literary Agency.

Although we have tried to trace and contact all copyright holders before publication, we will be pleased to correct any inadvertent errors or omissions.

****

Covered by disclaimer note
Aristophanes: *Acharnians* translated by Patric Dickerson in *Aristophanes Plays I* (OUP, 1970) originally in *Aristophanes against War* (OUP, 1957) - Mrs S. Dickerson [not traced].